The Science of Running

The Science of Running

How to find your limit and train to maximize your performance

Steve Magness

http://www.ScienceofRunning.com

First Printing: 2014

ISBN 978-0-615-94294-0

Origin Press

www.ScienceofRunning.com

Cover design by Mike Sayneko

www.SayenkoDesign.com

To Gerald Stewart, Tom Tellez,
And my family, Bill, Elizabeth, Phillip, and Emily

Table of Contents

Section 2: How to Train

Preface

The serious committed runner is neglected. There are very few books, magazines, or even advertisements aimed at the runner looking to maximize performance. Instead the running industry has focused on the recreational runner. The endless supply of articles explaining 'how to run your first marathon' or 'how to run your best 5k on 3 runs per week' dominates the magazine articles and the bookshelves. We were all beginners at some time, so it is no knock on those who need such information to get started. However, as we get further and further from the recreational runner, the resources become increasingly sparse.

For the highly competitive, elite, college, or serious runner looking to maximize performance, the options are few and far between. Unless you are lucky enough to call some elite runners or high-level coaches friends, the information on how top runners train is limited. My aim is to blow the doors wide open and provide the details that I've accumulated through running myself, coaching high level runners, working with great coaches and studying practically every elite coach in running history. My hope is that the information on training provided will not only help you maximize your or your athlete's running performance, but also lead to better and more innovative training practices. We have a long way to go until the training process is figured out, and hopefully this book serves as not a final destination but as a stepping-stone and catalyst for future improvements in training.

The first section of this book focuses on the details on the science of running. This section started out as an in depth literature review for my Master's thesis, but due to circumstances I could not use it. Instead of letting it go to waste, it served as the foundation of the Science section of the book. Similar to the training section, I felt that the running physiology that was available in the mass media was "dumbed down". I set out to look at everything we knew about the science of running and offer a critical review of that information. Most running science books take an explanatory approach. Instead, my goal was to try and answer the question "What limits running performance?"

Despite my background in sports science, this section was not written from a scientist's point of view. Instead I wanted to look at the science from a different perspective, that of a high-level athlete and successful coach. This allowed me the unique opportunity to analyze everything as a member of two opposing groups, a coach and a sports scientist. What caught my attention was the level of disagreement between the two groups and the degree in which they worked seemingly oblivious to the other group. There are exceptions of course, but it blew my mind that I would read paper after paper about the benefits of low mileage/high intensity training and how the Kenyans success was based on this system, while at the same time coaches were espousing the complete opposite and having phenomenal success with that approach. The two groups, real world application vs. laboratory science, seem to work independently of each other without either group acknowledging the others' work.

My hope is that this book will serve to bridge the gap. The coaches will get in depth scientific knowledge and a new training paradigm for distance running, while the sports scientists will get a look at what actually works with runners in the real world. I hope that you find this informative, useful, and above all, thought provoking.

-Steve Magness

www.ScienceofRunning.com

stevemagness@gmail.com

Introduction

This is not your typical watered-down, mass-market training book that relies on cookie-cutter programs. There will be no formulaic training regimes or easy to follow training plans included. Instead, this book is designed to challenge the athlete, coach, or scientist. It is designed for those looking to not solely get better, but instead to maximize their performance. That doesn't mean it is only for the elite, quite the contrary: it is for those of you who, like me, were frustrated with the redundant information given out in every coaching and training book. My hope is that this book will provide new insight and direction in the world of running and make the reader think critically about all of the traditional notions held in coaching, running, and science.

In the world of running, the science and the practical side are at war. Research scientists constantly lampoon the coaches for their lack of reliance on the training methods proven in their research studies to improve performance, while coaches ridicule the scientists for having no idea how the body works in the real world and laugh at their training ideas. Read enough from both sides and you'll see how far apart they are. Whether it's training volume, intensity, frequency of runs or even peaking strategies, the sides are so far apart on a variety of key issues that it is laughable. Most coaches and scientists give up on trying to understand the other side and instead delve deep into their own beliefs while simply ignoring what the other side is doing. Both sides go about their days seemingly oblivious to the others' work, so what we end up with is two completely contrasting theories on all things running.

I'm here to attempt to integrate both worlds. My goal in this book is to show you that while one side might be clued in a little better, we cannot reach the limits of human performance without understanding both sides. While this task might seem daunting, I'm uniquely qualified for this role as I've been on both sides of the coin. I started this sport as a phenom high school runner, running the 6th fastest High School mile time in U.S. history. That early promise quickly disappeared, as my college career was a wreck, marred with over training and injuries. Looking for solutions I turned to studying the best coaches in the world in distance running, both past and present. Not completely satisfied with their answers, I turned to trying to learn everything there was about the science of running, eventually completing my master's in the subject. In studying the science, I looked at it through an athlete's and coach's perspectives and couldn't help but notice the contradictions between what I had learned as an athlete, a coach, and in studying other coaches and what I was being taught in class. Unlike what often happens where your prior notions give way and you accept the dogmatic teachings of your chosen field, I couldn't let go of either the coaching or science side, thus creating a constant struggle between the two. When I started coaching others I had to confront this struggle, and it came to me: there's a place for both; they just have to be integrated properly.

This book is split into two sections, one focused on the Science side and one on the coaching side. What is unique about this book as that I have worked hard to integrate the two competing sides by providing the opposing sides' view and the practicality behind that information. The best coaches and Sports Scientists are those who actually understand both sides of the coin. Instead of two separate groups working independently along parallel paths, we need a unified understanding so that we can all work together towards helping athletes run faster and more efficiently.

Understanding how we run and how the body adapts to training allows for the development of better methods of coaching and training. Without this knowledge, coaches get stuck into the "followers" pattern, meaning they copy workouts from others for the sole reason that another coach did it. My goal is to instill independent thinking and above all to get other runners and coaches to start asking questions.

In a surprising twist, knowing the science opens up the door for the coach to be an artist. You learn to utilize the natural responses of the human body to solve problems in ways that the traditional coaching model would never allow for. Let me give a few quick examples. In 2009, my best runner was recovering from a case of mono while still trying to get in shape to win a state championship. I needed a way to get him in specific shape very quickly without overstressing his body. Without being able to do longer runs or traditional intervals like 800m repeats because it overstressed his weakened system, I used my scientific knowledge to come up with workouts that would accomplish the same sort of goals but be less stressful and easier to recover from. Instead of traditional intervals, he ran a lot of very short intervals at moderate speeds with short rest between intervals and then a long break between sets. This allowed him to spend a larger amount of time at race pace and to build his aerobic system gradually, while keeping the stress low.

Two of history's great running coaches were experts at integrating science and training. Italian coach Renato Canova used his knowledge of muscle fiber recruitment to develop a method that uses hill sprints and strength endurance circuits to teach the runner to recruit more muscles and then extend their endurance. By knowing the science, he knew that muscle fibers began to "fail" at the end of the race and that if he could increase the total fiber pool and then extend their endurance, this would enhance his runners' performance. Similarly, the great Hungarian coach Mihaly Igloi used his knowledge of muscle fibers to theorize that if runners changed their stride patterns from what he called a short swing to a long swing pattern, they would switch the muscle recruitment pattern and thus be able to delay fatigue slightly. This ingenious idea of being proficient in two slightly different ways of running has largely been forgotten but shows the value of having scientific knowledge. In essence, knowing the science frees you from the constraints of the "followers" coaching method. Once you know how the body works, your imagination can run wild, and you can then solve the problems that you face in coaching your athletes.

Hopefully by now you see the benefit of knowing both sides. While this book is primarily focused on how to train runners and maximize their performance, it would be impossible to accomplish that task without the science, as I hope you will come to understand. On the scientific side, my goal is not just to explain the research, but also to take a critical look at it, supplying context to the research and explaining what it means in practical terms. On the coaching side, this is not a paint by numbers training book, so instead of telling you exactly what workout should be done when, the goal is to teach you how to train using a method that elite runners and coaches use.

Before getting into the meat of the book, I'd like to go over what I call my rules of everything and my rules of training. The rules of everything are a series of tenets that I've developed over the years that should be kept in mind when evaluating the scientific research, new training ideas, equipment, and fads. Their purposes are to help you as the coach to make better-informed decisions. These go beyond just looking at science or even training and can be applied to a vast array of different situations. My rules of training are some simple overarching concepts that boil down the complex task of training into several succinct statements. I introduce them now so that you have some knowledge of my training philosophy while reading the science section of the book.

My Rules of Everything:

1. Hype Cycle: When an idea is new or gains popularity, it follows a cycle of initial overemphasis before eventually leveling off into its rightful place.

It does not matter whether the idea is new or being recycled, if it goes viral or reaches fad-like status, chances are that more importance will be ascribed to it than it really deserves. As something gains importance, it is easy to take one of two extremes and either jump on the bandwagon or discard the idea as worthless. The reality is that its importance is somewhere in between, and you must not let its fad status cloud your objective judgment. Eventually the fad will wear off, and the idea will slowly settle down into its rightful level of importance. Worthwhile ideas tend not to have as dramatic a fall and stick around longer.

2. Research is only as good as its measurement.

If the measurement system is flawed or relies on false premises, then the subsequent research or ideas that develop based on that measurement are flawed. This happens all the time in science and explains why there is so much conflicting data out there. We only read the conclusions and results without considering the theory or measurement on which it is built. Therefore many conclusions based on scientific data lead to incorrect conclusions and bad practices. Prime examples of this that will be discussed thoroughly in the text are VO2max and Running Economy.

3. We overemphasize the importance of what we can measure and what we already know while ignoring that which we cannot measure and know little about.

Every new breakthrough brings about euphoria as if this will be the finding that makes everything clear. This happens in medicine, nutrition, biology, genetics, you name it. Whenever something new is discovered or a new measuring device is developed, there is a corresponding increase in interest and thus subsequent study on that subject or using that measurement tool. What happens is that new info or measurement tool receives so much importance that it defines which way the field goes.

4. We think in absolutes and either/or instead of the spectrum that is really present.

The common saying goes "The world is not black and white." The human mind seems to prefer simple analog, yes or no, type thinking. This can be seen throughout exercise science and training. Some common examples include muscle fiber types and an infatuation with finding the one limiter of performance or that magical workout that maximizes performance. One of my favorite examples is the nature versus nurture debate. For decades all we heard was that genes controlled everything, then research and books like Malcolm Gladwell's *Outliers* came along and told us that it is almost purely nurture that makes us great and all we need is 10,000 hours of practice. The reality is that it is not this black and white and that it is a combination of nature and nurture that combine to determine our "talent" and success.

5. We underestimate the complexity of the human body (and almost everything else).

I'm painting with a broad brush here, but as humans we are arrogant. It's easy to get caught up and think that we have all the answers and have everything figured out. The truth is we don't. In every field of study there is much to be learned. Be very wary of anyone who claims to have everything figured out. You don't have to look very hard to find numerous instances in our field of exercise science to see the constant underestimation of the human body.

6. We look at and analyze things from our perspective, overemphasizing what our knowledge base strength is.

As is becoming a theme, many of these rules have to do with our human nature. The goal is to be aware of these rules so that you don't fall into the trap, thus freeing yourself to think critically and creatively. In this instance, our background and perspective play a large role in how we see things, and it is important to be aware of that. This is why sprint coaches think all distance runners run too much and should do more biomechanical work, and why many distance coaches think that sprinters are "lazy" and don't do enough work. The important thing to realize is that you should avoid this trap and try to analyze ideas and concepts from an outside perspective.

7. Everything works in cycles.

This rule applies to almost everything, whether it is science or training as discussed in this book or fashion trends. Everything comes and goes in a cycle. It's important to understand this and not to ditch a particular training method that works just because it is going out of style. Look at the history of preferred running mileage in America and this trend can obviously be seen with low mileage programs being given in the 1940-50's and late 80's and 90's while high mileage predominated in the 60-70's and the 2000's. Similar trends can be seen with static versus dynamic stretching, weight training, core training, and even exercise equipment such as kettle bells. Remember not to just follow the crowd for the sake of change.

8. Taking the extreme view is seldom good.

Lastly, once again whether its training, science, or topics such as religion, taking an extreme view is seldom good. This statement ties into the rule of how everything is not black or white but really a spectrum. Similarly, taking extreme views on anything seldom turns out to be right. In training for instance, it's obvious that all high mileage slow running is not going to work; just as all high intensity low mileage isn't either. A recent example of the dangers of taking an extreme view in training can be seen in the CrossFit phenomenon.

My Rules of Training:

1. Build and Maintain

It is easier to maintain a quality then to build it up. Thus each particular training parameter should go through a cycle of being emphasized to build it up, and once its emphasis decreases, a small amount of training should be done to maintain it.

2. Never leave anything behind

Tying into the last principle, the emphasis given to each training parameter changes, but it is never completely taken away. The goal of training is to build on top of what has been done previously, not leave it behind and forget about it.

3. Progress everything

Training is giving a large enough stimulus that it creates an adaptation. In essence, training is completely changing a person, all the way down to the genetic level. If the same stimulus is given over and over, the body's response is less and less. Since training fundamentally alters a person, how they adapt and respond to a stimulus changes too. Therefore, if trying to build a certain parameter, progression is paramount to ensuring continual adaptation. This applies not only on a small-scale workout-to-workout level but also on a large-scale career level.

4. Balance

Training is the process of balancing seemingly opposing adaptations. In the simplest form, balancing speed and endurance is the key to proper training. The exact balance depends upon the person and the event they are training for.

5. Individualize

Every runner is an individual and should be treated like one. Their physiology and psychology will change what type of training they need, and it is a disservice to the runner to give the same training to every runner and expect the same results. We must treat each runner as an individual.

6. Take complex things and make them simple

A great coach once told me that good coaches take complex ideas and make them simple, while a bad coach who wants to appear like they know what they are doing takes ideas and concepts and makes them more complex. It is good to know the complexities of training or science, but you must break them down into simpler and easier to use models. Be very wary of those who try to intentionally make ideas more complex by using big words for the sake of using big words. Concepts have to be simple to be practical and usable.

7. You can love an idea, but don't be married to it

Getting married to an idea or concept limits objective or creative thinking. When you tie an idea to yourself, it becomes bigger than it should be, and this creates a situation where if for some reason your idea turns out to be incorrect, you hold onto the sinking ship for much longer than you normally would. Remember, the key is in making our runners fast or advancing our knowledge of the science, not in stroking our egos. Don't create a situation where you are not free to admit past mistakes if there is a better method. When we "fall in love" with an idea, we essentially make it our belief system. So we tie our self worth to the idea instead of the final outcome.

8. Training does not occur in isolation

Too often we take an isolationist approach, looking at only the effects of a single workout or training during a single season. This is not how it works in the real world. Keep in mind the surrounding runs and non-workout factors that blend together to impact every single workout. Similarly, too often we plan each season independently without acknowledging what preceded it. What a runner has done in the past impacts what the effects of the training he will do in the future are.

Section 1

The Science of Distance Running

"Anybody can understand anything, as long as it is clearly explained, but, more than that, if they are sufficiently interested." Ben Goldacre

The sport of distance running has a long history that has been closely tied with the rise of sports science. The founder of modern physiology, Nobel Prize winner A.V. Hill, chose running as his platform to develop the concept of oxygen consumption (Bassett & Howley, 2000). Even with this long history of investigating the mechanisms behind performance and ways to enhance it in sports science, many questions remain unanswered, and the exact factors that govern performance are still debated. In addition, unlike other activities such as weight lifting, the optimal way to train distance runners, including both the effects of training at different intensities and how to periodize that training, remains unknown. The current function of science in training is not to be used as a way to prescribe training but instead as a way to explain why training used by coaches or athletes works.

The purpose of this section is twofold. First, it is to establish the variety of mechanisms that control and limit performance in the sport of distance running. Second, it is to look at the current training methods used by trained athletes and evaluate their impact on the physiological factors that govern performance. By analyzing the factors that affect performance and the current training trends, limitations in the training of competitive distance runners will become apparent.

Additionally, a sub goal is to bridge the gap between the Sports Scientists of the world and the coaches. Both groups do outstanding work, but it is as if a gap exists with each group going about their business with an air of superiority while completely ignoring or dismissing the other group. This has resulted in two completely different ways of training endurance athletes, with the coaches prevailing up to this point in superiority of performance in my opinion. This strange battle with each other should not be happening, but rather there should be cooperation aimed at finding out how to optimize performance. Once egos are put aside and we acknowledge that we do not have all the answers, then new performance levels will be met.

This section is very dense with information. I do not hold back on the latest ideas or concepts surrounding exercise science. This is not meant to scare you away, but if you find it intimidating and are looking for how to apply it to training, I would suggest reading Chapters 2 and 3 to get a grasp on fatigue, and then skip to Section 2 of the book, which is on training.

1

How Running Happens

"Scientific testing can't determine how the mind will tolerate pain in a race. Sometimes, I say, 'Today I can die.'" Percy Cerutty

When broken down into its simplest form, running is nothing but a series of connected spring-like hops or bounds. A certain amount of energy needs to be imparted into the ground to propel the runner forward, continuing the running movement. The amount of energy needed depends on the pace that the athlete is running; as the pace increases a greater amount of energy is needed. This energy comes about through two primary mechanisms called active and passive mechanics. Active mechanics refers to what we all think about when it comes to what drives running, actively recruiting muscles that generate force via muscle contraction. On the other hand passive mechanics are a result of the body, namely the muscles, tendons, and ligaments, acting in a spring like manner, temporarily storing the energy that comes about from the collision of the foot with the ground. During the subsequent push off, or propulsion, phase of running, this energy is utilized and released contributing to forward propulsion. These two mechanisms combine to provide the necessary force and energy to power the running movement.

In simplistic terms a runner can keep going at the same pace as long as they can produce the necessary kinetic energy, whether this comes from force production or passive mechanical energy. Once they cannot impart enough energy, the pace has to slow, as they are not able to cover the same amount of ground with the same stride rate. Simply stated, they fatigue. Before looking at performance and fatigue, it's important to grasp the intricacies of the running movement. While the previous description provides the framework, let's delve into each step of how running actually occurs from the Central Nervous System all the way down to a single muscle contraction. Once this has been done, the potential limiters along the route can be identified.

Motor Programming

The brain, or to be more exact the Central Nervous System (CNS), is where movement starts. The simple act of moving one finger is an incredibly complex task involving multiple systems, so completely understanding a complex dynamic movement like running is a daunting task. What we do know is that movement originates in the nervous system. The nervous system consists of higher levels of organization, such as the brain itself, and lower levels of organization, such as the spinal cord and brainstem. These two levels of the nervous system combine to decide how movement takes place.

Movement occurs with a combination of pre-conceived motor programs and slight tweaks or alterations based on sensory information. Essentially, the body has a gross general plan of how to go about doing a certain movement and then tweaks that plan based on the sensory information it is constantly receiving. The movement pattern serves as the rough basis for how that particular movement should take place. The sensory information provides for the on the go adjustment like that seen when running on a road versus sand or when an unexpected root pops up in front of you. If the body simply worked by predetermined motor programming without the ability to use feed forward or feedback information to adjust, we'd all be in trouble.

On the higher level, the brain works in an integrated way in that several areas of the brain combine to work dynamically to create the running pattern, using feedback and feed forward information to provide the details on what the muscles should do. At the lower spinal cord level, movements that occur reflexively or without the need for sensory feedback or feed forward information are developed. At the spinal cord level, Central Pattern Generator's (CPG) guide movement patterns and muscle activity without the need for sensory input (Molinari, 2009). These two processes integrate using both active and passive mechanics to decide how movement ultimately takes place.

In establishing the movement pattern, what muscles to activate, how often to activate them, and in what order activation takes place are all determined. While running, the CNS uses a complex amount of sensory information including external stimuli such as the ground surface, limb movement and position such as how the foot is striking, and internal stimuli such as the lengths of various muscles throughout the movement or even the buildup of fatiguing products in the muscles themselves. All of this information, combined with the basic motor programming, results in an on the fly adjustment of how you are moving. A variety of adjustments are made including what type of motor units (groups of muscle fibers) are recruited, the recruitment pattern, how long of a rest to work cycle a motor unit has, the relaxation of opposing muscles, and the manipulation of non-propulsive fibers to minimize the effect the impact with the ground has. The CNS is constantly using all of the sensory information, comparing the intended movement with the actual movement, and making slight tweaks or adjustments. Not only does it make adjustments based on the movement but also on what to alter when fatigue is building up. While this will be covered in depth in the next chapter, how the body deals with fatigue is ultimately a motor control issue. Have you ever wondered why you might start leaning back, swing your arms wildly, or reach out with your foot during the end of an exhausting race? This happens because of a combination of conscious and subconscious control in which you are trying to compensate for fatigue by a variety of biomechanical adjustments. Part of training is teaching the body how to accurately adjust the movement pattern to fatigue. From a motor programming standpoint, doing all out workouts where form is broken down completely might lead to negative motor programming or, in layman's terms, bad habits.

At first the movement pattern is rough, uncoordinated and inefficient, but as a person becomes better trained, this process is refined and improved. Initially, the exact recruitment pattern or how to relax the opposing muscle is not known or refined. Slowly, the body becomes more efficient at determining exactly what muscles need to be working and for how long. This refinement results in a smoothing out of the movement and is an improvement in neuromuscular control, which creates an efficient movement pattern that enhances performance via improving efficiency. This process is called motor learning, and contrary to popular belief, running is a skill that needs to be learned and refined.

While previously it had been thought that improvement in motor learning only occurred at the higher levels such as in the motor cortex in the brain, recent evidence has demonstrated that even at the spinal cord level the movement pattern can be refined (Molinari, 2009). The movement pattern is generally improved by better coordination of activating just the right amount of motor units to do the work, improving the cycling of motor unit activation, and decreasing the level of co-activation (when the opposing muscle is active at the same time as the main muscle). Additionally, as a movement becomes well refined, it is believed that the CNS becomes better at using all of the sensory information that is receiving, essentially weeding out the pertinent from the inconsequential information better than when first learning how to move.

Running Around with your head cut off:
     The phenomenon of chickens running around after their heads are cut off shows that a general movement pattern for running is available at the spinal cord level. Studies with other animals and even historical reports with humans when the guillotine was in use have confirmed this phenomenon. This points to the conclusion that activities like running and walking might have an ingrained motor program that has developed through evolutionary process.

Sending and Receiving the Signal

The actual process of activating muscles occurs because of communication between the brain and the muscles. After all, we have to figure out how to get the message across a continual chain of linked nerve cells. Neural signals called action potentials act as the communication device as signals make their way from the brain through the spinal cord and eventually to the muscles themselves. An action potential works via differences between the electrical charge inside the cell and outside the cell. A cell has a resting voltage called the resting membrane potential. In its resting state, a cell is polarized in that inside the cell has a negative charge compared to the outside of the cell, which basically means that there is a greater concentration of negative ions inside the cell.

An action potential occurs when this charge is reversed, or depolarized, to a significant enough degree so that now the inside of the cell has a positive charge (Brooks & Fahey, 2004). It's this shift in balance from a negative to a positive charge that allows the action potential to take place. Therefore to initiate or continue this "signal," a significant enough stimulus needs to be received to change from a negative to a positive electrical balance inside the cell. Once the action potential is generated, repolarization occurs, returning the membrane potential to resting levels so that it can be potentially activated again. The action potential that was formed now flows down the cell and communicates to the next cell in line via neurotransmitters. If the next cell is significantly stimulated, then this process occurs over and over as the signal makes its way from its origin through the nervous system and down to the muscles. This chain reaction can be thought of as a continual exchange of the baton from one runner to the next to get the baton to the finish line or, in the body's case, the muscle.

The electrical charge inside and outside of the cell is altered mainly by differences in sodium and potassium inside and outside of the cell. The potassium maintains the negative internal charge while the sodium keeps the positive external charge. To get the aforementioned action potential to occur, we need some way to change the ratio of potassium and sodium inside the cell. To accomplish this we have a device in the cell called the Sodium-Potassium pump as well as changes in ease of movement through the cell membrane for potassium (Brooks & Fahey, 2004). When sodium gates are opened, we get a shift in electrical charge in the cell, which can cause depolarization.

But what is the key to unlock and open the sodium gates? In motor units it is caused by the neurotransmitter Acetylcholine (ACh). Neurotransmitters are simply chemicals that allow for communication between cells. Following the action potential creation, the potassium gates open causing potassium to exit the cell, which causes repolarization thus returning the cell to normal. What we are left with then is a neural signal travelling towards the muscle via a linked system of neurons. We need ACh to signal to the cell to open the doors so that we can shift the change in charge of the cell. Once this occurs, the signal (action potential) is allowed to travel to the next neuron until it finally reaches the muscle. As we become better trained, all of this signaling can improve. We can see changes in the excitability of the neuron or in how quickly the signal travels. It's almost like we build bigger, better highways with higher speed limits the more we drive along the neural pathway.

Muscle Contraction

The nerve signal eventually reaches the neuron that connects with the group of muscle fibers we are trying to reach, called an α motor neuron. The entire α motor neuron and connected muscle fibers make up what is called a motor unit. The action potential travels down the neuron until it reaches the gap between the neuron and the actual muscle fiber, called the neuromuscular junction. This junction is where communication between the neuron and the muscle takes place.

As previously mentioned, this occurs via the releasing of neurotransmitters (in this case ACh) that travel across a small gap between the neuron and the muscle and bind to special receptors on the muscle. The binding of the neurotransmitter causes an action potential to occur in the muscle cell, which can lead to the depolarization process described previously. If enough action potentials reach the muscle cell, then it crosses a depolarization threshold, and the muscle will fire.

In the muscle cell, the depolarization process that leads to contraction is a little more complicated. Depolarization causes Calcium that is stored in a structure called the sarcoplasmic reticulum to be released. The Calcium quickly spreads throughout the muscle fiber with the goal of eventually reaching the actual contractile parts of the fiber. Deep within the cell is its basic unit, the myofibril, which contains the two main contractile filaments, actin and myosin. Actin is referred to as the thin filament while myosin is referred to as the thick filament because it has myosin heads on it, which can attach to the actin. The way contraction works is that these heads on the myosin essentially latch onto the actin filament and yank it, then detach and pull it some more until the muscle is contracted.

At rest, the myosin heads cannot attach to the actin because the attachment site is blocked. However, the calcium released frees up the attachment site and allows the myosin head to attach to the actin. When it does this, it essentially pulls on the actin, causing contraction. The repeated pulling and releasing that goes on is what causes muscle contraction. Without calcium release this interaction cannot occur. To help conceptualize this process, think of a stationary person (the myosin) pulling on a rope (the actin) to try to drag a heavy object towards them. The person's hand represents the myosin head as they grab the rope, pull it some, let go, and then grab it again to pull the object closer.

But that's not the entire story. This whole contraction process requires energy. Energy in the form of ATP is required so that the myosin head can pull on the actin. This movement requires the release of energy. However, in terms of supplying energy, ATP needs to be supplied once the myosin head has completed its pull to allow for it to release and be ready for the next pulling cycle. Thus, the process of supplying energy is one of replenishment. Without the resupplying of ATP after the myosin head's pulling has occurred, the continual process of attaching, dragging, and releasing cannot occur. In our conceptualization, without energy, the actual pulling of the rope takes energy, but if we did not supply energy at the end of a single pull, then our person would not be able to move his hands further up the rope and pull again. This is the process of a single contraction of a muscle fiber. Once the contraction occurs, relaxation has to occur before a subsequent contraction occurs. Relaxation is dependent on the calcium being transported back into its holding site, the sarcoplasmic reticulum. Until the calcium returns, another contraction cannot occur.

Energy Needed

As you can see from the process of contraction, chemical energy needs to be generated in the form of ATP to resupply the myosin heads during the contraction process. We only have a limited amount of stored ATP in the muscle, so we have several processes to recycle ATP. Our body acts as a recycling plant. These processes are a series of chemical reactions that take the various products left over from the energy release that occurs when contraction takes place and recycles them into ATP. When the myosin head uses energy, the ATP, which consists of an Adenosine molecule and three Phosphates (Pi), is broken down to ADP (Adenosine + 2 Pi) and a separate Pi. The separation of one of the Pi causes energy release. In the end we are left with ADP and Pi floating around, or in some cases AMP (Adenosine + 1 Pi) and Pi. The energy systems work to use these and other building blocks to recreate ATP, so that it can then be separated again to release more energy.

We have several energy systems that all use a series of chemical reactions to produce ATP. With each chemical reaction, enzymes are required to convert the initial products into the final products. Enzymes accomplish this by speeding up the rate of the reaction. Therefore the quantity of certain enzymes is one trainable factor that can enhance performance, as the ability to perform certain essential chemical reactions is improved.

Each energy system differs in complexity in terms of how many reactions are needed to finally get to ATP and on what the initial fuel source is. Obviously, with a greater number of reactions, it takes longer to go through the entire process. Additionally, there are more steps involved, which means more chances of slow down and more substances needed for each reaction. On the other hand, the supply of the products used during the energy systems matters. With our simple, one or two-step reaction systems they can produce ATP very quickly, but the fuel supply is limited and thus used quickly. The complex multi reaction systems, however, have fuel supplies that are much larger which means while they cannot produce ATP as quickly, they can do so for a much longer time. Lastly, one other difference is in the by-products that are produced. Each system results in additional products besides ATP. Some of these products can interfere with energy production or muscle contraction, and function in signaling to the CNS that the body is out of homeostasis. Thus it is a balancing act between by-product buildup, the speed and power of the system, and the endurance of the system. Let's look at some specific details for each system.

The first system is actually several different small systems that are termed the immediate energy systems. The quickest and easiest immediate energy source is stored ATP; the muscle simply uses stored ATP as a quick and easy energy source. The problem is that the amount of stored ATP in a muscle is extremely low, enough to power contraction for only a second or two (Brooks & Fahey, 2004). The next immediate system is what is referred to as the Phosphagen system. It consists of the simple one step reaction of Creatine Phosphate (CP) and ADP, which yields ATP and Creatine. Once again, the supply of CP in the muscle limits the use of this highly powerful system to only 5-6 seconds of work (Brooks & Fahey, 2004). Lastly, the myokinase system takes two ADPs and creates one ATP and one AMP. Even when all of these systems are combined, they can only provide energy for muscle contraction for 5-15 seconds, far too short for any endurance event (Brooks & Fahey, 2004). Besides the short capacity of these systems, they also take a long time to recover. These immediate systems essentially act as borrowing systems and cannot be repaid unless intensity is low enough. For example, after total exhaustion of its resources the Phosphagen system requires the aerobic system to turn Creatine back into CP so that it can be used again. At rest this takes up to several minutes.

To supplement the immediate energy systems, Glycolysis, which is sometimes referred to as the anaerobic system, takes part of the workload. Glycolysis is a system that requires no oxygen and has intermediate speed, power, and capacity. Essentially, it is the middle distance runner of the energy systems. Glycolysis works by breakdown of glucose or stored carbohydrate, glycogen. The breakdown of glycogen requires an extra step and is called Glycogenolysis. Unlike the immediate energy systems, Glycolysis involves 12 sequential chemical reactions that take us from Glucose to Pyruvate. From here there is a fork in the road where pyruvate can either be converted to lactate or to acetyl-CoA. The conversion to acetyl-CoA allows for that substance to enter the mitochondria and be used by the aerobic energy system. Contrary to popular belief, the decision on which way the system goes at this point is not based on whether oxygen is present or not (Brooks & Fahey, 2004). Instead the quantity of enzymes that convert it to lactate or acetyl-CoA and whether or not there is sufficient mitochondrial activity to handle pyruvate and other products produced by glycolysis (namely NADH) are the major determining factors on which way Glycolysis goes. Thus mitochondria, which will be discussed shortly, are important in determining the end route of Glycolysis. More on this process and the conversion to lactate will be covered in subsequent chapters.

One major drawback to Glycolysis, especially when it goes the lactate route, is that by-products are produced which can interfere with the energy systems, contraction itself, or even serve as a signaling mechanism to the brain that fatigue is imminent. While lactate itself does not cause fatigue, certain accompanying products, namely Hydrogen ions (H+), have been shown to contribute to fatigue. Lactate is in fact a fuel source that can be used aerobically. In the next chapter, the buildup of these products will be discussed. While the buildup of fatiguing products is one down side to Glycolysis, the amount of energy produced is another downside. With each cycle through Glycolysis, 2 total ATP are produced, which is far less than the amount produced aerobically. Glycolysis is thus an intermediate system that delivers a moderate amount of ATP fairly quickly but with some negative consequences.

The last energy system is commonly referred to as the Aerobic system. You may notice that I am not terming it Aerobic Glycolysis. This is because Glycolysis is a process by itself that does not require oxygen. You have to go through Glycolysis to get the necessary products to proceed with aerobic energy breakdown, but it is confusing to think of aerobic and anaerobic Glycolysis, because in reality there is one Glycolysis, the last step just differs. As mentioned previously, pyruvate is converted to acetyl-CoA, which then has to be transported into the mitochondria for use. The mitochondria are a different organelle and are commonly referred to as the powerhouse of the muscle cell. Once inside the mitochondria, the acetyl-CoA enters what is called the Krebs cycle. The Krebs cycle is the first step of the aerobic system. It consists of a series of 10 chemical reactions that function to produce an ATP source and a series of products that can be used in the second step of the aerobic system. The important products are NADH and FADH.

From here, these products enter the second step of the aerobic system, the electron transport chain. The Electron Transport Chain consists of a series of reactions that basically take the NADH (or FADH) and another $H+$ ion and react it with Oxygen, creating ATP, NAD, and water. While the process is more complex than this, the important thing to remember is that it is only this last step in which Oxygen is required. As can be seen, the aerobic system requires a large number of steps and transport of products to and from a different part of the muscle cell than where contraction is actively taking place. Due to these factors, the aerobic system produces a large amount of ATP (~30 in total) but is more time consuming. An advantage of this is that the subsequent by-products are kept to a minimum. Thus the aerobic system has a large fuel supply, causes little by-product fatigue, but takes longer to produce energy.

While the above steps have dealt with using Glycolysis and thus carbohydrate to produce acetyl-CoA, fat and protein can also be broken down to acetyl-CoA, which can enter the Krebs cycle and produce aerobic energy. The problem with Fat is that it is an even more complex chemical process than carbohydrate breakdown, thus while the energy production is very high, it can only work at low to moderate intensities. Once a runner gets much beyond around half marathon pace, the fat usage is very minimal. With protein, there is no natural storage of protein, unlike fat or carbohydrate. Thus when using protein as a fuel source, proteins that are meant for another use are being consumed. An example would be the breakdown and use of muscle protein.

Lastly, let's look at how the energy systems work. As already mentioned, the energy systems are not mutually exclusive but interact with each other. To conceptualize how they interact, let's go through starting an exercise or a race. It's best to think of all the energy systems being started up at the very start of exercise; it just takes some of them longer to rev up and reach full capacity. The amount of contribution is dependent on the intensity, or energy required. The systems dynamically combine to provide the total amount of energy that is required with the exact contribution changing throughout. What we are left with then is the combination of systems trying to fill the energy demands. In the distance events, I like to think of it as the immediate and anaerobic energy systems being the gap fillers.

At lower or moderate intensities, the full immediate energy store is not used up as the energy requirement is low and Glycolysis quickly steps in. Glycolysis takes around 20-30sec to reach maximum capacity, while the Aerobic system takes around 90sec- 2min to reach maximum capacity (Duffield et al., 2005). In looking at a race, in terms of the dominant energy system, the crossover point where aerobic energy is the majority supplied occurs at around 45sec (Hill, 1999). For this reason, if we look at relative energy system contribution for different races, anything over 400m uses the aerobic system to supply the majority of its energy. For competitive males a variety of studies have found that the energy contribution between aerobic and anaerobic systems is 60% aerobic and 40% anaerobic for the 800m, 77%/23% for the 1,500m, and 86%/14% for the 3,000m races (Hill, 1999; Duffield et al., 2005).

The timing of the energy systems reaching capacity is not the only issue. The amount of energy required also plays a role. The aerobic system is limited in its total energy supply rate capacity. Therefore if the exercise is at an intensity that is higher than the maximum rate of energy production for the aerobic system, Glycolysis has to step in and cover the energy requirement gap that is present. This results in the ever-accumulating by-products that can eventually lead to fatigue. For this reason, increasing the capacity of the aerobic system to produce energy is a beneficial training adaptation to delay fatigue. If the gap between aerobic energy production and needed supply can be shrunk, that means less Glycolytic energy is needed to fill that gap and less by-product accumulation.

As you can see, contrary to popular belief, you do not get more "anaerobic" during a race but actually rely increasingly on aerobic means. This is a confusing issue for some, as they've been taught that lactate accumulation from going anaerobic causes fatigue. While lactate does not cause fatigue, the other by-products that can cause fatigue increase in accumulation at shorter high intensity races toward the end of the race. It isn't that they are being produced at a higher rate; it is just that the ability to use or clear these items is increasingly diminished. Additionally, some of these products cause a reduction in the ability to produce energy through Glycolysis, and as that system begins to "falter" and the aerobic system is maxed out, something has to give because the energy needed cannot be supplied. The thing that gives is the pace, as a slowing of the pace decreases the energy demand. More on the actual causes of fatigue are discussed in the following chapter.

Muscle Fiber Types

Having gone from the brain down to the microscopic organelles in the muscles themselves, let's look at the different kinds of muscle fibers we have. Fiber types are generally classified as Slow Twitch (ST) or Fast Twitch (FT) with several subdivisions of FT fiber types depending on the classification method (FT-a,x,c are common classifications). The main method for classifying fibers is based on what type of a protein called myosin the fiber predominately has. The problem is that each muscle fiber type does not contain only one kind of myosin form, but instead most have a mixing of a variety of fast and slow forms. Therefore it is not a distinct division in fiber types like most believe. As was stated in Brooks, Fahey, and Baldwin's seminal text on Physiology, "considering the number of possible combinations of MHCs (myosin heavy chain) and myosin light chains, there are innumerable fiber types (Brooks, 2004, pg. 412)."

While scientists like to break things down into a nice distinct fiber type classification system, the reality is that fiber types are more like a spectrum. On one side of the spectrum we have what we'd call a pure ST fiber and on the opposite is the pure FT fiber. In between these two extremes is a range of fibers with different ratios of FT/ST characteristics, and this is where the majority of fibers fall. Where exactly a fiber falls depends on its individual characteristics, which include mitochondria density, capillary density, oxidative and Glycolytic enzyme activity, creatine phosphate stores, and contraction velocity.

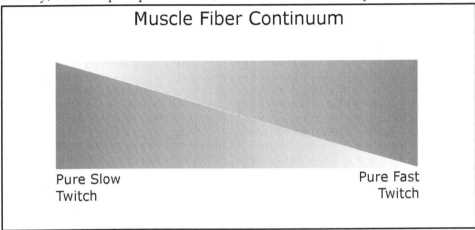

Along this continuum, training can shift fiber types to either the aerobic (ST) or anaerobic (FT) side. With acute training, the shifts are very small, but with long term training a larger change can occur. How large a change is up for debate. For a long time Scientists thought that we could not change fiber types at all. Once this was disproved, they thought that distinct conversion from FT to ST can't occur. The reality is that we most likely can change fiber types, but it can't be proven in humans because it is a long process. Several pieces of evidence lead to this conclusion.

First, animal studies on both rats and rabbits have demonstrated complete fiber type changes with chronic muscle stimulation. What researchers found is that a large amount of damage is required for a complete transformation (Pette & Vrbova, 1999). For example, in rabbits a complete transformation from FT to ST occurs with chronic muscle stimulation only if the researcher goes in and creates lesions in the muscle fiber. In rats, the FT to ST conversion occurs but takes a large amount of chronic stimulation causing considerable muscle damage. What these animal studies demonstrate is that a complete conversion probably can occur, it just takes a lot of damage, or in other words a long period of time of training.

Second, fiber type percentages have been altered in elite skiers as shown when they were tested during their beginning stages of training and then 8 years later. A longitudinal study by Rusko found that after 8 years of training and a doubling of training volume, the percentage of ST fibers in a group of Cross-Country Skiers increased by 11% (1992). Put these two together, and it makes sense that a large amount of volume (or in other words, damage) is needed to change fiber types.

This could partially explain why runners tend to reach peak performance levels later than sprint or power type athletes. It could be because distance runners need large amounts of training, or damage, to complete this muscle fiber type conversion. Additionally, this fiber conversion could also partially explain the success of African distance runners. Perhaps their large volumes of unofficial training early on, such as running to school or even the active lifestyle that they live, allow for this conversion to take place at a younger age. Africans tend to reach peak performance at younger ages then their Western counterparts and this could partially explain that phenomenon.

A Recruitment Issue

How muscle recruitment takes place is another important piece of the puzzle. As discussed earlier, each muscle has a number of motor units, which contain a large amount of individual muscle fibers. These motor units are what gets signaled to contract, and when this occurs, all of the muscle fibers in the unit contract. An entire muscle will never activate all the motor units it contains. If this occurred, catastrophic damage to the bone and surrounding tissue could occur. Thus the brain always keeps some motor units in reserve, even during maximal contractions. This reserve can be thought of as the body's safety system. We have all heard stories of people lifting boulders or mom's lifting cars to save a child. It is believed that in these rare occasions full activation of the muscles occurs. It's likely that the brain does a kind of cost benefit analysis and decides that using the full reserve and risking muscle or tissue damage is better than the alternative, death. The interesting thing is that trained athletes can use a larger percentage of their maximum recruitable fibers then the untrained. Essentially, the well-trained person slowly convinces the body that it's okay if it activates a little more muscle. But how does the body decide how many and what type of motor units are used?

First, muscle recruitment is dependent not on speed or intensity, although they are related, but on force output required. The amount of force needed is what predominately determines muscle activation. If more force is required, the brain activates a larger amount of the muscle fiber pool. This explains why running slightly slower up a hill activates more muscle than running on the flat ground at a slightly faster pace. But it's just not about how much muscle is recruited but what type and in what way.

What type of fibers are recruited has always been thought to work based on Henneman's size principle, which states that the easier to recruit fibers (ST) take up the work first while the harder to recruit fibers are activated as force or duration increases. But this isn't always the case. There are instances when FT fibers are recruited before ST fibers, particularly in situations when a high amount of force is needed in a short amount of time, such as ballistics exercises or during sprinting. Similarly, the force rule of muscle fiber recruitment can be violated during prolonged activity when ST fibers fatigue (glycogen is depleted for example) and then the FT fibers are recruited to take up the slack, despite the relatively low intensity and force recruitment.

Finally, the way recruitment occurs is important. Muscle fiber, or more properly termed Motor Unit, recruitment for endurance events happens in a cyclical manner. That means within a whole muscle, some units are recruited to do the work, and then they can cycle off and recover while other units cycle on and take up the workload. At low intensities, the number of units active at the same time is very low, but as intensity increases more units need to be active at the same time to result in a great enough force output, thus less units are recovering or inactive. Additionally, as recruitment increases the "resting" time between both when a fiber is recruited and between individual contractions of that fiber decreases. Understanding the muscle fiber type spectrum and the ways in which muscles are recruited will be important in designing training to combat fatigue and individualize training.

Passive Mechanics

Up until now, the focus has been on active mechanics, in that active muscle contraction initiated by the brain is supplying the force for movement. Traditionally this has been considered the main contributor to forward movement. The problem is that due to the short ground contact time and then the even shorter amount of time in which the body is in position to actually push and contribute to propulsion another energy source is needed. This is where passive mechanics come in. Passive mechanics can be separated into elastic energy storage, reflexes, and passive mechanical principles.

When a runner's foot collides with the ground, energy is absorbed from the impact. That energy can either be recycled, utilized, or dissipated. Instead of wasting the energy, the body has a remarkable system that allows for us to reuse the energy in a similar way to a spring. In this case, the muscles and tendons function as the spring, compressing and storing energy when ground contact is made and subsequently rebounding and releasing it upon push off. This spring like mechanism provides a large amount of the energy required for forward propulsion. The key is putting the body in proper position to get the most elastic energy return with the least amount of energy dissipation. This is one reason why running mechanics should be optimally developed. This concept will be developed further in the chapter on Efficiency.

Two similar concepts that rely on energy storage and return called the stretch reflex and the stretch shortening cycle (SSC) also help contribute to forward propulsion. The SSC basically refers to energy storage and release in the muscle themselves. It occurs when a muscle is actively stretched and then immediately contracts. During the pre-stretch portion, energy is stored in the elastic components of the muscle and then the energy is released during the contraction part. Essentially it is a spring-like mechanism with storage and release of energy greater than if just contraction took place. The amount of elastic energy return is dependent on several factors including the length and speed of the stretch, the stiffness of the muscle, and the time between the stretch and the subsequent contraction (Saunders et al., 2004). The most obvious example is the calf during hopping or running; upon landing the calf is stretched and then quickly contracts upon push off.

The stretch reflex is a similar phenomenon that occurs because of sensory receptors in the muscle called Muscle Spindles. The spindles detect changes in length of a muscle. When a muscle is rapidly stretched, the spindle basically sends a signal for the muscle to contract. This is done to maintain a relatively constant muscle length. It's common to experience this phenomenon during a High School or College class or when tired on an airplane. You may start to nod off slightly and then your head dips forward until you reflexively jerk it back up. In this case, the muscles on the back of the neck were rapidly stretched and thus the signal was sent to contract them, jerking the head back upwards and startling yourself and those around you.

One of the most overlooked contributions to human movement is how the lower legs function from a purely mechanical viewpoint. The leg can be thought of as multiple segments connected via simple joints. Taking the muscles out of it, these limb segments will function based on pure mechanical principles. This means that Physics and in particular Newton's laws of motions help dictate how the legs will move.

On this front, interesting research by Tad McGeer has demonstrated the passive dynamic properties of the lower legs. He built robots that were essentially just the lower leg segments of the body, and without an engine the robots can walk in a human-like fashion as long as a single initial force is applied. Once the single initial force is applied, or if the robot is on a slight downhill, the machine will walk in human-like fashion without any assistance. These robots are a great demonstration of the passive dynamic properties of the lower limbs. Just like in human walking, due to the physics of the two joint system, the lower leg will fold up slightly on the recovery phase allowing for it to clear the ground and land in front of the body.

The translation to running should be obvious. We tend to think of the entire running cycle happening because of active mechanics, but the reality is that simple mechanical principles dictate much of our movement. When walking for example, there is no need to contract the hamstring to a large degree to bring the lower leg up slightly towards the butt during the recovery phase. Similarly during running, if the push off and hip extension is large, the lower leg will fold up automatically and does not need to be pulled up with the hamstring. If the runner chooses to pull with his hamstring, then he's just wasting energy.

The combination of both passive and active dynamics helps create movement. In looking at running performance or the biomechanics of running, it is easy to focus on only one particular part of the picture. When discussing how to improve performance the conversation inevitably focuses on active muscle contraction, without giving any regards to the contribution of passive dynamics to performance. Similarly, when looking at how a person should run, often the stretch reflex or passive dynamics are not considered. Keep this in mind as we delve further into what limits running performance. Now that we know how running happens, let's look at why we fatigue or tire during running.

2

Fatigue: Friend or Foe?

"The winner is the athlete for whom defeat is the least acceptable rationalization." Tim Noakes

What limits performance? That is the central question that a coach, athlete, and sports scientist all want to answer, and the answer is fatigue. Fatigue is a nebulous catch all term that basically means we slow down or performance decreases. While we have a good idea of what causes fatigue under a variety of isolated situations, the exact mechanisms behind fatigue in a dynamic activity such as running are only now becoming clear. There is an old model and a new model of fatigue. The older model of fatigue was developed based on isolating fatigue. Originally, research focused on simple exercises such as handgrip or a simple bicep curl; then, when research progressed to dynamic exercise such as running or cycling, it was done in an unnatural way (run at X pace until you can't, instead of a self-paced trial). These two methodology quirks shaped our understanding of fatigue throughout the 20th century.

Understanding where fatigue comes from and how it develops is crucial for the coach and scientist. The name of the game is limiting fatigue so that we can race longer or faster. By knowing how it occurs, a coach can plan training to adapt the body to resist fatigue. A coach can then use this knowledge of fatigue to create workouts based on fatigue models, which is covered in the training section of the book.

How Fatigue Manifests Itself

The obvious consequence of fatigue is that you slow down. Why do we slow? The simple reason is that it is a way for our body to protect us. We slow because we are well beyond homeostasis, that nice natural equilibrium the body likes, and if we go much more beyond that homeostasis then dangerous consequences could occur. Fatigue is thus a protective mechanism.

We don't need science to tell us that we slow down, so what actually happens? When broken down, running is a series of spring like hops. A certain amount of force needs to be imparted into the ground to propel the runner forward. The amount of force needed depends on the pace that the athlete is running; the faster the pace, the more force is needed. This force comes about mainly through the muscles themselves generating force via muscle contraction. In simplistic terms a runner can keep going at the same pace as long as they can produce the force necessary on the ground. Once they cannot impart enough force, the pace has to slow as they are not able to cover the same amount of ground with the same stride rate. But what causes a drop in force? Muscle fatigue.

If we look at the biomechanical changes that occur over a 5k race, we get a clear picture of the effects of fatigue. Gerard (2013) and colleagues tracked changes in running mechanics as well as ground reaction forces over the course of a 5k track race. Not surprisingly, the main findings were that peak vertical forces declined throughout the race, ground contact time lengthened, and stride rate and length decreased while the runner slowed. We can't put in as much force as quickly as we get tired, so we slow and our mechanics change. What is happening on a musculature level to cause these changes?

First, when we look at total force output, we can look at it from both a single muscle contraction and an integrated multiple motor unit point of view. So when we look at total force production changes, we are looking at everything along the path from the brain sending the signal, all the way down to the muscle contracting itself. Fatigue can occur along many of the steps of the process, although much attention is focused on supplying energy for the actual contraction to occur.

From the single contraction point of view, we can see that the last portion of muscle contraction is important when discussing fatigue. Many theorize that since the last step of muscle contraction is dependent on ATP supply, energy supply is what limits performance. Or in other words, in order to delay fatigue, the recycling of ATP must keep up with the demand for ATP by the muscles. If supply cannot keep up with demand, then fatigue occurs. As you all know, we have several different energy systems to recycle ATP. This is where the energetic theory of fatigue comes into play. If we cannot regenerate ATP at a sufficient rate, fatigue occurs. The importance of the energy systems derives from these ideas.

While single muscle fiber contraction is how force is developed in isolation, the reality is that total force develops through the integration of many different motor units being active. Thus, the second factor that determines force is how many motor units are recruited to do the work. As previously mentioned, the Central Nervous System (CNS) sends the signal to the muscle to initiate recruitment. Thus, the CNS is in charge of deciding how many motor units need to be recruited to do the necessary work. The CNS can regulate exact force production in several ways. First, the type of motor units recruited and their individual characteristics play a role. Muscle fiber types are typically broken down into several distinct types, but it is best to think of them as a spectrum ranging from pure Fast Twitch (FT) to pure Slow Twitch (ST). The more FT a fiber is the higher force production from that fiber but the lower fatigue resistance. For this reason, ST fibers are generally initially recruited while FT fibers are reserved for later recruitment or very high force requirement activities like sprinting.

Second, the total amount of motor units recruited influences force production. A greater amount of motor units recruited means more muscle fibers able to do the work. Obviously whether they are FT or ST fibers also plays a role, but in general the more motor units that are recruited, the more force that can be developed.

Lastly, the way in which muscles are recruited plays a role. Muscle recruitment can either happen synchronistically or asynchronistically. For endurance events, recruitment generally happens in an asynchronous fashion in which we rotate the work among motor units as some contract while others rest. Once the working units become fatigued, the resting units take over the workload and let the fatigued ones rest (Maglischo, 2003). In this way, force output is kept constant. While these aren't the only ways the body regulates force output, for fatigue these are the main ones to consider.

We can use an analogy to understand the process of force development a little bit better. If you are in charge of a construction job, you know exactly how much work you need to have your workers do before the job is finished. Just as the brain uses resources efficiently, you don't want to hire more workers than you need, and you want to hire the right ones for the job. So what our fictional construction manager does is decide based on the job how many to hire, just as the brain decides how many fibers to recruit. The next step is to decide what type of worker, or in our analogy muscle fibers, to hire. We can either hire fast workers who only work a few hours a day before tiring or stronger slower workers. Based on our construction job, we decide which ones will do the best job, and then finally, we decide shift hours and whether we want everyone working the same 8 hour shifts, or if we want to stagger them. Our brain, just like our construction manager, makes all of these decisions in its best interest to accomplish the job in the most efficient way possible.

One other factor plays a role in how much force output occurs and it has to do with the biomechanics of the movement. There are certain biomechanical phenomena that aid in force output. The use of elastic energy is chief among them. The most well known is that of the Stretch Shortening Cycle (SSC). The SSC occurs when a muscle is initially stretched and then immediately contracts. When this occurs, the force output is much higher than if the muscle had simply contracted from a resting position. It essentially acts in the same way that a rubber band would. Not only do the muscles use elastic energy but the tendons do too. Another form of elastic energy storage and return occurs when ground contact is made. Upon ground contact, a large amount of energy is transmitted up the body that can be stored and used subsequently to push off from the ground. In particular, the tendons are useful in this respect. The two main contributors are the Achilles tendon and the arch of the foot (Ker et al., 1987). While the details of these will be discussed later, it's important to understand that elastic energy storage and return plays a large role in total force output. Additionally, this system can experience fatigue. Muscle or tendon damage is one way that the storage and use of elastic energy can decrease. Additionally, as we fatigue our ability to dissipate the muscle vibration that occurs with every impact is affected. This means we now have a decreased ability to utilize this so called "free energy." Now that we understand the basics of force output, it's time to move onto fatigue.

How Fatigue Occurs

In the next chapter we will look at fatigue as a whole, but for this section I want to break it down into its individualized parts before putting it back together. This is what the "old" model of fatigue does. We look at items that may cause fatigue in the periphery. While this isn't how newer theories suggest it works, it provides a framework off of which to work. The first is what I call the by-product buildup, the second is depletion, and the third is regulation, which includes the Central governor theory.

The By-Product Buildup

The By-Product buildup idea states that it is the buildup of certain by-products or substances that cause fatigue at several different levels. The most common, although wrong, example of this theory is the buildup of lactic acid. In essence, the buildup of certain products creates fatigue by impairing force output at any number of the different steps to get from muscle recruitment to contraction. Whether these products directly or indirectly cause fatigue is another subject that will be covered shortly.

There are many different products that can potentially cause fatigue. Many of the earlier ideas centered on the energetic model in which supplying ATP to the muscle for contraction is the main component. As is well known, the three basic energy systems are the immediate (Phosphagen and Myokinase), Glycolysis, and Aerobic system. Each system requires a series of chemical reactions that ultimately result in ATP reformation. The belief is that the energy systems, mainly the Glycolytic one, create by-products that inhibit subsequent energy production. As the use of these systems increased, by-products that cause fatigue increased to a degree that they interfered with total energy production from all the systems. In the energetic model, the enzymes that catalyze the numerous chemical reactions become less active, thus directly slowing energy production.

Looking at it from a contraction standpoint, these by-product increases can interfere with contraction via methods outside of energy production. Any number of the steps to get from sending the signal to actual muscle contraction can be impaired. The accumulation of such products as ammonia and potassium are prime examples, as these alter muscle fiber excitability. The impairment of muscle contraction can occur at any number of different sites, ranging from impairing the action potential to changes in Calcium release or uptake which can delay contraction and relaxation (Hargreaves & Spriett, 2006).

While lactate was initially seen as the culprit, hydrogen ions (H+) and the corresponding drop in pH are more compelling examples. As pH drops, the rate of ATP replenishment drops due to a reduction of two enzymes, PFK and ATPase, as well as an increase in the amount of Calcium needed during muscle contraction (Maglischo, 2003). This is just one example, and while it is beyond the scope of this book to review every product and site of fatigue, some include increased levels of: H+, ammonia, Potassium, Phosphate, Calcium and ADP (Hargreaves & Spriett, 2006).

Depletion

The idea of depletion is basically the exact opposite of the by-product buildup idea. Instead of the accumulation of products that cause fatigue, it is the depletion of products that lead to fatigue. It's best to think of this theory in terms of fuel sources. Whenever a vital fuel source is running low, fatigue is going to occur because the runner will need to slow down and switch fuel sources to make sure that total depletion does not occur.

Two prime examples of this are on the opposite ends of the energetic spectrum. The first is with the immediate energy systems. As we run out of stored ATP, we have to switch to get another energy system revved up and going. If that didn't occur, then we'd hit some sort of catastrophic failure. We end up slowing slightly as our next fuel system up can't provide energy at the same rate. The other example is in that of glycogen use. There is only a limited amount of glycogen stored in the body. When that fuel source starts to run low, the body has to switch to less productive fuel sources, such as fat, to keep going. This occurs during a marathon or longer races. Thus the depletion of glycogen causes fatigue. Other examples include a decrease in blood glucose or Branch Chain Amino Acids (Hargreaves & Spriett, 2006). The reality is that fatigue is a dynamic process and does not occur in isolation. Thus it depends on the individual and the race that they are running. It is likely that it is a combination of products that build up and other products that deplete which cause fatigue.

Oxygen's Role

This basic understanding on how and why fatigue develops is critical in understanding the development of the scientific models of endurance performance, and in figuring out what limits performance. Using the concepts expressed above, to prevent fatigue we must reduce the rate of by-product buildup or fuel source depletion, or alternatively increase the level of buildup or depletion that we can withstand before we consciously or subconsciously start reducing performance.

Exercise science has been based on the energetic model, which states that it is energy supply that is important in delaying fatigue due to the fact that contraction is dependent on having energy. As explained in Chapter 1, energy is recycled via three main energy systems: the immediate systems, Glycolysis, and the Aerobic system. Each has their benefits and drawbacks, but the common understanding is that the immediate system and Glycolysis lead to some negative drawbacks like by-products.

One key concept to understand with energy systems is that they don't work independently. As soon as hard exercise starts they are all on, it just takes longer for some to rev up to full capacity and take their workload. Thus the immediate systems and then Glycolysis carry the early load during the start of the race until the aerobic system gets revved up in distance races. Research has demonstrated that this crossover point where the aerobic system becomes predominant is usually around 90 seconds (Spencer & Gastin, 2001). Thus, contrary to what popular literature states, in middle and distance events, we get more energy aerobically as the race progresses. Due to the predominance of the aerobic system in middle and long distance events and the fact that it does not build up by-products that can lead to fatigue at the same rate as the other systems, oxygen has been given central importance in running performance. Oxygen allows the Aerobic system to function and do its job. Without the oxygen taken in, delivered, and utilized we have to rely more on Glycolysis and suffer the consequences of building up by-products. Therefore the supply and utilization of oxygen so that the aerobic system can recycle energy is crucial when it comes to fatigue.

Regulation

The last idea on fatigue is an integrated model which we will touch on in the next chapter. The idea is espoused by Tim Noakes in his Central Governor model and in other dynamic models such as Samuel Marcora's. The central idea of such models is that fatigue is not directly caused by any such buildup or depletion of certain products. Instead those products serve as feedback for either a conscious or subconscious controlling mechanism.

Whatever the controlling mechanism is, the point is that exercise is not limited but rather regulated. The body uses the changes in homeostasis of the various products to regulate fatigue. It does this through regulation of the various methods of muscle force output previously discussed, and different models tend to focus on different methods . Noakes' CGM states that the body uses the feedback it receives to regulate performance by controlling force output via the various methods already mentioned, chiefly muscle recruitment. If the by-products build up too quickly, muscle recruitment is decreased, and thus the runner slows. In Noakes' model, this occurs via a subconscious regulatory system.

For the conscious controlling mechanism, Marcora refers to pain perception and the level of motivation. The increase or decrease in by-products causes changes in pain perception. As the pain increases, runners consciously control their speed, and thus force output. The more pain we feel, the more we slow down. The body in essence is creating ever increasing levels of pain to protect itself and forces us to fold to its demands no matter how much drive we have for pushing on. At some point, pain levels will increase to such a high level that the athlete will be forced to give in and slow. The degree to which and when this occurs depends upon the level of each runner and is probably related to what we typically think of as 'mental toughness.'

The differences between regulation and catastrophic fatigue may seem subtle, but they change the way in which we should view certain aspects of training. For that reason, the next chapter will take an in depth look at this process.

3

The Brain: The Master Controller

"Facts do not cease to exist because they are ignored." Aldous Huxley

Integrating it All

Over the last decade, the way we perceive fatigue has radically changed. In some ways, this shift has mirrored trends seen in other scientific areas, such as neuroscience, as we gain a greater appreciation for the human mind and nervous system. Gone are the days of seeing fatigue as the result of a single product, such as the much-maligned "lactic acid". Instead, the current thinking relies on a complex integrated model with a dash of human emotion.

In 2012, Tim Noakes published a paper that's title included "Fatigue is a brain-derived emotion." (Noakes, 2012). While the paper itself is fascinating, the title sums up the shift in how we perceive fatigue. While there is much research to be done, the newer models of fatigue help explain not only the scientific evidence but, perhaps more importantly, the feelings that runners everywhere experience when they put their all into a race.

Violating Homeostasis

The central change in how we look at fatigue occurred as a result of Tim Noakes' Central Governor Model in the 2000's. Since its introduction, the model has been refined with new evidence, and similarly integrated models have been developed. Regardless of the model, the central difference is that exercise is regulated, not catastrophic. The traditional catastrophic approach would be that any of the sources of fatigue previously discussed would directly cause an athlete to slow down. The classic example would be lactate buildup would cause your muscles to slowly shut down. The integrated model flips the equation around and posits that the traditional fatiguing products don't directly cause fatigue. Instead, they are simply feedback that the brain uses to regulate fatigue. As an example, if we are exercising in the heat and our core temperature goes up, the brain receives this information and starts shutting down muscle fiber recruitment to slow the rise in core temperature.

The brain essentially acts as a safety mechanism with a goal of preventing your body's normal processes from venturing too far away from homeostasis. Its ultimate goal is to protect itself from harm or damage. Anytime we start venturing too far outside the norm, the brain steps in and curtails the workload. This can occur through a variety of ways and can be seen when glycogen is running low, core temperature is getting too high, or oxygen to the brain is diminishing. Whatever the system, there is a limit to how far away from normal it can go. This thermostat-like mechanism can be adjusted, and how far away one can go from norm can be influenced via training.

What is even more intriguing is that the brain works in an anticipatory manner. Instead of simply waiting until core temperature, for example, gets to a critically high level and then shutting things down and causing fatigue, the brain runs a complex calculation and slows you down in anticipation of reaching this critical core temperature. This is why in a time trial in the heat, your pace slows early on, despite not having enough time to reach a critical core temperature. Or in the classic marathon example, it's why pace slows before a runner truly runs out of glycogen. These are but a few examples, and in the rest of this chapter we will delve into the complex concept that is fatigue. First, we will look at the brain itself and how it functions during grueling exercise. Then, we'll explore what feedback signals may play a role and how this information may be processed. Finally, the goal will be to integrate it all together and show how the perception of pain might be the way in which the brain forces compliance to stay within the realms of homeostasis.

The Brain

According to this model, the Brain is the master controller, so it only makes sense to start there and work our way down. It has only been recently that neuroscience has been combined with exercise science to study what happens in the brain during and after exercise. This field will continue to grow and our understanding of this complex interaction will undoubtedly improve, but some interesting research has already shifted our understanding.

One approach to understanding the brain's role is to analyze how perception changes. A study by Ando et al. (2012) provides a glimpse into how the brain works under fatigued conditions. In a uniquely done study, they looked at visual information processing during steady exercise. By measuring reaction time to stimuli in the periphery of the visual field while exercising, they can get an idea of how the brain processes information under fatigue. The study found that while exercising at 75%Vo2max, reaction time in the periphery diminished. Reaction time remained relatively normal in the middle of the visual field but increased as the stimuli were moved to the periphery. The visual field essentially narrowed. It's almost as if our brain said, "we need to conserve resources, so focus only on what is right in front of us, and ignore what occurs outside of this range as it requires too many resources to process all of this information."

What was most interesting is that having a higher aerobic capacity attenuated this effect to a degree, meaning that the more aerobically fit athletes didn't suffer the drop in reaction time and processing that less aerobically fit athletes did. A reduction in oxygen to the brain during exercise could explain this change in visual perception. The fact that visual perception and reaction time decreases in hypoxic conditions would seem to lend credence to this idea.

The results of this study match up well with most runners' experience during races. In my own racing, during intense periods of the race, my visual field tends to narrow, and oftentimes I am unaware of anything outside of the race. The more intensely focused I am, which normally means a shorter more intense race like the mile, the more this tends to happen. I can distinctly remember several races where I didn't hear any splits being called or people cheering for me from the stands, yet every lap I could hear and see my coach standing in the stands on the backstretch among a crowd of others. My brain had filtered out certain visual and auditory stimuli and focused on or amplified others. It decided what is important and what is most likely background noise that takes too much energy to focus on right now.

This idea of cognitive focus and concentration fits well with concepts in neuroscience outside of the world of running. A simplified concept would be that the brain has to prioritize the information and stimuli that it has to process. During a race, information is being processed on the internal state of the muscles, heart, and so on, as well as information from the outside world through visual processes. As a runner gains experience racing, part of the improvement comes from the brain's ability to filter information and determine what is important versus what needs to be ignored for the moment. This can be seen outside the running world and in advertising for example, in the form of priming. If one is 'primed' for a certain word or color, then they are more likely to pick that word out of a paragraph or be able to spot a certain colored item in a visual scene. The idea can be translated over into running and may explain why when you are out there racing, it's not unusual to pick out your significant other's or coach's voice out of the crowd but not hear anyone else. This process of learning what degree of importance internal and external stimuli should be given is part of a person's development as a runner.

Looking further into the brain to see how activity and blood flow changes in certain areas provides some clues to why this altering of perception may occur and how the brain regulates performance and handles disruptions in homeostasis. Due to the limitations of the devices used to measure brain activity and/or blood flow, most of the research has been on isometric exercise or other simple exercise devices. Despite this limitation, the findings are intriguing and show how fatigue as a whole is handled.

Leading the charge in this area has been a group of studies by Hitly et al. (2011). In an initial study they used fMRI to look at brain activity during a series of fatiguing handgrip exercises. They set it up so that during about half of the handgrip trials the subjects would not be able to maintain the force required for the entire test. What they then looked for was what areas of the brain were active just prior to the subject's decision to "give in" and have "task failure." They found that the insular cortex and the thalamus showed increased activation and concluded that:

"In accordance with other studies investigating sensations that alert the organism to urgent homeostatic imbalance such as air hunger, hunger for food, and pain, we assume that an increased thalamo-insular activation in the context of a fatigue-induced handgrip exercise could reflect

increased homeostatic disturbance in the exercising muscle and may be of essential importance by
mediating task failure to maintain the integrity of the organism."

In other words, in this simple task, fatigue was a result of a desire to maintain homeostasis. In a follow up study, Hitly (2011) used EEG while performing a fatiguing cycling exercise to look at communication between the insular cortex and the motor cortex. They found increased communication between the two areas, and this combined with their previous study made them speculate that the insular cortex might play a key role in evaluating sensory feedback and communicating with the motor cortex to maintain homeostasis. While this research is still relatively new, it provides a framework for how the brain could regulate exercise. While it is too simplistic to expect these two areas to control everything, the point is that the communication between areas of the brain that deal with processing sensory input and areas that control motor output lends itself to the idea that exercise is regulated, and as we shall see these areas of the brain will keep popping up.

Playing Mad Scientist

With advances in science, we not only get new measurement techniques like fMRI, but also new treatment devices that would appear to be more science fiction than science fact to anyone a few decades ago. In particular, advances in technology now allow scientists to stimulate parts of our brain. This opens up a whole new world of study, and a whole new set of ethical problems to go along with it.

Two different methods have been developed to stimulate specific areas of the brain, transcranial direct current stimulation (tDCS) and transcranial magnetic stimulation (TMS). While each method differs, the idea is to deliver low level current to specific areas of the brain. While the devices are used in research to look at the function of brain circuits, there has been a rising body of research that uses them as therapeutic devices. In particular, several studies have shown that stimulating certain areas of the brain may be beneficial for people suffering from depression.

What is more pertinent is research that originated in psychology. In psychology studies, subjects would be put through a variety of cognitive or memory type tasks before and after being stimulated by tDCS or TMS. Across a wide range of studies, stimulating different parts of the brain resulted in improved memory, time to fatigue, and response time during a motor task (Davis, 2013). Additionally, it appears that the use of such devices allows for skill learning to occur more quickly and accurately following stimulation. Essentially, it cuts down the time taken to become an "expert" significantly.

Given the array of findings, it shouldn't be a surprise that someone finally tested it out on athletic performance. Okano and colleagues used tDCS over the temporal and insular cortex 20 minutes before doing a max cycling exercise (2013). The study participants, national class cyclists, improved their peak power output by 4%, which is a pretty large performance increase. While the complexity of the subject is astounding, the fact that stimulating the temporal and insular cortex can improve performance surely lends credence to the idea that the brain is the master controller. Whether the insular cortex ends up being the main part of the master controller or not, it seems like stimulation of the brain might help unlock that little extra reserve that our brain normally holds back. The future research in this area could be fascinating and unlock the mysteries of fatigue, performance, and why some people are able to summon up that final kick and push through depths of pain that others can only imagine.

While this is fascinating from a scientific and performance standpoint, it also leads down a deep dark hole. This research has led researchers like Davis (2013) to question whether Neuro Doping is the next wave of performance enhancement. My hope is that we don't have to go down this road, but with portable tDCS systems already on the market for "enhanced video game play," it's only a matter of time before this hits the world of athletics. For now, let's ignore the depressing side of this research and continue down the path of figuring out the brain's role in fatigue.

Neurophysiology

Another approach to dissecting the brain's role is to look at the chemicals that make communication possible, the neurotransmitters. In particular, the neurotransmitters serotonin and dopamine have shown particular promise. While the research is only beginning, analyzing how these chemicals may connect to fatigue provides further clues.

Serotonin is popularly known as the chemical in the brain that is associated with depression due to the most well-known antidepressant drugs, SSRI's (Selective serotonin reuptake inhibitors), having their primary action aimed at increasing serotonin levels in the brain. It's not surprising that serotonin has a wide range of roles, but for our purposes we will focus on how it seems to be connected to mood and anxiety. On the other hand, Dopamine is a chemical that's most well-known role is in the reward pathway, as it is one of the key chemicals that are released during any type of reward behavior. This can range from sex to food to social interactions with our friends. In very simplistic terms, this reward pathway is used to ingrain behavioral responses. So if Dopamine is released and pleasure is felt, the brain is primed to repeat the same set of actions or circumstances that it just did to get the reward. This is all fascinating, but what role do they play in fatigue?

To investigate this, researchers have used drugs to manipulate the levels of dopamine or serotonin in the brain during time trials. In a series of studies by Roelands et al. (2013), cyclists were put through self-paced time trials after the administration of an SSRI in hot conditions. What they found was that subjects needed longer (2.3min) to complete the same workload, but more interestingly the pacing strategies between the placebo group and the SSRI was different. The SSRI subjects were slightly slower during the middle portion of the time trial, but more significantly, they were not able to "kick" at the end. As we will see later, the "kick" is a result of a combination of reserve and drive. The fact that an SSRI eliminated the kick means that serotonin plays a role in fatigue and that perhaps, as Roelands put it, "increased serotonergic activity in the brain may block access to the reserve capacity."

Similar to serotonin, there have been several studies that have used Dopamine reuptake inhibitors before time trials to look at its effect on fatigue. In contrast to SSRI's, dopamine reuptake inhibitors seemed to improve performance in the heat (Roelands, 2013). In a series of studies done in hot conditions, dopamine allowed for better maintenance of power output throughout the time trial. Supporting the work using dopamine reuptake inhibitors, Bridge et al. (2003) found that dopamine activity in the hypothalamus was associated with exercise performance in the heat. In their summary of the studies on dopamine and fatigue, Roelands concluded that:

"From these studies, it seems fair to suggest that drugs acting to enhance brain dopamine would change the initial anticipatory setting of work rate by elevating arousal and motivational levels. RPE would be reduced, resulting in a mismatch between the actual and template RPE. Consequently, this would lead to an increased work rate and heat production, until the conscious RPE returns to anticipated levels for the time trial in the heat"

The conclusions above set the stage for how fatigue is regulated. It appears that using drugs that alter neurotransmitters in the brain has a profound effect on performance in the heat. The reason heat is often used is because it is the poster child for exercise regulation. We never really exercise until true heat exhaustion but instead are shut down early before we hit some critical temperature. In fact, as you will see later, when exercising in the heat, performance is regulated in an anticipatory function, with the body shutting down muscle recruitment and thus decreasing performance very early on in the race or time trial. Due to this fact, heat is often used as a way to look at pacing and anticipatory regulation of performance.

While serotonin and dopamine both have effects on thermoregulation, what is interesting is the effect they both have on pacing strategies. Manipulating serotonin in the brain seems to have a dampening effect on the kick. With the kick largely being a result of the brain letting the reins loose a bit because we are close to the finish and motivation and psychological drive are high, it seems plausible that serotonin may play a role in manipulating mood or drive. On the other hand, dopamine's contrasting performance enhancement seems to alter perception during exercise in heat. In looking at the pacing strategies, it is almost as if the dopamine-related drugs fool the body into thinking it is performing in a cool environment, causes an "ignoring" of the relevant feedback, or most likely allows for a person to tap into the "exercise reserve." Of all the possibilities, the latter is the most intriguing, and the one Roelands decided on. The fact that dopaminergic drugs allow people to exercise beyond the regular homeostasis limits demonstrates the power of regulation of exercise via the brain. Knowing how regulation may occur in the brain itself, what feedback in the body is actually monitored?

The Role of Feedback

In working our way down from the brain, the next step on this pathway is to look at what the brain actually monitors. After all, if we are stating that the brain plays a regulatory role, then its predictions and regulation are only as good as the information that it receives. That information can come from both internal and external sources, of which we will start with the internal cues, before delving into what happens when this feedback is blocked or manipulated.

The reality is that the brain likely monitors a large number of processes going on in the periphery, and for the purpose of this book, understanding every single item it monitors is not important, but rather the concept is what is crucial. Having said that, we will focus on the items that play a role in fatigue, and these internal factors include (Noakes, 2012; St Clair Gibson, 2013; Roelands, 2013):

- Partial Pressure of respiratory gases
  - Oxygen levels in brain and periphery
  - CO2 levels
- Muscular Metabolites (Hydrogen ion, lactate, Calcium, free radicals, etc.)
- Muscle pH
- Electrolyte concentration
- Lactate and metabolic by-products
- Biomechanical properties
- Muscle damage
- Heat storage and core temperature
- Glycogen and fuel stores
- Emotional state

External factors:
- Pace/Splits
- Visual Feedback
- Competitors
- Auditory feedback/ encouragement

Looking at the internal sources of feedback, it is not terribly different from the list of items that we thought directly caused fatigue. This shouldn't surprise anyone, as instead of an increase in hydrogen ion's causing the fatigue, the integrated model suggests that the brain monitors their levels and as they approach "dangerous levels", the brain causes fatigue to keep them within normal limits. This change in mindset seems subtle, but it has profound implications.

It's unnecessary to go through each source of feedback, but exploring some of the major sources helps demonstrate the concept. For example, we can look at oxygen content in both the periphery and in the brain during intense exercise or under simulated hypoxic conditions to see what role it plays. A series of studies help elucidate what is actually going on (Goodall et al.

2012). When exercising in hypoxic conditions, not only does oxygen delivery decrease but also cerebral oxygen content. What is interesting is that this decrease in cerebral oxygen is associated with a decrease in voluntary activation of both muscles involved in the exercise and muscles not involved in the exercise (Goodall, 2012). So a reduced cerebral oxygen level causes a decreased ability to recruit muscles beyond those that are already used and fatigued. Further corroborating this is the finding that central neurons can sense reduced oxygen delivery and alter their activity as a result (Ando et al. 2012). What all of this means is that cerebral oxygen content can change motor drive.

Another example of this process can be seen by analyzing exercising in the heat. When we exercise in the heat, critical fatigue occurs when core temperature reaches around 40 degrees Celsius. Unless there is a malfunction, the body shuts you down before you go beyond this critical temperature to prevent damage. Anyone who races in the heat knows that it isn't a case of race hard until you are hot and then you slow down. Instead, you slow down early on in the race. And not surprisingly, the research finds the same phenomenon, a slowing early on in the race. We will discuss this further in detail shortly in the pacing section, but what happens is that the brain uses a teleoanticipation system where the knowledge of how long the race is, the degree of rise in core temperature, and other factors are used to anticipate reaching that critical core temperature. Essentially, if your core temperature is rising too quickly for you to finish the race unscathed, the brain will start shutting you down early to slow your pace and thus slow the rate of heat accumulation (Schlader et al. 2013).

While these are but two examples of how feedback from the internal status of the body works, I hope you understand how the process works. We could go through the same with glycogen depletion, as we never hit full glycogen depletion, or any other source of feedback. These feedback sources are simply warning signs. If they rise or change too quickly, it sets off an alarm in the brain to do something to make sure that they don't get too far out of homeostasis. It's a safety mechanism, and it's one built with redundancy to minimize the chances of catastrophe.

Manipulating Feedback

While grinding through a particularly nasty set of intervals, we've all dreamed of what it would be like to block the signal of pain. Wouldn't it be wonderful if we could selectively ignore that sensation created by feedback? In one of the more campy Pierce Brosnan James Bond movies, one of his villains had sustained damage to the brain that prevented him from feeling pain. Upon watching the movie, I couldn't help but wonder how fast he could run. While blocking pain might not be as wonderful as it seems, after all how would we learn that touching a stove burns our hand or any other myriad of situations, the idea of manipulating feedback to the brain can provide some deep clues on how this feedback loop functions.

It took researchers a while, but they are finally having fun with some studies. There are several different ways of manipulating feedback involving either blocking it with drugs, introducing a fun dose of deception, or shifting attention to "block" feedback psychologically. Each provides its own clues that help elucidate what is actually going on.

In an experiment, Amann and colleagues (2006) used the drug fentanyl to block afferent feedback during a 5km self-paced cycling time trial. What occurred was not some super human performance because the information from the muscles could not be transferred to the brain, but instead pacing went out the window. Without feedback, the participants ran like your typical inexperienced freshman high school runner: out crazy hard. In the study, the participants went out much quicker and harder, building up a greater degree of "peripheral fatigue" because the brain had no reason to regulate the pacing strategy. The second half of the trial, the participants faded hard and interestingly had problems walking and standing afterwards. What this study showed was that the feedback was one of the ways in which the brain ensured that exhaustion occurred at the finish line and not before. Essentially, the blocking of afferent feedback had removed the initial counter balancing safety mechanism. With no feedback, there was no way for the person to know they were going too hard too soon. Thus, as we shall discuss shortly, feedback and anticipatory projecting play a large role in pacing, and pacing may be a window into our "central governor."

The more amusing way to manipulate feedback is simply to lie to your participants. While it may seem a little evil, deceiving subjects provides good information on how we process external feedback. As a coach, it would seem cruel to call out the wrong splits or tell our athletes they are lifting more than they actually are, but it is exactly what a group of researchers have done.

Starting with the simplest form of manipulation, a group of researchers put their subjects through a 6-week lifting test (Ness & Patton, 2012). They had everyone do a 1 rep max lift on the incline bench at the end of each week. At the end of the period though, they decided to be a little devious and changed the labels on the weights being lifted. Due to this act of deception, the subjects lifted on average 20lb more than they had at any other point in the study, simply by changing the labels.

Moving on to the world of endurance, Castle et al. (2012) decided to have some fun with cyclists exercising in the heat. They had their subjects do time trials on three separate occasions. Once in cool environment (22 degrees Celsius), once it hot conditions (31 degrees), and once in a deceived condition where they were told that it was cool, but in actuality it was 32 degrees. With this simple manipulation of the thermometer came profound changes in performance. Not surprisingly, the cyclists performed more work and covered a greater distance in the cooler temperatures, but as you might have guessed, when they thought they were performing in moderate temperatures but were actually performing in hot conditions, the cyclists covered the same distance and had the same power output as when they were actually in cool conditions.

This is an amazing look at both the psychology of performance and how external feedback matters.

Finally, in a study by Stone (2012), they took their subjects and simply manipulated their competition. They had nine cyclists complete four 4km time trials with the first two being used to ascertain a baseline. On the next two time trials, they had participants race an avatar and this is where the deception came in. They were told that the avatar simply represented their best performance at baseline, which was true for trial number three. But for the fourth trial, they programmed the avatar to go just faster (102%) than their baseline performance. As you might expect now, the deception resulted in a faster performance than any other time trial completed. What is notable about this study is that they found that difference was in anaerobic contribution to the exercise. The deceived trial resulted in a greater anaerobic output at 90% of the time trial. What does that mean? Simply that the cyclists were able to increase power output earlier, and more so, at the end of the time trial. In essence, they were able to kick longer and stronger. The implication for this is that they were able to tap into their "anaerobic reserve" to a much greater amount. It was almost as if their brains loosened the reins just a little.

This phenomenon of deception and manipulation raises many fascinating questions. One pertinent to this discussion is one raised by Stone (2012). How much information can we process? The field of sports psychology largely deals with those thoughts that come into our brain, which as we will see later could just be your brain vocalizing its internal struggle of psychological drive versus maintaining homeostasis. To deal with this there are numerous techniques of associative versus dissociative thinking. While a full discourse is beyond the scope of this book, one concept is the idea that given all this feedback, we can't possibly pay full attention to it all. In the world of neuroscience and cognitive psychology, this concept is prevalent, and there are numerous studies examining how much information we can process at a time. The idea is that our brains must filter that which is pertinent and minimize that which isn't. The classic psychological demonstration is that if I have you repeat and visualize the word red, let's say 10 times in a row, now that word and the constructs surrounding it will stick out slightly more. Your brain will notice red objects to a higher degree.

In the world of exercise performance, this concept that we have a limited capacity to pay attention to all the relative feedback has some interesting repercussions. First, it means that part of training is allowing the body to consciously or subconsciously learn what feedback is important and what is not. As we get better at this filtering, the gap between what the feedback is telling us and how far our body will let us go, or what pacing strategy we take, will narrow. Perhaps more intriguing is also that we might have the ability to "block" feedback simply through thinking. One theory is that by using dissociative thinking, we dampen down the amount of feedback received from the periphery because we are essentially clogging the pathway. Stone briefly mentioned that this dissociative strategy has resulted in an increase tolerance to fatigue in several studies and that it may be due to the "inability to simultaneously process distress related cues from sensory inputs." It doesn't mean that this type of strategy works all the time, but rather that what we pay attention to when we are dealing with fatigue matters. The possibility for shifting focus to manipulate feedback is one that needs to be explored.

While I haven't gone as far as deliberately misleading athletes, although I once worked with a very well-known coach who would fib to his athletes telling them splits and workout times faster than they actually were, you can see this phenomenon all around us. Many times I have watched coaches yell at their athletes that they only have 400 meters left in a cross-country race. Almost always, the actual distance is a little more than what the coaches relayed. I don't think the coaches were deliberately doing it, but it was a situation where you might have 470 meters left, but it sounds better to say 400, and hopefully that will snap the athlete into thinking he is okay to start kicking. Calling out that you "only" have so much left is simply a way of manipulating the athlete's perception.

I've seen this same phenomenon in coaching college runners. On numerous occasions, athletes have gone from looking like they were falling apart to having a huge spurt of energy, simply after me telling them that if they run X, they can PR. The realization that they can PR at just faster than the current pace is enough feedback to lift them out of the doldrums of fatigue, pain, and suffering.

The point isn't to go out and deceive your athletes but instead to understand the role feedback plays. It goes beyond the academic and has a practical purpose. What you tell your athletes or yourself while competing and, more importantly, how you deal with that information matters. That is a profound realization. In terms of practicality in coaching or training, it means that another variable of the coach's toolbox can be feedback. Don't lie to your athletes, but take away feedback. This is where "blind feedback workouts" where athletes run without knowing the pace, distance, or any number of variables, may be useful in teaching them to deal with the demands of racing, and in learning what sort of feedback to tune into or tune away from. Just like any ability, we can train how we receive, take in, and discard the information that comes to our senses. And this ability may just be the key to expert performance.

Perception of Effort

"Natural selection has set up the perception of pain as a token of life-threatening bodily damage, and programmed us to avoid it." Richard Dawkins

Perception governs reality. In the world of exercise, the perception of effort and fatigue is not just some unpleasant state that we have to deal with, but instead it is what ultimately may govern performance. We're all familiar with the concept of effort. It's relatively straightforward, and as runners we are familiar with the idea of dealing with ever increasing levels of pain. Recently, the concept of dealing with pain and increasing effort has shifted. Instead of seeing it as the old school, "let's see who is toughest and can suffer the most," thinking has shifted instead to maybe that sense of effort is our brain's way of telling us something important.

Rating of Perceived Exertion (RPE) is the common measurement tool used in the world of exercise science to measure effort. It uses a simple scale either from 1-10 or 6-20, with the higher numbers meaning that the exercise is "harder." This isn't some complex measurement and is no different than just asking the question: how hard would you rate this exercise at the moment? And if we look at the research, it shouldn't be that surprising that as you go through a time trial, race, or any bout of exercise towards exhaustion, RPE linearly increases until exercise is finished. This isn't mind-blowing work, as you go along in a race, exercise gets harder, and your effort increases. But where does this sense of effort come from and what does it mean?

In the previous section on feedback, we dealt with mostly a subconscious controller that integrated all of the feedback from the periphery. We don't consciously know where exactly our glycogen stores are at; it's all subconsciously controlled. What perception of effort is turning out to be is our conscious window into what is going on in the subconscious. In other words, what we perceive as effort is simply another form of feedback. It tells us how hard the body is working, whether our core temperature might be reaching high levels, or whether something is getting close to getting out of homeostasis in our muscles. The increased effort may just be one of the controlling ways in which our brains try to consciously slow us down. If this fails, as we will see later, it then "forces" us to slow down through subconscious control.

Research has made big breakthroughs simply by switching the viewpoint in which we see effort. One of the current theories on how effort arises is called the reafferent corollary discharge theory (De Moree et al. 2012). What it states is that central motor command (activity in the motor areas of the brain) helps control muscle activation during exercise and that because of this increased muscle activity, the muscle afferents send back a signal that is processed in the brain as increased perception of effort. It's a feedback loop where when we fatigue or speed up and need more muscle activation, the motor areas of the brain increase their signal to the muscle, and because there is more muscle activation, the sense of effort increases. Essentially, we are consciously aware when our body needs to send the signal to increase muscle activity.

But that is only half of the picture. What researchers realized is that they needed to separate the physical sensation of fatigue from the psychological effort. It may seem like a trivial distinction, but separating out the physical symptoms from the effort provides further clues to how the brain regulates performance. Swart and colleagues (2011) developed a novel rating system to separate out these two parameters. They then had cyclists do a series of trials rating Physical RPE (P-RPE) and a rating called Task Effort and Awareness (TEA) that they developed to measure psychological effort. What they were essentially looking at is how much cognitive effort was needed, or as an example, how much one had to "dig down" at each point. The cyclists performed a 100km time trial and another 100km test at 70% of their time trial speed. At set distances throughout the task, they included a series of 1km sprints during both trials. The goal and point of including the sprints during both a maximal and sub-maximal test was to determine the difference between effort and the physical symptoms of effort.

What they discovered was that both psychological and physical effort increases throughout exercise, but TEA only played a role in regulating performance when performance was near maximal. During the time trial TEA and P-RPE increased gradually, reaching its maximum at the end of the exercise. And during the 1km sprints, TEA increased dramatically, indicating that there was a large conscious effort to increase speed during that 1km burst. During the 70% speed trial the sense of effort remained low and in what they called the "subconscious zone." During the sprints, the sense of effort was increased to reach levels identical to that during the maximal trial, while the physical sensations remained lower until the very last sprint. What this demonstrated is that effort only governs performance when homeostasis is close to being violated. Once that point occurs, it takes more effort, or psychological drive, to convince the body to delve just a little closer to that edge. This sense of effort plays a crucial role in regulating performance, as we shall see.

The Mismatch Theory

What we're left with is our brain integrating all of the feedback from both inside and outside our body, as well as our conscious perceptions and sensation. So how does the brain make sense of all of this data and how is it all processed and used to govern performance? Before quite answering that question, let's look at one more study.

De Konig and colleagues (2011) used a simple index they called the Hazard score, which is a simple metric that looks at how hard we are working and takes into account how much longer we have to continue to work hard for. The Hazard score can be simply defined as:

Hazard= Momentary RPE * Fraction of the distance remaining

Their goal was to look at how people regulated pace and to explain the decision-making between speeding up and slowing down. They looked at several different experiments tracking RPE during a self-paced time trial, calculated the Hazard score, and then plotted the hazard score against whether the athlete sped up or slowed down. It turned out that using this simple measurement correlated well with changes in pacing. The higher the hazard score, the more the slowdown, and vice versa. Essentially, what it is saying is that if your RPE is too high for how far you have left, you are going to slow down.

Again, this should make complete logical sense, if we go out too hard and are working hard in the first mile of a 5k race, we're going to slow down because we still have 2 more miles to go. On the other hand, what the Hazard score predicts is that as we get closer to the finish line, it's easier to pick up the speed because the danger is decreased. We're almost done, so we can kick. In the study, they plotted hazard scores versus distance completed, and not surprisingly the hardest part of the race is during the middle portion. The effort is starting to get high, but it is still a long way away from the finish. It's no surprise that it is during this ½ to ¾ point of the race that many people fall off the pace. We reach a do or die point in a race, where we make a combined conscious and subconscious decision to fall off or fight on. This decision making point is largely based on your hazard score.

The key to the hazard score though is the comparison. In this simple little equation is something that is often overlooked. It is our expectations. How we feel at a given moment during the race is compared to how we expect to feel at that point in the race. If we feel better than expected, then the hazard score is lower and we can pick it up or last at the same speed. It is the mismatch between our expected feelings versus our actual feeling that governs performance. There is one additional component that we have touched on but have not explored and that is psychological drive.

Drive can be thought of as how far you're willing to push, and how important this race or contest is. They are intertwined and play a crucial role in determining performance. Racing is inherently a very painful endeavor, and we glorify toughness in pushing through that pain in our sport. The role drive and importance play is more about slightly shifting how far away from homeostasis we can push. A classic example I use is where a runner I coach, Jackie Areson, was falling off the leader of a race in a 5k. She hadn't been paying attention to splits throughout the race and suddenly with 400 to go looked at the clock and found out she had to "only" run a 67 to hit the Olympic A standard. She went from losing ground and falling 30m back to switching gears and running a 64 second final lap to win. It wasn't that she was "bagging" it, but instead the importance of the competition instantly changed once she saw the splits with 400m to go in the race. This is a unique example, but because the importance and her psychological drive increased, she was able to push her performance level farther from homeostatis.

Psychological drive doesn't always work in a positive manner as it could act as a hindrance. We aren't just talking about a meaningless competition, but instead having fear of failure. In a situation where we have a perfectionist distance runner, the drive could turn destructive. Drive and motivation could be extremely high but it could be in the wrong direction. In fact, some researchers have proposed that the "self talk" that goes on in our head during a tough race is simply a battle between psychological drive and homeostatic control (St. Clair Gibson, 2013). It is a war being raged inside our head on how far to go or when to let go and slow down. This is a topic more in line with sports psychology and beyond the scope of this book, but the key to understand is that importance and drive are critical parts of determining performance.

From the discussion above, we know that how we feel is a result of physical and psychological effort, which is derived from internal feedback from the muscles, heart, lungs, etc. and external feedback from splits, distance, and so forth. If this were mathematics, we would break down all of the above theories as follows:

Performance = Mismatch (Expected Effort/Actual Sense of Effort)

Where:
Expected Effort= Previous Experience+ Psychological drive (importance)
Actual Sense of Effort= (Internal + External feedback)* Hazard + current Psychological Drive

While this isn't a perfect demonstration, the key is understanding that our body integrates feedback consciously and subconsciously and transfers this feedback as a sensation of pain and effort. When we race this effort is then compared to how we expected to feel during the race at that point in time. It is then integrated with how much psychological drive we have to push through the pain, or as I'd like to call it, importance. If there is a greater degree of importance, then the body lets the reins loose just a little, and we can push to a slightly higher danger level. This is the essence of pacing. It is the degree of mismatch that determines where our pacing and ultimately our performance lie.

The brain is running a complex algorithm monitoring all of the above factors to keep us from violating homeostasis. How far we can delve into the danger zones is dependent on drive and importance at the moment, but we can never fully go all the way into the depths of the well. There is always a reserve because it is a protective mechanism. Hopefully by now you understand the complex nature of how exercise is regulated, but before leaving this topic let's use two phenomenon to look at how this regulation works in real life.

Kicking and Collapsing

If fatigue were a catastrophic event, once we hit fatigue that should be the end of us. We should slow down and not be able to pick it back up. Obviously, we know that doesn't always happen. More often than not when we reach the last stretch of the race, we can pick up the pace and manage a kick to the finish. In the research world they like to refer to this as the "end spurt" phenomenon. How it occurs offers a glimpse into the regulation of exercise.

If we use the aforementioned model of exercise regulation, we know that the peripheral fatigue by-products providing sensory feedback are increasing throughout the run, but what changes the last portion of the race is psychological drive and the hazard score. As we get closer to the finish, your ability to push increases partly because the danger levels drop. There is less worry about pushing too far because the end point is near. So what the body does is let the reins loose a little bit. The chance of dangerous fatigue happening too soon is greatly diminished, so the body provides just a little more leeway. The kick is a result of the interplay between anaerobic reserve, drive/reward, and a loosening of the safety mechanism from the brain.

This phenomenon can be seen in studies that show that at the end of the race a greater amount of fatigue is allowed. For instance, Ugrinowitsch and colleagues found that during the "kick" portion of the race, greater levels of brain deoxygenation were allowed (2013). Additionally, we can see that at the same time muscle recruitment increases. What this tells us is that despite increasing fatigue, the brain lets us recruit just a little more muscle and deal with just a bit more fatigue.

As previously mentioned, the ability to kick was tied to serotonin levels in one study. The manipulation of serotonin through drugs showed that once again everything is interconnected, as the change in serotonin levels was thought to affect drive and motivation. Not surprisingly then, a kick is not only dependent on being near the finish line but also on psychological drive and importance. If you have a runner 5 meters in front of you, your kick is likely to be much better than if you have no one to catch! It seems like a no brainer, but it's a wonderful demonstration of the regulation that occurs on a psychological and physiological level.

Putting it all together, to have a successful kick, there has to be some reserve left and enough reward or psychological drive. If this occurs, then the reins are let loose just a bit more. Oftentimes when we think of a kick we think of the ability to sprint at the end of the race, so most of the time coaches work on sprinting to improve it. But the reality is that it depends not only on our total capacity but also where we are in terms of using that capacity when we reach the time to kick. Research has shown that the kick is largely the result of tapping into our anaerobic capacity. The problem is that many runners use a large portion of their anaerobic abilities to maintain the pace during the race, so when it's time to kick, even with lots of motivation, they don't have as big of a capacity to increase performance. Thus the goal should be to have a larger capacity to use and training to be less fatigued and not having used that capacity when it comes down to the last 400 meters.

This is what happens when it goes right, but what happens when there is a malfunction in the system? In a fantastic paper by St. Clair Gibson (2013) they looked at why collapse happens during races. We have all seen the athlete get to the last finishing stretch and then suddenly go down and ultimately try to stumble or crawl to the finish. What they hypothesized was that collapse was simply a result of this battle between drive and homeostatic control. Collapse occurs when drive has forced an ignoring of the warning signals from the brain for longer than is normal. Then the brain begins to force a shut down and overwhelm drive.

The degree of collapse can vary between partial, meaning just to a knee or stumbling, to full collapse, lying on the ground. The idea is that the body has two systems of safety regulation. It has its primary system, which involves increasing the feeling of pain to try and get you to stop, as well as a reduction in muscle fiber recruitment to force slow down. But there is a system if that isn't enough, and that is a complete shutdown. It's the last ditch fail safe mechanism. Collapse might occur because it allows for an easier way to return blood flow to the brain since the body does not have to pump against gravity when the head is on the same plane.

Collapse, however, doesn't occur simply from "toughness". It's thought that it might be due to a failure to recognize the feedback that serves as a warning. According to St. Clair Gibson, this could be due to a failure of the receptors designed to integrate the signals or a down regulation of these signals. One example given is one that I've already mentioned. During dissociative cognitive thinking, the processing of feedback in the brain is manipulated, and in theory the feedback warning of fatigue in the periphery is not processed.

If St. Clair Gibson and colleagues are correct, then collapse is simply our last resort safety mechanism. It's the air bag for our body. What collapse gives us is a glimpse into how the body works. It shows what occurs at the extremes of fatigue and drive. The fact is that exercise is regulated. All of the peripheral fatiguing products that we have all heard about since first putting on our spikes and racing all still matter, but instead of directly being the culprits they are just information for the brain.

This isn't just relevant for us scientific nerds but instead opens the door for new possibilities in improving performance. No longer should training only be physiologically centered, meaning training for "lactic resistance," but instead it should include the other parameters that lead to performance. Namely, we can manipulate external feedback in workouts quite easily, as well as work on psychological drive at the right times (everyone's driven in the first mile of a marathon…) and "turning the brain off" at other points to minimize cognitive effort. If approached right, this change in mindset should allow for a different understanding of how to train for performance and possibly new types of workouts to solve that problem.

Perhaps the best demonstration of the regulation of exercise to sum things up are the news stories that occasionally pop up with mothers showing super human strength to lift a car off their child or some other similar scenario. While the authenticity of such stories may be occasionally questionable, the reality is that the body has a fantastic reserve capacity, and if drive and importance are sufficient than our body lets the safety mechanisms go because the risk is worth the reward. In racing, we'll never get to that point, but if we can steadily nudge how far away from homeostasis we can get, then we're on the right track towards improving performance.

4

An Oxygen Problem?

"We are going to relentlessly chase perfection, knowing full well we will not catch it, because nothing is perfect. But we are going to relentlessly chase it, because in the process we will catch excellence. I am not remotely interested in just being good." Vince Lombardi

Ask almost anyone what limits running performance and the inevitable answer is oxygen. That may suffice for the general public, but does that vague answer mean breathing in oxygen, transporting it, or utilizing it in the muscles? In the first two chapters, oxygen's role in energy production and fatigue was discussed. To understand oxygen's role let's first look at how we measure oxygen's impact and then at each step from intake in the lungs to utilization in the muscles.

As a coach, oxygen's importance is probably obvious, but it's important to delve deeper and realize that oxygen goes through numerous steps from intake down to utilization. Understanding this process and where the potential roadblocks lie will allow you to better train your athletes. Workouts can be designed to address the specific limitations for each individual athlete, as it is likely that some will have problems with oxygen utilization while others might have an intake limitation.

The Measurement: VO2Max

"What's your VO2max?" For any endurance athlete this common measurement seems to define your talent or potential. VO2max refers to maximum oxygen consumption and is one of the most commonly measured components when tracking changes in endurance performance. We've all heard of the stories of Lance Armstrong's or Bjørn Dæhlie's incredibly high VO2max measurements, but should it really garner that much attention? In short, no. Contrary to popular belief, VO2max is simply a measurement and does not define fitness or potential. In fact, among well-trained runners, it is impossible to discern who is the fastest by VO2max. That does not mean that oxygen transport and utilization is not important, it simply means that the measurement of VO2max does not accurately reflect these processes. Before dispelling some of the VO2max myths, let's look at the contributing factors of VO2max.

VO2max refers to the maximum amount of oxygen used and is calculated by taking the amount of oxygen taken in and subtracting the oxygen exhaled out (Bassett & Howley, 2000). The measurement of VO2max is commonly used to quantify the capacity of the aerobic system and is potentially influenced by a variety of factors as oxygen makes its way from the environment all the way to the mitochondria in the muscles. To calculate VO2max the Fick equation is used, where Q equals Cardiac Output, CaO2 equals arterial oxygen content, and CvO2 means venous oxygen content:

VO2max= Q (CaO2-CvO2)

While the details aren't crucial, this equation takes into account how much blood our heart pumps and uses the difference between the level of oxygen in the blood when heading to the muscles and then the level after having dropped off the oxygen at the muscles. It's no different than calculating how many supplies are being dropped off at a department store by comparing how many supplies a truck was carrying to the store and how many were left on the truck when it left the drop off.

In this equation, Cardiac Output is a measure of Stroke Volume (the volume of blood pumped with each beat) and heart rate so that we know the total amount being dispatched from the heart. Arterial oxygen content is the amount of oxygen in the blood that is being delivered to the muscles, while venous oxygen content refers to the amount of oxygen in the blood that is returning to the heart and lungs. When the arterial and venous oxygen contents are subtracted, the amount of oxygen being taken up by the muscles is known.

While the measurement of VO2max is of little practical interest for reasons to be discussed in the subsequent chapter, maximizing the body's ability to get and then use oxygen in the muscles is of the utmost importance in running performance. The components affecting and limiting this process can be divided into oxygen intake, transport, and utilization. Oxygen's route from the air all the way to the muscles is largely driven by pressure gradient differentials, meaning that oxygen likes to travel from an area of high concentration to one of low concentration. So as we travel the path from air intake into the lungs all the way down to the muscles, it is largely pushed along flowing from high concentration to lower concentrations. The major steps include:

- o Oxygen Intake
    - ▪ Air intake to lungs
    - ▪ To bronchioli and alveoli where it diffuses to capillaries (blood)
- o Oxygen Transport
    - ▪ Cardiac output-pumps blood throughout
    - ▪ Hemoglobin concentration
    - ▪ Blood volume/shunting
    - ▪ Capillaries to diffuse the Oxygen into muscles
- o Oxygen Utilization
    - ▪ Transport to mitochondria
    - ▪ Use in Aerobic respiration and Electron Transport Chain

Oxygen Intake

The first step along oxygen's journey is obviously getting it into the body and ultimately the blood stream, which occurs mostly due to the operation of the respiratory system. Air is taken in through the mouth or nose due to subconscious control that relies on the pressure differential of the outside air and that in the lungs. From here, the air proceeds down the pharynx and into the lungs. In the lungs, the air travels first through the bronchi and then into smaller tubes called the bronchioli.

At the end of the bronchioli tubes in the lungs are alveoli. This is the site where oxygen transport from the lungs to the blood occurs. Oxygen transport from the alveoli to the blood occurs with diffusion via pulmonary capillaries. The capillaries are very small blood vessels that allow for exchange to larger blood vessels via diffusion. The amount of oxygen diffused depends on both the pressure difference between the alveoli and the pulmonary capillaries and the total amount of pulmonary capillaries. The amount of capillaries plays a role, especially in well-trained athletes, because it allows for a longer period of time in which inflowing blood is in contact, meaning that there is a longer time for oxygen to diffuse into the blood.

Even at high intensities, the oxygen saturation in the blood is normally above 95% (Powers et al., 1989). This has been used as evidence that oxygen intake and transport from the lungs to the blood is not a limiting factor since saturation is near full. However, in some well-trained athletes, a phenomenon known as Exercise Induced Arterial Hypoxemia (EIAH) occurs. EIAH causes oxygen saturation levels to drop by as much as 15% below resting levels during heavy exercise. EIAH occurs because the large Cardiac Output of well-trained individuals causes the blood to move through the pulmonary capillaries so quickly that there is not enough time for full diffusion of oxygen and thus saturation to occur. Therefore, in some highly trained athletes, oxygen intake and diffusion can reduce the VO2max.

Do it yourself Physiology:

Is your limiter in your lungs?

A simple way to find out if you have Exercise Induced Arterial Hypoxemia is to buy a pulse oximeter. These devices simply clip on your finger and take the oxygen saturation in the blood in a noninvasive way. Most models give a pulse reading and an oxygen saturation level. These devices can be found for under $50. To find if you have EIAH use one of these devices during a set of progressively faster repeats. A good test would be to do 1,000m repeats with short rest at progressively faster speeds. In between each repeat clip the device on your finger and record an oxygen saturation level. If the level drops by 5 or more percent from the resting value of 98%, you likely have EIAH and may be limited by the diffusion of oxygen from the lungs to the blood.

EIAH is an overlooked phenomenon and could have implications in elite endurance performance. As researchers, we often look for one main limiter, however the limiter of a certain system or pathway changes based on the individual's physiological makeup and training. Due to the enormous training loads of elite endurance athletes that greatly increase oxygen transport, it is likely that there is a shift in the limiter from more of a transport issue to an intake and diffusion issue.

Diffusion is an issue that is dependent on both oxygen intake and on cardiac output (Wagner, 1996). The degree to which oxygen is saturated is often thought of only in terms of the pressure gradient between the air and the lungs and then the lungs and the blood. However, while the pressure gradient and the attraction, or binding affinity, of oxygen to hemoglobin play roles, the Cardiac Output of the heart also contributes. As already mentioned, with a larger Cardiac Output blood moves through the area where oxygen exchange occurs more quickly, resulting in less time available for loading and unloading. This can be partially offset by an increase in pulmonary capillaries. The larger cross section of the capillaries allows for a longer amount of time for oxygen saturation to occur. If you find that an athlete has reduced oxygen saturation levels, or EIAH, it might be beneficial to try and enhance pulmonary capillarization through various exercises designed to stress the pulmonary system.

Additionally, respiration could interfere with oxygen saturation. High rates of ventilation can result in a mixing of the gases in the lungs resulting in a ventilation-perfusion inequality (Wagner, 1996). In his review on VO2max, Wagner notes that in the majority of normal subjects there is evidence of some sort of pulmonary dysfunction (1996). The results of which can be seen in the increase in alveolar-arterial PO2 difference with increasing exercise intensity.

The muscles that aid in respiration also play a role during exercise. The oxygen cost of respiration contributes significantly to VO2max. At moderate intensities, respiration accounts for 3-5% of VO2, while at heavy intensities it accounts for ~10% of VO2max in untrained individuals (Aaron et al., 1992). However, in well-trained athletes, it was found that respiration accounted for 15-16% of VO2max during intense exercise (Harms et al., 1998). What this means is that the act of ventilation itself requires a larger oxygen and energetic load that must be accounted for. These findings that respiration has a higher oxygen cost in well trained athletes lends credence to the idea that demands and limits in trained versus untrained athletes are different.

Another potential reason that respiration could limit performance is that the respiratory muscles compete for blood flow with skeletal muscle. Due to this competition, diaphragm fatigue can occur at intensities greater than 80% VO2max (Johnson et al., 1993). In a study by Harms they investigated this possibility by artificially increasing and decreasing the respiratory muscle load (2000). They found that endurance was significantly increased by 15% in the decreased respiratory muscle load trial, while endurance was decreased by 14% when increased respiratory muscle resistance was applied. While such studies demonstrate in theory that respiratory fatigue occurs, what happens in the real world? A study by Romer provides an answer as it found that global inspiratory muscle fatigue occurred during 20 and 40km cycling time trials (2002).

If respiration can impact performance, can we do anything to train the respiratory muscles? The study by Romer set out to evaluate this as well, finding that using inspiratory muscle training improved performance over the 20km and 40km trials by 3.8% and 4.6% when compared to a control group and resulted in a reduction of respiratory muscle fatigue post trial. Other studies investigating respiratory training have been mixed. Several studies have seen increases in performance in cyclists and rowers (Volianitis et al., 2001; McConnell & Sharpe, 2005). On the other hand, several authors have found no change in performance with training (Williams et al., 2002; Inbar et al., 2000). In a review on the subject, Sheel found that out of eight studies done, six showed improvements in performance following respiratory training (2002). The contrasting results are likely due to whether oxygen intake and respiration were the participant's main limiter. As we have seen, the degree to which the respiratory muscles contribute to VO2max varies based on training level. For higher-level runners, it is likely that respiratory fatigue or EIAH occurs due to changes discussed previously. For this reason, higher-level runners should consider respiratory training, while lower level runners probably will not see the same degree of benefit.

> ### Applying it your training:
> Several new devices can be used to train the respiratory muscles. The cheapest way is to use pursed lip breathing focusing on breathing using the entire diaphragm. Start with long inhalations and exhalations, gradually increasing the speed of the pursed lip breathing until it is very rapid. Throughout be sure to use the entire diaphragm as most people neglect the lower half.
> Another option is the powerlung, which is a device that you breathe through that adds resistance on inhalation and exhalation. This device costs around $100. A third, more expensive device, costing around $900, is the SpiroTiger respiratory trainer. It is backed by several research studies and trains the respiratory muscles in a slightly different way. Essentially it uses more of an endurance training model.

Oxygen Transport

Since A.V. Hill's first experiments measuring VO2max, oxygen transport has always been considered the major limiter of VO2max (Bassett & Howley, 2000). Oxygen transport refers to transporting the oxygen from where it enters the blood stream all the way to the muscles that will take it up and use it. Di Prampero calculated that oxygen transport accounted for 70-75% of the limitation of VO2max (2003). The rate of oxygen delivery is dependent on several factors.

Heart Adaptations

The heart's Cardiac Output (CO) refers to the amount of blood that is pumped out of the heart each minute and is usually regarded as the major limiter of VO2max. CO is dependent on two factors, as it is calculated by multiplying Heart Rate (HR) and Stroke Volume (SV). Thus to increase maximum CO, one of these factors would have to be modified. Maximal HR is a factor that does not change due to training or even lowers slightly, while sub maximal HR is lowered with training (Brooks et al., 2004; Levine, 2008). However, with endurance training, SV increases at rest and all intensities.

The increase in SV is primarily due to an increase in heart size and contractility. These changes to the heart cause an improvement its ability to rapidly fill and an increase in the End-diastolic Volume (EDV), which is the amount of blood present at the end of filling. According to the Frank Starling mechanism, the greater the stretch on the heart (or EDV), the greater the subsequent contraction is. Think of it as a rubber band–like effect. This means that an increase in EDV, which would create a greater pre-stretch, would increase the subsequent ejection, or SV. Increasing EDV thus plays a central role in increasing SV. In addition, endurance athletes have an increased ability to rapidly fill the heart at high intensities, which is important as at higher intensities there is less time between heart beats for the heart to fill (Levine, 2008). Further supporting this idea, work by Levine et al. showed that in endurance athletes, their increased SV was almost entirely a result of EDV increases due to enhanced compliance of the heart (1991).

Traditionally, the increase of Cardiac Output during progressive maximum exercise has been seen to occur with an initial rise in SV, which then plateaus, while HR continuously increases to maximum. However, recent evidence points to some elite endurance athletes having a continual rise in SV and without exhibiting a plateau (Rowland, 2009). The data is conflicting on whether this phenomenon occurs and, if it does occur, the reasons for it. Rowland suggests that if it does occur the likely mechanism is an increase in End Diastolic filling, which when accompanied by an enhanced Frank Starling mechanism, would result in an increasing SV (2009). This increasing CO throughout exercise is an interesting phenomenon and could point, once again, to the individual nature of VO2max limitation.

One other mechanism that increases end diastolic filling is an increase in blood volume. A study done by Krip manipulated blood volume in endurance trained and untrained individuals and studied its effect on cardiac function (1997). They found that blood volume increases and decreases caused significant alterations in maximal diastolic filling rate, SV, and CO. These results demonstrate that increases in blood volume, which is an effect of endurance training, improve SV and CO via enhanced diastolic filling.

As mentioned previously, a high Cardiac Output can have negative consequences in regards to oxygen delivery. With a high output, the diffusion time for oxygen in the lungs and muscles is greatly reduced because of how fast the blood moves through the oxygen exchange zone. The body must do a balancing act to elicit optimal oxygen delivery. This balancing points to a limit of effective Cardiac Output increase if a subsequent increase in diffusion capacity does not occur. This can be seen at extreme altitudes where in theory, despite increases in Cardiac Output, oxygen uptake would not increase due to diffusion limitations (Wagner, 1996).

> **Future Advances in measuring Cardiac Output:**
> Traditionally, measuring CO is hard to do and not practical during intense exercise. However, a new device called the PhysioFlow has shown promise. It's a device that has EKG leads coming from a small battery pack that can be strapped around the waist. This allows for Cardiac Output, Stroke Volume, and other hemodynamic parameters to be calculated while running.

Hemoglobin

Another major factor in oxygen transport is the oxygen carrying capacity of the blood itself. This is dependent on the Red Blood Cell (RBC) mass and the Hemoglobin (Hb) concentration, which serve as the major carrier of oxygen in the blood. Red blood cells serve as the blood cells that carry oxygen, while hemoglobin is an iron containing protein within red blood cells that binds with oxygen to transport it to the muscles. The degree to which oxygen binds to hemoglobin is dependent on the partial pressure of oxygen in the blood and the affinity between oxygen and Hb. The affinity of Hb and oxygen is how strongly attracted to each other each component is, and it is affected by temperature, pH, hydrogen ion concentration, and carbon dioxide concentration. Hb affinity is once again a situation of balance. While having a high affinity would seem like a positive adaptation, as it would allow more oxygen to bind to Hb, it would also make it more difficult for the oxygen to detach from the Hb when going from the blood to the muscle.

An increase in Hb would improve performance via allowing for an increased transport of oxygen to the muscles. Research has demonstrated this relationship via seeing how reductions in Hb affect performance (Calbet et al., 2006). For example, a reduction in Hb because of anemia has been shown to decrease VO2max (Lamanca & Haymes, 1993). Interestingly, in a series of studies by Ekbolm, after reducing hemoglobin levels via withdrawal of blood and seeing the initial drop in Hb, VO2max, and endurance, after 2 weeks VO2max returned to normal despite Hb and endurance performance being still reduced (1972). This may point to an adjustment made when blood withdrawal occurs that acutely compensates for the drop in Hb that restores VO2max. The fact that VO2max could be restored while still having low Hb raises some interesting questions and shows the remarkable adaptation potential of the body and reminds us that there are many different ways to optimize oxygen delivery to reach VO2max. In addition, the return of VO2max but not performance, points to the idea that VO2max and endurance performance cannot be considered synonymous.

On the other end of the spectrum, in studies artificially increasing Hb levels, VO2max and performance have been shown to increase (Calbet et al., 2006). In one particular study by Buick, elite distance runners showed significant improvements in time to exhaustion and VO2max following a blood transfusion that increased Hb levels from 15.7 to 16.7 g . 100 ml-1 (1980). In a study on blood doping, which artificially increases Hb levels, improvements in VO2max have been between 4% and 9% (Gledhill 1982). Given the reliance on blood doping of such drug cheats as Lance Armstrong, it should come as no surprise that artificially increasing the hemoglobin levels improves performance.

> **Common Misconception with Blood tests:**
>   When you get a regular blood test, Hemoglobin and Hematocrit (the ratio of RBC to the rest of the blood) are the ones endurance athletes obsess over. The problem is that these tests give Hemoglobin per 100 milliliters and do not represent total Hemoglobin levels.
>   With endurance training, Hemoglobin increases, but plasma volume usually increases to a greater extent. Thus, trained runners will usually see Hemoglobin and hematocrit levels drop. In fact, elite Kenyan runners have had levels far below normal of both of these parameters. What this means is that you should not obsess over these two parameters as they mean little without knowing changes in plasma volume.

Blood Volume and Blood Shunting

With an increase in the hemoglobin, the blood itself becomes more viscous, or thicker, as more of the blood contains red blood cells as opposed to plasma. The hematocrit is a measure of the ratio between red blood cells and plasma. With this increase in viscosity, the rate of blood flow is slowed, thus decreasing oxygen and nutrient delivery to the muscles. Therefore, too high a hematocrit could potentially decrease performance via a slowing of the delivery rate. As can be seen, it is once again a balancing act between the rate of blood flow and the carrying capacity of the blood on what best delivers the most oxygen and nutrients to the muscles. This process can be compared to either having a large truck that can carry a lot of goods but only reach 55mph or having a fast sports car with little space that can reach 120mph. If the goal is to deliver the most goods continuously, the optimal combination is likely a vehicle with moderate storage room and moderate speed.

With endurance training, blood volume is normally increased along with hematocrit and Hb. The body seems to self regulate in creating an optimal hematocrit to allow for increased carrying capacity of the blood while also having adequate blood viscosity. However, it is not clear whether a high hematocrit with higher viscosity or a lower hematocrit with lower viscosity is better for endurance performance. Athletes using illegal drugs, such as Erythropoietin (EPO), to artificially boost red blood cell production have performed well with dangerously high hematocrits (Calbet et al., 2006). On the other hand, several world-class African runners perform well with very low hematocrit and Hb levels that would normally suggest anemia (Canova, Oct. 2007). It is likely that this is because of their large blood volumes from endurance training, and it is possible that this reflects an alternative way of adaptation to altitude, which will be discussed below. The question on which delivers oxygen the best and improves performance the most is unanswered.

It is possible that the optimal way to deliver oxygen in terms of blood Hb and hematocrit varies based on the individual. In looking at the way particular groups of people adapt to altitude, it is not a stretch to see a similar variation in whether groups respond best to higher Hb/hematocrit or lower hematocrit/higher plasma volume. There is an Ethiopian-specific pattern of adaptation to altitude to go along with the previously found Andean and Tibetan patterns (Beall et al., 2002). The Andean response consists of erythrocytosis (RBC increase) with arterial hypoxemia (reduced oxygen saturation), the Tibetan pattern shows normal Hb concentration with arterial hypoxemia, and the Ethiopian pattern consists of maintenance of Hb concentrations and oxygen saturation levels. The maintenance of oxygen saturation levels at high altitudes points to some improvement in oxygen diffusion ability from the lungs to the blood or increased Oxygen-Hb affinity. The exact mechanisms are unknown, but the fact that several different patterns of adaptation have been found at altitude points to the idea that different adaptation mechanisms could occur in optimizing the blood parameters mentioned above.

One other consideration is that when exercising the body reroutes a larger portion of the blood volume to working muscles and essential organs. This is called blood shunting and allows for more blood and oxygen to be available for the working muscles. At rest only 15-20% of the total blood volume goes to the muscles, while 85-90% goes to the muscles during exercise (Maglischo, 2003). This process occurs because of dilation and constriction of the arteries, with dilation opening up the arteries thereby reducing restriction of blood flow to the working muscles.

Capillary Density

Lastly, oxygen in the blood stream has to get into the muscles. This process is aided by capillaries, which are the body's smallest blood vessels. In this case, they surround muscle fibers providing a place where substances can diffuse from the capillaries into the muscles or vice versa. This diffusion is how oxygen gets into the muscle fibers, and lactate and carbon dioxide are transported from the fibers to the capillaries. As mentioned already in regards to oxygen saturation in the blood, a larger density of capillaries allows for a longer amount of time for oxygen diffusion to occur. Capillary density has been shown to increase with endurance training, particularly intensive endurance training (Billat, 2003). In addition, capillary density has previously correlated with VO2max (Basset & Howley, 2000).

Oxygen Utilization

Once oxygen is delivered to the muscles it then must be utilized. Oxygen utilization takes place in the powerhouse of the cell, the mitochondria, which is where it helps produce energy. We can quantify the oxygen utilized by the muscles by looking at the arterial-venous oxygen (a-vO2) difference, which tells the difference between the oxygen in the arterioles and the content in the veins. Oxygen utilization by the muscles is generally not considered to be a major limiter of VO2max. This conclusion has been reached from two main lines of reasoning. First, peak a-vO2 differences in elites and non-elites are not very large (Hagberg et al., 1985). Secondly, in looking at the a-vO2 difference, it can be seen that there is not much oxygen leftover in the veins. Arterial oxygen content is around 200 mL of O2/L, while venous oxygen content is approximately 20-30 mL of O2/L (Bassett, 2000).

In simply looking at the numbers listed above, common sense would have us ask why there is even 20-30mL of O2 leftover. While it may not be the main governor of VO2max, a-vO2 is a factor that can be improved with training. While contributing much less to VO2max, it is important to remember that even a fraction of a percent improvement is crucial in the world of elite athletics. In several studies, a-vO2 difference has been shown to increase with long-term endurance training by as much as 11% (Bassett & Howley, 2000; Saltin, 1973; Wilmore et al., 2001). Recognizing this fact, it appears that while not a major limiter to VO2max, it does play a role and therefore should be considered a relevant training adaptation.

In addition, the question still remains as to why there is not full extraction of oxygen by the muscle. Venous Hb concentration has been reported as ~15% in normal subjects (Wagner, 1996). There are several possibilities for limitations in oxygen transport from the blood to the site that uses it in the muscle, the mitochondria. These include the capillary density, which would allow for greater contact time and diffusion, the diffusion distance, and myoglobin concentration, which serves to transport oxygen from the cell into the mitochondria. In his review on the subject, Wagner concludes that distance to the mitochondria is not a major factor because of the high intracellular oxygen conductance (1996). Animal studies, for example one by Bebout using dogs, suggest that muscle capillary density is the main structural factor affecting muscle oxygen conductance (1993).

Future advances in measuring muscle tissue saturation:
Recently a way to measure muscle tissue saturation that is both portable and non-invasive has been developed. The MOXY Near Infrared Spectroscopy (NIRS) is a small device that you strap next to the muscle you want data from. It uses NIRS to measure tissue saturation, oxy-hemoglobin, deoxy-hemoglobin, and total hemoglobin. The system transmits data wirelessly, so it allows for data on what is going on in that muscle while exercising with zero invasiveness. The applications for such technology are almost endless, both from a sports science and a coaching perspective. It's one step closer to knowing exactly what is going on in the muscle during exercise.

Oxygen's final destination in the muscle cells is the mitochondria. The Mitochondria is the site in the muscle cell in which aerobic energy generation takes place. To be transported across the muscle cell to the mitochondria, myoglobin is required. Myoglobin transports oxygen from the cell membrane of a muscle fiber to the mitochondria. Greater myoglobin concentrations would allow for more oxygen transport to the mitochondria, potentially enhancing oxygen delivery and thus performance.

Oxygen is used in the mitochondria during the Electron Transport Chain. Therefore the amount of mitochondria plays a large role in aerobic energy generation. In theory, the more mitochondria, the more oxygen utilization and extraction that can occur in the muscle. However, many studies have shown that while mitochondria enzymes increase significantly with training, the corresponding change in VO2max is much less. Mitochondrial enzymes function to aid the chemical reactions needed to eventually generate energy. In one study monitoring changes with training and detraining, mitochondrial capacity increased by 30% with training, while VO2max increased by only 19%. However, VO2max improvements lasted much longer during the detraining phase than mitochondrial capacity (Henriksson & Reitman, 1977). Mitochondria enzyme concentrations are much more likely to affect other factors in performance to a greater degree than VO2max, like Lactate Threshold and substrate utilization (Bassett & Howley, 2000; Klausen et al., 1981).

The VO2max Limiter

Having gone through the possible limiters of VO2max, it is important to remember that there is not a single limiting factor and that VO2max can be impeded at several points as oxygen travels from the ambient air to the mitochondria. In his review on the subject Wagner eloquently stated that:

> "The concept of 'the' limiting factor to VO2max is no longer an appropriate concept. All parts of the O2 transport pathway are involved in determining VO2max. Thus a change in O2 conductance of any one component will change VO2max in the same direction (1996, pg. 29)."

This idea should be expanded out to include that the impact of each step will vary based on the individual, training status, exercise, and environment. Several examples of this can be seen in comparing different groups of subjects, some of which have been briefly mentioned. Oxygen diffusion from the lungs to the blood is rarely considered a limiter of exercise in healthy individuals at sea level. However, the phenomenon of EIAH occurs in many well-trained endurance athletes. This drop in oxygen saturation in well-trained individuals significantly impacts VO2max. Thus the relative importance of oxygen saturation's impact on VO2max changes with training status (Dempsey & Wagner, 1999).

In a similar demonstration, a study by Powers showed the variation in the main limiter of VO2max between highly trained and normal subjects (1989). They tested VO2max while inhaling normal air and oxygen enriched air in both groups. In the normal group, VO2max was not significantly different while inhaling either type of air. In contrast, the highly trained group saw a significant increase in VO2max (from 70.1 to 74.7 ml/kg/min) when inhaling oxygen-enriched air. This leads to the conclusion that oxygen intake plays a role in limiting VO2max in highly trained people but not in normal subjects, thus showing the impact of training status and endurance capacities. Lastly, the different adaptation responses to altitude in Ethiopian, Tibetan, and Andean groups shows that several different mechanisms can occur to reach the same goal of maintenance of Oxygen delivery.

While the focus for almost a century has been on oxygen transport being the limiter, oxygen utilization could play a role to some degree as increases in peripheral factors, such as oxygen extraction measured by a-vO2 difference, have been shown to cause a small, but significant, increase in VO2max (Wilmore et al., 2001). In conclusion, the take away message is that the individual physiology, the training done by a person, and potentially other factors can shift the limitation of VO2max to a number of different sites or alter the degree to which the various sites limit oxygen transport and even oxygen utilization. The bottom line is that VO2max represents a summary of many different processes that affect fatigue and thus performance. The absolute total number is not as important as how each path along the route to oxygen utilization in the muscles functions.

Instead of worrying about the absolute number, for performance worry about ways to increase the amount of energy that is produced aerobically, and that means improving each step of the process. By understanding the different spots of potential slow down along oxygen's route, a coach can design training around an athlete's specific needs. As can be seen, the weak point is likely to change as a runner develops, so the training will have to shift slightly too. Without understanding the entire process of oxygen delivery and utilization, we end up relying on generic one-size fits all training recommendations for improving the aerobic system, which as you can hopefully see is incorrect.

What does this all mean?

It means the limiter to VO2max changes based on the individual's physiological makeup and training status. The takeaway is that if each person has a different "weakness" in their VO2max, different types of workouts should be used. Yet with most training programs suggested by coaches the same workouts or workout types are targeted as VO2max workouts. Similarly, in the research there has been a large focus on finding the key workouts to maximize VO2max. There is no such magic workout. It is going to vary quite vastly based on the individual.

The takeaway message should be don't focus your training on improving some parameter like VO2max, instead focus on providing the right training stimulus to improve race performance.

5

The Fallacy of VO2max

"If you are a scientist and believe in truth, you've got to say you don't know when you don't know. There's always a temptation, especially if you have a theory, to try to prove it rather than to find out what is the truth." Frederick Sanger

In a comprehensive review on training, Midgley and McNaughton's first sentence states "The maximal oxygen uptake (VO2max) has been suggested to be the single most important physiological capacity in determining endurance running performance" (2006). Based on this notion, training for distance runners has become fixated on the concept of VO2max. Training to enhance VO2max is the subject of numerous review articles and popular coaching material. A whole theory of training has evolved based on the idea of training at the speed that corresponds with VO2max and at certain percentages of VO2max (Daniels, 2005). Given the emphasis on this particular parameter one would assume that it must be very closely tied with performance and fatigue. It's not.

In the following chapter the limitations of VO2max will be discussed. Including the legitimacy of the variable itself, why it arose to such prominence, the efficacy of basing training paces off of it, the question of should we even train to improve it, and how closely it ties to performance. The discussion focuses on VO2max as a measurement, not necessarily the importance of oxygen transport and use. This is of the utmost importance for coaches because VO2max training has become a staple in the training lexicon.

How the VO2max Concept Developed

The route scientific progress takes is highly dependent on what we can measure at the time, and with the ability to measure oxygen consumption first arising in the early 1920's, VO2max became an early darling of the physiologist world. It was in 1923, when A.V. Hill and his partner H. Lupton came up with the idea of there being an upper limit on oxygen consumption. In true pioneer fashion, Hill was the participant in his own study. Hill ran at various speeds around a grass track while measuring VO2 and found that he reached a VO2max of 4.080 L/min at a speed 243m/min (Bassett, 2000). Despite increases in speed, his VO2 did not increase, leading Hill to conclude that there is a maximum limit to oxygen consumption, or in his words:

"In running the oxygen requirement increases continuously as the speed increases attaining enormous values at the highest speeds: the actual oxygen intake, however, reaches a maximum beyond which no effort can drive it… The oxygen intake may attain its maximum and remain constant merely because it cannot go any higher owing to the limitations of the circulatory and respiratory system" (Noakes, 2008, pg. 575).

These findings led to two lasting conclusions. First, that VO2max is limited by the circulatory and respiratory system. The second conclusion was the result of trying to devise a laboratory test for determining VO2max, in which thirty years later, Taylor and colleagues decided that during a graded exercise test a VO2max was obtained when a plateau occurred in VO2 (Noakes, 2008). However, in Taylor's original definition, a plateau was not a true plateau but rather consisted of a VO2 increase of less than 150ml/min from one workload to the next. These findings led to the idea that in order for a true VO2max to be reached, a plateau of the VO2 should occur.

Understanding how the VO2max test came about is important as it impacts the way we currently view and use the parameter. The fact that VO2max was first measured during exercise by one of the pioneers of Exercise Science in the 1920's goes a long way in explaining the level of importance ascribed to it. Whenever a new parameter is discovered or introduced, a large degree of emphasis is put on that parameter in the research. The initial reaction by many scientists is to ascribe a great deal of significance to the newly discovered parameter, as if it will answer all of the questions that we have. It is almost as if it is human nature to go through this process of discovery and then exaggeration of the importance of the new finding. This can be seen in many instances in a wide degree of scientific fields. In Exercise Science, this may best be demonstrated by the rise of the anaerobic or lactate threshold during the 1970's, 80's, and 90's. With the ability to portably test lactate, research was centered on ways to improve lactate threshold and the various methods to test for it. Coaches also devised ways of using lactate testing as a way of manipulating the training of their athletes. Over time, the use of lactate testing and the lactate threshold have slowly decreased and settled into the level of importance that it most likely deserves. Whenever something is new, it is overemphasized, before it eventually settles into its rightful place of importance over time.

Due to the very early development of the VO2max concept, a large amount of early research and study was focused on it, escalating the importance given to the parameter. In addition, theories were developed utilizing the VO2max concept very early on as it was one of the only things that was measurable. The problem is that early development of the VO2max concept created a situation where there was an enormous amount of data and research surrounding it, in essence creating a concept that is too large to break down. It is almost as if the field of Exercise Science was built upon the VO2max concept.

Recently, the legitimacy of VO2max as a measurement and the acceptance of VO2max as a practical measurement of cardio-respiratory endurance have been called into question. The contention is that VO2max is not actually a representative measure of the maximum ability to transport oxygen but is rather controlled by a central governor. In Tim Noakes' Central Governor Model (CGM), the CGM predicts that the body regulates exercise to prevent myocardial ischemia during exercise. This is accomplished by limiting the blood flow to the periphery which the brain accomplishes by regulating muscle recruitment (Noakes & Marino, 2009). Therefore, VO2max reflects this regulation of muscles recruitment. In essence, a central governor acts as a regulator for exercise instead of exercise being limited by some parameter.

The basis of the CGM was described in a previous chapter, but it can be explained with the quote from Noakes that states that "The CGM predicts that a wide range of biological signals are monitored to ensure that exercise always terminates before the loss of homeostasis in any bodily system. (2009, pg. 339)." In essence, the key to understanding the CGM is that exercise is regulated, not limited, and that this regulation is done to ensure protection of vital organs. Instead of the production of so called by-products such as H+ directly causing fatigue, these substances act as feedback to a central governor which then adjusts the workload to ensure that homeostasis is maintained.

There are several theoretical arguments for this model or another similar integrated model. Noakes and other CGM proponents point to the fact that fatigue is seldom catastrophic as would be predicted in traditional models. Instead, the body uses various feedback information and past experiences to modulate power output or, in the case of running, pace. The idea of pacing being prevalent in endurance events and the fact that a finishing kick, or end spurt, occurs are given as further evidence to support this model (Noakes, 2003). Interestingly, evidence of alterations in pacing strategy and EMG, which measures muscle activation, can be seen from the very beginning of performance, such as that seen when racing in warm versus cool weather, lending credence to the anticipation model of fatigue (Noakes, 2008).

An increase in muscle activation is also seen during the last segments of races which should not occur if the muscle is "failing" due to fatigue. Noakes' hypothesis is that at the end of a race the body's feedback says that it is near completion so that it can push slightly deeper into its capacity (Noakes, 2008). Evidence for this hypothesis can be seen in a study that found that when completing a 20-km cycling trial in normoxia versus hyperoxia, the improvement in power output in hyperoxia was proportional to the increase in iEMG that also occurred, which the authors cited as evidence that control of muscle activation was one way in which performance was regulated (Tucker et al., 2007).

Another interesting point raised in the CGM debate is the effect hypoxia has on Cardiac Output. Exercise in hypoxic conditions show a reduction in peak Cardiac Output, due to both a decrease in HR and SV (Calbet et al., 2003). According to the conventional model Cardiac Output, since it is regulated by muscle oxygen demands, should not be reduced. However in the CGM, Cardiac Output is reduced as a regulatory mechanism and is determined by the work done by the muscles (Noakes, 2004). Thus, a reduction in Cardiac Output in hypoxia is due to a decrease in muscle activation. When supplementary oxygen is taken, Cardiac Output immediately increases to normal levels (Noakes, 2004). This immediate increase in Cardiac Output demonstrates that there is a regulatory mechanism in control, and one has to question why Cardiac Output is reduced at altitude when oxygen demand by the muscles should be higher.

The Testing Plateau Problem

In regards to VO2max and how it is tested, Noakes has pointed out that in most cases the original requirement of seeing a plateau in VO2max during an incremental exercise test does not occur (Noakes, 2008). Demonstrating this lack of plateau, in a study on world class cyclists only 47% reached a plateau, prompting the authors of the study to state that their limitations might not be oxygen dependent (Noakes, 2008). It is amusing that some authors have commented that motivation may be the reason some athletes do not reach a plateau (Shephard, 2009). This could be a valid statement if the subjects were sedentary; however, since the above study was with world-class cyclists, it seems a bit ludicrous to suggest that motivation during a maximum test would be a problem with such athletes. In addition, in other studies including one by Hawkins, there have been individual variations in VO2max levels between the traditional incremental test and a supramaximal test (Noakes, 2008). While in the average of the whole group there were no differences between the tests, the fact that certain individuals showed different VO2max is interesting and shows that the traditional test does not always give the highest VO2.

Combining the fact that a plateau does not occur in many subjects and the fact that some individuals reached higher VO2max values during a supramaximal test than the standard incremental one, the use of the standard incremental VO2max should be called into question. Other studies show that knowing or not knowing when a test or trial will end significantly affects physiological parameters, which lends credence to the aforementioned idea. In a study by Baden they demonstrated that during a sub maximal run Running Economy significantly changed, along with perceived exertion, based on whether or not the group knew they were running for 20 minutes, even if they ended up running 20 minutes (2005). The VO2max test is one in which participants do not have an exact finish distance or time, so it is likely that this degree of uncertainty could affect the physiological parameters measured. The study also points to the importance of feedback and anticipation and that it can affect physiological variables.

One final theoretical problem is the question of why variation exists based on exercise testing mode (Basset & Boulay, 2000). A runner tested running versus another modality such as cycling will have different VO2max values. There is great individual variation too, between 0 and 13% in the aforementioned study. If we recognize that regardless of exercise the oxygen cascade from the air through delivery via Cardiac Output are central adaptations and should not be different between the exercise modes, then the change in VO2max must either happen on the muscular level or it is regulated via muscle recruitment. This would explain why elite cyclists reach higher percentages of treadmill VO2max when testing cycling VO2max compared to lower level cyclists (Basset & Boulay, 2000). Lastly, the fact that muscle mass activation seems to be the major reason for variations in VO2max among a whole variety of testing methods shows that muscle activation may play a significant role in determining VO2max, at least to a certain point (Dalleck et al., 2004).

Considering this new theory of fatigue, and the fact that the requirement used for reaching VO2max does not occur in many subjects, the use of VO2max as a testing parameter should be called into question. In addition, if VO2max is regulated, then the question arises if it even accurately reflects cardio-respiratory endurance. If we accept this to be true, then using VO2max and percentages of VO2max for training might not give the training response that we think it does.

Efficacy of Basing Training Paces Off of VO2max

With the rise of VO2max research, training systems developed based on the parameter in two ways. First, training at the speeds that elicit VO2max has become the magic training intensity, which supposedly elicits the most improvements. Secondly, training at percentages of VO2max has become en vogue as a way to quantify training intensity.

In regards to training at VO2max, this arose because of a review of research that showed that the largest improvements in VO2max occurred when training at an intensity that corresponded with the parameter, regardless of duration of the exercise (Wenger & Bell, 1986). This finding was subsequently used to demonstrate that training at VO2max was the best intensity for improving endurance in all groups of people. There are two problems with this conclusion. First, the study's findings are generalized to all groups, even though, as we will talk about later, VO2max does not improve in well-trained individuals. Second, VO2max and endurance performance are used almost synonymously, which is not true; as discussed earlier VO2max may not even measure cardio-respiratory endurance and is certainly not the only factor in endurance performance.

Despite these concerns, training at VO2max has risen to prominence. In looking at the research, there are countless studies and reviews that focus on training at this intensity (Midgley et al., 2006). It has gone so far that maximizing the time spent at VO2max during a training session has garnered much attention (Midgley et al., 2006). Researchers have studied the various interval-training programs with the sole goal of seeing how much time at VO2max each subject spent during the training, which in itself is interesting because it shows the emphasis on the parameter instead of performance. The thought is that time spent at VO2max is the stimulus needed to improve VO2max. However, this theory has not been substantiated by research. For instance, in a study by Billat after four weeks of training using an interval program designed to elicit time at VO2max, VO2max and, more importantly, performance did not improve (1999). In addition, even in untrained people, the original review by Wenger and Bell stated that improvements in VO2max at high intensities were not dependent on the volume of training (1986). Despite these facts, researchers continue to press on with the idea that time spent at

VO2max is the key ingredient for improved endurance, even though no research backs up this theory.

Using %VO2max and %vVO2max to quantify intensity is an accepted practice in research and is used in many training programs, such as those prescribed by Jack Daniels and Joe Vigil (Vigil, Daniels, 2005). The problem with this approach is that each individual will have a wide range of adaptation, even if training at the same percentage of VO2max. This occurs due to differences in the individual's physiology. For instance, lactate threshold can occur at a wide range of %VO2max, even in trained individuals (Brooks and Fahey, 2004). As an example, if two trained runners both performed at a fixed intensity at 80% VO2max, one can be below lactate threshold and one above. This would substantially impact the energetics of the workout, as can be seen in a study that showed there was a 40-fold range for increases in lactate levels at 70% VO2max among individuals (Vollaard et al., 2009). In a recent study by Scharhag-Rosenberger they tested whether exercising at the same %VO2max resulted in similar metabolic strain. They found large individual variance in the lactate response at the fixed intensity, even if groups were matched for similar VO2max values. This led them to conclude that the use of percent VO2max values for training or research should not be used if the goal is to have similar metabolic strain by the exercisers.

In addition to lactate differences, factors such as the individual's substrate use, fiber type, and other physiological variables will all vary considerably at a fixed percent of VO2max. This phenomenon was demonstrated in a study by Vollaard (2009). The study showed that while on average improvements were seen in a variety of endurance parameters after six weeks of endurance training, the individuality of the response was widespread with some showing even negative responses to the training, even though the training was at the same 70%VO2max intensity for all subjects (Vollaard et al., 2009). The study showed that there was a wide range of adaptation in maximal and sub maximal tests including VO2 parameters, muscle enzyme activity, and metabolite levels. An interesting finding in the study is that low responders for an increased VO2max were not low responders in other parameters. The change in VO2max did not correlate with the change in performance on a time trial, which is a significant finding demonstrating that perhaps more attention should be paid to changing performance instead of manipulating physiological parameters such as VO2max. One has to question the training recommendations based on training designed at improving parameters such as VO2max, with the assumption being that performance will improve because of it, when studies show that change in VO2max are often not linked with a change in performance. This phenomenon of varied response is not new and can be seen in a wide array of training situations, such as altitude training for example (Chapman et al., 1998).

Knowing the wide variance in adaptation that can occur when training at a fixed percent of VO2max, its use has to be called into question. In fact, Vollard questioned the use of %VO2max as a way to standardize intensity and suggested standardization on parameters that more directly affect power output (2009). These findings combined with those by Scharhag-

Rosenberger et al. suggest that the use of %VO2max should be eliminated if the goal is to standardize intensity. One has to really wonder about training programs that use %VO2max to prescribe training as what adaptations will take place are almost a crapshoot. This does not seem to be a scientific way to train, as it is portrayed. In practical terms for trained distance runners, it probably makes more sense to standardize paces in relation to their recent race performances or based on percentages of goal race pace in well-trained runners.

Should We Train to Improve VO2max?

As mentioned previously, studies have shown that training at VO2max elicits the most improvement in VO2max. This has been used as reasoning for training at VO2max because, as previously discussed, VO2max is the traditional measurement for endurance. The logic is that if VO2max is increased, endurance performance increases. This is not the case. In addition, the question arises if VO2max actually improves in well-trained runners? It doesn't.

Showing the separation of VO2max and performance, the Vollaard study found that the change in VO2max was not related to the change in time trial performance (2009). Other studies demonstrate improved performances without changes in VO2max (Daniels et al. 1978). Also, studies show that VO2max can improve without changes in performance, which is seen in a study by Smith that showed improvements in VO2max by 5.0% without an improvement in performance over either 3,000m or 5,000m (2003). In addition, in looking at long-term changes in performance in elite athletes, changes in performance occur without subsequent changes in VO2max.

In highly trained athletes, many studies have shown that VO2max does not change, even with performance improvements. In one of the only studies done on a large group (33) of elite runners, Arrese tracked changes in VO2max across three years. Performance improved by an average of 1.77% in men and 0.69% in women, with VO2max remaining essentially unchanged (~76.56 vs. ~76.42 in men, and ~70.31 vs. ~70.05 in women) (Legaz Arrese et al., 2005). This points to improved performance in elite runners without changes in VO2max. Furthermore, it has been shown that among homogenous groups, such as well-trained runners, VO2max does not correlate well with performance and cannot be used to distinguish which runners are faster (Legaz-Arrese et al., 2007).

Further evidence can be seen in two case studies on elite runners. In a study on a female Olympic level runner, Jones showed that while the athlete's 3,000m time improved by 46 seconds, her VO2max decreased from 72 ml/kg/min down to 66 ml/kg/min (Jones, 1998). Another study by Jones, this one on the current women's marathon world record holder, found that while VO2max varied some based on the time of testing, it was essentially stable at 70 mL · kg–1 · min–1 from 1992 to 2003 (Jones, 2006). The fact that Radcliffe's Vo2max was essentially stable despite her training volume and intensity increasing substantially is intriguing. Her training increased from a modest 25-30 miles per week (and her VO2max was already 72 at the time) to 120-160 miles per week. The fact that VO2max did not change despite this massive increase in volume and intensity shows the short time course of changes in VO2max. Most importantly, Radcliffe's performance improved dramatically during that time period.

The rapid change in VO2max can even be seen in untrained individuals. In a study by Smith and Donnell, they evaluated the changes in VO2max over a 36-week training period (1984). VO2max substantially increased by 13.6%, but all of those gains were seen in the first 24 weeks of the study with no further increases during the final 12 weeks. Similarly in a study by Daniels, in untrained subjects VO2max increased during the first 4 weeks of training but did not increase after that even with a further increase of training, despite continued improvements in performance (1978). Given the evidence that VO2max does not change in elite runners and does not correlate with performance, training focused on improving VO2max does not seem like a logical idea for well-trained runners.

Vollaard might have put it best when they came to the conclusion that "Moreover, we demonstrate that VO2max and aerobic performance associate with distinct and separate physiological and biochemical endpoints, suggesting that proposed models for the determinants of endurance performance may need to be revisited (2009, pg. 1483)". Their recognition that aerobic performance and VO2max are not direct equals or even well linked is a step in the right direction and needs to be acknowledged to a much greater degree. Combining these findings with Noakes' CGM creates a situation where VO2max may not be measuring what we think it is. Adding the facts that using %VO2max to classify training results in a wide range of adaptations and that changes in VO2max do not occur in trained athletes, one has to question basing entire training programs on VO2max. The point isn't to question the importance of oxygen or the aerobic system but instead to show that VO2max does a poor job of representing the aerobic contribution

The bottom line question that needs to be asked is why is so much of training focused on a variable that does not change in well-trained athletes, barely changes in moderately trained athletes, levels off after a short period of time, and does not even correlate well with performance? Does this sound like a variable that we should be basing all of our training off of?

6

Lactate, Acid and Other By-Products

"You build the best possible story from the information available to you, and if it is a good story, you believe it. Paradoxically, it is easier to construct a coherent story when you know little, when there are fewer pieces to fit into the puzzle. Our comforting conviction that the world makes sense rests on a secure foundation: our almost unlimited ability to ignore our ignorance." Daniel Kahneman

For decades the main culprit of fatigue and the nemesis of all athletes was a foe called lactic acid. Unfortunately, for decades we were dead wrong. Instead, lactic acid, more correctly termed lactate, has given way to the idea that the buildup of other products could potentially cause fatigue. If you recall the chapter on fatigue, this is the buildup theory. The revelation that lactate is not the enemy doesn't mean that our training needs to be thrown out or that all of the research based on lactate should be banished. While lactate does not directly cause fatigue, it highly correlates with it, so that as fatigue increases lactate increases. This is partially due to the linear relationship between by-products such as H+ increases and lactate increases. One of the keys to running performance is to delay the buildup of these accompanying products. If the rate of accumulation of those products can be decreased, fatigue can be delayed. So while lactate is not the culprit, it corresponds with the buildup of by-products that can cause fatigue. Given the vast amount of research done on lactate, we'll delve into what causes lactate buildup and what can be improved to delay its buildup. First let's look at how the buildup of such products affects performance.

Coaches commonly use workouts to enhance lactate tolerance or the lactate threshold. While the traditional method of hard intervals for the former and tempo runs for the latter has merit, knowing the underlying mechanisms of this process will help a coach better design workouts to enhance those variables. For instance, in the training section you will learn about a progression of workouts designed to improve threshold from the knowledge of how the lactate threshold develops.

Buffering Capacity and Dealing with Acidosis

In events that are run at speeds that require more energy than the aerobic system can provide, anaerobic energy sources must take up the slack. As previously mentioned, middle distance events have a significant anaerobic component. Due to this anaerobic component, certain products will accumulate in the body, potentially causing fatigue. Previous studies have demonstrated that an increase in H+, which is a proton that dissociates from lactate and would decrease the pH, may impair muscle contractility (Mainwood & Renaud, 1985).

While the previously accepted notion that lactate played a direct role in fatigue, essentially acting as a "poison" to the muscles, has been disproven, it does not discount the entire acidosis concept of fatigue (Noakes, 2007). While lactate itself may not cause fatigue, it corresponds with other products in the body that may contribute to fatigue, thus lactate can still be used in studies as a marker of fatigue. For instance, as mentioned already, an increase in circulating blood lactate corresponds well with a decrease in pH and an increase in H+. An increase in H+ has been shown to reduce the shortening speed of a muscle fiber, while a reduction in pH impairs Ca2++ reuptake in the Sarcoplasmic Reticulum and may inhibit phosphofructokinase (PFK) (Hargreaves & Spriett, 2006; Brooks et al. 2004). In addition, a decrease in pH could stimulate pain receptors (Brooks et al., 2004). All of these actions could potentially cause fatigue.

The ability of the muscle to buffer the H+ could potentially delay fatigue. As mentioned above, a rise in H+ concentration causes many processes that could potentially lead to fatigue. In particular, its inhibitory effect on PFK would impact ATP production through Glycolysis. Training has been shown to increase buffering capacity in both recreational and well-trained athletes (Laursen & Jenkins, 2002). Furthermore, in one study, the buffering capacity of 6 elite cyclists was found to be significantly related to their performance in a 40km time trial (Weston et al., 1996). This demonstrates the importance of dealing with by-products and buffering capacity when it comes to performance. Due to the impact of acidosis on energy production and performance, much of the coaching and scientific literature focuses on delaying this process. Of particular interest is the concept of the lactate threshold.

The Lactate Threshold

In this book, Lactate Threshold (LT) is defined as the fastest running speed at which blood lactate levels remain in a relative steady state. Or stated in another way, it is the fastest speed in which lactate production and clearance are in equilibrium. LT has been given many different names, from Maximum Lactate Steady State (MaxLass) to Anaerobic Threshold, and has been given many different definitions based on fixed lactate readings and extrapolation from a lactate curve. Originally, LT was defined as a fixed lactate reading at 4.0 mmol/L, but more recent research has shown that lactate levels at LT can vary as much as 6 mmol/L, between 2 and 8 mmol/L (Beneke, 2000). In addition, LT can be expressed as a percentage of VO2max.

The lactate threshold is dependent on many factors relating to the production and clearance of lactate. This interaction is what governs the amount of lactate in the blood and ultimately the LT (Billat et al., 2003). Lactate production within the individual fibers occurs via Glycolysis. At the end of Glycolysis, pyruvate is formed, which can go one of two routes: it can be converted into lactate via the enzyme Lactate Dehydrogenize (LDH) or into acetyl-CoA via PDH and enter the mitochondria to be used in the Krebs cycle and produce energy aerobically. Whether Pyruvate is converted to acetyl-CoA and enters the mitochondria or is converted to Lactate depends on several factors, including LDH and PDH enzyme concentration and activity (Hargereaves 2006). Contrary to popular belief, conversion to lactate occurs even when in the presence of adequate oxygen.

Path of Lactate

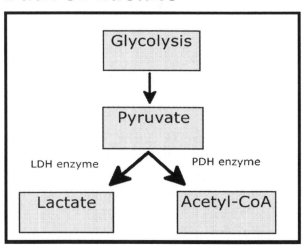

It is important to note that we are measuring blood lactate when defining LT, not muscle lactate. That means that LT is dependent not only on how much lactate a muscle produces but how much actually makes it into the blood stream. When lactate is produced it can stay in the muscle, travel to adjacent muscle fibers, move into the interstitial space between muscles, or travel to the blood stream. How much travels to the blood is partially dependent on both the difference between lactate levels in the blood and muscle and on the lactate transporter activity, which will be covered later. Lactate appearance in the blood also depends on exercise intensity and the amount and type of muscle mass activated. Greater intensity means a greater reliance on Glycolysis without as much aerobic respiration taking place. Also, the more intense an effort is, the greater the amount of Fast Twitch fibers that are recruited, and because of their characteristics, they are more likely to produce lactate.

On the other side of the coin is lactate removal, which occurs via several mechanisms. Within the muscle cell itself lactate can be used as fuel by being taken up and oxidized by the mitochondria. Therefore lactate can be consumed by the muscle fiber, or it can be transported to adjacent fibers to be used. Additionally, it can be transported to interstitial spaces (the space surrounding/between muscle cells). In these instances, lactate produced in the muscle would not increase the blood lactate levels as it would either be consumed by the producing muscle or adjacent fibers, or it would be sent to interstitial spaces.

Lactate that makes it to the blood stream can be removed in several ways. Muscle fibers that are on the Slow Twitch side of the muscle fiber spectrum can act as consuming fibers that take the lactate from the blood and use it as an energy source. Muscle fibers that are not taxed to a high degree also are used to take up lactate from the blood stream. In addition the heart, brain, and liver all play an active role in clearing lactate from the blood. The heart and brain use lactate as a fuel source, while the liver, through the Cori cycle, acts to convert lactate to pyruvate and then ultimately the fuel source glucose. This process has been termed the lactate shuttle, in which lactate is produced in a muscle then sent through the blood stream where it can be taken up and used as a fuel source by muscle fibers or other tissues and organs. It has been theorized that this is one of the body's way of transporting energy stores to different muscles as glycogen in its stored form cannot be transported.

Common Misconceptions and Lactate:

Contrary to popular belief, lactate does not cause fatigue. In fact, as explained in the text, lactate is a fuel source and likely delays fatigue. While acidosis may play some role in fatigue, it is other products such as Hydrogen ions that contribute to decreasing muscle pH. Lactate actually helps by consuming those Hydrogen ions.

Lactate also does not cause muscle soreness. Lactate removal after exercise occurs fairly quickly and does not linger for days like many people think. Following an intense exercise bout lactate can be back to near normal levels after an hour or less and even sooner if easy aerobic exercise is done as that speeds removal.

Why measure lactate if it doesn't cause fatigue? The answer is because the appearance of lactate corresponds almost exactly with by-products that do cause fatigue that are harder to measure. A goal of training can still be to decrease lactate, although what you are really trying to do is decrease products like Hydrogen ions.

Muscle Fiber Characteristics

Muscle fiber type also plays a role in lactate production and ultimately LT. Fast Twitch muscle fibers are more likely to produce lactate due to the individual characteristics of the fiber that make it prefer Glycolysis, such as having a larger amount of Glycolytic enzymes (Bishop et al., 2000). In addition, having less mitochondria, myoglobin, and greater LDH activity makes it where the pyruvate is more likely to go the route of lactate. Similarly for Slow Twitch fibers, mitochondria concentration plays a role in enhancing the LT (Billat et al., 2003).

An increase in mitochondria allows for more pyruvate to be converted to acetyl-CoA and enter the mitochondria. Because of these factors, the fiber type of the athlete and mitochondria concentration will help determine the amount of lactate produced and the LT. Not only does an increase in mitochondria size cause a decrease in lactate, but an increase in mitochondrial enzymes decreases lactate too (Bassett & Howley, 2000). This is likely due to an increase of the pyruvate that is converted to Acetyl-CoA instead of lactate or an increased ability for lactate oxidation. Going beyond just changes in lactate concentration, several studies have established a relationship between mitochondrial enzyme activity and the LT (Coyle, 1995). Lastly, a study on detraining found that the drop in LT that occurred closely mirrored the drop in mitochondrial enzyme activity (Coyle, 1985). These results show the close relationship between lactate levels and mitochondrial enzyme levels.

Monocarboxylate Transporters

Lactate clearance occurs via the lactate shuttle. Lactate produced in a muscle fiber can be used as a fuel source by several different organs; including being shuttled to adjacent muscle fibers, the liver, cardiac muscle, and other muscles via the blood stream (Stallknecht et al., 1998). This shuttle system allows for the transport of an energy source, which is important because stored glycogen in a muscle fiber cannot be converted back into glucose to be transported. Lactate transport proteins mediate this transport.

So far, two different primary lactate transporters have been found that help facilitate transport into and out of the muscle cell. Monocarboxylate 1 (MCT 1) has a high affinity for lactate and is primarily found in ST muscle fibers. It is believed that MCT1 has a role in the oxidation of lactate and therefore the transport of lactate into the cell (Billat et al., 2003; Hargereaves, 2006). For this reason, MCT1 quantity has been found to correlate with endurance performance (Bentley et al., 2009). MCT4, another transporter protein, is found primarily in FT fibers. It has a lower affinity for lactate and is believed to have a role in lactate transport out of the muscle cell (Billat et al., 2003; Hargereaves 2006). Both of the MCT types increase with training, thus showing that lactate dynamics can be improved.

<u>**My Training Cheat Sheet: How to improve Lactate Threshold**</u>
Here are my general guidelines for improving the LT. Start with step one and add in the next steps to your workouts as you progress:
1. Basic mileage
2. Steady runs at around Marathon Pace
3. Level 1- LT runs- Run at around the pace you could race at for one hour- start with 15min total and increase the total time as you progress, progressing to a max of 35-40 minutes total. Can be split up (i.e. 15min, 10min, 5min with 2min rest between).
4. Level 2- LT runs uphill- Do your threshold runs by feel, uphill or on a hilly terrain. Works great on a treadmill.
5. Level 3- Workouts slightly faster than LT- Do split up repeats at just faster than threshold.
6. Level 4- Do the following workouts:
   a. medium length runs at 10k pace
   b. long intervals at just slower than 5k pace- 4x1mile w/ 3min rest
   c. medium intervals at 3k pace- 3 sets of 4x400m w/ 45sec rest at 3k pace 3min between sets

For Fast Twitch type runners (like 800m runners) do very short repeats at near race pace on step 6. For example 10x100m at 1mi pace w/ 30sec rest.

Maximum Lactate Steady State

Lactate steady states are generally only considered to happen during longer duration running. In particular, it is often cited that the fastest speed that one can run while keeping lactate readings steady is a speed that a runner can hold for about one hour (Billat et al. 2003; Daniels, 2005). However, field data provided by Italian coach Renato Canova during a simulated 5k and 10k race in elite Kenyan athletes, one of which is a world record holder, suggests that elite runners may be able to run at a lactate steady state in the middle kilometers of a 5k or 10k, which take ~13 and ~27 minutes for these athletes to complete. This goes against conventional wisdom as it is generally accepted that blood lactate levels increase steadily throughout the race. This may be true for most athletes, but if the elite African runners have this ability to run at a steady state in the middle of the 5k or 10k race this could partially explain their dominance.

In addition, there was a relationship between the ability to increase speed in the final kilometer and the ability to increase lactate by a large degree in the final kilometer. Essentially the athletes were able to run at a moderate amount of lactate during the middle of the race and then during the final stretch of the race increase their speed and lactate levels to a large degree. Perhaps this gap between lactate during the middle of the race and the ending lactate explains the ability to kick at the end of a race. The African runners are notorious for being able to finish very fast last laps in both championship and fast races. Many times their last lap times are very close to their self-reported fastest times they can run one lap fresh. This phenomenon is one that needs to be explored in a controlled environment.

How do you create a MaxLASS?

While it is only theory, it is believed that only high level runners can create a lactate steady state at 5k-10k speeds. One theory is that the high active lifestyle in many African countries combined with high level training allows them to create this effect. However, even the rest of us can create more of a steady state (lessen the steepness of lactate accumulation) in shorter races. Below are guidelines based on Renato Canova's work:

1. First develop Lactate Threshold to a high degree
2. Add in moderate surges during the middle of runs, and at the end of long runs.
3. Intervals just faster and just slower than 5k pace
4. Threshold runs with short surges. Example: 5mi threshold run with 60sec surges down to 10k effort every mile
5. Alternating intervals- Alternate 10k or 5k Race Pace (depending on your goal) with a steady pace (close to marathon pace). Example 5miles of 400m at 10k pace, 1200m at marathon pace
   a. Progressively increase either the distance of the race pace work or the speed of the steady part

Lactate Testing

The best way to measure LT is up for debate (Billat et al., 2003). Traditionally, the lactate test has consisted of a series of ~5min steps that gradually increase in pace. However, research is unclear on what the best testing method is, and if using a step test, how long each step should be and how much velocity should be increased with each step. It all comes down to how much time is required to reach a reasonable degree of steady state. This has led some researchers to suggest long stages of up to 20min (Billat et al., 2003). However, the problem with this suggestion is that it is not practical, and if one does not have a reasonable approximation of the velocity of the individual's LT, then it could take many long stages to find an LT.

At best, the tests used to find a true lactate threshold are essentially educated guesses. The only true way to find a lactate threshold (or Max Lass) is to run at a constant speed for around 20-30min and take blood lactate samples and make sure there is very little increase in lactate from start to finish. Then, do this again at a faster pace. You have to keep doing this until you find the fastest pace that you can maintain without an increase in blood lactate. Practically, it's pretty much worthless and too time consuming. So we throw that idea out the window. Instead scientists have developed all sorts of ways to guess what the LT is based on a lactate curve. Some ways are more accurate than others, but most involve a step test. For example a common test is to run 5x mile with 1-2min rest, starting at an easy/moderate speed and increasing speed by 15sec per mile or so. For example running 5:35, 5:20, 5:05, 4:50, and 4:35 for someone who has a threshold of around 4:55-5:00. This gives you a lactate level for each speed, which is then plotted on a speed vs. lactate level graph. A variety of methods are used to determine where lactate threshold is, but they all essentially look at what speed lactate readings start to increase significantly over baseline. Some involve simply looking and guessing while others involve mathematical formulas, but the bottom line is all are educated guesses.

Since we've established that there is a problem with finding the lactate threshold, let's look at the next problem with lactate threshold research. That would be the problem of knowing what that nice little lactate curve actually means. The traditional way to read a curve is that a shift to the right in the curve means a better LT, or better endurance, and a shift to the left means deteriorating endurance. The problem with that idea is it is too simplistic. According to Jan Olbrecht, who outlines lactate testing in his excellent book *The Science of Winning*, there are two opposing forces that mainly act upon the lactate curve. These opposing forces are the aerobic and anaerobic capacity. Aerobic capacity is essentially how well the aerobic system functions to minimize lactate levels. If you recall the previous section on lactate dynamics, lactate can be minimized via several mechanisms. First, when pyruvate is formed, it can be converted to acetyl-CoA and be used to produce ATP aerobically, thus minimizing the amount of pyruvate that becomes lactate. Also, lactate that is produced in the muscle can be taken up and used aerobically by adjacent muscles or other tissues, and lactate that is in the blood stream can be taken up by Slow Twitch muscle fibers to be used as fuel aerobically. Thus aerobic capacity can be changed based on any improvements that enhance these processes, such as increased aerobic enzymes, mitochondria, or oxygen delivery.

In essence Anaerobic Capacity refers to the maximum amount of pyruvate that can be produced. An increase in Glycolytic capacity through improvements such as increases in Glycolytic enzymes is one example. The theory is that maximum pyruvate production impacts the LT because if more pyruvate is produced without a change in the amount that can be turned into Acetyl-CoA (or aerobic ability), then more pyruvate automatically gets converted to lactate. Therefore a change in LT can occur without any change in aerobic abilities.

These two factors interact to produce the lactate curve. An increase in anaerobic capacity would shift the curve to the left (meaning more lactate produced at each speed), while an increase in aerobic capacity would shift the curve to the right (meaning less lactate produced at each speed). The strength of each of these opposing forces determines where the curve ends up. While this view is still a simplistic actualization, it acknowledges the anaerobic contribution to the lactate curve and provides a better model for looking at the lactate curve. That is an important point, because traditionally all changes in the lactate curve have been thought to be because of changes in aerobic abilities. This model by Olbrecht shows that changes in the curve depend on the push and pull of two factors, not just one. You can clearly see that not only do aerobic abilities, such as how much pyruvate gets converted to lactate or how much lactate can be used by other muscles or organs, play a role, but so do anaerobic abilities such as how much pyruvate is produced. Shown on the following page is a simple diagram of this model.

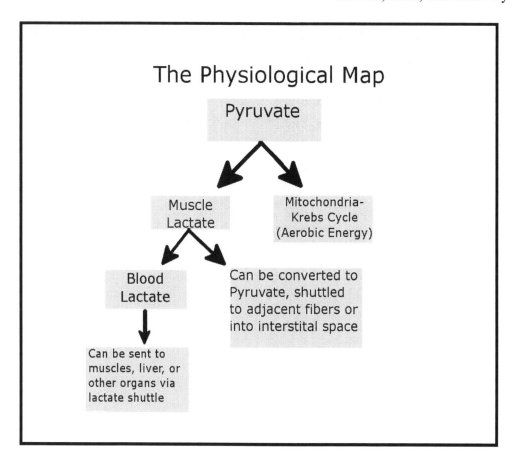

Now that we have this model, what does it mean and how do we use it? Starting at the top of the diagram, the first thing that can be affected is pyruvate production. From this point forward, I will refer to maximum pyruvate production as Anaerobic Capacity. Aerobic Capacity can be seen in the amount of pyruvate that is taken up by the mitochondria and leads to aerobic energy.

Looking at these two capacities, it can be seen how the model works in diagnosing training. In order to increase energy available we can increase the Anaerobic Capacity. That will allow the athlete to produce more pyruvate. However if the aerobic capacity stays the same, then this means more lactate will be produced at that effort level. If we increase the aerobic capacity, then we can see that more of that pyruvate is shuttled into the mitochondria resulting in aerobic energy increase and less lactate at the given effort. This model shows lactate has an interaction with both the anaerobic capacity and the aerobic capacity, not just the aerobic capacity, which is widely recognized as the only source in traditional training models.

The question then becomes how do we analyze the LT curve to see if it was a change in aerobic or anaerobic capacity that caused a change in the LT? While there is no simple foolproof way, the use of an anaerobic capacity test makes everything a bit clearer. An anaerobic capacity test consists of running an all out 400-600m and taking lactate readings every 2-3min afterwards until a maximum reading occurs. This usually occurs within 5-9 minutes following a max test. Combining the maximum lactate number and the speed of your time trial, you get a good baseline idea of your anaerobic capacity. The higher the lactate and faster the speed, the higher the anaerobic capacity is. A decrease in maximum lactate levels and speed shows a decrease in anaerobic capacity.

Once you have this information, do a traditional LT test to get a lactate curve. My suggestion would be 5x5minutes with 60-90 seconds between repeats, starting at a moderate speed and increasing the speed by 10-15sec per mile until the last two repeats are faster than LT. Plot the results in a speed versus lactate graph to get a curve. The first test serves as a baseline. The real information comes when you repeat this test in a month or two. To analyze it, first look to see if there was a change in the lactate curve to see if it shifted left or right. Next, look at the anaerobic capacity to see if it changed. Remember that an increase in anaerobic capacity shifts the curve to the left, while a decrease shifts the curve to the right. The degree to which each capacity changes also matters in that a moderate increase in anaerobic capacity with a stronger increase in aerobic capacity would result in the lactate curve moving slightly to the right. The interaction is what matters. Below is an example interpretation:

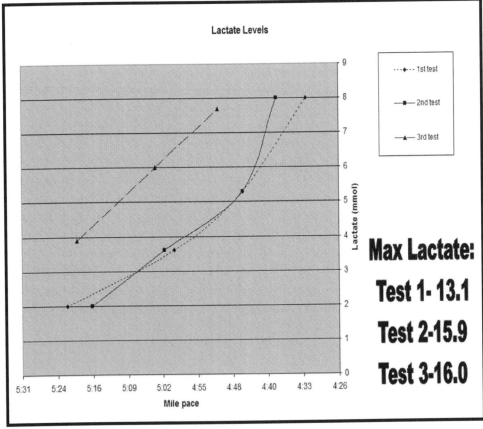

In the above graph, we have three separate lactate tests performed. The first test provides a baseline for the subsequent tests. In test two, it can be seen that lactate levels are essentially the same throughout, with a very slight difference only at the fastest speed. In the traditional way of evaluating the test, these two tests would give the same LT and the conclusion would be that LT did not improve so the training was ineffective. However, note that the max lactate increased dramatically from 13.1 to 15.9mmol. We can conclude that since anaerobic capacity improved by so much thereby pulling the curve leftwards, the aerobic capacity must have improved by a similar amount since the lactate levels did not change. Thus the conclusion is that anaerobic and aerobic capacities were both improved and the training was effective if that was the goal.

Next, test 3 shows the lactate levels shifted upwards and left, as more lactate was produced at each intensity. If we look at the maximum lactate, it shows a very similar number to the previous test so the anaerobic capacity did not change. Therefore, since the lactate levels increased without a change in anaerobic capacity, it must be concluded that the aerobic capacity deteriorated. This is just one example of how lactate curve analysis can be done using this new model. The takeaway message is that lactate levels reflect a balance of opposing aerobic and anaerobic forces.

Do it yourself Physiology
You can buy your own lactate testing equipment. You can get a portable lactate analyzer, test strips, and lancets for a total of around $400. Be sure to read up on how to easily and safely do a test. The device is similar to the devices used by Diabetics to measure blood sugar. It requires a simple prick of the finger, which might sound bad, but trust me it isn't!

7

Efficiency

"The search for understanding, wherever it roams, is a search for better simplifications. Simplifications which explain more and distort less…All human understanding is based on simplifications of more complex realities." Bill James

While most of the time the focus is on capacities, or how big the engine is, the real key is often how efficient a runner is. Coaches and scientists often talk about the importance of efficiency, but what it actually is and how to improve it is not well understood. Instead of one catchall term, there are actually several types of efficiency including metabolic, neural, and biomechanical. These three types of efficiencies combine to create total efficiency. Total efficiency is useless unless the components that make it up are understood. By understanding the three different types of efficiency, a runner can find and improve their particular weakness. Before delving into the different types of efficiency and how they can be improved, let's look at the measurement commonly used for total efficiency.

The Measurement: Running Economy

The last of the traditional big three physiological parameters for running performance is Running Economy (RE). Running Economy is the measurement used to classify total efficiency in research. The measurement uses oxygen intake to represent energy use and is commonly defined by how much oxygen it takes to cover a given distance at a fixed speed (Saunders et al. 2004). RE significantly correlates with performance and has been used in conjunction with other factors as a model to explain running performance. In a study on well-trained runners (VO2max of ~72), Conley and Krahenbuhl showed that RE could explain 65% of the variation in race performance among the group of 12 runners (Conley et al., 1980). While the problems with the measurement of RE itself will be discussed later, it is often forgot in the research that RE is a measure of gross efficiency, meaning that it is the result of both internal and external components, so that mechanical, neural, and metabolic efficiency play a role. The RE measurement simply reflects a combination of these three efficiency components.

Biomechanical efficiency refers to the mechanical cost of running and includes such factors as energy storage and how wasteful the movement pattern is. Neural efficiency can be defined as an improvement in the communication between the nervous system and the muscles themselves. As an example, an improvement in neural efficiency could occur via more refined motor programming. Lastly, metabolic efficiency refers to factors that impact the production of energy for the muscles to use, such as fuel source or oxygen delivery. This concept of multiple types of efficiency is often overlooked, as it is possible to become more efficient in one area yet have total RE be negatively affected because of a larger decrease in another aspect of efficiency. Thus it is a balancing act to maximize total efficiency. The measure itself of gross efficiency may be flawed as it tries to integrate too many variables based on oxygen consumption, but the idea that efficiency is important is correct. Let's look at some of the components that affect running economy.

Biomechanical Efficiency

Biomechanical efficiency refers to anything that impacts the mechanical cost of running. If you think back to the chapter on how running happens, you'll recall that active and passive dynamics combine to provide the energy needed for movement. Biomechanical efficiency is mainly concerned with the passive dynamics side, while the active side, which relies on muscle contraction for movement, is accounted for in metabolic and neural efficiency. There are several factors that contribute to biomechanical efficiency. If these factors are optimized then less energy is required to cover a given distance. They include elastic energy storage and return, the mechanics of the stride itself, how the foot lands, and the structure of the runner.

Stretch Shortening Cycle and Elastic Energy Return

While the most efficient way to run biomechanically is discussed in a later chapter, there are several mechanisms that improve biomechanical efficiency, one of the most important being the Stretch Shortening Cycle (SSC). The SSC occurs when a muscle is actively stretched and then immediately contracts. During the pre-stretch portion, energy is stored in the series elastic components of the muscle, and then the energy is released during the contraction part. Essentially it is a spring-like mechanism with storage and release of energy greater than if just contraction took place. The amount of elastic energy return is dependent on several factors including the length and speed of the stretch, the stiffness of the muscle, and the time between the stretch and the subsequent contraction (Saunders et al., 2004).

In general, a stiffer muscle will store more energy than a loose muscle, although there is likely an optimal stiffness. This idea can be conceptualized by thinking of a very loose rubber band compared to a very tight rubber band. If the tight rubber band is stretched it stores a much larger amount of energy and will fly much further if let go than if a loose band is stretched and let go. In addition, the longer the delay between the stretch and the subsequent contraction the more energy dissipates. Therefore the SSC works best when a stiff muscle is rapidly stretched and contracted with little time in between. A good example of this is the calf muscle upon landing and subsequent toe off during running or the extension of the hip while sprinting. Evidence of the impact of the SSC on RE can be seen by the fact that muscle stiffness strongly correlates with RE (Dalleau et al., 1998). The fact that muscle and tendon stiffness is one factor that can improve RE leads to the question "is an increase in flexibility is such a good thing?" Contrary to popular belief, a stiffer muscle is more efficient during running than a flexible one.

The stiffness of the muscle-tendon unit is dependent on several factors including active characteristics such as the muscle concentric/eccentric contraction state and passive characteristics such as the length and condition of the muscle, tendon, and fascia during impact. Demonstrating the impact of muscle stiffness, Kyrolaine found that stiffer muscles surrounding the ankle and knee created an increased SSC response, which resulted in greater force on the subsequent push off (2001). The keys to obtaining optimal stiffness and energy return are to put the body in optimal position upon impact, training the muscle and tendon to be able to absorb and utilize the forces, and training to pre-activate the muscles.

Pre-activation of the muscles before landing is a way to actively manipulate stiffness of the system, resulting in greater storage of elastic energy. Dalleau demonstrated this in showing that the energy cost of running was related to the stiffness of the lower leg (1998). Pre-activation occurs as the muscles in the lower leg prepare for impact. This is done to adjust for the impact forces, essentially acting as an internal cushioning mechanism, and to decrease the stress caused by muscular vibration. This pre-activation, or muscle tuning, can be thought of as the body's way to prepare for landing. If we are running on soft sand versus hard concrete, the degree of stiffness in the muscle just before landing will change.

In addition to the muscles themselves contributing to energy storage and release, the tendons also play a role. During impact such as the braking or contact phase of running, tendons store energy and then subsequently release that energy via recoil during the take off phase of running. The tendons and muscle complexes essentially act as a spring, storing energy upon ground strike and releasing energy as the runner nears take off.

In a study by Ker, it was found that the Achilles tendon stores 35% of its kinetic energy, while tendons that are in the arch of the foot store 17% (1987). It has been estimated that without the two aforementioned mechanisms of storage and release of elastic energy, the VO2 required would be 30-40% higher (Saunders et al., 2004). To properly utilize these elastic mechanisms, the body has to be in optimal position biomechanically and the tendons have to be trained to utilize the forces. Rapid movements such as sprinting or plyometrics will train the tendons to be better able to utilize the energy.

Additionally, the use of these elastic energy systems depends greatly on a person's biomechanics. Running in a certain way can potentially elicit a greater elastic storage and return, as it will put the muscles and tendons in a better position to be able to store and use energy. For example, forefoot running (or barefoot running) has been shown to improve RE when compared to heel striking with shoes in certain populations (Squadrone & Gallozzi, 2009). One possible explanation is that forefoot running results in the runner landing with the ankle more plantar flexed; this may allow the subsequent stretch reflex on the calf and Achilles-calf complex to utilize more elastic energy than landing in a dorsiflexed position at heel strike where the calf complex is already in a stretched position thus minimizing the SSC. Another possible explanation put forth by Dr. Daniel Lieberman of Harvard is that forefoot striking utilizes the elastic components of the arch of the foot more so than a heel strike does. Lastly, in a heel strike the ground contact time is longer as the foot has to transition from the heel touching the ground to pushing off with the ball of the foot. This lengthened ground contact means more time between energy storage and release. Thus more energy likely dissipates and is lost. Regardless of the explanation, it appears that a non-heel strike would be beneficial to maximize efficiency if a runner is highly dependent on elastic energy return. This is but one example of how the position of the body impacts energy usage.

Maximizing Elastic energy use:

1. Biomechanics- How you run plays a large role. Ideally, foot strike would be mid or forefoot underneath your knee and close to your center of gravity. An often overlooked use of elastic energy is in the muscles in the hip. Good hip extension allows for the use of this rubber band–like effect that takes care of the subsequent forward recovery leg movement.

2. Reactive or Plyometric training- Short hops, jumps, and bounds with the focus on minimizing the time spent on the ground will work. Sprinting is about the most specific form of plyometric activity that can be done for runners, yet it is often underutilized. Doing 60-100m accelerations is a great way to work on using elastic energy. This type of work will train you to reach force development faster, minimize ground contact, and optimize the stiffness of muscles and tendons.

Racing on grass vs. mud vs. track:

Have you ever wondered why some runners are better in Cross Country than track? The use of elastic energy plays a role. When running on a softer surface, such as mud or grass, more energy is dissipated instead of being returned. Runners who rely a lot on energy return tend to do worse in races where the surface is soft, like cross country, and better on surfaces where they get good energy return, like the track or road.

Stride Characteristics

There are several biomechanical characteristics that impact the efficiency of the running gait. One factor is individual stride length. Since speed is equal to stride length x stride rate, optimizing and manipulating those variables is important. In a study on fatigue during a marathon, it was found that RE decreased in the later stages of the marathon partly due to a decrease in stride length (Hausswirth). This leads to the question of whether manipulating stride parameters can optimize RE. Evidence has shown that runners are most efficient at their self-selected stride lengths and that when made to run with shorter or faster stride lengths, RE was worse (Cavanagh & Williams, 1982). However, it should be noted in the Cavanagh study that not all runners self-selected their optimal stride length. In another study they found that 20% of their subjects selected stride lengths that resulted in an elevated RE (Morgan et al., 1994). It is of interest that all of these subjects were over striders. Similarly, in the Cavanagh study, of the 10 subjects who did not select optimal stride lengths, 7 were over striders. It has been hypothesized that over striding results in a reduction in the ability to use stored elastic energy. This hypothesis was backed up by the findings of Kyrolaine who found that increased braking force, which would occur in over striding, results in an increased RE (2001). In regards to optimizing stride length, it appears that it functions based on a U-shaped curve, where too short and too long of a stride length for a given speed results in increased VO2, therefore hampering RE (Morgan et al., 1994).

In addition to stride parameters such as length and frequency, vertical oscillation contributes to RE. Excess vertical oscillation decreases RE and is one of the factors that helps explain why long distance runners are typically more economical at slower paces than middle distance runners (Saunders et al., 2004). In fact, several studies have found that runners are more efficient at running velocities at which they frequently train (Jones & Carter, 2000). There are two important things to remember with vertical oscillation that are sometimes missed. Remember, that it is excess vertical oscillation that decreases RE, not vertical oscillation itself. A certain amount of vertical lift will be needed to cover ground. Additionally, vertical motion is needed to gain a higher amount of potential energy. If we were to stay flat, the amount of potential energy to be used elastically would decrease.

Tying into this idea, it should be noted that RE is measured at slower speeds due to the need for a steady state in oxygen consumption when doing the measuring. Since runners who focus on shorter events, such as middle distance athletes, tend to have greater vertical oscillation, it is likely that this is a more efficient way to run at faster speeds. A greater vertical oscillation is needed to cover ground in the air and reach their optimal stride length. Based on these two ideas, I would advise against minimizing vertical oscillation and instead recommend finding the optimal vertical component. It is not unlike the basic physics problem we all got in high school to determine the optimal angle to shoot a cannon to reach the farthest distance. Too great of an angle would result in a large vertical component but very little distance covered. On the other hand, a very small angle would result in a line drive shot that would again fall short of maximum distance. The running stride is very similar in that we need to come off the ground at an optimal angle to maximize stride length.

Foot Strike

Whether a runner should use a heal strike or a midfoot/forefoot strike is often debated and it can play a role in biomechanical efficiency. Williams and Cavanagh suggested that a heel strike is more economical due to decreased muscle activation required to provide cushioning, because heal strikers let the shoe do the cushioning (1982). However, it has not been established if the muscles used to alter cushioning play a role in fatigue during a race. Also, as previously mentioned a forefoot strike potentially utilizes elastic storage and return to a much higher degree than a heel strike thus negating the muscle activation consequences. Research by Ardigo backed up the benefits of a forefoot strike, showing that a forefoot strike results in a shorter ground contact time and time of acceleration, both beneficial adaptations (1996). Given these facts, forefoot or midfoot strike are likely to be more economical, especially at faster speeds which require rapid force production and short ground contact times, such as middle distance events, or even distance events at the elite level.

It is likely that there will be individual differences in regards to foot strike, but forefoot striking may be more efficient mechanically, and perhaps more importantly may be needed for the increased force production coupled with a short ground contact time that is seen in faster running (Kyrolaine et al., 2001). Additionally, forefoot striking allows for greater use of elastic energy storage and return from both the Achilles tendon and the arch of the foot. Lieberman also found that a forefoot strike allowed for more conversion of translational energy into rotational energy (2010).

Looking at the foot strike characteristics of elite athletes may provide some clues. Unfortunately there are only a limited number of research studies on the topic. Hasewage looked at foot strike at the 15km mark in a Japanese half marathon (2007). In the study, out of the 283 runners, 74.9% were rear-foot strikers. The rest were mid-foot and forefoot strikers. That leads many to conclude that rear-foot strike may be the way to go. However, if we look at a couple of other factors the picture gets a little cloudier. When you separate out the top 50, instead of using the entire group, those who mid-foot or forefoot strike jumps from ~25% to 38%. That significant difference showed that there was a tendency for more mid/forefoot strikers to be faster.

If we look at ground contact time, there was a linear relationship with the faster runners having less ground contact time and GC increasing as runners got slower and slower. In addition, forefoot/mid-foot strikers spent significantly less time on the ground than their heel strike counterparts (183ms vs. 199ms). These findings led the researchers to conclude:

"The percentage of RFS increases with the decreasing of the running speed; conversely, the percentage of MFS increases as the running speed increases. A shorter contact time and a higher frequency of inversion at the foot contact might contribute to higher running economy."

However, the story is not complete. There are still two other factors that one has to take into account when looking at this study. First off, the video was taken at ~9.3mi into a 13.1mi race. In other words it takes place late in the race when fatigue has already set in. As fatigue sets in more mid-foot and forefoot strikers become heel strikers. Thus, when you look this deeply into a race, it could potentially skew the percentages.

Second, the study was done in a large Japanese road race. While there were several elite Kenyans and other nationalities, of the top 283 the vast majority were Japanese which is very significant. This means that technically the results are only generalizable to Japanese runners. Why is this significant? Because of how the Japanese have historically trained and how they historically run. Due to the heavy emphasis on very high mileage and to moving everyone to the longer distances (half marathon and marathon) while neglecting the shorter distance races (1500,5k), the running style of Japanese runners is very different from Americans, Europeans, and even Africans. Similarly, the traditional ideas taught by Japanese coaches at the time favored a running style that was more flat/scoot around type running. One of my coaching mentors spent time going to Japan educating Japanese coaches on running mechanics at around the time of this study. We've spent many hours discussing what their views were, what the runners were being taught, and how their athletes were running, and his experiences confirm this idea.

Due to these factors, it's impossible to take this study and generalize it to anyone except Japanese runners. In addition, the study shows that speed is correlated with both foot strike and ground contact time. In the only other studies to look at foot strike in faster runners, Hayes and Caplan evaluated foot strike during high level 1500m races in Britain. These studies are unpublished at the moment but were presented at the European College of Sports Science meeting in 2009. They looked at foot strike and ground contact time on each lap. This will not only give us an idea on foot strike implications but also on how that changes with fatigue. The conclusions that can be drawn based on the research about fatigue and training are very interesting.

In the 1500m, the range of times was from 3:45 to 4:22 with the average being 3:56. Once again, ground contact time was related to foot strike. Forefoot strikers spent 161ms on the ground compared to 169ms for mid-foot and 192ms for heel strikers. The difference between heel strikers and the other two are pretty remarkable. What is interesting is that ground contact increases on every lap.

Foot strike also changed based on lap. Initially on lap 1, 34.6% were forefoot striking, 46.2% mid-foot, and 19.2% heel striking. On lap 4 the picture changed slightly. More of the mid-foot strikers in particular had switched to heel striking (heel striking increased to 27 %.) What all of this means is that fatigue presumably caused a change in foot strike. Before delving into the meaning of this, let's look at the results of the other study on 800m runners quickly. Average time 1:55 (range: 1:47-2:01)

	Foot strike	Ground Contact
Forefoot	35%	156ms
Mid-foot	48%	161ms
Heel	17%	177ms
	Lap 1	Lap 2
Ground Contact	156ms	168ms

What does this all mean? It's hard to come to any firm conclusions, but the possible implications are very interesting. In regards to foot strike, there is a relationship between running speed and foot strike. Do all fast runners forefoot strike? No, but there is a tendency for the faster runners to forefoot/mid-foot strike more so than the slower runners.

Critiques of the fore/mid foot striking idea say that foot strike is a function of only speed. While speed certainly plays a role in where you strike to an extent, it's unlikely that it plays as much of a role as people make it out to. This means that someone is not going from a straight heel strike while running easy to a forefoot strike while running 800m pace. The previously mentioned Lieberman study provided the first evidence showing that forefoot strikers struck forefoot regardless of condition. Similarly, if we look at the data in the studies above, you can see that the percentage of foot strike types is remarkably similar despite the significant increase in average running speed between the events (from 63-64sec per lap down to 57.5sec per lap). Even though these are different people running each event, if foot strike were solely a function of speed, like many have claimed, then you would expect to see a definite trend away from heel striking as the group got faster.

Perhaps most interesting is what seems to happen during fatigue. Ground contact times increase in both studies, regardless of foot strike. If we remember back to what typically impacts ground contact time, it provides some interesting clues. Ground contact changed even when foot strike did not, so we can eliminate that possibility. The other two possibilities are that leg stiffness and use of elastic energy changed, which is entirely possible but impossible to know, or that rate of force development was diminished. There is some research showing fatigue changes leg stiffness and stretch shortening cycle fatigue. The most likely scenario is that fatigue is impacting the body's ability to produce force in as short of a time period. The foot has to be on the ground longer in order to generate sufficient force to maintain the pace.

Lastly, in the 1500m study it was interesting to see a change in foot strike pattern. During the last lap, you saw an increase in heel striking. This would seem surprising, as generally one of the faster laps in the race is the last as people try and kick it in. The question is why do runners switch to a heel strike under heavy fatigue? One possibility is that stride length tends to decrease with fatigue and runners are trying to compensate by lengthening their stride, but instead of doing it by pushing off and covering more distance, they simply let their lower leg reach out. Another possibility is that fatigue may impact fine control of the lower leg. As fatigue builds up, the body tends to ignore less critical functions, so the sensory feedback that tells the higher motor centers that we are heel striking are filtered out and ignored. While early on, the brain paid attention to the feedback and didn't want us to heel strike so that injury was avoided, under heavy fatigue the body is more worried about protecting critical functions so impact forces due to heel strike are seen as unimportant. Lastly, in a surprising twist, our body could make us heel strike subconsciously as a way to slow us down. While this seems contradictory, on a subconscious level it knows that if we slow down fatigue will start to dissipate, therefore heel striking might be a sort of protective mechanism when we are venturing too far away from homeostasis. Regardless of the cause, it's obvious that lower leg biomechanics can play a role in not only performance but also in resisting fatigue.

Structure

One last factor can impact biomechanical efficiency and that is the individual variance in the structure of a person. There are certain structural characteristics that make a person more efficient. A reduced lower leg mass in elite African runners has been hypothesized to partially explain their superiority in RE (Larsen 2003). This would be due to the fact that a reduction in mass at the extremes would reduce the energy cost of swinging the lower leg through during running. A study by Scholz found that runners with shorter heels had better RE (2008). This is due to the fact that a shorter Achilles tendon moment arm results in greater elastic storage. Additional structural factors that affect running economy include body fat percentage, pelvis width, and foot size (Saunders et al. 2004). Since an individual's structure cannot, or can only minimally, be changed, I won't go into great detail on the subject. The good news is that there are a wide variety of runners with varying body shapes who have been successful on the elite level.

How Much Does Each Factor Contribute?

Each contributing factor to efficiency is not equal. As discussed, the human body is a wonderfully complex machine that has many mechanisms that work in conjunction with each other. So teasing out how much each item contributes to the energetic cost of running is a tall order.

In a series of elegant experiments, Dr. Rodger Kram has done an amazing job of trying to tackle that question. I first heard of Dr. Kram's unique experiments when he spoke to my undergrad biomechanics class while I was at the University of Houston. He described a contraption that he and his grad students had built to determine the cost of horizontal forces during running (Chang & Kram, 1999). They created a device that used a treadmill and a type of pulley system. In this particular study, they found that around 39% of the energy used was for forward propulsion.

Over the next decade, Kram and his colleagues devised different apparatuses to tease out the how much is attributed to supporting your body weight (Teunisson et al. 2007) and swinging your legs through (Modica & Kram, 2005). These were the three big components that contributed to the energy cost of running that could be measured. They found that supporting your body weight cost around 73% of the total energy required, while swinging your legs through cost ~20%. In each of these experiments, a device was made to eliminate or negate the component they were trying to study so that they could calculate the energetic requirement. For example in the leg swing study a device assisted with pulling the leg through, so that the subject didn't have to, thus eliminating the energy requirement.

The one problem with this model is that it segments out each individual component, and we know the body works as a well-tuned whole. If you have ever dealt with running form, it is obvious that changing one component significantly affects another part of the body. To combat this, all three devices were combined, so that Kram could study the energetic cost of body support, leg swing, and horizontal propulsion all at once. In this grand study, it was calculated that combined these parameters equaled almost 90% of the cost of running (Wardripp & Kram, 2007).

Not wanting to stop there, Kram's group also looked at the cost of swinging your arms (Arrellano & Kram, 2011), maintaining balance (Arrellano & Kram, 2012), and of running on different cushioned surfaces (Tung et al.,2012). Interestingly, the results for arm swing actually found that swinging your arms gives you an energy saving effect of around 4% compared to not swinging your arms. The reason for this is likely that the arm swing counterbalances the leg rotation, and there could be an additive effect that swinging your arms provides towards force application to the ground. The cost of maintaining balance was ~2%, and the cost of running on a hard surface versus one cushioned with 10mm or 20mm of EVA differed by roughly 2%. The interesting part was that the 10mm cushioning "saved" more energy than the 20mm cushioning, demonstrating that there is a sweet spot between dampening the amount of work your body has to do to cushion for impact and the amount of hard energy return needed from the ground.

While these studies are rough models and are not going to give exact figures, they do demonstrate quite uniquely what the main energetic contributors are biomechanically. It's also a nice demonstration of how our body functions as a whole with the many different movements of our upper and lower body working in concert to produce the most efficient movement pattern possible.

Optimizing Biomechanics and Running Economy

Looking at how biomechanics affects RE is a difficult proposition. Most scientists ignore the fact that runners have years of motor programming that has already developed neural pathways for their individual stride, thus they are very efficient neurally at that stride. It is possible that a runner could be running less mechanically efficient, but has adapted to that stride after years of training so that their RE is relatively good. For example, in looking at Cavanagh's study, the question becomes are runners most efficient at their selected stride length because that is their optimal stride length mechanically or is it because they have adapted to that stride from years of running and thus it has become their "optimal" because it is an ingrained motor program? In other words, with training could a different stride length become more efficient? Unfortunately, no long-term training studies have been done to clear up this picture. As will be discussed shortly, there could be a flaw in measuring economy or efficiency that may be clouding the research results. The way economy is measured greatly affects the conclusions that can be drawn.

Comparison studies between elite and non-elite runners may help to provide clues on what optimal running mechanics consist of. In a study by Leskinen, world-class 1500m runners (~3:35 for 1,500m) were compared to national class runners (~3:49) (2009). It was found that the elite runners demonstrated a more efficient use of the hip joint and potentially more elastic energy utilization. The importance of hip extension was also noted in the study by Kyrolainen (2001). This should make sense, as hip extension can both generate a lot of force and, if done correctly, results in a stretch reflex occurring that helps cycle the leg through the recovery phase.

How to Run misconception:

A lot of runners get caught up in trying to manipulate the recovery or swing phase of how they run, when to a large extent what happens is a result of passive mechanics. As Weyend et al. put it, "based on recent research, the energy used to move the legs through the swing phase is largely because of passive mechanics, instead of active muscle action" (2010). What this means is that phenomenon such as the stretch reflex, SSC, elastic energy return, and simple passive biomechanics supply the energy for moving the legs through the air, not contractions. In particular, it is believed that the leg cycling through is highly dependent on a stretch reflex at the hip, which has the rubber band–like effect of being extended and then shot forward.

What this means is that for the most part, except for putting your foot down for foot strike, how your leg swings through the recovery phase is a result of what you do when your foot is on the ground. Things such as how far the hip is extended or forward lead angle will determine how the leg swings through.

The bottom line is that ideas such as kicking your butt, driving the knee, lifting your foot, or pawing at the ground are all bad ideas and bad cues. If someone's recovery leg swinging through doesn't look right, it is most likely because of something he is doing earlier in the stride when he is in contact with the ground.

The manipulation of biomechanics to improve RE in distance runners is often a subject of controversy. As mentioned previously, the complexity of efficiency makes discerning the effects of changes in biomechanics on RE a difficult one. This is due to fact that when changing biomechanics it should be expected that a short-term reduction in economy would occur due to the fact that new motor programming has to take place and muscle recruitment patterns may change. Therefore, doing short-term studies on changes in RE via mechanical manipulations might not be a good idea. However, evidence exists that some mechanical changes may improve RE. The study by Morgen and colleagues changed stride length using audio and visual feedback that resulted in optimizing step length and an improvement in RE (1994). This study points to the idea that mechanical manipulations can improve RE. Lastly, the practical experience of many of the world's best track coaches who focus on manipulation of technique provides evidence from the practical world.

Neuromuscular Efficiency

In addition to the various components that impact mechanical and metabolic efficiency, neuromuscular characteristics need to be taken into consideration. This efficiency can be broken into two categories, factors that improve the neural signaling and motor programming of the running motion and those that improve the muscle force production itself. Recall how the running movement occurs. Reflexes and motor programs at the brain and spinal level combine to result in the running motion. Although it is often not considered one, running is a skill, just like hitting a baseball or swinging a golf club. As with those skills, practice is needed to improve efficiency at the activity. As the movement is practiced the body becomes more efficient by refining the motor program, learning exactly what muscles to recruit, what ones to inhibit, and the exact number of muscle fibers needed. It is through this refinement that the movement becomes better coordinated and efficient. Research has demonstrated these claims, consistently showing that repeated practice results in improved muscle fiber recruitment and movement control (Bonacci et al., 2009). A more efficient recruitment pattern decreases RE because of the intricate linking between VO2 and RE.

Neuromuscular efficiency can also be seen through muscle activation studies comparing untrained with moderately or well-trained individuals. In a study done comparing cyclists, differences in muscle recruitment were found. Novice cyclists showed greater variability in muscle recruitment between pedals, more variations of recruitment between each individual, more muscle co-activation, and longer muscle activation periods than well-trained cyclists (Chapman et al., 2008). These results point to the idea that training can improve neuromuscular characteristics. The fact the neuromuscular adaptations do occur gives an explanation for how resistance or explosive type training could improve RE, which will be discussed in detail later.

Applying Force to the Ground

The muscle contraction itself also plays an important role in neuromuscular efficiency. The ground reaction forces (GRF) and contact time influence both neural and biomechanical efficiency. GRF is explained by its namesake, it is simply the forces that occur when the foot makes contact with the ground. These forces are typically shown in their vertical form as the force exerted upward as the foot hits the ground and then as the person applies force to the ground. GRF can also occur in two other planes, side-to-side and front to back. Ground contact time is self-explanatory and refers to the amount of time that the foot is in contact with the ground. These two factors combine to partially determine speed. To be successful, not only does a runner need to impart a large amount of force into the ground for propulsion, but they need to do so in a short period of time, often around a tenth of a second. Thus, it is not only about force production, but also about rate of force production.

A study by Weyand uniquely demonstrated this by comparing ground reaction forces in running, hopping, and backwards running (2010). They demonstrated that during the other activities higher peak forces could be developed but ground contact time was longer, thus it took longer to develop such forces. During running, the forces weren't as high, but they were generated in a very short amount of time due to the short ground contact period. Their study demonstrated that total force development is not the limiter in how fast someone can run, but rather the limiter is how quickly force can be developed.

In terms of RE and long distance running, a runner would be most economical if they produced only the amount of force necessary to run at a given pace. In a study by Wright and Weyand, they found that the determining factors for VO2 were rate of ground force application and the amount of muscle mass activated (2001). Therefore these two factors combine to impact RE. Backing up this idea, Heise and Martin found that the amount of vertical GRF, when combined with the time it took to apply this force, explained 38% of the variability of RE between individuals in their study (2001). Therefore, maximizing rate of force development so that ground contact is minimized creates a more efficient runner.

Muscle Fiber Characteristics

Lastly, the characteristics of the muscles themselves impact efficiency both metabolically and neuromuscularly. In particular the muscle fiber type is of particular interest. There have been several studies that have found a correlation between Slow Twitch (ST) fiber percentages and improved RE (Svedenhag & Sjodin, 1994; Saunders et al., 2004). Other studies have found correlations between cycling efficiency and ST fiber content (Coyle et al., 1992). This is partially due to the ST fibers being better equipped to utilize oxygen due to its increased mitochondria, myoglobin, and Krebs cycle enzymes. With an increase in mitochondria, less oxygen will be used per mitochondria chain. This would result in a more efficient use of oxygen, resulting in a decrease in VO2. Another explanation is based on the mechanical efficiency of the different muscle fibers. For a specific muscle fiber its peak efficiency occurs at one-third of its maximum contraction velocity (Coyle et al., 1992). Given that endurance training and competitions rely on slower muscle contractions, ST fibers will be closer to their peak efficiency during endurance activities. Backing this up, Coyle found that during endurance cycling, the contraction velocity of the vastus lateralis was close to the peak efficiency rate of ST fibers leading to greater mechanical efficiency (1992). Thus, ST fibers are likely more efficient when an activity requires slower contractions, while FT fibers are most efficient during activities that require very rapid shortening.

In addition, the makeup of the individual muscle fibers themselves could impact RE. Titin has been shown to have elastic properties, which aid in the storage and then subsequent utilization of that energy. Thus Titin could potentially spare chemical energy use (Kyrolaine et al., 2001). It is possible that each fiber type stores elastic energy to a different degree.

Metabolic Efficiency

The processes that result in energy production determine metabolic efficiency. How much oxygen is needed by the muscles, the efficiency in delivering and utilizing that oxygen, and how well substrates can be utilized all play a role. Each of these factors can be improved to a large degree with training.

Oxygen's role should be readily apparent after reading the chapter on how oxygen is delivered and utilized. Additionally, the traditional measurement for running economy relies on VO2 at a given speed to quantify efficiency. That explains why efficiency is often looked at in terms of the percent of VO2max that a person can run at for a given race distance. The lower percent of maximum he can run at it, the more efficient the runner is thought to be. Efficiency is impacted by many of the steps from oxygen intake to transportation to utilization that were discussed in the previous chapter on oxygen's role.

Substrate Utilization

The preferred fuel source in endurance races that last less than a couple of hours is glycogen. The body has a finite supply of glycogen stored in the muscles, while it has a relatively large supply of fat. Due to the limited glycogen stores, in longer distance races, such as a marathon, glycogen depletion is a major source of fatigue. However, in races of under an hour, which includes most of the distance races (3k, 5k, 10k, half marathon), glycogen depletion is generally not considered a major source of fatigue, but instead plays a large role in determining the training load (Costill & Trappe, 2002). Given its importance and limited supply, how efficiently glycogen can be used is an important factor in training runners. Reducing the rate of glycogen use at a given speed will improve the metabolic efficiency of a runner.

For the marathon, substrate use and total glycogen stores greatly influence performance. While glycogen is never fully depleted during such a race, it seems that the body induces a slowing of the pace as glycogen levels drop, presumably to limit the reduction in glycogen stores. Well-trained runners use a mixture of fuel sources such as carbohydrate, fat, and a minimal amount of protein. Thus to delay fatigue from low glycogen, either an increase in total glycogen storage, or a shift in being able to use more fat as a fuel source at marathon pace is necessary. Long runs and high mileage training tend to increase the total glycogen supply of the muscles. A change in the fuel source ratio also comes from long aerobic running and moderate paced aerobic running. Additionally, research has demonstrated that dietary manipulation such as training in a fasted state is one way to increase the use fat as a fuel. Therefore, for a marathon runner, some runs and long runs should be done without taking supplemental fuel, as low glycogen during the run seems to be the signal for a shift in substrate use.

Even though glycogen depletion is not a direct cause of fatigue in shorter events, adaptations that change substrate utilization can aid performance in middle distance events. With the high volumes of training done, glycogen depletion during training can impact training intensity and adaptation. A large percentage of training is done at easy to moderate paces (Esteve-Lanao et al., 2007). The intensity of this running allows for significant contribution of fat as an energy source, which would help alleviate the strain on glycogen stores during high volume daily distance running. One training adaptation that shifts the balance of fat and carbohydrate use towards fat usage is mitochondria density (Brooks & Mercier, 1994). An increase in mitochondria and mitochondria enzymes, which occurs with endurance training, allows for greater use of fat as a fuel.

However, it is also possible that glycogen depletion could play a role in fatigue in shorter races. While glycogen depletion is usually only thought of in terms of long duration exercise where total glycogen depletion is a problem, it can occur at a local muscular level. Glycogen breakdown occurs within each working muscle fiber, in addition to some total body glycogen breakdown stimulated by hormones. It cannot be transported from fiber to fiber, except when converted to lactate, transferred, and then reconverted to glycogen. Given this, glycogen depletion can occur in individual fibers before total glycogen depletion occurs, and the selective depletion depends on the intensity of the activity and the use of that fiber (Abernathy et al., 1990). Therefore it can play a role in fatigue in much shorter events. With glycogen depletion of a muscle fiber, that fiber can no longer perform work at the same intensity; therefore with fibers getting glycogen depleted, there are fewer total fibers to cycle in and do work, potentially causing fatigue due to the increased demand put on the other fibers. This can be seen in animal models that showed that after partial glycogen depletion anaerobic performance was impaired (Lacombe et al., 1999). Research done by Jacobs showed the specificity of glycogen depletion when they compared a group that almost exclusively depleted ST fiber glycogen with one that partially depleted both ST and FT fibers (1981). In the ST only group, maximum strength was not impaired but muscular endurance was. In the FT and ST depleted group, maximum strength was impaired, presumably because of the glycogen depletion in the FT muscle fibers.

Substrate Utilization and the Actual Running Economy Measurement

Due to the way RE is commonly measured, what the energy source is will effect the measurement. RE is commonly calculated by dividing the rate of oxygen uptake by running speed. VO2 is used because, when measured at a speed using almost entirely aerobic energy sources, it represents the amount of ATP used. However, the common measurement does not take into account that the energy equivalent of O2 depends on which substrate is used. Fats, carbohydrates, and proteins all provide a different amount of energy per liter of O2.

When expressed as a unit of caloric cost, RE is more sensitive to changes in substrate use. This is particularly important in distance events that are limited by fuel issues, such as glycogen depletion. Thus while substrate utilization might not be as big of a worry for a middle distance athlete in terms of efficiency, for a marathon runner it is one of the most important factors. A marathoner who is able to utilize fats more will spare his glycogen stores, delaying fatigue. For the marathoner it is not only about total glycogen stores, but the rate at which those are used. His goal is to run as fast as he can while using glycogen at a rate that will put him depleted just after the finish line. Training to be able to utilize a greater amount of fat at marathon pace will increase performance. Our marathoner should be more concerned with looking at RE in terms of caloric cost, because he is less concerned with RE as measured in terms of VO2 since that is not his race limiter. That brings us to one of the problems with RE measurements. It can be expressed in several different ways that all take into account different efficiencies (metabolic, biomechanical, or neural) to a higher degree.

My Own Running Economy:

	10.5 mph	11 mph	11.5 mph	12 mph	12.5 mph
VO2 per km	176	175	178	185	185
Caloric Unit Cost	.86	.86	.88	.92	.92

Problems with Running Economy

As mentioned previously, one problem with RE is that it can be measured and expressed in several different ways. The most common ways are expressing it in terms of VO2 at a given speed, and VO2/distance. There are two ways to report VO2 using running speed. One is to express it in terms of the VO2 at an absolute speed, while the other is to express it as VO2/speed. These rely on the idea that below a certain speed (around Lactate Threshold) the oxygen cost is independent of speed. However, Vickers demonstrated that this is not the case (2010). When measuring economy at an absolute speed, runners will be running at vastly different relative intensities which will change several factors. Biomechanical factors such as ground contact, ground reaction forces, stride lengths and frequencies are all speed dependent. One individual at 6 minute mile pace may need a very low percentage of their max force development, while another runner might need a much larger percentage, thus changing ground contact times. That is but one example of how speed affects biomechanics. In addition, substrate use would be vastly different among groups of individuals at an absolute speed. Since races are of a given distance, expressing RE as the oxygen cost per unit of distance seems to make more sense, but it still neglects the effect substrate use has.

One last way that RE is reported is caloric cost. In this measurement, the Respiratory Exchange Ratio (RER) is used to calculate the caloric equivalent of VO2, which can be used to determine the amount of energy used per unit of distance. A study by Fletcher compared RE expressed as VO2/distance and caloric unit cost (2009). They stated that the traditional way of measuring RE appeared to be flawed for several of the reasons discussed earlier, and for the practical reason that faster runners tended to have worse economy, which makes little logical sense. In their study, Fletcher found that the better runners had a lower energy cost of running (better economy) and that RE expressed as caloric unit cost was much more sensitive to changes in speed. One of the interesting findings was that RE determined using the VO2 measurement showed that RE was independent of speed. The caloric unit cost showed that RE got worse as speed increased, which would be the expected outcome as when speed increases reliance on carbohydrates also increases. This debate on how to measure RE demonstrates that we have a long way to go in understanding efficiency. It also makes one question the conclusions based on studies looking at what improves RE.

One other problem with measuring RE is whether to use gross or net VO2. Gross VO2 refers to the total oxygen consumption, while net refers to the total oxygen consumption minus the resting value. It has been hypothesized that net would better reflect active energy usage and correct for a speed-related bias that is present when measuring RE as VO2/speed (Vickers, 2005).

RE is used as a means of quantifying total efficiency. However, given that one is basing efficiency off of VO2, the merits of this approach may be in question. According to Noakes' CGM VO2 may be a result of a central governor regulating VO2 by muscle activation. If this is true, then RE reflects the degree of muscle activation at a given pace. This still means it is a valid measurement, and it may reflect efficiency of muscle activation. However, the degree that it can be used to measure and quantify mechanical, metabolic, and neuromuscular efficiency is unknown. Separating efficiency into these three different categories might aid in clearing the quiet muddy picture of what affects RE, or in this case total efficiency. The interactions of the different types of efficiency may also explain the mixed results in changing biomechanics or why there are contrasting results on what is the most efficient way to run in the literature. In a study by Purkiss they demonstrate a model of calculating internal work that allowed for distinguishing efficient and inefficient running styles in elite runners (2003).

Also, the measurement of RE may be suspect if we look at a recent study by Baden. In that study, RE changed when the participants did not know when they were stopping exercise, even though they ran for the same amount of time as they did during the test when they knew for how long they would be exercising (20 minutes) (2004). The results of these studies demonstrate that another mechanism may regulate RE based on feedback. The fact that RE could change solely based on outside feedback such as when exercise would be completed is interesting and may lead to reevaluation of the way we test RE. Lastly, efficiency needs to be put into context when using it as a performance measure. The fact is that performance is the main concern, and efficiency should not be the only thing taken into consideration. It is possible, because of the way we measure efficiency, that a parameter that improves RE could be detrimental to performance. For example, increased vertical oscillation decreases RE, but if that vertical oscillation results in a far greater stride length, it is possible that the person has increased efficiency per unit of distance traveled. Taken by itself, vertical oscillation might be detrimental, but taken in context of the whole locomotion a slight increase could prove beneficial. An example of this can be seen in a study done in converting runners to the POSE technique of running. After 12 weeks of training, the runners reduced their vertical oscillation significantly, by 1.52cm on average, but their RE was significantly impaired (Dallam et al., 2005). This was due to a significant reduction in stride length. Thus, it is the optimization of the variable, and giving hard recommendations may not be appropriate.

In conclusion, the measurement of RE may need to be called into question as a measure of total efficiency. This would have significant repercussions in the interpretation of many studies. Looking at other methods of calculating efficiency may be more beneficial, as the two groups mentioned above have done (Fletcher et al., 2009; Purkiss et al., 2003). Furthermore, evidence from the world of cycling may shed some light on using a measure based on VO2. Using a measurement of VO2 economy, cyclists were most efficient at pedaling rates that were relatively low, 40-65 revolutions per minute (rpm), while professional cyclists preferred pedal rates that were much higher, over 90rpm. These higher rates consistently show a much higher submaximal VO2. Rather than coming to the conclusion that the elite cyclists were wrong and needed to have lower pedaling rates, Belli and Hintzy instead expressed efficiency as the energy cost of cycling, in terms of joules per kilogram per minute (2002). Using this method, it was found that the energy cost was lowest at pedal rates that matched those preferred by elite cyclists. The authors concluded that energy cost represented biomechanical efficiency much better than the economy measurement. A similar scenario could easily play out in running if we looked at stride rate and length instead of pedal rate. These results may explain some of the discrepancy between what coaches suggest is correct biomechanically and what appears in the research; the heel strike versus mid-foot strike and the degree of vertical oscillation would be prime examples. The problem isn't with the importance of economy or efficiency but with the actual measurement used to define economy.

8

The Brain-Muscle Connection

"The subjective experience of pain is constructed from both our physiological state and contextual data...when nerve cells send a signal to the pain centers of your brain, your experience of pain can vary even if those signals don't." Leonard Mlodinow

The aforementioned VO2max, Running Economy, and Lactate Threshold make up the traditional trio of running performance, but there are several other factors that contribute to performance such as anaerobic, neuromuscular, and psychological factors. While distance running and even middle distance running is primarily an aerobic activity, anaerobic systems play a significant role. In the 1,500m estimates of anaerobic contribution have generally been found to be about 20%, while in the 3,000m event for men 16% anaerobic contribution was found (Hill, 1999). Despite this fact, for years the traditional research ignored the anaerobic contributions to performance in their models. In the following chapter, we'll delve into some of the neglected contributors to running performance work.

Understanding the entire picture is crucial for athletes and coaches looking to maximize performance. It is easy to focus on the main contributors, but when we consider that well-trained runners are thankful for any improvement they can get, the smaller contributors cannot be ignored. Traditional training programs focus mostly on the aerobic aspect of running, neglecting the neuromuscular and even anaerobic. Since the time of Lydiard, the anaerobic contribution has been misunderstood. It is not the evil system that it is often portrayed to be, but instead it requires a little more fine-tuning and balance than the aerobic system. Let's take a look at these nontraditional factors and see what they mean in regards to performance.

Neuromuscular and Anaerobic Factors in Performance

Since the majority of distance running performance is tied to traditional factors focused on aerobic components, most of the research has followed that route. However, recent research has shown that anaerobic and neuromuscular factors play a role in improving distance running performance. One such study was done by Paavolainen which found that better performance in a 10km run was partially due to increased pre-activation and decreased ground contact time (1999). Pre-activation could potentially increase RE due to a tightening of the muscle-tendon system that would increase elastic storage. In another study by Paavolainen, performance on a maximal anaerobic running test was significantly correlated with running performance over 5,000m (1999a). Lastly one study found that anaerobic work capacity and power contributed significantly to a model explaining running performance in Cross-Country and over a 10km race (Sinnett et al., 2001). These studies demonstrate that anaerobic factors are crucial for distance running success.

There are many components that affect anaerobic capacity and power. Anaerobic power refers to the rate of energy turnover for the anaerobic systems, while capacity is the total energy turnover. Factors that affect both of these include muscle fiber type, recruitment, and force production.

Muscle Fiber Type

Muscle fiber type will largely influence anaerobic capabilities. The differences between Slow Twitch (ST) and the various Fast Twitch muscle fibers (FT-a,x,c) make this clear. Fast Twitch fibers offer several advantages for force and power production, with the tradeoff being a reduction in aerobic abilities. FT fibers have a higher Myosin ATPase activity, which means they also have a quicker shortening velocity (Fitts & Widrick, 1996). Due to this increased shortening velocity, FT fibers have greater power outputs. FT fibers also have more muscle fibers per motor neuron, which allows for greater force production than ST fibersthat have fewer fibers per neuron. Lastly, FT fibers have a larger Creatine Phosphate store, more Glycolytic enzymes, and a larger Sarcoplasmic Reticulum. The larger Sarcoplasmic Reticulum will result in enhanced Calcium delivery (Stephenson et al., 1998). All of these differences give FT muscle fibers an advantage in anaerobic related activities. However, it is a blend of FT and ST fibers that can lead to optimal performance because of their various strengths and weaknesses. Can we train for an optimal balance of fiber types or are fiber types predetermined and should we instead find the sport that matches our fiber types?

Conversion of muscle fiber type was previously believed to be impossible. It was thought that whatever muscle fiber types you were born with, you were set with these. However, recent research suggests that that view is erroneous. Changes within Fast Twitch fibers in humans have been demonstrated in numerous studies, so that conversion from FT-x to FT-a or any other subset is now commonly accepted. A full conversion from FT to ST is still debated in humans. If we look at research in animals, this conversion can be seen (Pette, 1999). So why don't we see it in humans? First, in animal studies it takes a large amount of chronic low-frequency stimulation to get this conversion to occur. And, in particularly resistant fibers, it sometimes takes muscle damage combined with chronic stimulation of the fiber to get a full fiber type conversion (Pette, 1999).

If we use common sense, then we would have to believe that every distance runner pre-selected themselves into distance running since almost every runner tested shows a large percentage of Slow Twitch fibers. While some pre-selection obviously occurs, when we test fiber types of populations, we only see the end result. There are no studies that test someone before they begin their journey down the path to distance runner stardom for obvious reasons. If we look at longitudinal studies that looked at muscle fiber types in high level endurance athletes, changes can be seen. A longitudinal study by Rusko found that after 8 years of training and a doubling of training volume, the percentage of ST fibers in a group of Cross-Country Skiers increased by 11% (1992).

Why do I bring up the possible change in muscle fiber type? One reason is that it could partially explain why runners tend to reach peak performance levels later than sprint or power type athletes. It could be because distance runners need large amounts of training, or damage, to complete this muscle fiber type conversion. Secondly, this fiber conversion could also partially explain the success of African distance runners. Perhaps their large volumes of unofficial training early on, such as running to school or even the active lifestyle that they live, allows for this conversion to take place at a younger age. It is well established that there are certain physiological and even epigenetic components that are more susceptible to imprinting and changing earlier in life. Africans tend to reach peak performance at younger ages then their Western counterparts and this could partially explain that phenomenon.

The long-term changes in muscle fiber type are important for the coach to understand. It points to the idea that training cannot be seen through a segmented season to season viewpoint but should instead be seen through a lifetime and long term view. The athlete changes from the start to the end of his competitive career and training should be adjusted to accommodate and even facilitate those changes. That is why we cannot get stuck in a cookie cutter–coaching plan or have one dogmatic philosophy.

Fatigue and the CNS

From a neuromuscular standpoint, fatigue can occur either centrally or peripherally. Central fatigue means that it occurs sometime between the CNS initiating and the muscle receiving the signal for contraction to occur. Peripheral fatigue occurs between the time when the muscle receives the signal and actual contraction takes place. Fatigue at both levels is generally reflected by changes in motor unit recruitment, decrease in relaxation time, and a decrease in neural signaling among other changes. A buildup of metabolic by-products, depletion of fuel sources, or a decrease in central drive can all affect the neuromuscular system by decreasing force output. Attention will be given to changes that occur along the route of the CNS signaling for muscle recruitment to take place. The focus is not on what exactly causes neural fatigue, as that differs for each event, but on how it manifests itself during a race and how to combat it. There are several different factors that can be altered to prevent fatigue from a neuromuscular standpoint. Changes that can occur neurally that may enhance performance include increased muscle fiber recruitment pool, a decrease in time to activate muscle, and an increase in rate of force development.

The CNS decision on the specifics of muscle fiber recruitment affects both anaerobic attributes and neuromuscular characteristics. There are several potential ways that muscle fiber recruitment can delay fatigue. First, an increase in the muscle fiber pool allows for more fibers to be available to do the work, thus delaying fatigue. Second, during fatigue a decrease in the Action Potential signal strength and velocity occurs (Leppers et al., 2002). Training to decrease the degree of activation needed for those fibers to be recruited allows for the ability to recruit such fibers when fatigue is high and the neural recruitment signal is not as strong.

In a study by Nummella a significant correlation was found between EMG levels at the 3km mark of a 5km time trial and the average velocity that the 5k was run at (2006). Essentially, the runners who could maintain a higher level of muscle activation during the middle section of the 5k had better finishing times for the entire distance. This shows that maintaining muscle recruitment during a distance race is an important factor for success. If we tie this back into the fatigue models, it's clear to see why. The runner whose recruitment is dropping is having fatigue buildup earlier than the others. Depending on the fatigue model, training to increase muscle fiber recruitment during hard training may be one way to combat this problem. If we can "force" recruitment during heavy fatigue with high force activities, it will train the maintenance of recruitment during a race. Some preliminary evidence for this can be seen with strength endurance work, which is discussed in the training section of this book.

Another interesting find in this study is the increase in EMG at the end of the race when the runners demonstrated the "end spurt" or "kick" phenomenon. The ability to recruit additional motor units under heavy fatigue at the end of the race impacts one's ability to increase the speed in the closing stages of a race. This idea could explain why heavy resistance training or sprinting improves distance running performance, as it increases the total muscle fiber pool that can be recruited. Some evidence for this idea is that in the Nummela study, the velocity of this final lap end spurt was not related to VO2max or RE, but to the vMART, suggesting that neuromuscular abilities are what determine the end spurt, and not the oxygen dynamics.

In distance running, the various muscle fibers work so that they are rotated so that some fibers do the work while others rest and then the others cycle in and take over. This works well at low intensities, but as intensity increases more force is required, so more fibers have to be activated to do the work, and the time that they can "cycle off" and rest is reduced. As fatigue sets in, fibers begin to fatigue, and harder to recruit fibers are called upon. When fatigue gets intense, there is a decrease in the number of muscle fibers recruited as the neural drive decreases and the number of fibers that are fatigued has reached a high level. This is where increasing the muscle fiber pool comes into play. Even during maximum voluntary contractions, a person can never fully recruit all of his fibers. There is always a reserve, which makes sense if we realize the body's design to always have a safety net. Research has demonstrated that well-trained athletes are able to tap into a higher percentage of that reserve than untrained athletes. For distance runners who rarely ever do high force activities like sprinting, their total recruitable fibers will be lower than those runners who have trained to recruit fibers during high force activities. The increase in fiber pool allows for more muscle fibers to be recruited or cycled in, thus delaying fatigue.

Another neural factor is rate of force development. As has been covered already, the amount of time that a runner has to produce force while the foot is on the ground is very limited. Weyend demonstrated that we do not have time to reach max force levels even during sprinting (2010). Therefore, it is more a matter of rate of force development than total force application. If distance runners can be trained to increase their rate of force development, this allows for several beneficial adaptations. At slow speeds it means they are working at a lower percentage of their max force production capacities, which should extend endurance. During race speeds, it also means that they can generate the necessary forces required to run at their faster pace. This means that ground contact times can be reduced as not as much time is needed to generate the force. Previous research has shown that decreased ground contact times result in less time having to support the weight of the body and thus improved Running Economy. One result of training that improves rate of force development is a decrease in the time required to activate a muscle. Research using explosive strength training by Mikkola demonstrated that with training endurance athletes could be trained to enhance rapid muscle activation (2007).

Further research in the area that anaerobic and neuromuscular factors play in regards to distance running is needed. The ability to close fast in the later parts of the race has been suggested to be what separates the best runners, and it has been speculated that this might be due to an ability to increase motor unit activation in the later parts of the race (Noakes, 2003). The aforementioned data by Nummella seems to support this notion (2006). The previously mentioned field observations in elite Kenyans being able to run at a MAXLass during a race and then dramatically increase lactate at the end might also lend credence to this idea.

As distance coaches we are used to recognizing fatigue that results from running lots of mileage or hard workouts. What we don't grasp is CNS fatigue. The fatigue experienced after doing 50m sprints is a totally foreign concept. We need to recognize CNS fatigue and implement a recovery strategy for it just like we do for recovery from a long run. Additionally, coaches can plan strategies to improve the neuromuscular performance of an athlete by exploiting training practices to improve muscle recruitment and coordination.

Recognizing CNS Fatigue:

Any activity that requires a large neural demand will result in CNS fatigue. For instance, all out sprints, heavy weight lifting, or very taxing interval work all will result in various amounts of CNS fatigue. Adequate rest and recovery from such high demand CNS work is needed. It is why sprinters do not do a large volume of repeated all out sprints day after day.

Several strategies can be used to determine if CNS fatigue is present. Explosive tests such as a broad jump are useful. As are reactive tests such as a repeated hopping exercise in which you measure ground contact time. If ground contact time is increased, it's likely that there is CNS fatigue present. Lastly, how an athlete feels or looks during faster strides before a workout or run can give the coach an indication of fatigue. Oftentimes using one of these methods prior to a workout or the day before can tell a coach if the athlete is prepared for the next workout or needs more time to recover.

Temperature Regulation

An increase in body temperature is another mechanism that can cause fatigue. When core temperature gets to a dangerously high level, people either slow down dramatically or stop exercise. An interesting fact is that people terminate exercise at very similar temperatures of around 40 degrees Celsius. This termination of exercise happens regardless of starting temperature, pre-cooling of the body, or rate of heat loss and storage (Gonzalez-Alonso et al., 1999). There is a theory that exercise in hot conditions, where fatigue is likely due to reaching high core body temperatures, is governed by an anticipatory regulator. This anticipatory regulation system monitors rate of heat storage and adjusts muscle activation to delay or prevent overheating. Evidence for this theory comes from studies that have studied EMG levels in a variety of temperatures. Lower EMG levels have been seen in hotter temperatures, which should not be surprising, but the anticipatory regulation can be seen in that EMG levels are lower early in the exercise when core temperatures were essentially the same (Tucker et al., 2004). Regardless of the exact mechanism, it can be seen that slowing the rate of heat storage can enhance endurance. In addition, other mechanisms related to heat and core temperature increases can potentially impair performance, even before the critical core temperature is reached.

At higher temperatures more of the blood is redistributed to the skin to aid in cooling. When this happens, blood flow that is normally going to the muscles is reduced, potentially hampering performance. Also, at high muscle temperatures, ATP production is decreased due to a loosening of the coupling between oxidation and phosphorylation in mitochondria (Brooks et al., 2004).

Delaying heat gain and core temperature increases depends on the body's cooling mechanisms. Heat loss can occur via radiation, conduction, convection, and evaporations. Radiation allows for heat loss due to a difference in temperature gradient. When the skin temperature is higher than its surroundings, more heat radiates from the body. This process accounts for 60% of heat loss. Conduction is the transfer of heat via direct contact and accounts for around 3% of heat loss, while convection is the transfer of heat to air or water and accounts for about 12% of heat loss at room temperature (Brooks et al., 2004). Blood flow to the skin aids the process of convection. Heat travels with the blood from the core to the skin, which then allows for heat loss to the air. In this way, heat is transferred from the core to the environment, aiding in temperature control.

Lastly, evaporation accounts for about 25% of heat loss in normal conditions (Brooks et al., 2004). For heat loss to occur, sweat must evaporate. In humid conditions, evaporation of sweat is greatly reduced, thus decreasing heat loss through evaporation. In addition, in very hot temperatures where the outside temperature is greater than the body temperature, evaporation is the only means of heat loss since the other methods are dependent on having a temperature gradient. An acclimatized person can sweat up to 4 liters per hour; while a person not acclimatized can only sweat about 1.5 liters per hour (Brooks et al., 2004). Therefore, heat acclimatization to get this effect could potentially enhance endurance performance.

For athletes competing in hot environments recognizing that heat and temperature regulation may be the cause of fatigue is paramount. Practices can be designed to minimize the effect of temperature on fatigue. For instance, during the 2004 Athens Olympic marathon several elite runners used ice vests pre race to decrease their core body temperature because the temperatures were extremely warm for a marathon. Their coaches recognized that heat regulation was going to play a bigger part than usual and designed a strategy to combat that. Recent research has suggested that drinking ice-cold fluids helps to combat the core body temperature rise. Using strategies such as these can make a large difference in hot weather races.

Additionally, heat training can be used to improve performance even in cooler conditions. While altitude training is the "sexy" thing to do to increase performance, training in hot and humid conditions has similar training benefits. When training in warm and humid conditions, the processes described above are put to the test. Because more of our energy is being spent on cooling ourselves and more blood flow is being diverted away from our working muscles, we have an increased stressor at slower paces. We get an almost altitude like effect of reduced blood flow and thus oxygen to the working muscles. One of the adaptations that occurs because of this is an increase in blood volume following training in heat and humidity. Although the combination of heat and altitude during periodization is thought of as a newer invention, it is, in fact, what Olympic champion Frank Shorter employed in the 1970's by splitting his training between Florida and Boulder, Colorado. Heat training should be thought of as an additional stressor to be used to enhance performance. It might not have the trendiness of altitude, but it has its place.

The Psychology of it All

Racing is a very intense activity. Dealing with pain or mental toughness is often cited as a reason for success in the sport of distance running. The ability to deal with fatigue and pain could lead to improved performance. Despite the rigors of training and racing, running remains one of the most popular activities in the U.S. A look at the motivation of runners and how they deal with pain is essential in understanding what makes a successful distance runner.

Motivation

The motivation of runners has been analyzed with a variety of different approaches. Clough (1989) took an interesting approach looking at running in terms of other leisure activities. They found that runner's motivation could be divided into six groups: Well-Being, Social, Challenge, Status, Fitness/Health, and Addiction. The most important factors were challenge followed by fitness/health and well-being. While the first four factors were similar to those seen in other leisure activities, the last two factors were different. This study set the stage for acknowledging that there was something extra that set running apart from other similar activities.

While studies initially compared runners as a whole group, latter studies pointed to the idea that there are different groups of runners motivated by different factors. One such study was done by Slay (1998) in which they found that obligatory runners' motivations differed from non-obligatory runners. The obligatory runners were more motivated by negative or external factors such as guilt of stopping and weight control. In another study on committed runners who ran more than 40 miles per week, it was found that the committed runners were more motivated by mastery, competition, and weight regulation (Scott and Thorton, 1995). Lastly, Ogles and Masters (2003) found that marathon runners could be divided into several groups based on their motivation profiles. These groups were: running enthusiasts, lifestyle managers, personal goal achievers, personal accomplishers, and competitive achievers. These studies demonstrate that runners' motivations differ based on their level of running, goals, and experience.

Motivation also tends to vary based on skill level. Although not done with runners, a study by Chantel (1996) looked at the differences in motivation in elite athletes. They looked at motivation in terms of Deci and Ryan's Self Determination Theory, using the Sports Motivation Scale (SMS) as a way to measure Self Determination. The Self Determination Theory states that there is a continuum of motivation that includes three different levels of internal motivation, three levels of external motivation, and one level of amotivation. Internal motivation refers to participating in the activity for its own satisfaction or pleasure. In other words, it is motivation based on the activity being an end in itself. External motivation includes doing the activity as a means to an end or for some external reason. Finally, Amotivation is a lack of motivation and is first on the continuum.

Chantel found that the best athletes had higher levels of amotivation and non-self–determined extrinsic motivation. Non-self–determined refers to external regulation and introjected regulation. It should be noted that this study was on Bulgarian athletes who were likely influenced by communist practices. Looking at what motivates elite Kenyan runners, Onywera (2006) found that they were primarily motivated by economic incentive, followed by talent and tradition. This finding would seem to match up with elites having higher extrinsic motivation.

The motivation to run is different at each level of running, so coaches have to deal with a wide range of motivations. The key is finding out what motivates each individual runner and to exploit that. In an ideal world, runners would have both high intrinsic and extrinsic motivation, meaning they are motivated by internal and external factors. However, the reality is that coaches need to understand where each runner falls and exploit it. Additionally, as a coach, it is important to try to influence the motivation of an athlete so that he can enjoy the sport in the long term. For example, trying to slowly change someone who is motivated by a fear of failure to a more healthy motivation is important. The bottom line is that knowing what makes your athlete tick is valuable information that can be used to enhance their performance.

Pain Tolerance

Dealing with pain is an everyday occurrence for an endurance athlete. So it should come as no surprise that how we deal with pain is different than the everyday person, and it plays a role in our performance. But it goes beyond simple mental toughness and gritting it out. Let's take a brief look at pain research on athletes and see how that translates to racing.

When researchers study pain, they generally look at pain threshold, which is when the first initial detection of any pain arises, and pain tolerance, which is how much pain a person can withstand. To investigate these areas, researchers apply one of many ever-increasing painful stimuli. These range from cold immersion to mechanical pressure application to electric shocks. When we look at the effects of running on pain, we have to separate it into acute versus chronic effects. Acutely, endurance exercise creates "exercise-induced hypoalgesia" which basically refers to a reduced sensation of pain following longer or intense exercise. This is thought to primarily occur because of opioid secretion and is related to the "runner's high" that many people feel.

On the other hand, we have chronic adjustments in pain perception, which are long lasting adjustments in how our body perceives and deals with pain. Chronic adjustments deal with modifications in our processing of the pain signal and enhancement of our pain inhibition system. The pain system is far too complex to give an entire overview in this section, but it can be best thought of as a simple sensory feedback system, where feedback is sent from the periphery to the brain to interpret and create the sensation of pain. Along the way we can increase or decrease that signal sent and alter our brain's interpretation of it.

When we look at chronic changes, there are definite differences in how athletes versus non-athletes interpret pain. In a metaanalysis looking at all such studies, Tesarz and colleagues concluded that athletes had a higher pain tolerance to a wide variety of stimuli (2012). For the most part, however, athletes did not have a difference in pain threshold. This means that athletes first sensed pain at the same level but could tolerate pain for much longer. When looking at runners the picture is much the same. In one study looking at marathon runners, it was found that they have a higher pain tolerance and a reduced experience of pain. Similarly, research on triathletes shows higher pain tolerance levels. In particular, high-level triathletes had higher pain tolerance when compared to active athletes, and other research shows that pain perception was related to aerobic fitness levels (Garcin, 2004). These and similar studies show that level of prowess may play a role. What explains this elevated pain tolerance?

An additional component called Conditioned Pain Modulation (CPM) is used to evaluate the capabilities of the pain system to adapt. A CPM test consists of the use of two pain stimuli with an almost pre-test stimuli followed by a secondary stimuli to see how the pain perception changes. In triathletes, CPM was enhanced, meaning they showed less pain when both heat and cold stimuli were applied on different arms. While this improvement might seem obvious, what it tells us is that triathletes have a more efficient pain modulation system (Geva, 2013). They are better at modulating the inhibitory effects.

Knowing that athletes have higher pain tolerance and that it is partially due to a more efficient pain modulation system, can we actually train and improve these parameters, and, if so, how is that accomplished? If we again turn to the research the answer can be found. In the study on triathletes, it was found that there were strong negative relationships between duration of training and fear of pain, as well as between fear of pain and inhibition. What this tells us is that longer training duration was related to lower levels of both fear of pain and pain inhibition. Other studies have found similar correlations with pain tolerance and training, so if increased training improves pain management, how does this actually occur?

If we look at a study by Ord on rowers, pain tolerance correlated with the number and quality of coping strategies (2003). The better the rowers were at coping with the pain, the higher their pain tolerance was. This shouldn't be surprising as athletes who have to endure pain regularly in both racing and training would be expected to develop some sort of coping strategy. Similarly, in a study of marathon runners, the higher pain tolerance was related to higher associative coping skills and lower dissociative skills. While we can't use this as a blanket piece of advice, the research does provide clues on how we might get better at dealing with that pain: developing effective coping skills.

Coping skills are critical, and they generally come about by happenstance and necessity as when we encounter pain during races we develop ways to deal with and process that psychologically. Instead of simply relying on whatever natural coping mechanisms you developed, it would be wise to increase your arsenal and develop a wide range of coping skills. The coping skills are developed for more than just generic pain tolerance. Mental stress, fear of pain, and a process called catastrophizing all influence our pain perception.

A study by Marcora demonstrated that mental fatigue could impair performance (2009). In comparing groups who performed 90min of cognitive demanding tasks to a control group that watched documentaries, they found that the group that performed the cognitive tasks performed significantly worse on a cycle to exhaustion. Fear of pain can create a negative feedback loop in which our fear of pain creates an anti-analgesic effect and counteracts our body's attempts to inhibit pain. Catastrophizing is a process in which we exaggerate negative appraisal of the pain sensations. We have an almost overactive response to the pain, which creates emotional distress. We've all encountered this at some point, maybe even in a race, and it can almost be thought of as a minor panic attack. If we learn how to deal with and cope with such instances, we can modulate our pain perception and improve our pain tolerance.

The altered pain perception in athletes might have an impact in other ways. One theory is that since athletes constantly challenge themselves in terms of dealing with pain, they may constantly activate their pain inhibitory system. This could potentially create a situation where the pain inhibitory system becomes overworked and becomes "exhausted," which generally occurs in those who suffer chronic pain (Tesarz, 2013). If this occurs, it could explain select cases of overtraining or even sensitivity to injuries. As an often-overlooked component of pain tolerance is that it applies to the physical pain felt in muscle pulls or stress fractures too.

The Psychological and Physiological are intricately linked, and we have much to learn in these areas of study. High-level runners are likely to have higher degrees of both intrinsic and extrinsic motivation, which may allow them to delve into the deeper depths of perceived pain. Additionally, well-trained runners probably experience a callusing sort of effect, where they get used to certain levels of discomfort and pain during practice, so that they perceive it as being less painful than other runners. The important take away message is that they are psychologically and physiologically linked. It is a mistake to blame poor results on an athlete being "weak" as that is too simplistic of a viewpoint. Instead, recognize that pain is the result of a combination of many factors and work towards improving an athlete's ability to handle it in the correct fashion. Pain is a perception that can be influenced by both internal and external stimuli, and appropriate coping strategies should be developed.

9

The Genetics of Training

"Our ability to spot patterns is what allows us to make sense of the world, but sometimes, in our eagerness, we are oversensitive and trigger-happy and mistakenly spot patterns where none exist."
Ben Goldacre

Knowing all of the physiological components that can change with training is important, as is knowing what kinds of training improves those components, but how do we get from the workout to those functional changes? The body must go through a series of steps that takes it from the training stimulus all the way down to the genetic level and then back up to a functional change. This process is called the signaling pathway and is demonstrated in the chart below.

While the coach who reads this may get discouraged by the references to certain complex sounding names, it is important to not get caught up in the minutia and to understand the general concept. Knowing how a training stimulus results in a tangible adaptation such as increased endurance is paramount for making good decisions on workout planning. By knowing the adaptation steps that the body goes through, the specific aims of a workout and the recovery post workout can be set up to optimize this process. For example, if we know adaptations related to fuel use are triggered by low glycogen stores, then that gives us information that we can use to create a training stimulus that creates low glycogen stores. In this case, a long run would be the training stimulus, which would seem obvious, but what might be overlooked is that knowing low

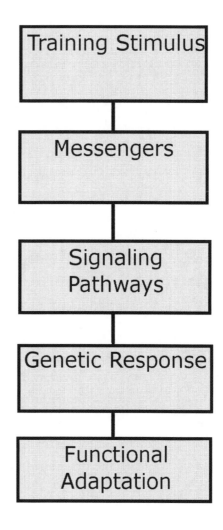

glycogen stores is the signal for adaptation we might want to forgo a carbohydrate drink on that long run.

Steps of Adaptation

Training Stimulus

The first step is that a training stimulus is applied; this is what occurs during the workout. In order for the workout to elicit adaptation, it has to be significant enough both in terms of intensity and volume to disturb the body's homeostasis. The body's homeostasis can be disturbed in a variety of ways such as stressors that will impact the mechanical, metabolic, neural, endocrine, and cardiovascular systems. In reality, all of these systems function together. Two examples of this process are a high intensity endurance workout at altitude might decrease the oxygen saturation levels, while a lengthy endurance workout might result in a depletion of glycogen. In these cases, the endurance workout at altitude changed the natural levels of oxygen in the blood, and in the long endurance workout example the workout caused a change in glycogen levels. These changes, glycogen and oxygen levels, will act as triggers for the rest of the adaptation that will be discussed shortly.

Essentially, the body must be put in a state of crisis to trigger the stages of adaptation. The workout's goal is to bring about this "crisis." Outside factors determine the degree of training stimulus needed for adaptation. We all know that an untrained person can go walk for 30 minutes and get some sort of training effect, while it is unlikely that would produce any effect for a well-trained runner besides possibly enhancing recovery. Training state must matter then. This effect can be seen on the genetic level, as research by McConnel found that AMPK activity, which is one of the signaling pathways discussed later, increased by 9-fold after 2 hours of cycling in untrained people, but after the subjects completed 10 training sessions, AMPK activity did not increase after the same amount of exercise (2005). This demonstrates the importance of what a person is accustomed to in training. A larger stimulus is required to disturb homeostasis. In addition to training state, the physiological makeup of the person and their nutritional state determines the effects of the training stimulus. An example of this effect is seen when runners take some sort of carbohydrate during a run versus taking nothing. The carbohydrate changes the subsequent signaling pathway response entirely.

Messengers

Once the stimulus is provided, they create a disturbance in the body. If enough disturbance occurs, a change in homeostasis can occur via numerous mechanisms ranging from changes in fuel levels to the buildup of various products in the muscle. These alterations in physiological parameters act as messengers. When these messengers reach a critical level they act as triggers to the various signaling pathways. It's best to think of the messenger's role as being like a type of alarm. Whenever there is a large change in a messenger, it's as if an alarm goes off that triggers action. In this case, the action is to activate subsequent pathways. The messengers act to tell the body that homeostasis has been disturbed and that action should be taken to fix that problem. It is our body's safety net and tells the body that repair and strengthening need to occur. It would be no different than having an alarm for a leak in pipes in a power plant. If the alarm went off, we would know that we need to get in there and repair or replace the leaky pipe so that it doesn't happen again. Thus, most of the messengers are triggered either by depletion or too high of a buildup of certain substances or by drastic changes in the ratio of substances.

These signaling events are important for both coaches and scientists, as knowing what events need to happen to trigger adaptation allows for the manipulation of training to try to accomplish this. These messengers are what must change in order to get adaptation. They are our workout's targets on a physiological level. With that in mind, the following is a list of the messengers that have currently been discovered, and the signaling pathways that they trigger. This is an ever growing field, so this list is not comprehensive:

Messenger	Pathways Initiated	Functional Results
Mechanical Stretch-frequency and intensity	CaMK, MAPK and IGF pathways	Hypertrophy, fast to slow fiber type conversions,
Changes in Calcium levels in the cell	CaMK, MAPK, Protein kinase C	Hypertrophy, slow twitch fiber type conversion
NAD: NADH ratio		
Low muscle glycogen	AMPK and MAPK	Increased mitochondria
ATP:AMP ratio	AMPK	Increased mitochondria
Decreased blood Oxygen levels	HIF-1	Increased EPO and Red Blood cells
PI3-k and Akt	mTOR	Muscle Hypertrophy

MAPK=Mitogen activated protein kinase
IGF-Insulin Like Growth Factor
PI3-k= Phosphatidylinositol 3-kinase
CaMK=Calcium/Calmodulin pathway

Signal Pathways

Once homeostasis has been disturbed significantly enough, the messengers activate various signaling pathways. Signaling pathways are basically the steps taken to initiate adaptation. In order to proceed to the step of functional adaptation, these pathways must be activated. In our analogy, the pathways represent the response to that alarm and the protocol that has to be followed to ensure that next time the same thing happens the alarm won't go off again. The signaling pathways are like the collecting of the materials needed to fix the problem.

Then, the next step of genetic adaptation is the process of using the materials collected to build our final product that will ensure the alarm doesn't go off.

The signaling pathways consist of a series of reactions and steps that ultimately result in some sort of gene expression. Essentially it creates the blueprint for functional adaptations. The exact steps differ with each pathway. It is this gene expression that ultimately leads to the functional changes and will be discussed next; some of the better-researched pathways will be discussed as well as what functional changes are the results of these pathways.

Pathway	Gene changes	Effects
AMPK	Increase in AMPK= 1. ↑ PGC-1 2. inhibit MTOR	1. ↑PGC-1=↑mitochondria 2. inhibits protein synthesis
HIF-1	EPO gene	Increased Red Blood cells
mTOR	1. results in either EIF4E or p70S6k	1. Muscle hypertrophy
CaMK	1. ↑ PGC-1	↑mitochondria
MAPK	1. ↑ PGC-1	↑mitochondria

MAPK- mitogen-activated protein kinase
PGC-1=peroxisome proliferators-activated receptor gamma coactivator C
CaMK=Calcium/Calmodulin pathway

Genetic Adaptation

While each signaling pathway differs, most work by increasing gene expression. As mentioned earlier, think of the pathways as collecting the material, and the step of genetic adaptation as building the final project. The building process is accomplished first by transcription. Transcription is the process of copying a string of DNA into mRNA. This gives us the blueprint of what we want to build. mRNA can then go through the process of translation. Just like it sounds, translation is taking all that information that we copied and translating it (or it may be better thought of as assembling it) into a nice usable package. Translation turns the mRNA into a protein. In regards to training, the protein formation is often the step that results in some sort of functional adaptation. For example, mitochondria biogenesis will improve endurance via several mechanisms.

It is important to note that I have only mentioned the pathways that we know a good deal about right now. It is likely that there are many other pathways through which adaptation occurs. The important take away is to learn how adaptation works. This allows you to design training based on the desired outcome. You do not need to know the specifics to apply this concept. Look at the glycogen depletion example. Just use logic and a good training workout can be deduced. If the marathon is an event that is dependent on the optimal fuel use ratio between carbohydrates and fats, how do we signal the body to change that ratio so that there is more reliance on fat. We need to "embarrass" it and send the signal that more fat needs to be used. How do you do that? Simple, by running a workout that depletes the glycogen stores to a significant enough amount that the body adapts to make sure that it does not run low on glycogen the next time. It accomplishes this by increasing the use of fat as a fuel and/or increasing glycogen stores. This example just took you through the process of adaptation without mentioning a single complex name. Use this technique to design solutions for to how to train for the upcoming race.

Long Term Adaptation

Until now, we have focused on just one training session, but that is seldom how it works in the real world, and in reality one training session is not going to be enough to elicit much adaptation. Following a single bout of training, mRNA levels increase and peak between 3-12 hours post exercise. The levels will remain elevated until around 24hrs post workout (Coffey & Hawley, 2007). With each increase in mRNA, a new level of protein synthesis is reached. So, while mRNA levels may fall back to resting levels after a day, the proteins that are created in this process remain elevated for much longer periods of time. For example, mitochondria protein turnover half-life is about 1 week. As mRNA levels return to baseline, protein levels level off. With each subsequent training stimulus that increases mRNA levels, the protein amounts are increased to a new level. Therefore, for long term training adaptation to occur, repeated bouts of exercise are needed to increase mRNA levels and continually keep progressing protein levels to the next level. If there is too long of a gap between training bouts, protein levels can potentially fall to the preceding level, and thus detraining occurs. This information helps explain why we need maintenance doses of workouts aimed at the variety of parameters to ensure that we don't go into a detraining state.

Training Applications

Although the study of signaling pathways is relatively knew, we are starting to understand the training that affects these pathways. As previously mentioned, low glycogen training has been validated in the research recently. The idea is to train low, compete high, or, in other words, do some training in a low glycogen state, while competing fully stocked with glycogen. In events like the marathon, this approach would seem to enhance performance. Once again, the research knowledge is behind the coaches and is simply explaining a phenomenon known for years in training. As far back as the 1950's, Ernst Van Aaken coached several elite marathoners who would practice low glycogen strategies by doing doubles without eating in between or doing long runs with no supplemental food. The fact is that often coaches figure out what works in training and then the scientists come in later and explain why it works.

Where the study of signaling pathways really contributes to the practical world is in its demonstration of why the never ending debate of volume or intensity is not an either/or situation. The AMPK and Calcium-Calmodulin pathways both ultimately result in an increase in mitochondria development. What is interesting is that the AMPK pathway seems to be highly activated by short intense workouts such as 30sec sprints, while the Calcium-Calmodulin pathway is activated by prolonged endurance exercise (Laursen, 2004). What this demonstrates is that there are multiple ways to get the same adaptation. Two entirely different workouts activate two different pathways that give the same result. That explains why runners in particular need a wide variety of training stimuli. It also could explain why athletes who switch coaches from one emphasizing lots of long steady running to one emphasizing high intensity lower volume, or vice versa, seem to have breakthroughs for the first year before stagnating. Perhaps the mitochondria increases of one pathway are near maxed out, and when there is a dramatic change in training, the other pathway has more adaptation potential.

These signaling pathways do not work in isolation. They can interact, and this may partially explain why strength gains are affected by endurance training. In particular the mTOR pathway seems to interact with the AMPK pathway. In looking at these two pathways, the main interaction explains why it is harder to gain strength while doing endurance training than it is to gain endurance while strength training. The AMPK pathway inhibits the mTOR pathway thus inhibiting protein synthesis. The inhibitory effect explains the interference effect between the two types of training.

How Nutrition affects Genes:

Beyond the obvious example of low glycogen training, your nutritional habits can impact these pathways and the resulting adaptations. For strength gains, supplementing strength training with Amino Acids works to increase strength because Amino Acids activate the mTOR pathway.

AMPK activation can be manipulated via nutrition too. AMPK activation is partially dependent on glycogen stores. AMPK generally stays active during a workout, but as soon as a workout is complete, it can be turned off by taking carbohydrate post workout. This quick shut off for AMPK would be a good idea for strength training athletes who want to minimize its effects, but for distance runners that may not be a good idea. While glycogen replenishment is a good idea, one has to wonder if deactivating AMPK as soon as exercise is done by chugging some Gatorade is a good idea all of the time?

The EPO Example

To demonstrate how the process of adaptation, signaling, and genetic response works in full, I'll briefly take you through the process of how altitude increases EPO production and ultimately red blood cells.

To set some hypothetical parameters, we will look at a moderately intense aerobic training stimulus (done around the lactate threshold) in a hypoxic environment. Going to a hypoxic environment, whether natural or artificial, puts a new stress on the body causing the various systems of the body to react and adapt to its new environment. Training, even at sea level, similarly causes numerous changes to occur within the body as it attempts to react to the stress of the particular training load. Therefore, when exercising at altitude, the body not only has to respond and adapt to one stimulus, it has to respond to two, a training and hypoxic one. When these two stressors combine, the body's primary objective becomes ensuring adequate oxygen delivery to the working muscles. It accomplishes this through a variety of mechanisms.

First, let's look at some of the larger changes that occur when training in a hypoxic environment. Two main factors will determine the physiologic and metabolic response: the intensity of the exercise and the level of hypoxia. Both of these factors will affect the amount of oxygen delivered to the muscles through a variety of factors. The level of hypoxia will first affect the hemoglobin oxygen saturation due to the decrease in the pressure gradient that occurs because of the reduction in the partial pressure of oxygen at altitude (Rusko, 2004). This greatly affects VO2max as each 1% drop in oxygen saturation below 95% decreases VO2max by 1-2% (Dempsey and Wagner, 1999). This drop in oxygen saturation even occurs at moderate to low intensities, as was demonstrated in well-trained athletes seeing drops even when training at 60-85% VO2max (Peltonen 1999). The drop in oxygen saturation is linearly related to the drop in maximal heart rate that occurs at altitude (Rusko 2004). Due to this drop in HR max, cardiac output is reduced at altitude.

The nervous system also plays a role in controlling the response to hypoxic conditions. Due to the decrease in oxygen concentration, muscle activity is reduced in hypoxic conditions (Peltonen, 1997). This reduction in muscle recruitment may be a way of the CNS governing performance. It has been suggested that the decrease in VO2max at altitude is the result of the CNS controlling exercise, instead of the decreased recruitment being a cause of the reduction in VO2max (Noakes et al., 2001). What the exact controlling mechanism of the response of the CNS to hypoxic conditions is remains unknown, but the CNS does play a role in the overall response to training in hypoxic conditions.

All of these changes that occur while training in hypoxic conditions lead to an eventual decrease in oxygen levels in the blood, and a decrease in the muscles themselves. This reduction in oxygen concentration in the blood and at the muscular level is the stimulus for the mechanisms behind our eventual desired outcome, an increase in RBC mass. A reduction in oxygen concentration of the blood activates the Hypoxia Inducible Factor-1 (HIF-1) pathway in tissues where EPO production can take place (i.e., kidney, liver, and the brain) (Stockmann et al. 2006).

HIF-1 is a main oxygen homeostasis regulator in the body. Two subunits, HIF-1α and HIF-1β, make up the HIF-1 complex. Under normal conditions, HIF-1β is present, but HIF-1α is constantly being degraded by the proteasome (Dery, 2005). When oxygen levels are lowered, the degradation of HIF-1α is inhibited and HIF-1α stabilizes. The stabilization allows for HIF-1α to bind to transcriptional coactivators and enter the nucleus of the cell. Here, HIF-1α binds to HIF-

1β, forming an HIF-1 transcriptional complex (Marzo et al., 2008). This HIF-1 complex then binds to the Hypoxia Response Element (HRE) on the EPO gene. This in turn leads to EPO expression (Stockmann et al., 2006).

EPO then needs to be transported to and bind with EPO receptors. EPO receptors can be found on erythroid stem cells in bone marrow (Marzo et al., 2008). The binding to the receptor on the cell membrane results in a signaling cascade that results in the activation of the transcription factor STAT-5 and two enzymes, PI3K and MAPK. These enter the nucleus and induce transcription of specific genes that result in the inhibition of apoptosis, programmed cell destruction (Marzo et al., 2008; Jelkmann, 2004). The end result is that this prevention of destruction of developing RBC results in an increase in RBC.

A larger RBC mass means a larger oxygen carrying capacity, which ultimately results in increased oxygen delivery to the muscles. Oxygen delivery has been shown to be a major limiter of VO2max (Bassett & Howley, 2000). In studies done on blood transfusion of RBC in elite endurance athletes, increases in endurance performance and in some cases VO2max have been significant (Calbet et al., 2006). In one particular study done on elite athletes with an average VO2max of 80 ml kg−1 min−1, time to exhaustion in an endurance test and VO2max were both significantly increased (Buick et al., 1980). Therefore, increased oxygen delivery results in increased aerobic capacity and the functional change of improved endurance.

This leads to the reasoning behind the selection of the training intensity. The idea behind the selection of a training intensity around lactate threshold is due to our desired outcome. In order to elicit the reduction in oxygen levels in the blood and muscles, the intensity needs to be high enough that it will do this. As was stated earlier, Peltonen et al. found that oxygen saturation was reduced at even sub maximal intensities of between 60-85% of VO2max (1999). In well-trained individuals, this intensity corresponds well to that of LT. Secondly, the intensity has to be low enough to allow for a significant volume of training to take place. The duration spent training has to be long enough to allow for activation of the pathway responsible for the desired adaptations. The signaling of the HIF-1 pathway under hypoxic conditions has been shown to already show increases in HIF-1α in the first 2 minutes. However, maximum HIF-1α did not occur until 1 hour of hypoxia, with max half times occurring at between 12 and 13 minutes. In addition, the reduction of HIF-1α with reoxygenation occurred quickly, also within 2 minutes, and was back to normal within 32 minutes (Jewell, 2001). These results suggest that a sufficient duration is necessary to elicit maximum gains via the HIF-1 pathway. Lastly, in a study by Zoll they found that training at an intensity that corresponded to the ventilatory threshold increased mRNA concentrations of the HIF-1α, giving credence to the theory discussed above (2005).

In looking at the research and the pathways involved in EPO production and RBC increase, it can be seen that in order for hypoxic training to increase RBC mass a sufficient intensity and duration is needed. The intensity must be high enough so that a drop in oxygen saturation occurs, while being low enough so that sufficient time can be spent training at that intensity for the pathway to be activated. In addition, enough repeated bouts of this type of training are needed in order to ensure that EPO synthesis achieves continued increase to new levels. Without repeated bouts, it is likely that mRNA will return to baseline levels, and EPO will quickly follow, thus not allowing for a sustained increase in RBC.

10

Theories of Training Adaptation

"It is not the strongest or the most intelligent who will survive but those who can best manage change." Charles Darwin

The training of endurance athletes is a complex process that is not entirely understood. Coaches of endurance athletes have generally taken an approach of focusing on improving various physiological parameters, a system based on tradition and trial and error, or a system based on race pace being the central focus with various percentages of race pace used to elicit different training adaptations. The wide variance in distance running training is the result of a reliance on training methods passed on by coaches that have been successful and skepticism of the science behind training. Before delving into what the current models of training are, a look at the volume of training done, the intensity of training, and the distribution of the training load and how all of those affect physiological parameters will give insight into what it takes to be a successful distance runner.

General Adaptation Syndrome and Dose-Response

Before analyzing the research done on the various ways to manipulate training for increased performance, it is essential that the overall process behind how the body responds to a stimulus and adapts be discussed. Hans Selye's General Adaptation Syndrome (G.A.S.) provides the basis for the process that the body goes through to adapt to a stimulus, regardless of whether it is training, an environmental stressor, or a psychological stressor. In Selye's original work, he provided a variety of stressors to rats and found that despite the change in how the animals were stressed, there response to the stressor followed a similar pattern. He saw similar changes in the lymph nodes, adrenal glands, and a few other systems, and this generalized response became the G.A.S. (Selye, 1978). It consists of three distinct stages.

The first stage is the Alarm stage. This refers to the initial response of the body to a stress where a lowering of resistance is seen and is often classified as our "fight or flight" response. The next stage is the Resistance stage, which consists of the body adapting to the stressor and an increase of resistance to the stress. The last stage occurs if the stress is continually applied and is the Exhaustion stage. In this stage, resistance to the stress lowers considerably, and the body cannot respond effectively to the stress (Selye, 1978).

Supercompensation

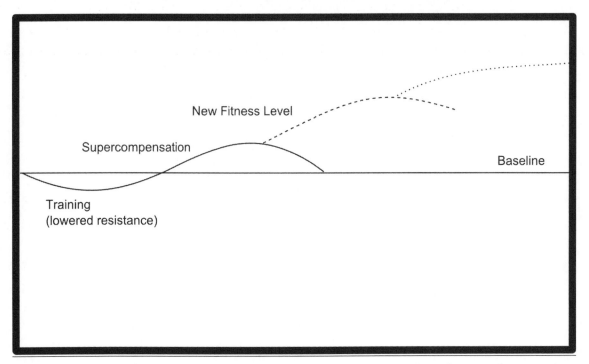

Selye's principle of adaptation can be applied to exercise training. In popular exercise literature, the application of the G.A.S. is often referred to as the principle of supercompensation (Bompa & Haff, 2008), which provides a theoretical guideline for the response and adaptation to an exercise stimulus. Similarly to Selye's theory, when some sort of training stimulus is applied, there is an initial alarm phase where fatigue occurs and the performance level is decreased. Following this alarm stage, with recovery, there is an adaptation phase where fatigue subsides and adaptation takes place so that there is a supercompensation where performance increases to a level above that which it was before the training stimulus was applied. A new training stimulus can then be applied to go through the process again. If too little recovery is allowed, then the body never fully recovers or adapts and can enter Selye's exhaustion phase; this is what is commonly referred to as overtraining (Bompa & Haff, 2008).

This model on stimulus and adaptation allows for the planning of the work and recovery during the training process. Obviously, recovery is needed to allow for adaptation during the resistance or adaptation phase, without which the person would enter an overtraining phase. In addition, a strong enough stimulus is needed to elicit adaptations, and on the other hand the stimulus cannot be too intense, thereby lowering resistance to a level that requires too much recovery time and does not result in an adequate supercompensation. Thus assigning the correct intensity and volume of a workout to elicit an optimal response is essential in proper training.

The dose response relationship is another model that helps explain the optimal load of a workout. The dose response relationship originates from medicine and explains the interaction between the dose, the total lode of a stimulus (i.e., intensity, volume, frequency), and the response, or resulting training effect (Iwasaki et al., 2003). In looking at a typical dose-response curve, it can be seen how the training dose affects the resulting outcome. Too low of a load given will result in little or no adaptations, and contrasting to that, too high of a load will give diminishing adaptations. Busson created a model that showed that an inverted U-shape best explained the optimal dose-response relationship between training and performance (2003). The top of the inverted U demonstrated an optimal dose of training, while either too little or too much training dose decreased the effect on performance.

It is also important to consider what affects this relationship. Just as a child needs less Advil than an adult for the same effect, a particular individual will need more or less of a training stimulus depending on a variety of factors. In doing research on large groups of participants it is easy to sometimes forget this relationship. An individual will react differently to a stimulus based on his physiological make up and his training history, among other factors. This individual response is an often-neglected parameter when discussing training dose and can shift the dose-response curve. Manzi demonstrated this by showing that Autonomic Nervous System parameters were dose related when accounting for the individual training dose, instead of taking a group only approach which had previously shown no relationship (2009). This can be seen in the constant search for an optimal intensity or volume which can be seen in both the popular literature, such as Arthur Lydiard's proclamation of 100 mile weeks being optimal, or in research, such as the search for an optimal training intensity, which seems to have varied between VO2max and Lactate Threshold (Midgeley et al., 2006; Lydiard, 1998). The recognition that each individual will respond differently to a stimulus, instead of giving recommendations that appear to be a one size fits all recommendation, would be one step towards closing the gap between research and coaching in the sport of distance running.

Individuality of Adaptation

In a viewpoint article, Kainulainen points out the individuality of the training response and the relative neglect of this phenomenon (2009). In this article, the author points to a study by Vollaard that showed that while on average improvements were seen in a variety of endurance parameters after six weeks of endurance training, the individuality of the response was widespread with some showing even negative responses to the training, even though the training was the same for all individuals and done as a percent of VO2max to provide some measure of individuality to the training program (Vollaard et al., 2009; Kainulainen, 2009). The study showed that there was a wide range of adaptation in maximal and sub maximal tests including VO2 parameters, muscle enzyme activity, and metabolite levels. Another interesting finding in the study is that low responders for an increased VO2max were not low responders in other parameters. This means that just because someone responded positively to training in one parameter, it didn't mean they'd respond positively in others. The change in VO2max did not correlate with the change in performance on a time trial, which is a significant finding demonstrating that perhaps more attention should be paid to changing performance instead of manipulating physiological parameters such as VO2max. One has to question the training recommendations based on training designed at improving parameters such as VO2max with the assumption being that performance will improve because of it when studies show that change in VO2max is often not linked to a change in performance. This phenomenon of varied response is not new and can be seen in a wide array of training situations, such as altitude training for example (Chapman et al., 1998).

The individual response goes beyond short-term adaptation. In a study by Gaskill they tested the yearly training model for 14 Cross Country Skiers (1999). During the first year all skiers performed the same kind of training that consisted of high volume training with only 16% of the training being performed at or above LT. At the end of the year, subjects were split between responders, those who showed the most improvements, and non-responders. The responders trained the same way the following year, while the non-responders slightly reduced their training volume and increase the total intensity. Following the 2nd year, the non-responders showed significant improvements in race times, VO2max, and LT. The responders also showed similar continued improvements in race times. These results point to the individual nature of training adaptation and show that some subjects will thrive off of different training stimuli. The mechanism behind this different response has not been found yet. It is speculation, but a difference in the fiber type distribution and strength of aerobic and anaerobic capacities might explain the different reactions to training. Perhaps an individual with a tendency towards more FT fibers responds better to higher intensity training that recruits those muscle fibers. Similarly, an athlete with a predominance of ST fibers might respond better to more volume.

The neglect of the importance of the individual dose-response relationship could be of consequence when trying to determine the effects of various training modalities. Furthermore, as pointed out by Kainulainen, perhaps the problem is the standardization of training paces as percents of VO2max. The aerobic and anaerobic contribution at a fixed percent of VO2max can vary widely from individual to individual, as can be seen in the fact that the Lactate Threshold can occur at a range of percent VO2max (Brooks et al., 2004). Similarly, in the Vollaard study there was a 40-fold range for increase in lactate levels at 70% VO2max, showing the wide individual range of response to the exercise stimulus (2009). They acknowledged this point and suggested standardization on parameters that more directly affect power output. In practical terms for trained distance runners, it probably makes more sense to standardize paces in relation to their recent race performances or based on percentages of goal race pace in well-trained runners.

11

Volume and Intensity of Training

"Western societies are taught to avoid and fear fatigue. Everything we do is geared towards avoiding fatigue in society." Renato Canova

While the second half of this book is devoted to training, as a coach it is important to understand what the scientific research says about training and more importantly to answer the question as to why what it says is different from what most coaches recommend. In this chapter, we'll explore the two different viewpoints on volume and intensity of training and see if we can make some practical sense out of the two contrasting views.

Volume of Training

The volume of training is generally quantified as miles per week ran. How much is needed to optimize performance has been a source of great debate in popular distance running training for many years. Following World War II, the contemporary training was based on a lower mileage higher intensity training program, which can be seen in the training of Gerschler and Franz Stampfl. It was not until the late 1950's, early 1960's that the volume of training became a focal point. With the success of Arthur Lydiard's athletes, typical training volumes that eclipsed 100 miles per week (mpw) quickly became the norm (Lydiard, 1998). Up until the early 1980's, high mileage was predominant among the elite distance runners of the world. In the 80's and early 90's, a new line of thinking focused on moderate mileage (~50-70mpw) with more high intensity work gained popularity. This was led by the British coaches Peter Coe (with his success in coaching his son Seb Coe) and Frank Horwill (Coe & Martin, 1997). The rise of sports science during this period of time also seems to have led to the emphasis on higher intensity work with lower volume. While Coe and others had success with this approach, the dearth of American distance running success on the world level during the 90's is sometimes blamed on this change in emphasis.

With the rise of Kenyan and Ethiopian distance runners, ideas on training volume shifted again towards higher mileage totals. The East African runners demonstrated that relatively high volumes of training might be necessary for reaching the levels that they were at. Some authors have speculated that East African runners are actually in the moderate volume, high intensity line of training, but this neglects the popular literature and more importantly the scholarly literature on the subject (Berg, 2003). Billat found that East African runners in their classified Low Speed Training group averaged 172km per week, while high speed runners averaged

158km per week (2003). Both of these values are substantially higher than the values done by lower mileage programs such as Coe's. In addition, these values were recorded while the subjects were in racing season, which is not the period of highest volume. Therefore, the idea that East African runners are of the lower volume model is not substantiated. Lastly, training programs by authors who have coached elite Kenyan runners also demonstrate that they take a relatively high volume approach (Canova & Arceli, 1999). One important note is that their intensity is also fairly high, and in this author's opinion, much higher than the higher volume programs of the 1960's and 70's; perhaps this is due to their large volume of running and activity during their childhood. This could potentially allow for them to handle higher intensities while still maintaining higher volumes. While examining the historical volumes of training of elite runners gives us an idea of what might be best, the question is what does research say about volume of training?

There have been a few studies that have tried to determine the impact of training volume on performance and physiological factors. Daniels found no change in VO2max while increasing training from 20-30km/wk to 50-70km/wk (Daniels, 1978). Similarly, a study by Costill comparing changes in VO2max with two marathon runners coming back to training after a 6-month layoff, VO2max increased progressively as mileage increased up until ~100mpw, while further increases in mileage, all the way up to 200 mpw, resulted in no further changes in VO2max (Costill & Trappe, 2002). The fact that VO2max does not seem to change after a certain amount of mpw is sometimes cited as a reason that higher mileage is not needed. However, it is important to remember that VO2max is not the be all and end all and does not accurately reflect performance. Two studies have shown that with increases in mileage performance was improved even with no change in VO2max (Costill, 1967; Daniels, 1978).

Two different studies have also looked at the relationship between the amount of training done and Running Economy (RE). Theoretically, one adaptation that could occur with a large volume of running is an increase in RE due to increased efficiency, both mechanical and metabolic, because of the repetitive nature of running. In a comparison of a spectrum of runners spanning from untrained to elite, the findings suggest that high volumes of running could increase RE (Costill, 1967). Similarly, Mayhew found that the number of years running significantly correlated with RE (1977). Contradicting this data, Pate did not find a correlation between RE and training volume (1992). The connection between RE and volume of training remains inconclusive.

Lastly, it's important to recognize the limitations of research studies on the impact that volume of training has. Many of the adaptations that may occur due to increases in volume may take longer than the couple of weeks that most studies last. For instance, a longitudinal study by Rusko found that after 8 years of training and a doubling of training volume, the percentage of ST fibers in a group of Cross-Country Skiers increased by 11% (1992). While obviously not solely due to the volume increase, these changes show the long-term adaptations that take place in endurance athletes. Another study by Fiskerstrand and Seiler found that the performance changes (+10%) in world class rowers from 1970 to 2001 occurred not with an increase in intensity of training but with an increase in volume of easy training (2004). The amount of low intensity training per week increased from 30hrs to 50hrs per week, while the amount of supramaximal training decreased from 30hrs to 7hrs per week. The lack of longitudinal studies prevents making any research based recommendations on what the ideal volume of training is for distance runners.

Intensity of Training

While volume of training is often the first factor most think of, intensity of training plays just as important of a role. Distance runners typically perform several higher intensity workouts per week, which are separated with easier runs. The intensity of both the harder and easier runs affects the adaptations that take place and lead to improved performance. The intensities used range from easy jogging all the way up to sprinting. There has been much research aimed at finding the effects of different training intensities. Most of these studies separate training intensities into sub maximal, LT, VO2max, and supramaximal training. While the efficacy of separating training into zones is debatable, we will look at the effects of training at these various intensities for the sole reason that this is how most of the research splits the training up.

In general, the knowledge of what intensity to train at is in the dark ages as far as research goes. This is definitely one area where coaches appear to be ahead of the scientists. Given that fact, I will lightly touch on some of the pertinent research done on training at various intensities and then give a brief overview of a practical approach to assigning training intensities.

Lactate Threshold

For distance runners, training at or around LT has risen in importance in recent years. This is partly due to a few different reasons. First, the observation that VO2max does not seem to change in elite athletes, yet performance and LT continues to improve (Legaz Arrese et al., 2005). Second, advances in measuring lactate threshold meant more research came out showing the effects of training on that parameter. Once again, since we could measure it, it gained significance. For these reasons, training at LT has become en vogue.

For recreationally trained runners, training at around the threshold seems to impact LT, RE, and VO2max. Four different studies with recreational athletes found that adding between 1 and 6 LT type sessions per week increased VO2max by between 2.5-8.1% after 6-8 weeks of training. In addition, two studies measured changes in LT and found that it increased by 3.3% and 10.7% respectively. It is worth noting that the 10.7% increase was seen when 6 sessions of LT training were done per week, while the other study added two such sessions per week. Lastly, improvements in RE were measured and seen in two studies with improvements of both 1.8% and 3.1% (Billat et al. 2004; Franch et al., 1998; Hoffman et al., 1999; Yoshida et al., 1990).

While the improvements in all three variables are impressive, we should expect the novel and somewhat stressful stimulus of threshold work to improve runners. The question becomes what happens in well-trained runners? Acevedo and Goldfarb investigated adding training sessions at an intensity near LT in well-trained runners (average VO2max=65.3 ml/kg/min). The added training sessions resulted in a nonsignificant improvement in VO2max of 0.7% but a significant increase in LT of 5.1%. In addition, performance in a 10k race improved by 3.1% (1989). In an interesting study Jemma found that after 3 weeks of interval training at an intensity that usually corresponds with LT (~85%VO2max), performance over a 40km time trial in well-trained cyclists was improved (2005). They measured EMG changes and found that the performance improvements could have been due to changes in muscle recruitment.

This improvement in LT and performance without an increase in VO2max is consistent with the idea that VO2max seldom changes in well-trained athletes and performance improvements come from other factors. The changes in EMG found during the Jemma study are interesting and point to the notion that factors outside the traditional endurance performance model need to be considered when conducting training studies.

VO2max

Many studies have focused on training at around the velocity of VO2max. The belief is that spending time at VO2max may help increase VO2max or stress the aerobic capacity maximally, thus serving as the most effective stimulus for adaptations. There have been numerous research studies on the effects of training on VO2max. In untrained subjects, training at or near VO2max increases VO2max (Berg, 2003). In two separate studies, adding intervals at or around vVO2max in recreational trained athletes increased VO2max by 5.0% and 6.0%, and RE by 2% and 3% (Franch et al., 1998; Smith et al., 2003).

In well-trained athletes, as previously mentioned, changes in VO2max are rare, as can be seen by a study by Legaz Arrese which found improvements in performance without changes in VO2max in elite runners (2005). Several specific studies have been done on a variety of interval training programs at the velocity at VO2max (vVO2) in well-trained runners. Out of four studies that tracked changes in VO2max, only one study found any significant changes in VO2max. Three of these studies showed improvements in performance, with one showing no change. Only one study measured changes in RE, and it showed an improvement. Lastly, two showed an improvement in vVO2, while two showed no change (Acevedo & Goldfarb, 1989; Smith et al., 1999; Billat et al., 2002; Billat et al., 1999). The data on training at vVO2 remains inconclusive on a number of levels. Performance seems to improve the majority of the time, while the exact mechanism of this performance improvement is unknown. Since only one study measured changes in RE and those were positive, it is possible that this could be the main benefit. The Jemma et al. study also points to the idea that neuromuscular changes such as altered recruitment pattern could play a role in alteration in performance during high intensity training (2005). Even though the training is generally termed VO2max training since it corresponds with that parameter, it should be remembered that training at that intensity will result in adaptations other than those related to VO2max.

Supramaximal Training

Training at speed faster than vVO2max has been shown to improve endurance performance. It is possible that this occurs through several mechanisms. Training at speeds faster than VO2max could potentially alter many of the previously discussed anaerobic and neural factors that impact endurance performance. In addition, faster training could have an impact on the traditional factors in performance: VO2max, LT, and RE.

There have been a limited number of studies with supramaximal training involving runners only. The limited number of studies involved recreationally or moderately trained individuals. Two different studies found contrasting results. In a study by Franch, they had participants do intervals at 132% vVO2 and found a significant increase in VO2max of 3.6% and a nonsignificant increase in RE of .9 (1998).On the other hand Bickham found that doing sprint intervals at 90-100% perceived maximum effort increased time to exhaustion at 110%VO2max and decreased VO2max by a nonsignificant 2.2% (2006). Interestingly, this study showed an increase in MCT1, which, as mentioned earlier, may play a role in assisting with the oxidation of lactate. These results point to the need for more studies on supramaximal training in distance runners and the measurement of more variables that may impact performance.

It is possible that supramaximal training could induce changes that could negatively affect distance running performance. High intensity interval training could elicit Glycolytic adaptations that could impair aerobic processes. In several studies using very intense interval training, increases in lactate production and the enzymes PFK and LDH have been found (Billat, 2001). As mentioned in the LT section, an increase in lactate production, and an increase in LDH, which could represent more pyruvate being converted to lactate, could alter the balance between lactate production and clearance. This in turn would negatively impact LT. The degree to which this theoretical argument holds up in well-trained runners needs to be investigated, because it is likely that in untrained subjects any sort of training stimulus that had some aerobic component would improve LT.

Cycling studies provide us some clue of the general effects of such training on endurance performance. Several studies have looked at the impact of supramaximal intervals of 30-60sec in length. Laursen found an improvement in power output by 5.3% over a 40km time trial after 4 weeks of interval training, an increase in power following an incremental test (+4.0%), and an increase in VO2max by 2.2% (2002b). Stepto found an increase in power over the 40km distance by 3.4% without a significant change in VO2max (-0.6%) (1999). In another study, Laursen found an increase in power by 5.7% at Ventilatory Threshold (VT), which closely relates to LT, an increase in maximum power attained in the step test (+4.7%), and an increase in VO2max by 3.5% following four weeks of training (2002a). Finally, in a study by Creer, EMG measurements were taken before and after 4 weeks of interval training to assess neural factors (2004). They saw significant increases in peak power and VO2max, as well as an increase in EMG readings showing increased motor unit activation.

The cycling studies all point towards improved performance following the addition of supramaximal training. The exact mechanisms for these improvements vary with each study. The measured increases in maximum power in the Laursen studies, combined with the Creer study measuring increased motor unit activation, could lend credence to the idea that neural adaptations may be the main reason that supramaximal training improves performance in endurance athletes. In addition, if Noakes CGM is taken into consideration the increase in VO2max seen in relatively untrained individuals after supramaximal training could be a result of increased muscle activation.

Training at speeds faster than VO2max is a regular part of most distance runners training, yet there is a lack of information regarding its effects on well-trained runners. This is probably due to the heavy emphasis on training at VO2max and LT. That emphasis is likely due to the fact that those quantities are easily measured and provide points of reference. Cycling studies help show that other factors besides these may be the true mechanisms responsible for why supramaximal training improves performance. More running specific research is needed on this topic to discern the exact mechanisms.

Interaction of Volume and Intensity of Training

In the research literature there has been a trend towards the recommendation of high intensity versus high volume training (Berg, 2003). This is likely a result of the short-term nature of research studies. Given the changes that occur with high intensity versus lower intensity and longer duration training, it is not surprising that high intensity training shows greater benefits over only the standard 6 week timeframe of most training studies. This has led to the conclusion that high intensity training is preferential over higher volume to reach the same adaptations. However, it is questionable whether this preference has merit. Seiler and Tønnessen found that elite endurance training consists of about 85% of the training being performed at low to moderate intensities in several different groups of elite endurance athletes (2009). Regardless of whether their sport was cycling, running, cross-country skiing, or a similarly aerobically demanding sport, the amount of light activity was very high. Furthermore, they point out that elite training is more likely to represent optimum training than what is demonstrated in the lab setting because of a likely evolutionary process of training by elites.

Contrasting with the research theory, Esteve-Lanao demonstrated that it was the amount of easy running that impacted running performance over a 10km race not the amount of high intensity training (2007). The experience of elite endurance athletes also contradicts the research findings that high intensity, low volume training is optimal. As pointed out already it seems that the best runners combine a higher volume of training with some higher intensity training. Due to the high volume of training, the large percentage is low intensity, but the absolute volume of relatively high intensity training still reaches levels of 20mi or more per week (Billat et al., 2003). In a paper by Laursen, he points out two key findings. First, without a background of high volume training, high intensity training can maintain but seldom improve performance (2009). Second, while the adaptations of high intensity and high volume training may be similar, they may occur via two different pathways. Most of the training studies manipulating intensity of training add high intensity work to an athlete's training schedule who has been doing a large volume of low intensity training. This approach where high volume training must precede high intensity training is fundamental in popular literature on distance running, but it is neglected in the research. What we are left with in most research then is taking someone who has a base of endurance and adding some high intensity training. Should we really wonder why they improve with that periodization model?

The idea that high intensity training is more beneficial when preceded by a base has been around since the days of Arthur Lydiard. In a study by Quinn, two different groups performed either continuous exercise or interval training for 12 weeks (2002). At the end of the 12 weeks, the groups switched, so that the continuous group now did 12 weeks of interval training. It was found that the group that did continuous and then interval training improved significantly more in terms of time to exhaustion (15% to 5.3%) and VO2max (7.4% to 3.6%) than the group that did interval and then continuous training. While this shouldn't surprise any coaches, the finding supports the idea that a base of moderate work needs to be established before intense training is done in order to achieve maximum benefits. This could also explain why in most studies that simply replace a portion of the low to moderate training in their subjects' routine with high intensity training, performance is improved by so much. This interaction of prior training's impact on training during a study should be taken into consideration when evaluating study results.

According to Laursen, high volume training may signal for adaptations through the calcium-calmodulin pathway because of the increase in intramuscular calcium seen in long duration, high volume training (2004). In contrast to this, high intensity training may signal adaptations through the adenosine monophosphate kinase (AMPK) pathway because of the increase in AMP seen following high intensity training. Both of these pathways eventually lead to PGC-1α, which is a transcriptional cofactor that will result in the typical adaptations seen in endurance athletes such as mitochondria biogenesis (Laursen, 2004). Laursen thus concludes that there are two very different ways to achieve similar adaptations. This points to the idea that to maximize these adaptations both stimuli are likely needed as one pathway may be more difficult to activate than the other depending on the individual and their training status.

In conclusion, it is likely the disparity between the time course of changes and the length of the research studies that is creating this discrepancy between real world recommendations and the findings in the lab. High intensity training is likely to show quick adaptations, explaining its greater impact on performance within a short period of time. The long-term effect of repeated high intensity training is not something that has been researched in the literature.

The experience of coaches points to a long block of high intensity training leading to decreased performance, mostly likely due to overtraining (Lydiard, 1998).

Training in the Real World

While studies on training are interesting, they should be taken with a grain of salt. In research we have to isolate one variable to see its effect. In the real world, variables are never isolated. This creates a situation where training in the lab is completely different than training in the real world. The training effect is the result of a combination of all of the training stimuli applied to the athlete.

Research on concurrent endurance and strength training has demonstrated this effect by showing that the genetic adaptation that occurs is partially dependent on whether the strength or endurance training was done last during the day's training. This is but one example of the limits of research-based endurance training. Another problem is that the research looks at averages and everyone as a group, while a coach has to look at people as individuals. This creates a situation where researchers are looking for the magic workout or training intensity that improves performance on average. It does not exist.

In the real world, we know that training cannot be classified into easily manageable zones. Yes, certain workouts will have a greater effect aerobically or anaerobically, but as discussed previously an individual's reaction to training will vary drastically. This might partially explain the drastic difference in opinion of optimal training between most Scientists and most coaches. The scientist viewpoint has been explained in detail, so a brief counterpoint of the coaches' viewpoint on intensity of training is in order.

From a coaching standpoint, there should be no zones of training. All paces are connected in some way and elicit slightly different adaptations. The central premise of deciding training intensity should depend primarily on two factors, the race distance the individual is aiming for and the individual makeup of the runner. The race distance and goal pace should give the coach a pace that can be defined as specific. From this pace, as we get faster or slower, the intensity becomes more general, all the way out to the extremes of jogging or full out sprinting.

Generally, coaches start with using very general training, on both sides of faster/slower spectrum, and work towards specificity. Further details on this are discussed below in the periodization section. The key difference is that all the intensities build upon each other or, in other words, are supported by each other. The term base is often used and applies to this idea. A base of easy aerobic running needs to be established before more intense aerobic running can be done. Similarly, a base of pure speed and muscle fiber recruitment provides the foundation for slightly slower but longer work. The goal of training is to use both sides of the spectrum to increase the speed that you can handle over a specific distance or, in other words, to extend the length of time you can run at your goal pace until it reaches the full race distance.

The workouts themselves are not done in the way that most research based workouts are in that you run a single set of repeats at a given pace. Instead there is mixing of intensities for a desired goal. Workouts also have built in progression to take the athlete to the next adaptation level by manipulating pace, intensity, rest interval, etc.

This is a very brief and general overview of the training process from a coach's standpoint, and just one of many theories. The key differences between research designs and real world training can be summed up with the idea that research is looking for the magic workout and magic training intensity that enhances performance whereas coaches use a large mixture of workouts at a variety of intensities to reach peak performance. In addition, research is focused on the group average, while coaches recognize the individuality of training.

Supplementary Training

Training that is not running specific also has been shown to improve distance running performance (Jung, 2003). Resistance training and plyometrics are the two types of training that are the most studied and beneficial. Despite the evidence pointing towards performance benefits, there has been a hesitation by many runners to include these types of training. Part of this hesitation is due to the idea that resistance training increases size and weight The belief that only VO2max, RE, and LT impact running performance has also held back the acceptance of supplemental training. However, as discussed already, it is now known that anaerobic and neural factors contribute to success in distance running.

There are many different types of resistance training, which complicates quantifying its effect on endurance performance. The types of resistance training that will likely aid runners are those that do not result in a significant increase in body weight and muscle size. A significant increase in muscle size would result in a decrease of the capillary and mitochondria density (Brooks et al., 2004). For these reasons, training that focused on improving the neural and anaerobic factors that improve distance running performance without a subsequent increase in weight or size would be desirable. Following this idea, plyometrics and heavy training are likely to be the best for endurance athletes.

The majority of studies using traditional weight lifting have shown no change in VO2max in well-trained athletes (Jung, 2003). The studies that have found a change in VO2max were on untrained subjects. For example, on well-trained subjects, Hickson found no change in VO2max when resistance training was added to cyclists training (1988). In trained individuals it is unlikely that VO2 will be high enough to elicit a change in VO2max. However, if one applies the theory of Noakes' CGM, it is possible that changes in VO2max following resistance training could be attributed to changes in muscle activation which transfer to the task of running. Of the traditional factors, RE and to a lesser extent LT appear to be the most affected by resistance training.

RE seems to be the primary factor that is improved with this training. Three studies using trained runners and replacing part of their training with plyometric or explosive type training have shown improved RE, while one study using heavy lifting demonstrated improved RE. Spurrs found an improvement in 3k time along with an improvement in RE following plyometric training (2003). Similarly, Saunders found that following plyometric training improved RE by 4.1%. In addition, neuromuscular factors were improved, such as decreased time to reach maximal dynamic strength and increased average power during a plyometric test (2006). Lastly, in well-trained runners, Paavolainen found that following 9 weeks of plyometric type training, the runners improved their 5k races by 3.1% and RE by 8.1% (1999). They also improved their vMART, and that improvement significantly correlated with their improvements in performance.

One study has been done on the effects of heavy weight lifting on endurance performance. Millet studied the effects of 14 weeks of heavy weight training on various parameters in triathletes. They found that RE, maximal strength, and power during a hopping test were all significantly increased (2002). Another study by Esteve-Lanao found that a periodized resistance training program resulted in the maintenance of stride length compared to a control group and a non-periodized resistance program (2008). This study shows another potential benefit of resistance training.

These findings on the effects of plyometric and resistance training lead to the idea that neural and anaerobic factors from strength training could be responsible for performance improvements. As discussed in the neuromuscular section, it is likely that changes in motor unit recruitment, changes in anaerobic capacity, or alterations in ground contact time or muscle-tendon stiffness could explain improvements in performance following resistance training.

Training Frequency

How often runners train and the distribution of training intensities across training are two other factors that are debated. In distance running, it is accepted that well-trained runners train every day or at least six days out of the week. This is needed to reach the higher volumes of training that are done. One debate surrounds whether training once or twice per day is most beneficial. There have even been reports of elite Kenyan athletes running up to three times per day (Tanser, 2008). Billat found that elite Kenyan runners trained between 10-14 times per week (2002).

To the author's knowledge only one training study has been done comparing training once versus twice per day in moderately trained runners. In a study by Mostardi and Campbell they added a 7mi run to one group's training on 4 days per week, while the other group ran only once per day continuing their daily regimen. After 4 weeks, no differences in improvements in VO2max were found. However, VO2max was tested on a bicycle ergometer, which may impact results since the participants were track athletes and ran during their training. Both groups saw significant improvements in mile time, but there were no differences between the groups (1981). More research needs to be done on this topic as obviously the research results conflict with the real world training suggestions.

Several theoretical arguments can be made for twice versus once per day training, especially during in-season training. During in-season training, a large bulk of the training of distance runners is used as recovery or general aerobic running (Daniels, 2005). In well-trained runners, at this point of the season, it is unlikely that a low training stimulus would elicit further adaptations. It is possible that splitting these recovery runs into doubles would further promote recovery while maintaining volume.

In theory, glycogen depletion could be minimized to a greater degree than with one single run, as glycogen repletion would be easier to achieve following two separate 5 mile runs instead of one 10mi run. Two separate runs could lead to greater glycogen repletion due to a greater window of insulin sensitivity following each run. Additionally, the hormonal response of such hormones as Growth Hormone, which plays a role in recovery and adaptation, could potentially be greater in two separate runs instead of one longer run. Significant GH release in endurance runs at low and moderate intensities occur in relatively short runs (Gilbert et al., 2008). In addition, some researchers have suggested that training in a fatigued state may enhance subsequent adaptations. It has been found that training in a glycogen depleted state enhances gene transcription of several markers of training adaptation (Yeo et al., 2008; Hansen et al., 2005). In two studies on training every day versus training twice every other day, increases in enzyme activity have been more significantly increased in the twice every other day group. In the study by Hansen, they used knee extensor exercises with one leg being trained every day and the other twice every other day (2005). The twice every other day leg showed significantly better time till exhaustion at the end of the training, along with the increased enzyme activity. In the study by Yeo and colleagues they compared two different groups using cycling as the means of training (2008). In their study enzyme activity was higher in the twice every other day group, but performance was equally increased in both groups. More research needs to be done using study designs that more accurately reflect the training done in the real world, meaning that training once every day versus twice per day, even with equal volume, should be researched instead of twice every other day.

In addition to the frequency of training done, the frequency of the more intense workouts also plays a role. Recommendations in the popular literature suggest that 2-3 intense workouts should be done per week (Daniels, 2005). However, little research has been done on this subject with runners. As will be discussed later, recovery plays a central role in the adaptation process. Without adequate recovery, athletes could be pushed into a state of overtraining or overreaching (Billat et al., 1999). Therefore, finding the optimal distribution between low intensity and high intensity workouts should be considered. In a study by Billat, they put this to the test having subjects perform 3 low intensity workouts, 1 LT workout, and one high intensity training (HIT) workout per week (1999). They then increased the intensity of the training by having the subjects perform 2 continuous, 3 HIT, and one LT workout per week. The subjects did not show any further improvement with the increased density of hard workouts and showed markers for overtraining. This study gives an idea on the density of hard workouts that subjects can handle.

12

Periodization of Training

"Lots of things work. The question is, what's the most practical and efficient way to train for a certain task?" Again to Carthage

How we plan and implement our training is of the utmost importance for ensuring success. It is important to remember that periodization does not refer to some exact method of training planning but instead simply refers to how one goes about planning the training. Training volume, intensity, and frequency are manipulated throughout a season to bring about peak performance. There are numerous theories of how to plan and manipulate training to bring runners to maximum performance, yet there is no research testing any of these periodization models. On the other hand, periodization is well studied in strength training (ACSM 2009).

Periodization is the process of dividing the training into smaller periods of training where the emphasis, or the target, of the training is altered during each period. Generally a manipulation of the volume, intensity, and frequency of workouts is done to bring a person to peak performance. Traditionally, periodized training has been broken down into several phases. The largest of these is a several year cycle that was originally based on the 4-year cycle of Olympic athletes. Below this is the Macrocycle, which consists of a period of training that lasts from months to up to a year. The next level is that of the mesocycle which consists of several weeks of training. A microcycle is the next phase that consists of several days to a week or more of training. The last level is that of the individual workout (Issurin, 2008).

Training can be periodized on several different levels. On a microcycle level, the variation of volume and intensity of workouts on a day-to-day basis is often done. In endurance training this often means the alternation of harder workouts, those performed at intensities near or above LT, with easier runs performed at relatively light intensities. In popular coaching literature, there are many different theories on how to manipulate training. It is generally accepted that harder days are followed by one or two easier days before another hard day is repeated (Daniels, 2005; Hudson, 2008). There has been no research or studies that the author is aware of that have investigated this manipulation of training on the microcycle level. It is not known whether this alternation of hard and easy training is optimal or whether some other manipulation is more effective. This is one of the many research limitations in endurance sports. One study on strength training clearly shows that altering what is done each day is more effective for the development of strength than altering only every 4 (Rhea et al., 2003).

On a larger scale of mesocycle and macrocycle level, debate surrounds how to manipulate volume and intensity over the course of a season. In endurance training, only one study has been done comparing periodized training and non-periodized training. The study by Soungatoulin found that after 16 weeks of training the periodized cyclists performed significantly better in a time trial (2003).

The intricacies of periodization can be debated on many different levels. Looking at a macrocycle level of training, the manipulation of overall volume and intensity is often debated as volume and intensity are inversely related (Bompa & Haff, 2008). Several contrasting views are seen in the manipulation of these variables. The traditional approach, emphasized by Arthur Lydiard, consisted of very high volumes of work early in the season that consistently lowers as the season progresses with a proportionate increase in intensity (Lydiard, 1998). In contrast to this approach, Simmons has suggested an ever increasing total volume of training with a corresponding steady increase in intensity (Simmons & Freeman, 2006). There is no research to suggest how the volume and intensity of training should progress on a macrocycle level, so we have to mainly rely on how training has evolved in the real world.

Volume and intensity can be manipulated on a meso and microcycle level too. Several different approaches to manipulating these variables are seen in the popular literature and even in theoretical literature. Some coaches subscribe to a consistent approach to volume in that within a period, volume is kept relatively level from microcycle to microcycle (Lydiard, 1998). In contrast to this, in other approaches volume is altered every week with a high and then a low volume week of training. Another approach is an escalating approach to volume where volume is increased every week during a mesocycle. Some of these programs also institute the inclusion of a down or recovery week where volume and/or intensity is decreased to allow for adaptation (Bompa & Haff, 2008). This approach makes sense in theory in regards to Hans Selye's General Adaptation Syndrome that explains the mechanisms behind stress and adaptation. In theory, the down week would allow for recovery, adaptation, and progression to a new level of resistance. How many weeks of higher volume or escalating volume should be done before a down week is not known. There has been no research done to investigate any of these theories or ideas. This leaves the manipulation of volume on a mesocycle level largely based on experience and trial and error.

How one should periodize the training to target specific adaptations is also a source of debate (Issurin, 2008). The debate surrounds whether a linear/block or non-linear/mixed periodization scheme is more beneficial. In a linear/block periodization scheme, periods of training that are almost solely devoted to developing a select few biomotor abilities, while work on other abilities are kept to a minimum. The next period or block of training would then shift its emphasis to a different biomotor ability to be its focus. For example, during the first period of training, a several week period may be spent doing exclusively endurance training. This may be followed by a period of training done to develop high-end aerobic endurance, and then by a period designed to develop speed endurance (Bompa & Haff 2008).

In a non-linear/mixed periodization scheme, the emphasis during each period would change, but nothing would be almost entirely neglected (Hudson, 2008). Essentially, in each period there would be an element of endurance training, speed, speed endurance, etc.; only the emphasis on each one would change. For example, during the first period of training, endurance may be emphasized with lots of aerobic running, but a weekly sprint session may be included. In a later period, speed training may be more emphasized and thus a higher volume or frequency of that work is done, but training focused on endurance would also be done, just not to the degree it was done during the period when it was emphasized.

In regards to endurance training, the benefits are largely theoretical and anecdotal. In resistance training one study has been done comparing linear and nonlinear approaches. In a study by Monteiro nonlinear periodization showed higher increases in strength and more consistent increases in strength across a 12 week training period when compared to a linear and a no periodization group (2009). In this study, three different workout types, consisting of 3-4 sets of either 4-5 reps, 8-10 reps, or 12-15 reps that were aimed at different adaptations were used. The periods of training were split into 3 blocks of 4 weeks each. The linear group did all 3 sets of 12-15 reps the first period, then all 8-10 rep sets the second, and finally all 4-5 rep sets the last. The non-linear group did two of the three rep types each period, with it altering each period. The non periodization group did solely 3 sets of 8-12 reps. While the design of this study was for strength increases, it shows that a non-linear approach was more consistent in strength increases after each period and produced greater total increases, which both are criticisms of a non-linear approach (Issurin, 2008). No similar studies have been done using endurance training so whether the results would be similar in endurance training is unknown, but it does provide theoretical support for a non-linear approach of training. This calls into question the merits of having a period of training focused solely on one adaptation such as is seen in many endurance sports where a large base period focuses only on steady aerobic running.

Periodization is a complex process that occurs on many different levels. In looking at the coaching literature, the general periodization for distance runners can be divided into down into two theoretical models. The two models include a linear model and a funnel to specificity model.

Linear Periodization

Linear Periodization

The linear model is considered the classic approach to distance training. It gained popularity and influence following the success of Arthur Lydiard's athletes in New Zealand. The Lydiard approach, which is the basis for the linear approach, started with a several month period called Marathon Conditioning where high volumes (~100mpw) of easy to moderate running were done. In addition long tempo or fartlek sessions were done during the end of this period. Following this phase, mileage was decreased and the intensity was increased with a one month period called Hill Resistance which focused on strength endurance by using a variety of hill repeats and hill circuits. The next phase consisted of track training, starting with longer intervals on the track (800's, miles) and progressively working towards shorter intervals (200's and 400's). This was followed by a sharpening and peaking phase that consisted of shorter faster work, such as 50m in and out sprints or an all out 200m, and a further drop in volume (Wilt, 1964; Lydiard, 1998).

This method is still used today by many coaches. Greg McMillan, coach of an elite training group in the U.S., characterizes his training as going from Base to Stamina to Speed (Greg McMillan, personal conversations). Similarly, Esteve-Lanau described the periodization used by well-trained Spanish runners in their study as a type of linear periodization (2005). While the traditional linear system consisted of a large drop in volume, modern linear programs tend to have a more gradual drop in volume.

This linear periodization model can be characterized as a system that starts with a high volume of training and progressively decreases this volume, while at the same time intensity of the workouts starts low and is progressively increased. In this case, volume and intensity are inversely related. Looking at the hard workouts themselves, it can be seen that the pace of these is generally increased from the start of the training until the end. Training might start with the harder workouts being done at LT or similar tempo intensities, progress to 10k-5k speeds, then to vVO2 speeds, and finally speeds that are at mile pace or faster.

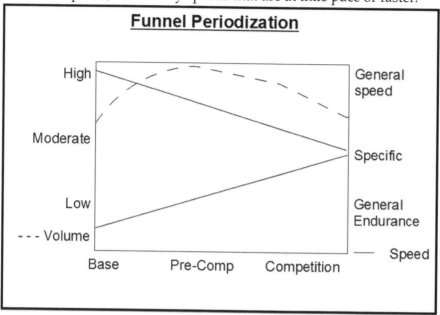

Funnel/Mixed Periodization

The funnel model of periodization is a newer training theory that is taking hold in distance running. Its modern origins appear to be from the Italian system of training and have been popularized by coaches Renato Canova and Luciano Giggliotti. This program focuses on the specificity of the harder workouts. In Canova's terms the harder workouts progress from General to Special to Specific (Canova, 1999; Hudson, 2008). Specific is defined as the goal pace for the peak race the athlete is training for. The further away from this pace, in both faster and slower directions, the more general the workout becomes. The workouts come from two different extremes and funnel towards specificity. On one extreme, workouts start out with highly aerobic work such as longer steady runs and then progresses towards the specific race pace with workouts getting progressively faster and shorter. On the other extreme, workouts would start very short and very fast, such as 60m sprints, and then progress upwards to longer and slower workouts toward the specific workouts.

For example, if an athlete were training for a 5k race, his goal 5k time would be the specific pace. From the aerobic side, the workouts might progress from steady runs at marathon pace to LT runs to 10k paced intervals and finally to a 5k paced interval workout. On the other extreme, workouts might progress from 60m sprints, to 200m at 800m pace, to 400's at 1500m pace, to 800s at 3,000m pace, and finally to specific work at 5k pace. Essentially, the workouts start at the extremes and work towards each other, like a funnel. Volume is manipulated in a different way than the classic linear model too. Overall volume of training is progressively increased during the first period of training, and then peaks and stays relatively constant until the peaking phase where there is a drop but only a slight one (Hudson, 2008).

13

Where Do We Go From Here?

Differences Between Scientists and Coaches

"The human body is centuries ahead of the physiologists." Roger Bannister

Before moving on to the training section, I'd like to briefly outline some of the unanswered issues we have in the field with regards to running and why coaches and scientists seem to be at opposite ends of the spectrum with their beliefs.

Unanswered Questions

There are many unanswered questions in our knowledge of the limits and training of distance runners. Considerable debate exists on the exact mechanisms which limit or cause fatigue during running. From a scientific standpoint, it is hard to see how we can recommend ways to delay fatigue if the exact mechanisms that cause fatigue are still debated. Research such as the work done on Noakes' Central Governor Model and Samuel Marcora's model based on motivation are steps in the right direction in working towards this goal. Similarly in their study Vollaard came to the conclusion that "Moreover, we demonstrate that VO2max and aerobic performance associate with distinct and separate physiological and biochemical endpoints, suggesting that proposed models for the determinants of endurance performance may need to be revisited (2009, pg. 1483)". Perhaps this shift in thinking will get us away from the propensity for relying almost solely on VO2max as a measure of endurance when it is only one factor, has exploded due to its ease of measurement, and does not even change in elite runners. Which raises the question why is so much training focused literature done on trying to impact a parameter that does not change much, if at all, in well-trained runners? In addition, the validity of giving training recommendations based solely on improving parameters such as VO2max, LT, and RE, should be called into question when changing those parameters does not result in changes in performance (Vollaard et al., 2009; Daniels, 2005). On the same subject of VO2, using percentages of VO2max as a way to quantify training should be called into question given the wide range of stimulus it may provide. It is tough to give advice on training to improve performance when the exact mechanisms that limit performance are not known. Given this, for research that is geared towards being able to give practical guidelines to coaches on how to train runners, the focus should be on changes in performance and not some parameter.

Furthermore, for runners, I'd argue that researchers should shift away from trying to find the magic workout that improves performance and instead try to explain why workouts that successful coaches use work. When looking at the innovations in track and field training or in techniques, almost all of them come from the athletes or coaches first and then the science comes in and explains why it works. One prominent example is in the High Jump technique the Fosbury Flop. There is a large gap between the research studies' ideas about training and the real world coach's approach to training. For instance, many researchers and studies point to a lower volume, higher intensity approach, yet practically none of the best distance runners follow this approach. It is easy as a researcher to say that maybe the athletes would be better if they followed the opposite approach, yet as pointed out by Seiler and Tønnessen, it is more likely that elite athletes have developed more efficient training means than those developed in the lab (2009). There are several reasons for this difference, such as the length of training intervention studies. These limitations of studies are not easily overcome, so rethinking the approach or even purpose of training studies needs to be done.

This disconnect also happens in regards to the impact of training intensities. Most research studies classify training based on physiological variables such as LT and VO2max. Yet, most coaches classify training based on different race paces or percentages of race paces. This means that coaches seem to be more specific during workouts with their training paces than training studies. A coach sees differences between running 800m intervals at 2:15 as compared to 2:12, yet in most training studies for someone running around 8:50 for 2miles, these paces would all be considered VO2max training intensities. The classification of training in certain zones does not take into account the differences between various paces. Similarly, the classification of training based on %VO2max should be called into question based on recent studies. This could potentially explain the wide range in results of training intervention studies and is another factor that needs to be taken into consideration.

This leads to the logical conclusion that research should shift in design to actually mimic what is done in the real world. It is very seldom seen that an athlete does the same exact interval session 2-3 times a week for 6 weeks, yet that is what is done in training studies to discern the effects of a particular workout. Perhaps the effects of that workout would be different when surrounded by a variety of other stimuli, which is what is found in the real world.

Getting away from training studies for a minute, there is little to no research in regards to the planning and periodizing of training on the microcycle, mesocycle, and macrocycle level. Although it is a common practice, there are no research studies that show that alternating hard and easy running days is more beneficial than some other manipulation. In addition, there are no studies on the different periodization models used in training. In fact, there are few running studies showing that periodization is better than doing the same thing every day. Several studies have pointed towards the need for periodization, but none have evaluated its effectiveness. For instance, in Laursen's review, he points out endurance adaptations can occur via two different pathways that require two completely different stimuli (2004). This finding may help clear up the debate on volume versus intensity and show that it is not whether one is better than the other but when each is used during training that is important. In other words, the periodization of the training is the key.

Lastly, given studies showing the individual response to training and the contrasting views on volume and intensity seen in both research and in popular training literature, one has to wonder whether not enough attention is given to the individual differences in people. As researchers we tend to look at things as averages of a group and ignore the individuals. The wide variety of training programs that are successful in increasing performance is perplexing. One possible answer is that adaptation to a training stress is highly individual. Attributes such as fiber type distribution may play a role in determining whether a person responds best to a high intensity or high volume type of training. This possibility needs to be investigated and more attention to the individual response to training needs to be given.

Despite the large volume of research that has been done on endurance training, the fact remains that training runners based on research only is not a successful way to train. Breaking away from laboratory type studies and looking at some of the training methods used by coaches of runners in the real world would be a step in bridging the gap between research and practical application. As of now, little credence is given to research studies by coaches or athletes, most likely because two factors. First, the studies on training seldom are applicable to real world training. Second, on many issues, such as volume of training, due to the measurements used and the length of studies, the research does not match up with real world experiences by world-class athletes. This creates a situation where even those coaches who have a scientific background rely on theory rather than actual research. Perhaps by mimicking what is done by coaches, such as the periodization schemes used, research could gain credibility in terms of practical application by coaches and athletes.

The Problem with Applying Research to the Real World

When a scientist looks at distance training they break it down and try to isolate a variable. The goal is to find out how a single workout affects a variable. It is what I call the isolation approach. This is how we get the information on what kind of training seems to increase the lactate threshold or improve buffering capacity for example. Let's look at a quick hypothetical situation of what typically occurs when athletes or coaches read such studies.

The next step in the process once a coach or runner hears of the research is that they look at the data and come to the seemingly logical conclusion that if X training improves buffering capacity, for example, then runners should do X training or workout to get an improvement in buffering capacity, and because buffering capacity is a limiter to certain races, that race time will improve. So the coach who does this goes out and implements this training with his runners and smugly throws around scientific explanations for why his athletes are performing the intervals they are to anybody who will listen, but something goes wrong, and his runners do not improve their race times. The coach then becomes perplexed and either reasons that the science was wrong and becomes an anti-physiology coach or that the training did not succeed because the athlete did not work hard enough. If the coach took his athletes to a lab, he most likely would see an increase in buffering capacity. Then he may become further perplexed and think that the athletes are "weak" runners and not tough enough because the workout obviously accomplished what it was meant to.

The real reason for failure, however, is in the logic, not in the athletes or the coach or the science. Buffering Capacity did increase as the science said it would, but you have to look at the global effects of a workout, not just a singular effect. The singular effect was an increase in buffering capacity, but there are many other singular effects that the science did not look into or explain and all of these singular effects make up the global effect. It is this global effect that is most important. In our example, the intervals had one singular effect of increasing buffering capacity. If you did research, another effect would probably be a decrease in aerobic capabilities due to the heavy acidosis that the athlete endured to increase buffering capacity. Thus these two effects combined (and any others for the workout) would make the global effect an increase in buffering capacity with a decrease in aerobic capabilities.

This example illustrates the differences in approach between scientists and a coach. Scientists must think in isolation as they are trying to discern the exact effects of one variable. Good coaches on the other hand are concerned with the end result or, in other terms, the global effects of a workout. We have to stop thinking of the singular effects a workout might have and start thinking about the global effects it will have on the athlete. Not only do the global effects of one particular workout need to be considered, but also how the workout interacts within a training program needs to be considered. One example that has already been researched is the interference effect with concurrent strength and endurance training.

The takeaway message is that to be useful in the real world of training athletes, the isolation method cannot be used. Training does not occur in isolation. Instead, a global and integrated approach to training should be taken. It's my belief that this difference in perspective or approach between the researchers and the successful coaches is why for the most part the training of the best runners reflects practices established in the real world and not the laboratory. This leads to the next section of the book, which is a look at how to train to maximize performance.

Section 2
How to Train

"We don't have the time or the mental bandwidth to observe and consider each detail of every item in our environment. Instead we employ a few salient traits that we do observe to assign the object to a category, and then we base our assessment of the object on the category rather than the object itself." Leonard Mlodinow

It is time to step away from the science and instead focus on what most people care about, the actual training. This portion of the book is designed to teach you how to train at a high level to maximize performance. I'll go through every step in designing a training program, with particular emphasis on how to individualize training for every runner. The purpose is not to have you blindly follow a training program but rather to teach you how to train. Unlike most training books, I have not held back or dumbed down the training in any way. It is written for serious runners trying to reach their limits of performance.

If you have skipped the science section, I suggest going back and reading the chapters on fatigue and on The Genetics of Training and Adaptation as it provides a foundation for the processes that one goes through from training to adaptation. I hope that the following information helps you maximize performance or become a better coach. Lastly, I'd like to recognize some of the numerous coaching influences who provided the foundation for the training section:

Coaching Influences:

Gerald Stewart	Tom Tellez	Renato Canova
Arthur Lydiard	Scott Raczko	Jan Olbrecht
Harry Wilson	Ernie Maglischo	Antonio Cabral
Peter Coe	Marius Bakken	Theresa Fuqua
Joe Vigil	Geoffrey Dyson	Fred Wilt
Percy Cerutty	Joe Douglas	Mihaly Igloi
Jay Johnson	Brad Hudson	Vern Gambetta
Charlie Casserly	Jason Winchester	Bob Duckworth
Mike Del Donno		

14

The Philosophy of Training

"It is much easier, as well as far more enjoyable, to identify and label the mistakes of others than to recognize our own. Questioning what we believe and want is difficult at the best of times, and especially difficult when we most need to." Daniel Kahneman

While the first half of this book focused on science, I'd like to take a philosophical approach to training in the second. All of the information in the first half of this book is needed, but we have to be able to translate that knowledge into something that is usable; something that we can quickly conceptualize. As we did in the previous chapter, we can use models to simplify the complexity and in turn make concepts easy to use. Dan Dennett in his book *Intuition Pumps* describes the process as oversimplification:

"Oversimplifications can be in science; they can cut through the hideous complexity with a working model that is almost right, postponing the messy details until later."

The central tenet is to break down all the complexity displayed in the first half into something that is pretty close to right, but taking out all of the needless details that don't have a large impact on the practical result. It's not that the details aren't important; they certainly are. It's that trying to account for every minute factor leaves us with an unwieldy model, which then leaves us unable to distinguish the forest from the trees. Using this idea, let's look at training, attempting to break it down as simply as possible. If you remember back to the genetics of training, we had a flow chart that took us from training stimulus to messengers formed and eventually to functional adaptation.

If we eliminate the details what we are left with is the simple path of:

Training Stimulus ➡ **Adaptation GIVEN adequate recovery and nutrition**

It seems simplistic but the adaptation that we get from any training method is a result of whatever stimulus was applied. In other words, our body adapts to the stimulus it is given and in the direction that the stimulus is applied. By eliminating the "mess" in the middle, we are making some assumptions. The biggest of which is that the process goes according to plan, and in most cases that means that we have proper recovery going into and coming out of the training stimulus that allows our body to adapt. What we are left with then is two assumptions.

Assumptions Made

1.   We assume that the person follows a normal route of adaptation.

2.   We assume that the recovery is correct and long term adaptation takes place.

Given this information, we can now use it as a road map in figuring out what the key factors are that a coach needs to decipher. At this point, let's ignore our assumptions and focus on the stimulus to adaptation part of the equation. Given that focus, we are left with three important factors that a coach needs to know to solve this part of the problem:

1.   The training adaptation we are looking for.

2.   What stimulus leads to that adaptation?

3.   How much is enough?

What we've just done is try to make our way through a logic problem. If stimulus leads to adaptation given enough rest, then what matters is applying the *correct* stimulus to get the adaptation the athlete needs and then knowing how long it takes before a similar stimulus can be applied. The first step is knowing what adaptation we are in search of, then deciding what the stimulus is that leads to that adaptation, and finally figuring out how much of that stimulus we need to get the necessary adaptation.

It may seem like an exercise in futility to go through this logic problem, but what it does is alter the coaching process to a degree. It defines what the coach needs to know. And if we know the questions that we need to be asking, then we can actually answer them. Too often, we skip the idea of asking the questions and go straight to trying to find the answers. To figure out the answers to the above questions, the coach needs to figure out several things about their athlete. What we are left with then is what I define as the absolute things a coach needs to know, and then the concepts that he probably should know but aren't a requirement for some success. When we bring back in the assumptions of recovery and nutrition, then we are left with the following variables that a coach needs to consider in designing the workouts and training plans.

What a Coach Needs to Know

1.   What adaptations are needed for your individual athlete training for an event.

2.   Timing—At what period and how often should the athlete be working on these adaptations.

3.   How much stimulus (volume, intensity, density, etc.) needs to be applied for your individual athlete.

4. How much recovery and what type of training can be done while the athlete adapts.

Advanced Understandings

5. What external factors can influence adaption (nutrition, recovery, physio, timing, etc.)
6. Interactions between confounding adaptations.
7. Amplifiers and Dampeners of adaptation process.

Knowing the Adaptation

The first, and probably most obvious step is to figure out what adaptations are needed for your event and athlete. There are three steps to answering this question. First, the event itself provides a physiological blueprint. Obviously each event requires different demands, whether it is in terms of aerobic versus anaerobic contribution, tactics, psychology, or mechanical demands. Using knowledge of physiology presented in the first section and the models of fatigue in the last chapter, we can come up with a generalized picture of each event.

The next step is to look at how the individual affects this generalized model. Each individual will bring a slightly different biomechanical and physiological profile to his or her race distance. Whether it is a varied muscle fiber type, reliance on elastic energy return, or mentality, their individual physiology affects how we approach training for each event. Individuals' physiological make up causes shifts because it changes the event demands and what stimuli might lead to an adaptation. Therefore we need to take the event demands plus the individual characteristics and use that to design our training model.

This is quite different from a traditional model of coaching. While it may seem subtle, it is important. Traditionally, the idea is that we come up with a grand overarching training philosophy, and then somehow force each athlete into that model. What I am suggesting as a theme throughout this book is to turn that idea on its head. Know the event demands and how the individual affects those demands and then build your training model around that. This can be depicted in the illustration below.

<u>Traditional Model</u>

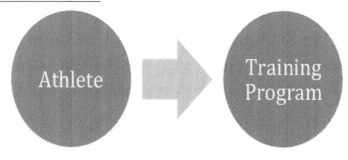

Athlete Centered Model

Throughout the rest of the training section of this book, we delve into the details that surround the principles of adaptation discussed above. The individualization chapter will cover in detail how the makeup of each runner affects the event model, while the chapter on workout design will cover how to manipulate workouts to create a stimulus for a specific adaptation. For now, it's enough to understand the influence that they have.

Timing it Out

Once we know what adaptations we are trying to develop, the next step is determining the timing of developing each. Not to sound like a broken record, but again this depends on both the event and the individual makeup of the runner. These are the key determinants in deciding how much, when, and how quickly we develop a particular adaptation. That being said there are some general principles that should be adhered to. While we will cover the details on this process in detail during the periodization chapter, let's focus on the process of deciding the timing of various adaptations.

The first step is to look at how long it will take to develop a particular adaptation for that athlete. This of course depends on how much we are trying to progress an adaptation. If we are looking at making huge gains in general aerobic endurance, then we might need to devote more time than if we were looking for moderate gains. There are adaptations that occur very quickly, such as neural adaptations to a balance program, and there are adaptations that take very long to develop, such as general endurance. Remember that we are not talking about how long it takes to maximally develop an adaptation, as that may take years of work, but instead, in this context we are talking about how long it will take within this periodization time frame to reach a level necessary to hit this season's goals.

Additionally, we have to know the individual timing of development and how that might change over a career. For instance, the amount of anaerobic development for distance runners is highly variable. Some athletes need a long and gradual buildup of anaerobic work, while others need only 4-6 weeks of simple sharpening to increase their anaerobic capacity to an acceptable level at that time period. And this might change as the athlete ages and develops a better aerobic system. The same can be said with specific endurance, strength, speed, or any other adaptation. There will be individual variability within the general time frame that it takes to develop those adaptations. Figuring out what kind of runner you are, which will be covered in the individualization chapter, helps take some of the guesswork out of this decision. We can broadly classify runners based on their physiology and make educated guesses on how they respond to certain training stimuli and how quickly they adapt. Then we can use feedback from the athlete and experience of coaching them to make further adjustments or to make sure they are adapting in the same manor and fashion in which we "guessed".

Stress and Recover

The final two factors that a coach needs to know are how much stimuli to apply and how much recovery is needed to come out of that stimulus. In the subsequent chapter, workout design will be covered in which details of how to increase the stimulus will be covered, so again, I will leave that to be covered shortly. But in terms of recovery, the main factors to look at are how strong or weak an athlete is at that particular stimuli and then how much larger of a stress is that workout than the last workout targeted at that adaptation.

It should be obvious that the amount of stress that a workout causes should be in proportion to how much recovery is needed following that workout. It only makes sense that if we do a large session that completely drains the athlete, then more recovery should be used than if we did a standard moderate workout. The question is how much is enough when it comes to recovery.

The first question that needs to be answered is what is the recoverability of the athlete. We can generally classify athletes from strong to weak in terms of their ability to recover. Their ability to bounce back may differ based on workout type. When we are assessing recovery, we need to ask the question of what is it that causes an athlete not to be able to bounce back. If we look at what running workouts do, then the limiting factors become apparent.

The first major contributor is mechanical damage to the muscles themselves. If muscular damage occurs, the muscle cannot function as efficiently and the sensation of soreness will decrease our body's ability to recruit as many muscle fibers, as well as influence our "central governor." When assessing recoverability, we should look at how much damage occurs for each type of workout or race. In general, muscle damage is highest during high eccentric loads, new exercises or activities, and activities that are above and beyond what an athlete has done before.

Another contributor is depletion of fuel sources. An athlete may not be recovering because the workout depleted various fuel sources. So if we go on a 24 mile run, we expect to be heavily glycogen depleted, but the degree of depletion depends on how efficient that athlete is in fuel use, his total glycogen capacity, his fueling strategies, and a host of other factors.

Lastly, we can look at how psychologically strenuous a workout is. If an athlete has to delve deep and really gut out a workout, they will deplete their psychological drive or will power to a high degree. Recent research has shown that our will power decreases over the course of a day and we are less likely to do things like exercise later in the day due to our depleted will power. The case is similar with running and working out. If we do a highly depleting workout, it takes a while before we can emotionally and psychologically delve back into the same depths. It's almost as if our brain is regulating how many times we can go to the well and come out of it.

This phenomenon is not simply psychological though, as it should make sense that if one invests a lot emotionally and psychologically there are physical consequences. For instance, if we are anxious about a workout, we may activate our stress response to a slightly higher degree, which means we start flooding our body with stress hormones like cortisol. Then we need a subsequent recovery period where we switch out of that sympathetic nervous system dominated state and return to homeostasis. The stress response is not simply a reaction to physical stress but instead to stress in general. In running we are keenly aware of the physical stress, but we need to realize that psychological or emotional stress also contributes to the total stress load.

Therefore we have to look at both the physical and psychological to assess how well they recover from each workout. After all, a workout can be relatively moderate physically but have a huge psychological demand if a runner fears a particular type of workout. Therefore, it's important to look at all aspects of stress load and how a runner recovers from them. The best way to monitor recovery is not by some top-secret scientific gadget, but instead by simply listening to your body. It is a skill to understand the feedback that your body is providing.

That being said, there are certain tests that can be used to assess damage, stress, and recoverability. These are listed in the chart below and are categorized into four sections. Emotional and mental readiness can be assessed via various psychological questionnaires or simply by asking the athletes about their mood. Additionally, mental reactions tests traditionally used in psychology or neuroscience hold some promise in assessing readiness. In looking at the generalized stress response we can look at cortisol, heart rate variability, or a T to C ratio which all give us an imprecise but general view of where the overall body is at. In terms of physical damage, the most reliable marker is simply soreness, but we can also look at markers for inflammation and damage. Lastly, when assessing neural fatigue, we can look at ground contact times or counter movement jump performance as a surrogate measure. Or we can once again look towards psychology research and look at simple reaction tests such as a repeated finger tap to give a rough assessment of neural fatigue.

Assessment Tools for Recoverability:

Emotional/Mental Readiness	• Mood state questionnaire • RPE • Mental reaction test
Stress Response	• Cortisol (Blood test) • Heart Rate Variability • Testosterone to Cortisol ratio (saliva)
Physical Damage	• Creatine Kinase (Blood test) • Inflammation markers • Muscle soreness • Lactate levels
Neural/Central Fatigue	• HRV • Counter movement jump • Reactive strength index (contact time/flight time) on drop jump • Reaction test (repeated finger tap) • Ground Contact during repeated hops

Once we have assessed the recoverability of the individual athlete, then we combine it with our knowledge of how stressful the workout is to determine how much recovery is needed after a workout to ensure adaptation. As was mentioned previously, each type of workout takes a varying amount of time to recover from. For instance, we don't need as long to recover from a 9 mile easy run as we do from doing a 4 mile tempo run. That should be obvious, but within workout types there is variation too. Jan Olbrecht, in his book *The Science of Winning* presents data that give a rough estimate of how much recovery is needed for each workout type. While these are rough estimates, it's a good starting point for deciding how many easy days are needed after a hard workout. The end result though is that the degree of stress is the deciding factor for recovery. Regardless of workout "type", the stress level that takes into account the volume and intensity as well as external factors decides how much recovery is needed to adapt.

External Factors Affecting Adaptation

The contents of the workout itself are not the only thing that matters. Up until this point we have worked under the assumption that we proceed normally from stimulus to adaptation without any external force acting upon that process. We have also assumed that nutrition and recovery were adequate to allow for making this journey towards functional adaptation. Now we need to shift focus and look at the details that may either amplify or dampen the training effect of a certain workout.

Amplifiers of Adaptation

Amplifiers of adaptation are anything that may boost our subsequent adaptation either by acting early and increasing the stimulus or by increasing the conversion of that stimulus to an adaptation by bolstering recovery from the workout. When we think of boosting the stimulus of the workout, it's not just about making that workout harder so that our bodies are forced to adapt to a higher stress load. Instead it's about forcing a higher stress in a particular direction that we know we can handle.

There are a few main ways to accomplish this. The first way is to perform workouts in a pre-fatigued state. Instead of being completely fresh for all hard workouts if we start them in a slightly depleted state, we can now delve deeper into the depths of glycogen depletion and access muscle fibers we seldom recruit. So, we get a slightly different training effect thanks to the pre-fatigue. To accomplish this we can manipulate the training cycle so that athletes aren't fully recovered going into a workout or insert workout days where they perform two separate intense workouts on the same day. The possibilities are endless, but remember that we are trying to increase the stress of the training slightly, and it's important to make sure that we don't push that stress over the edge and fail to recover.

The last amplifier that influences the training stress part of the equation is manipulating fuel to shift adaptations. If we are looking to improve our ability to run with reduced glycogen or shift to being more efficient using fuel, then we can manipulate our fuel stores via nutrition to amplify this shift. The best way to do this is either via fasted runs or longer runs with no supplemental fuel. When we do runs when running lower on fuel, our body realizes that it needs to become more efficient so that it doesn't reach the depths of fuel deprivation again.

Traditionally, we've relied on long runs for this effect. But we can further aid this process by doing runs in a fasted state because we have essentially pre-fatigued ourselves fuel wise. So our bodies are forced to find a way to deal with and adapt to this. Similarly, instead of taking your carbohydrate drink or gels during every long run, consider running some with only water. The goal here is to similarly allow for glycogen depletion to get pretty low on the long run so that the body is forced to adapt.

The other amplifiers all refer to improving the recovery side of the coin. If we can supply the right nutrients and help the body's natural recovery process we can positively influence adaptation. The obvious one is recovery nutrition. We all have been inundated with information about taking our carbohydrates or protein after a workout, so I won't cover that in detail, except to say that it works and that protein is showing to be more important not only for muscle repair but also for tendon growth. It starts the process and helps shift the balance towards an anabolic state of buildup and repair.

A further way to take advantage of the effects of protein is to take "hits" of protein throughout the day. Taking five hits of ~20g of protein throughout the day will keep protein synthesis elevated throughout the day. Additionally, taking a large dose of protein before bed will keep protein synthesis elevated during sleep, which is when a large portion of recovery and repair takes place. This hit of protein before bed has been shown to significantly aid recovery. So it's a good strategy to use when trying to recover from a particularly hard bout of training.

While on the topic of sleep, it too can potentially amplify the recovery process. The recovery process largely takes place during sleep, and it is during the sleep cycles where a unique combination of repair, processing, and learning occurs. As mentioned previously, we can manipulate protein synthesis during sleep via nutrition supplementation, but sleep also plays a role in hormone secretion. Research has shown that testosterone levels rise during the first REM cycle, while Human Growth Hormone (HGH) goes through a cycle of peaks and valleys corresponding to the sleep cycles. The point is not to obsess over when HGH or testosterone is produced but instead to know that delays in falling asleep or interference in the sleep cycle can severely affect the production of both of these hormones, which in turn can influence recovery and repair. Additionally, sleep is often the time when neural programming seems to be ingrained and learning processes that occurred during the day are cemented. It is for these reasons that sleep can be an amplifier in terms of recovery and adaptation.

Finally, before moving on to dampeners of adaptation, the last amplifier is massage. While massage has been used throughout history as a recovery device, it's never fully been scientifically backed because the mechanisms touted such as increased blood flow never really materialized. We know that massage can manipulate the muscle in the short term by adjusting muscle tension, but what about long term adaptations? Recent work by Mark Tarnopolsky out of McMaster University in Canada found that massage actually increases the activity of PGC-1a while dampening NF-kB. NF-kB is a protein involved in inflammation in the muscle, while PGC-1a was heavily mentioned in the first half of this book. Its role is a precursor along the way to creating more mitochondria. While this work is preliminary, it shows that massage might have a potential role as an enhancer (and possibly dampener) of adaptation.

Dampeners of Adaptation

The other side of the coin is that there are certain things that can negatively influence the adaptation process. These processes can act in two different ways; either dampening down the stimulus or by affecting the recovery in a negative way. We have already mentioned the balance of making training easier or more difficult based on taking nutrition or even performing a workout on pre-fatigued legs, so instead we will focus on external items which might affect the stimulus and recovery. Ironically, this dampening effect often comes as a result of someone trying to improve recovery.

Damage is generally thought of as a bad thing, but the reality is that it acts as a signaler for adaptation. If we did not create any damage or overwhelm homeostasis, then our body has nothing to adapt and respond to. The class of adaptation dampeners largely consists of items that affect the damage created. We can start with the inflammatory response. When we create micro tears in a muscle, the body responds by going through an inflammatory cycle to initiate repair and strengthening. This is all natural and good, but oftentimes we try to speed up the process artificially by taking anti-inflammatories or plunging into the dreaded ice bath.

What happens here is that the anti-inflammatory drugs or substance clears out some of the inflammatory biomarkers which act as signaling pathway triggers. When we clear these markers out and thus dampen the pathway activation, what we are left with is less translation to a functional adaptation. In simpler terms, if our body senses a lot of inflammation, it brings in the heavy-duty repair equipment to shore up the defenses and build it stronger. If all of the sudden, we have a 3rd party that takes care of some of the damage, then the body simply says, "oh the problem wasn't as bad as we thought, so we don't have to do as big of a fortification job as we anticipated."

In addition to anti-inflammatories, antioxidants work in much the same way. Oxidation occurs during running and acts as one of the major triggers for increasing mitochondria to deal with all of these pro-oxidants. If all of a sudden we take in an artificial anti-oxidant, then we again have a 3rd party that acts as a cleaning crew and shuts down the signal that the body needs to majorly adapt. What is interesting is that, according to research, only artificial antioxidants vitamins seem to have this strong effect. Natural antioxidants coming from fruits do not cause this effect.

Using anti-inflammatories, antioxidants, or even too much of other recovery modalities, is all part of a phenomenon I call over-recovery. It's an epidemic that has occurred largely due to our want to just do something. You see this in the training room of any university, where modalities that have no proof are used on injuries, just to do something for it. We've essentially taken recovery and made it too much of a good thing. Instead of always dampening the training stimulus, and therefore possibly limiting adaptation, a coach should periodize the recovery. A coach should decide when it makes sense that the adaptation is king and when it makes sense to not care about eking out an extra percentage point of adaptation and instead focus on recovery. These aren't the only dampeners of adaptation, but instead provide a snapshot and a guide to realizing that there are other similar recovery modalities out there that probably act in the same way.

Mixed Modifiers

This last set of modifiers can be either amplifiers or dampeners of adaptation depending on how and when they are used. This is slightly true for all modifiers, even those discussed previously, but for the select ones below, there can be a large difference in how they act on an adaptation depending on the circumstances.

Caffeine is a central nervous system stimulant that improves performance. It therefore can increase race performance, as well as performance in a training session. Thus it can amplify the adaptation by artificially letting you run faster splits or pushing further in a workout. The problem is that it comes at a cost. We highly adapt to caffeine as it can change adenosine receptors in the brain if chronically consumed. We adapt so much to it that for habitual coffee drinkers the energy buzz they get from drinking their morning coffee is simply a return to baseline from the withdrawal effects of caffeine. The facts that we can get adapted to it and that if we use it every workout we artificially stress the CNS beyond its normal control means that we can somewhat "fry" the nervous system by constant chronic caffeine intake. Additionally, we lose its effectiveness to a degree. That's why caffeine can acutely improve performance and adaptation but can chronically impair adaptation if we do not keep it in balance.

Similar to caffeine, we can manipulate the stress of a workout via psychological stressors. According to Hans Selye's General Adaptation Syndrome, we respond to a stressor in a generalized similar way regardless of whether it is a physical, emotional, or even perceived stress. So when we add psychological stress on top of the physical stress of running, we can either enhance adaptation or suppress it. The next trend in training will be related to cognitive training where we stress the cognitive limits of our brain both in terms of concentration and fatigue resistance. Referring back to the chapter on fatigue, you can see why. The physical manifestation of fatigue is largely related to mental fatigue. So we can probably use psychological or mental stressors to challenge adaptation. An example might be doing simple arithmetic during long runs, or using a computer game to do mind numbing mental tasks before going out and doing a hard workout. Performance of that workout will be impaired, but psychological adaptation will be challenged.

On the other hand, psychological stress could impair training adaptation via either pre-fatiguing so much that an athlete over-trains and cannot adapt to the workload or by leading to negative psychological adaptations to fatigue such as a mental phobia to certain workouts or races. It is important then to understand when to push the boundaries of psychological or cognitive stress and when to ensure a well-rested mentally clear performance. We can see the drastic effects by the fact that placebos and nocebos can greatly influence perception of pain and fatigue. Simply believing that something will increase or decrease pain can alter training and adaptation.

Carbohydrate intake can also amplify or dampen adaptation based on the timing of it. I have previously discussed the concept of train low, compete high in regards to carbohydrate intake. There is a growing body of evidence that shows training in a low glycogen state activates signaling pathways that influence both aerobic gains and fuel efficiency. It makes sense that pressing lower into the depths of glycogen depletion would cause the body to find a way to be better at using it efficiently. On the other hand, constantly training low would limit how fast or long we could go and therefore dampen adaptation. Similarly, taking carbohydrate during a workout might dampen fuel efficiency adaptations, but it may help with adaptations in the gut in allowing the gut to take in, process, and use the carbohydrate quicker on the run. Once again, this is why timing and purpose of the run is critical.

Strength training can also help or hinder adaptations. In looking at the main signaling targets for strength and endurance gains, they essentially act as antagonists, but mostly in the direction of strength. It's one of the reasons why strength gains are limited when combining with heavy endurance work. Timing is once again critical. For instance, a low amount of strength training can influence recovery via changes in hormone concentrations when done after a run. While doing it the other way around, strength first and then running right after, will increase strength endurance but dampen down the muscle growth gains from the strength work because endurance exercise will shut down the mTOR pathway, which could be good or bad depending on the goal of the training. While it would require an in depth look to go through all of the outcomes and interactions, the point is where you schedule strength matters.

Lastly, especially with the invention of artificial altitude, we can easily use altitude to modify adaptation. We can challenge workouts and hope for spikes in aerobic adaptations by performing a workout at altitude. Or, an idea that has not yet been researched, we can manipulate the recovery and presumably the adaptations by making the post workout recovery take place in altitude. These could be positive or negative influencers on adaptation.

Altitude should be thought of as another stressor, just like heat, humidity, or including a hill in a run. Once it is thought as a stressor and not as some magic device or formula, it becomes easier to understand why it might help or hinder an athlete. The use of altitude then depends on the goal of the training session or training block. It can either help by forcing adaptation in the aerobic direction, or it could hinder by causing an overload of stress or by inhibiting recovery.

While this is not an exhaustive list, the goal should be to start thinking outside of the X's and O's of the workout itself and instead consider the important variables that surround those workouts. The friends that I have had who have gone to East Africa always remark on the East African's stress free approach to training and racing. The workouts are incredibly tough, but there are no long nights spent awake dreading the next workout or nervous eyes fearing what is to come. Similarly, there's no huge emotional dwelling on a bad race after the fact. I can't help but think that this reduction of psychological stress may play a role in their success. So keep in mind that what surrounds the workouts can indeed effect what you get out of the workout itself. Now we need to discuss perhaps the most important part of coaching and training.

Balancing Act

Before moving on to the details of how to create and manipulate workouts, we need to cover one more overarching concept. Training at its simplest form is a balancing act. As a coach, the goal is to simultaneously build and develop seemingly opposing forces. In the world of distance running, we need to balance speed versus endurance, strength versus efficiency, and flexibility versus stiffness, to name a few.

This conundrum of having to develop systems that are almost playing a game of tug of war against each creates some unique challenges. Training isn't simply the idea of continually building fitness in each separate area. If it were, life would be easy. We would simply keep increasing the stimulus for endurance or speed or whatever component individually for as long as we could until its time to peak. The problem though is that everything interacts.

This pattern of competing interactions starts at the physiological level before being translated into a functional difference. For example, we can see how the mTOR pathway, which plays a role in strength gains, can be inhibited after being activated simply by doing endurance training. If we were to go lifts weights for muscle hypertrophy, part of the trigger for that adaptation is activation of the mTOR pathway. We try to keep the activation of this pathway high even after we finish the workout so that we can translate and maximize the strength gains. If we were to do a 30 minute up-tempo run immediately following the lift, then the mTOR pathway would be down regulated as the aerobic workout would inhibit this pathway. Thus, we probably wouldn't get the full benefits of the lift.

The mTOR pathway example is but one interaction of opposing forces and as it was explained above relates to the short term programming of training. While this is important, the long-term balance of opposing forces is more important and plays a critical role in training periodization. While there are many major components that interact, the major key concepts to keep in mind when considering balance are speed, endurance, strength, and power. If you recall from the chapter on Lactate, we can clearly see this opposing tug of war happening in a lactate curve using the ideas of Jan Olbrecht.

Using the lactate curve, we can see that if we do a lot of endurance and threshold work, we will generally see less lactate produced at each intensity, and we assume that we improved our endurance. This might be true, but what other event could cause us to see less lactate produced at every intensity? A decrease in our anaerobic capacity, or how much lactate we can produce in full. If we did so much endurance work that now we produce 15mmol instead of 20mmol, then we'll see lower lactate levels throughout, even if we didn't improve our aerobic abilities at all. We simply got way worse in our anaerobic abilities. This is a classic case of doing too much endurance work, not enough speed or anaerobic work, and killing speed. This might be fine, IF that is the desired balance, which might be the case for a marathon or longer event.

In the following graph, we show a scenario of balancing the stimulus, or stress load, and the recovery throughout the year. The units are arbitrary, but we can use them to represent the concept. In the base phase, we have a relatively high stimulus perhaps mainly due to the volume of work, but our recovery is deemphasized. As we progress, you see that the stimulus reaches the highest point during the pre-competitive phase before tailoring off slightly during competition, while the recovery becomes increasingly emphasized. This is just a snapshot of what we expect the overall program to look like, and we can break down the balance for each individual component, such as speed and endurance, in the same way across the season.

Stimulus vs. Recovery Balancing Act

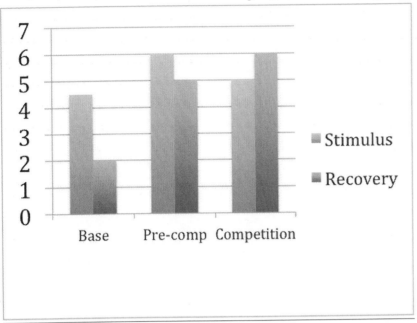

So obviously we have several components that interact. And we all intuitively know that speed and endurance, as well as many other systems, play opposing roles. We also know that different components need to be built at different rates and time of the year. There's a reason why the base phase, which traditionally includes a lot of general endurance training, is done early in the season. And regardless of your beliefs, we generally follow a base phase with something more intensive or more speed orientated. As coaches, we all know that we should periodize in roughly the same way, but why does that timing and periodization work? If we look closely, what we are really trying to accomplish makes sense in terms of the balancing act needed.

What we are intuitively trying to accomplish is to get the balance right for a particular event and runner at the right time. That is all periodization is. During the base phase we may increase general endurance a ton, and sacrifice speed a little, but the hope is that during the speed phase, we regain that speed and have built our endurance up so much that it doesn't suffer much at all. The key though is asking how much do we let something suffer, such as speed during a base phase, and how much do we try to maintain a component.

In the older days of Lydiard, the idea was to have extreme swings of balance. During the base phase athletes would do tons of endurance work, neglecting speed, and then shift gears completely and do 4-5 days a week of "speed" training 6-8 weeks before the competition to hopefully build that speed back up. In modern training, we take the approach of smaller swings in balance. We try to gradually shift the strengths of components around without completely neglecting any of them or letting them fall too far behind.

The Goal of Training

The goal of training is therefore simply to know what the correct end balance for the event and individual is and then modulate training to arrive at that balance on the correct day. Earlier in this chapter we looked at race modeling and then correcting that for the individual to come up with the race demands for each athlete. So if we have the race demands, we know roughly where that individual's balance needs to be in terms of speed, endurance, aerobic/anaerobic, or strength and power. The next step then is figuring out the logical sequence of improving each component which includes: knowing what is a prerequisite, at what time of the year a component needs to be maximized, and at what point might it need to be sacrificed a little.

A prerequisite is exactly what it sounds like. In order to maximize some particular component, we may need to develop another component beforehand. It only makes logical sense that we cannot develop speed endurance without first developing speed to a degree. We can't improve a quality that we have not created or developed. Well, technically we can, but we are limited in its development. As an example, if we haven't developed a large general endurance base, then how do we build on that base with more high end aerobic or threshold work?

The general rules of thumb for what are typically prerequisites are listed in the chart below. As mentioned above, the idea behind a pre-req is that the further we build up the pre-req, then the more we can develop the subsequent adaptation. In fact, sometimes we cannot progress a particular adaptation without going back to the pre-requisite adaptation. As a quick example, if we have an 800m runner who has run 1:47 but can only run a 50.0sec 400m, then no matter how much specific endurance work we do, his 800m time likely won't improve. He's capped out on that development because he has maxed out that ability because he's already holding 53.5sec pace and likely coming through in 52sec. In order to give him some more room for development, we'd have to work on anaerobic capacity to get that 400m down to 49.0 so that we could then have some room to improve his specific endurance for the 800m. Given this scenario, a pre-req for his 800m specific endurance development would be work on his anaerobic capacity to give him a bigger gap between his 400m and what he comes through in his 800m. This is but one example, and the list below is not exhaustive, but instead meant to give you an idea on how development interacts.

Prerequisites

General before specific (on both speed and endurance)
Strength before power
Strength before Strength endurance
Neural
Speed before speed endurance

Once we know the prerequisites, we then look at timing out the balance to reach our optimal race model during our peak racing season. The event and individual guide this process. We need knowledge of how quickly a component can be developed, how much someone needs to maintain a component, and how quickly a component deteriorates when it isn't being fully trained. The details on when and how much for each component will be discussed further in the chapter on periodization, but for now it's important to see how this concept works.

Let's use a simplistic model that looks at our 400m time versus our threshold times to represent our speed versus endurance development. Let's say we have a miler, Brian, and he's able to run a 49sec 400m, his threshold work is around 5:10 pace, and he is a 4:08 miler. We're trying to improve his mile time and decide he is weak aerobically, so that's what we emphasize. Let's look at three different scenarios that in the tradition of goldilocks have one that is too much shifted towards the endurance side, one too much towards speed, and one that is just right.

Heavy Endurance

	Base	Pre-Competition	Competition
400m	51.0	50.5	50.0
Threshold work	5:02	4:58	5:05
Mile Time	4:10	4:08	4:08

Heavy Speed

	Base	Pre-Competition	Competition
400m	49.3	48.5	48.0
Threshold work	5:07	5:10	5:15
Mile Time	4:12	4:09	4:10

Just Right

	Base	Pre-Competition	Competition
400m	49.7	49.0	48.5
Threshold work	5:05	5:02	5:05
Mile Time	4:10	4:07	4:04

In the heavy endurance model, let's say we overload our athlete on the endurance side, doing nothing but pure aerobic work during the base phase. Then progress to a pre-competition phase that is heavy on aerobic support or threshold-like work, before finally sharpening up in the competition phase. What happens generally is that our balance gets skewed heavily towards the endurance side. We improve our general and then high end aerobic abilities a lot, but we neglect the speed side of the equation during the large majority of the training cycle. It isn't until the last

5-6 weeks that we do a heavy load of sharpening work and try to hurriedly get our speed back. What happens in this example is that we let our speed slip way too much, and we can't get it back. So our end balance results in the same performance we had before this season, even though we improved our threshold a lot due to our neglecting of the speed side for so long.

The next example is if we shifted the balance more towards the speed side. It doesn't mean we do only fast interval work throughout, but in this example it might mean that we do a base phase to improve our aerobic abilities, but it's heavily inundated with fast and anaerobic work throughout. So what happens is we improve our aerobic abilities a bit during the base, but then they steadily deteriorate as we increase the speed component. What we are left with is that we got a lot faster on the speed side, but our aerobic abilities deteriorated, and we run the same or slower.

In the last theoretical example, we get the balance right. We do just enough work to prevent the deterioration of speed while we improve our aerobic abilities during the base phase. Then during the pre-competition phase we shift slightly towards being more speed focused while still working on our aerobic support, and then during the competition phase, our speed improves more while our aerobic abilities only fall off slightly thanks to us maintaining them. In this simple example, we end up with the fastest mile time of the three scenarios. It is a simplistic look at the process, but the point is that this athlete reaches a nice balance point and that it isn't simply about maximizing each component. Instead it's about knowing how to balance the development of speed and endurance and knowing when each needs to be at their highest during the season.

While this is just an example, the point is that training is essentially the process of creating the optimal balance of contrasting systems in an athlete. The event and the individuality of the athlete will shift what balance is needed and how to achieve the desired balance. It is therefore the coach's job to not only figure out what the optimal balance is but to plan and then adjust as the training proceeds to insure that the proper balance is key.

The purpose of this chapter is to present the philosophical basis for coaching. It's to break down the decision making process that goes into designing the training for your athletes. It might seem tedious, but it's important to know what we need to know, what questions we need to ask, and what we do about it. The rest of the book breaks down how to accomplish these tasks. We will end with briefly summarizing what the process entails. I break it into five categories: Identify, Know, Decide, Design, and Adjust. These represent the steps taken from beginning to the end.

It starts with identification of the demands and individual adjustments to create a model. We are creating a model of what the demands are and how we manipulate the individual's physiology, biomechanics, and psychology to master that model. Once we have identified the model, there are a series of "facts" that we need to know in order to fully understand the training process. With the combination of identifying our model and having our background knowledge in place, then the process entails deciding the details of the plan. In essence, we are looking for how far we are going to push adaptions, in what direction they are going, and the details that surround them. The fourth step is branching out from those details and putting workouts into their proper place within the broader periodization plan. Finally, we put our plan into action and then use feedback from that athlete, races, and workouts to continually adjust throughout.

The basic outline of this book is to help you understand how to tackle each of these sections. Up until now we have looked at the philosophical side. We've identified overarching principles that form the foundation of training design, and laid the foundation for making knowledgeable decisions on what it is we are trying to do. From here, the following chapters will begin to transition away from the philosophy and into the world of detailed planning. The next chapter will be concerned with the identification process. We will look at creating models of races, defining workouts, and setting the stage for developing a training program. From there we will progress to workout design and manipulation, and we will follow this up with a chapter devoted to individual adjustments, and then proceed into chapters on periodization and training plan development to finish off the detail level. The process of coaching can be broken down as follows.

Philosophical to Details approach:
1. **Identify:**
   a. Event/Race Demands
   b. Race schedule
   c. Individual adjustments to demands
   d. Training adaptations we are looking for based on Model constructed.
2. **Know**
   a. What stimulus leads to those adaptations
   b. Interactions between stimuli
   c. Prerequisites for development
   d. Amplifiers and Dampeners for adaptation
   e. Periodization/Timing of development of adaptations
3. **Decide**
   a. How much stimulus
   b. How much Recovery
   c. What direction to take adaptation
   d. Correct Balance throughout year
4. **Design**
   a. Workout progressions
   b. Periodization/shifts in emphasis
5. **Adjust**
   a. Continual adjustment of workload, emphasis, balance based on:
      i. Physical
      ii. Emotional
      iii. Psychological

15

What Are We Trying to Accomplish?

"When faced with a difficult question, we often answer an easier one instead, usually without noticing the substitution." Daniel Kahneman

Models of Fatigue

While knowing the complexities of the science of running is good, it is easy to lose the forest for the trees, as it is hard to wrap your head around it all so that it can be practically applied. To circumvent this problem, we take those complex ideas and make them into simple models. In our case, we take the scientific knowledge and come up with simple models of fatigue, which gives a road map on how to train to avoid fatigue.

The great New Zealand coach Arthur Lydiard once commented that almost anyone could run a 60 second quarter, yet very few could run four of those in a row to string together a 4:00 mile. His point was that most of the time endurance was the key to performance. In a similar vein, Renato Canova stated that every event is an event of extension. The goal of training is to be able extend your ability to last at a given pace. If your goal is to run a 2:00 800m and in your current shape you can run that pace for 650m, then your training goal is to extend your ability to run at that pace until it matches your desired goal of 800m. Once that goal is reached, you work at extending your ability to last 800m at a faster pace. This occurs via delaying fatigue. If fatigue can be delayed at race pace, then a runner can last longer at that pace before fatigue slows them down. On the other hand, if one can handle greater amounts of fatigue, performance will increase too. It is therefore the rate and maximum tolerance of fatigue that combines to determine performance. Several models of fatigue can be used to apply this practically, but, first, what is fatigue?

Fatigue is a catch all term that basically means we slow down. The exact mechanisms of fatigue are unknown and vary widely for each event. First, I'll briefly go over the concept of fatigue, and then look at some practical fatigue models. Fatigue has traditionally been thought of as an issue of depletion or accumulation. Either products build up that cause fatigue, or we run out of products that are necessary for function and fatigue. Initially it was thought that these products were the direct causes of fatigue, meaning if Hydrogen ions (H+) got high, it directly caused fatigue. However, more recent research has led to different beliefs, as discussed in the first half of this book. Some of the products believed to play a role in fatigue are listed below:

- Increase in H+ (decrease in pH), core temperature, ammonia, Pi, and Magnesium
- Decrease in blood glucose, glycogen, BCAA, and Calcium release and uptake in the Sarcoplasmic Reticulum.

While these products can contribute to fatigue, the more recent understanding is that none of these products directly cause fatigue, and instead they are (or cause changes in substances that are) simply signals to the brain that homeostasis has been changed. An increase or decrease in these products does not directly cause the fatigue but instead signals the brain that if we don't change what's going on, we'll be in danger. So the brain then forces the person to slow down both consciously and subconsciously. Subconsciously it may regulate intensity via recruitment of muscles fibers. So that when the brain is receiving signals that fatigue is building up, it decreases muscle fiber recruitment to protect the body. Another proposal says that fatigue is regulated consciously, in that as these products build up or decrease, the body creates the sensation of pain, so that then the runner slows down consciously because of the high pain levels. Certain runners are able to delve deeper into the realms of pain than others, but all of us eventually give in to the ever increasing pain levels. Exactly what occurs is unknown but it is likely some combination of conscious and subconscious interaction.

All of this is nice and good, but in training we aren't overly concerned with whether the products directly cause fatigue or if they indirectly cause fatigue via feedback. The bottom line is that if we delay the buildup of fatigue products, or delay the reduction in neural recruitment, fatigue is delayed. If the buildup in the products themselves causes fatigue then we are directly delaying fatigue by decreasing their buildup with training. If the buildup of products indirectly causes fatigue through pain or subconscious control, then delaying the product buildup still delays the signaling to the brain to cause fatigue or pain. Either way performance is improved. Given this information, we can take the complex idea of fatigue and boil it down into three useful simple fatigue models.

The Lactate or By-product theory works on the idea that fatigue is caused by the buildup of some fatiguing by-product. We use lactate because it is easily measurable and corresponds with fatigue, not because it causes fatigue itself. The theory is that there is a maximum amount of these products that can accumulate during a race, so if we can decrease the rate of accumulation or increase the maximum amount that can be accumulated, fatigue will be delayed and performance will improve. Based on this theory, the training goals are as follows:

Lactate/By-Product Theory Training Goals:

1. Decrease Lactate (fatigue by-products) overall
2. Decrease Lactate accumulation at Race Pace
3. Increase maximum Lactate that can be accumulated over race

The second fatigue theory is based on muscle fiber fatigue. In this model, fatigue is looked at as happening because of both neural recruitment of fibers and the endurance of the fibers themselves (or how long a fiber can stay recruited without fatigue). As fatigue sets in, muscle fibers begin to "fail" and other fibers are recruited to take up the slack. Eventually, there is a point where the majority of the muscle fibers are fatigued and cannot maintain the necessary force production, thus fatigue occurs and the runner slows. Based on this theory, fatigue can be delayed via increasing the recruitable fiber pool, training to be able to use those fibers during a race, and lastly extending the endurance of those fibers thus delaying fatigue. This theory is an integration of both peripheral (the muscles themselves) and central (the Central Nervous System) fatigue. As with the lactate fatigue theory, it does not matter whether there is a central regulator or if fatigue happens peripherally in the muscles themselves, as the training goals are still the same.

Muscle Fiber Theory:

1. Increase Maximum Fibers you can recruit
2. Increase Percent of fibers you use over race
3. Increase length those fibers can last (endurance)
4. Tying it together: Increase/maintain recruitment of fibers under heavy fatigue

Lastly, we have the overall fatigue model, which ties together local and central fatigue in a useable form. This theory integrates the brain and the muscles in a sort of sensory feedback loop.

Simple Integrated Fatigue Model:

1. Products of fatigue build up in the muscle.
2. The brain monitors this increase in fatigue products and regulates muscle recruitment to prevent muscle from reaching dangerous level of fatigue products.
   a. Fatigue products that may signal to the brain include lactate, H+, Ca+, heat/temperature, glycogen levels, and numerous other triggers.
3. Can train to:
   a. Delay buildup of these products thus delaying brain's signal to shut down
   b. Delay signal from brain to "shut down and protect" by proving you can safely handle slightly more of that product.
   c. Increase maximum amount of these products that can be accumulated or lost before the brain starts shutting things down.

These models of fatigue allow for practical integration of science and training. The models provide an easy to understand way of looking at what causes fatigue and in turn how to train to delay fatigue. As a quick example of how to apply these models, let's look at the muscle fiber theory. To delay fatigue we need to increase the muscle fiber pool and increase the endurance of those fibers. To accomplish these goals, we need to do workouts that cause a large increase in muscle fiber recruitment such as sprints, hill sprints, or heavy weight lifting. Following this, we need to extend the endurance of the newly recruited fibers, so the next set of workouts adds an endurance component. An example might be doing hill sprints in between sets of 800m repeats at race pace. The hill sprints would serve to recruit fibers, and then those fibers would be trained during the 800m repeats. Another option is to do long uphill repeats as more muscle fibers are recruited during uphill running then flat running.

Event Modeling

The goal should be to use these simple theories of fatigue and combine them with a template for each race. We can use our knowledge of physiology and then also look at traditional pacing of the event to understand how to combat fatigue. Let's go through a few events as examples.

First, we know that in the middle distance events (800/1500) we have a rapid buildup of fatigue contributing by-products. If we are to look at the energetics of it we know that the anaerobic system revs up first, covering the gap in energy needed until the aerobic system catches up to cover the majority, but not all, of the energy provided before once again calling on whatever anaerobic reserve we have at the end to kick.

In the 800m, the energy supply is higher so more anaerobic energy is needed to cover the gap between energy required and what the aerobic system can contribute. Additionally if we look at pacing strategies in the 800m, it is essentially a gradual decline in speed with maybe a maintaining or, at best, a very slight increase in the last 200. What that tells us is that compared to the longer events, we use our anaerobic reserve earlier in the 800 to maintain the pace, and therefore there's nothing to call upon. In the 1,500m, it's just slightly slower, and thus most times we are able to call upon some extra anaerobic reserve to kick.

If we look at what happens muscle fiber wise, there's a steady increase of muscle fiber activation of both fast twitch and slow twitch fibers, before we try recruiting as much as we can as fibers fatigue in the closing stages. Generally, what we see is a decrease in force into the ground, which can be seen by increased time spent on the ground or changes in stride length or rate. We've got plenty of glycogen and other stores of energy, except for phosphocreatine, but that's almost a bonus, so depletion isn't really an issue. It also isn't long enough to have overheating be an issue. So what we are left with is mostly buildup of by-products causing an increase in pain/RPE that eventually shuts us down.

In the distance events of the 5k and 10k, we have a similar yet subtly different picture. We can get a glimpse of the demands by looking at the optimal pacing, which essentially looks like a mostly even paced race with a larger kick in at the end. The energetic demands can largely be met aerobically, so that the anaerobic reserve is just used to fill the gap in the beginning and then once fatigue sets in or it's time to kick. The muscle fibers recruited are still a mix, but we can rely on a larger proportion of slow twitch fibers in the beginning and rotate through recruiting them to a degree, before calling upon the harder to recruit fibers as fatigue grows. Additionally, if we look at the buildup of products, there isn't a rapid rise, but instead a slight and gradual increase throughout the race, with maybe a peak at the end once we delve into our anaerobic reserves.

However, there is an exception in a select group of elite athletes who have really well-developed aerobic systems, where we might even see a leveling off of the buildup of things such as lactate mid race. The athletes reach a steady state that is normally reserved for longer races. Though this is rare, the point is that it's a much more nuanced increase in most athletes who fit the bill of a 5k or 10k specialist.

In addition to the normal fatigue causing "stuff" such as lactate, pH changes, acidosis or whatever buzz word you want to describe it as, we also see buildup of heat and changes in core temperature affecting these races, especially the 10k. Depending on the ambient temperature, if it is warm enough, reaching a critical core temperature could be a real possibility. Then we see fatigue occurring as a result of this rise in temperature, and often get an anticipatory slowing down because of it.

Psychologically, dealing with concentration and focus becomes a larger component of the fatigue picture as we have a larger period of time under strong, but not extremely high (as in the 800m), duress. So what we are left with is distance events where buildup plays a role, as does changes in muscle fiber recruitment and neural activation, but at a more gradual/subtler pace than with the mid distance events.

Lastly, we're left with the longest event that I'll cover, the marathon. The marathon changes the fatigue paradigm. While building up fatigue products is still an issue, what they are changes. Instead of it being things that people mostly associate with anaerobic metabolism, such as changes in pH, we are left with buildup of more central parameters, such as heat, changes in certain chemicals in the brain, or a few other items. The rise in core temperature is one of the more likely causes of fatigue in conditions that are either warm or humid.

The main cause of fatigue though is the depletion of fuel. While we never fully run out of fuel, it is the anticipation of running out of fuel that ultimately causes the slowing. Think of it as if your car ran a calculation using your current fuel economy and how long you have till your destination. With this calculation it projected whether you could make it to your destination before the low fuel light turned on. If it can, great, you continue at your same fuel economy and speed. But if it can't, then it will automatically slow you down until your efficient enough to make it to your destination before you get that flashing warning light. You never run out of fuel, but your car is being overprotective to make sure that you have just enough left in case it's life or death, and that's what the low fuel light represents.

This process is more or less what your brain and body do, except that as humans running a marathon, our efficiency can get significantly worse as we go along in our trip. So our brain might make some late adjustments that cause us to have to make drastic slow downs. One way in which this might happen is through mechanical damage. The damage caused by 26.2 miles of pounding could cause muscle fibers that you were expecting to do work to not be able to handle their load due to micro tearing or other damage. Even if you don't get full blown muscle cramping because of fatigue, it may be enough to change your gait and thus increase the energy cost per mile. So what we are left with is worrying mostly about depletion, a moderate amount of concern for whether we can withstand the mechanical demands, and then, depending on the circumstances, a small amount of buildup.

The last step is to adjust these models for the individual, which will be covered in depth in a chapter to come. But the basic premise of it is that our individual differences will shift the race model more aerobic or anaerobic, power or strength, or any other combination of differences. As a quick example, if we have a speed orientated 800m runner versus an endurance one, for the speed athlete, the 800m is more anaerobic, will create a larger buildup of by-products, and most likely recruit a larger percent of their fast twitch muscle mass.

All of these factors shift the model and how we train for the event. It is perhaps even more pertinent in the longer distance events because individual physiology can shift the components of the race model to a very high degree. A marathoner who is efficient at 10k, may not have the fuel capacity, or the ability to withstand the damage, that someone with more of a longer background and shuffling stride. While this is not meant to be a complete overview of each race, I hope that it is enough of a guide to create a template for the demands of each race. Now that we understand what the goals of training are and have models from which to work, it's time to look at classifying the training.

General to Specific: A Classification System

There are an endless number of workouts that can be done. How do you decide which one to do and at what time to do it? It's an overly complex task that needs to be simplified. A workout classification system is used to aid in this simplification. The majority of workout classification systems work off of creating zones based on physiological parameters. For example, a classic structure would be to have a supramaximal, VO2max, Lactate Threshold, and Easy zone system. The problem with such as system is it works off the premise that these zones are the only or the optimal way to enhance those parameters, which we know is false. In addition, it assumes that these parameters are what matters in race performance, which is not entirely true as even when combined these parameters fail to explain performance better than a test using running speed.

Instead of using such a zoning scheme, we'll use a system that was popularized in Renato Canova's *A Scientific Approach to the Marathon* but has been used in Europe for over 30 years and is common in sprint and power events for classification. The advantage of such a system is that the focus is on what matters: running speed. Instead of using physiological parameters, it focuses on how closely the workout or run you are doing replicates the desired race. Why does that matter? Because of the training law of specificity.

The ultimate goal of training is to race a particular distance at a certain pace. The goal race pace and distance are specific training. According to the law of specificity, it is what matters most. This makes sense from a physiological perspective too, as running at race pace is the only way to mimic the exact muscle fiber recruitment pattern and fatiguing by-product buildup that will occur in a race. Does that mean that all we should do is train at race pace? Absolutely not, other paces and intensities are needed to elicit adaptation and support the specific training. Specific training, which can be defined as your goal race pace plus or minus a few percent, simply serves as the basis from which to start our classification system. If our goal race were the 5000m, then specific would refer to goal 5k pace plus or minus a few seconds per mile on either side.

Before looking at the classification system, a couple of points need to be made. First, there are no magical training zones that maximize adaptation or "dead" space where adaptation is less. The body responds to the demand it is placed under, thus every training pace will impart a slightly different stimulus. Certain stimuli will be needed at different times throughout the season, but the take away message is that there are no magic stimuli or "dead" zones. Many runners get caught up in only running at certain intensities, while completely neglecting the in between speeds. This is often seen in American runners where there is little training, if any, done at the speeds between lactate threshold and normal distance run pace. When such a wide range of speeds is neglected, there is a wide array of stimuli and adaptations that the runner is missing out on.

Second, every pace is connected. We tend to think of training in isolation. Instead of having abrupt training zones, whether it is based on physiological zones or race paces, there is a large degree of interaction between every intensity. What this means is that the classification system should be thought of as a spectrum starting with your specific race pace and branching out, without any abrupt zones. Instead of abrupt zones, each category blends into the next. Each training intensity supports the preceding and proceeding intensities. The only reason we have defined zones is to make it practical and useable. Even when training in a certain "zone," it's important to remember that progression must exist and that there is no exact pace that needs to be hit within that zone. Instead, the pace of the workout or run is dependent on what the goal of the session is and where you are at in the training phase, which will be discussed in detail later in the book. With the idea that the classification system is really more of a spectrum with a connection of all of the so-called zones, the chart below represents the entire classification system.

Classification Name	Pace level	5,000m runner example
Recovery	Anything slower	Anything slower
General Endurance	3 race distance up +/-	Steady pace to marathon pace +/-
Aerobic Support	2 race distances up +/-	Lactate Threshold/ Half Marathon pace +/-
Direct Endurance Support	1 race distance up +/-	10k pace +/-
Specific	**Race pace +/-**	**5,000m pace +/-**
Direct Speed Support	1 race distance down +/-	3,000m pace +/-
Anaerobic Support	2 race distances down +/-	1500m pace +/-
General Speed	3 race distance down +/-	400-800m pace +/-
Neuromuscular	Pure speed/sprints	Pure speed/sprints

Specific training is defined as the goal race pace for your particular event, plus or minus a few seconds per 400m. The plus or minus refers to the fact that in a given race it is very unlikely that a runner will have exactly even splits. Therefore, specific pace represents the goal pace with an allowance on either side for expected differences in pace. An example for an 800m runner aiming for 1:48, which is 54sec per lap, would be to consider anything from around 52 to 56sec per lap to be specific because those are the paces that he will expect to hit in an 800m race. Branching out from specific, we get what is termed support training. Note that we are branching out on both the speed and the endurance side. In the original German classification, this was termed special training, but the term support has replaced special in the American training lexicon. Support training refers to the training that is just a step or two further away from specific training and serves the purpose of supporting the specific work that is done. Support training can be divided into two classifications, direct support and anaerobic/aerobic support. Direct support refers to the training intensity that is directly connected to specific speed. In this case it refers to about one race distance slower and one race distance faster than specific speed. On the speed side I refer to this as direct speed support, and on the endurance side it is direct endurance support. Working down the ladder, the next step is aerobic support, which is that training which is connected to direct endurance support, or the race distance about 2 distances slower than specific speed. On the other side is anaerobic support, which refers to an intensity about 2 race distances faster than the specific pace.

Support Training Paces:

	800m	1500m	5,000m	10,000m	Half Mar.	Mara.
Aerobic Support	10k-5k pace +/-	Slightly slower than 10k to 10k pace	Lactate Threshold +/-	Marathon pace +/-	Steady pace +/-	Easy to steady
Direct endurance support	3k to 1mile pace +/-	5k to 3k pace	10k pace +/-	Lactate Threshold +/-	Marathon pace +/-	Lactate Threshold +/-
Direct speed support	400m-600m pace	800m pace	3k to 1500m pace +/-	5k to 3k pace	10k pace +/-	10k pace +/-
Anaerobic support	Speed endurance (200-300m pace)	400m pace to speed endurance	Faster than 1500m pace	3k pace to 1500m pace	5k to 3k pace	5k pace +/-

General training refers to intensities that are 3 to 4 race distances faster or slower. At General endurance training we run out of typical race distances to use to define the pace in many instances. For that reason, we'll use the words "steady" as the next pace up from marathon pace and "easy" as the next pace up from that. Steady refers to a pace that is generally 5-10% slower than marathon pace, or, in other terms, it's a good consistent pace that requires some focus to run but is not tiring. Easy refers to paces that are up to around 25-30% slower than marathon pace and represents what is used on most normal distance runs. Finally, recovery refers to any training that is slower than general training and is meant not to build fitness but instead to aid in recovery and adaptation. Neuromuscular refers to pure sprint work.

General Training Paces:

	800m	1500m	5,000m	10,000m	Half-Mar.	Mara.
General-Endurance	HM pace to steady	HM pace to steady	Marathon pace to easy	Easy to steady	Easy running	Easy running
General-Speed	Pure sprints	Pure sprints to 400m pace	Pure sprints to 800m pace	Pure sprints to 1500m pace	Pure sprints to 1500m pace	Pure sprints to 3200m pace

Please note that I used the word "about" to describe the paces each classification refers to. This was on purpose because I do not want to give the impression that these are intensity zones that are strict and absolute and that anything falling outside these zones is worthless. The reality is that each classification level should blend into the next one. Contrary to the zone theory of training, we now know that there are no magical training intensities and that instead the intensities are connected, with each intensity influencing the next. In essence, there is interaction, not isolation. In the subsequent chapters, each classification level will be explained. For now, let's focus on how they interact and why this is important.

A Different Kind of Base: Training Intensity Interaction

Traditional training models have used a pyramid system that states that a large block of endurance is the base and then that layered on top of that is blocks of ever increasing intensity until you reach the top, which is the "speed" training that brings about top shape. The central asset of this theory is that it acknowledges that there is interaction between training intensities. Certain types of training should precede other types. An example is a large block of endurance work is needed before moving to faster threshold type work. The reason for this is because of the connections and interactions among training intensities.

If one were to jump straight into faster work with no base, one of two things would likely happen. First, they would get injured because they were not adapted to the workload. Second, they make it through the workouts without injury, but the total amount of work is severely limited. In this sense, peak shape could not be reached, and whatever shape they do reach would not last very long. The general endurance training would help to alleviate these two problems. It would develop the runner's musculoskeletal, metabolic, and neuromuscular systems to be able to handle the faster training and allow them to handle a much higher workload before they break down. Each training intensity interacts in this way. Each level of intensity described in the classification model discussed earlier serves to support the next level of intensity. If the end goal is increasing an athlete's specific endurance, then there is a chain reaction that occurs, starting with general training. If we increase general training that in turn increases the quality and amount of aerobic support training that can be done, which increases the amount and quality of direct support, which finally increases the amount and quality of specific training. With an increased ability to handle specific training, specific endurance is improved. Or stated in another way, the runner can now handle more work at a specific pace before fatigue sets in, which we know directly enhances performances.

As you can see, each level of training has an effect on the subsequent level. The flow is only as good as its weakest link. Therefore, in certain situations increasing the amount of general endurance will do nothing in terms of increasing specific endurance if the weak link is at direct support. Instead, training of aerobic support or direct support may be needed to stop the clogging that occurs at direct support. That is where the art of deciding how much emphasis should be focused on each level comes into play, which will be discussed in a later chapter.

The original pyramid does a fine job of demonstrating this process from the endurance side. The problem is that it ignores the whole other side of the spectrum. As speed and intensity are increased, the athletes have the endurance background to handle it, but not the speed or neuromuscular background. What normally happens when athletes follow the traditional pyramid model is that they get to the speed work and either get very sore or they rapidly adapt to the workload, peak, and then have a rapid decline in performance. Why spend so much time gradually adapting on one side of the spectrum while letting the other side be thrown into the fire when it is time to introduce "speed". What we need is a different kind of base.

The Multifaceted Base

The multifaceted base means that instead of creating a base of just aerobic running, we are establishing a metabolic, neuromuscular, and structural foundation. As discussed earlier, the idea of constructing an endurance base is sound, but what needs to be added is the base on which to build speed. In other words, the endurance base works from the top down towards specificity, while the speed base should work from the bottom up.

A speed base will provide several benefits. First, it will establish a neuromuscular foundation off of which to work. Thinking back to the muscle fiber fatigue theory, two of the central premises are that an increase in total muscle fiber pool will enhance performance and that extending the endurance of newly recruited fibers will enhance performance. The ideal way to increase muscle fiber recruitment is through high force activities like sprinting. During the base phase of training, just as you do a lot of general aerobic running, you should do a lot of general speed training, which includes workouts such as sprints.

Working up the pyramid, it only makes sense that if speed endurance is to be trained, speed must be trained first. Thus, a base of pure speed training is needed before attempting to extend that speed. Speed endurance is a critical factor for shorter distance races like the 800m and 1500m and of importance for Fast Twitch (FT) type runners. For Slow Twitch (ST) runners or longer distance runners the support phase of the pyramid serves not as a hard anaerobic workout but as a way to get the runners relaxed at a faster speed, maintain their FT fibers while doing high volumes, and improve biomechanics and muscle fiber recruitment patterns. For ST runners, this support phase could consist of a simple workout such as 8x200m at 2 mile down to mile pace with 200m jog. The idea in such a workout is to get them comfortable at slightly faster speeds, that way when it is time to do specific training or "speed" training like in the traditional model, it is gradually brought about and the runners are ready for it. This will be discussed in detail in later chapters.

The bottom line is that not only do runners need to have an endurance foundation off of which to build, but they also need a speed foundation. This does not mean that they should be doing hard interval sessions during the base phase. That is not speed training for the base phase. Please refer to the charts to see what a foundation of speed is all about. Lastly, it should be noted that the original pyramid referred to volume and intensity, in that volume should be high at the beginning and decrease as the season progresses. The Multifaceted Base Model does not refer to the volume/intensity interaction.

Multifaceted Base Pyramid Model

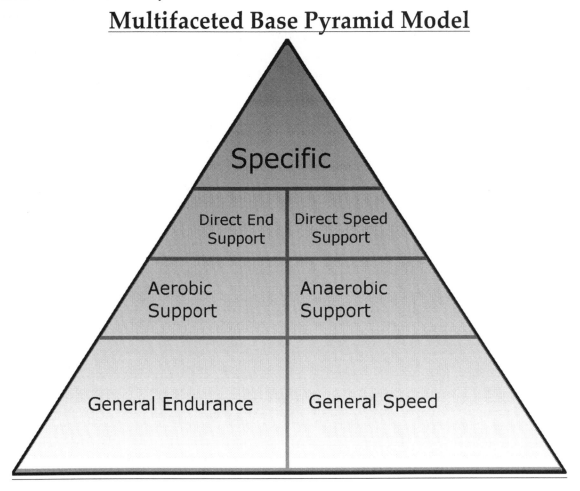

Periodization

While a more in depth discussion on how to plan the training will be done in a later chapter, it is important to understand some of the ideas before discussing the details of each training classification. The multifaceted base pyramid should provide a good summary on my views. A base of both speed and endurance is required before funneling towards specificity on both sides, eventually meeting in the middle. As making complex concepts simple is the theme, the following statements can succinctly summarize proper periodization:

Start backwards. Work the extremes. Bring it together. Never leave anything behind. Progress everything.

Let's break each statement down a little bit. 'Work the extremes' and 'bring it together' have already been discussed and should be obvious. They refer to starting out on the extremes of speed and endurance and bring them together working towards specificity. That is the general direction that the main workouts will go. 'Start backwards' refers to the idea of knowing where you want to end up. It is impossible to plan training if you don't know where you want to go. Thus first look at the goal races and decide what it is you want to accomplish. Only then is it possible to start gearing the training towards that goal.

Perhaps most important is the statement 'never leave anything behind'. This statement focuses on what I call the build and maintain principle. Rather than moving from one type of training to the next and leaving the preceding training behind, I believe that instead of subtracting something, we should always try to add and build off of our training. Once a type of training is introduced, it stays in the training program.

I know what you're thinking, how do we fit it all in? While the training stimulus remains in the program, its emphasis changes. That's where the maintain part of the 'build and maintain' idea comes in. Research has demonstrated that it takes a lot more training to build a particular parameter than it does to maintain it. Maintenance only requires a little spurt of that type of training every now and then. The key is that we don't neglect it so that detraining occurs.

The 'never leave anything behind' statement also pertains to the idea that we almost never should have a period of training when it is entirely one stimulus. Other stimuli should not be neglected for that long. It doesn't have to be much, sometimes 100m strides will do for a speed stimulus, but there should not be total neglect. Obviously there are some times when this principle is violated such as when coming back from injuries or a layoff, but for athletes in serious training it holds true. This concept can best be remembered and summarized by the idea that every component of the training system is included in the training at all times, just the emphasis on each component changes throughout the year.

Lastly is the idea of 'progress everything'. Thinking back to the theories of adaptation, one of the central tenets of adaptation is the idea of supercompensation. Your body reacts to a particular stress by adapting to it and rising to the next level. When this occurs, a new stimulus must be applied to raise adaptation to the next level. Given this idea, progression is paramount. Workouts should be progressed to ensure adaptation. This can occur one of many ways, including a change in total volume, speed, decreased recovery, repeat length, or even how an athlete goes into the workout. This last idea is often neglected, but an athlete can repeat the same workout and still have it be a progression if they go into the workout more fatigued or have the workouts surrounding it contain more mileage or intense running than usual. This is particularly important in regards to specific training. If the goal is to increase specific endurance via delaying fatigue, then a gradual increase in the stress is the only way to accomplish this goal. This gradual progression means that the athlete is adapting to the workload. If at any time the athlete is not able to handle the progression for an unknown reason, then it is time to back off and recover, as the athlete's adaptation ability is probably low. There is one exception to the rule of progression. When a training type enters maintenance mode, we are no longer trying to build, so progression is not needed.

A more in depth look at periodization cannot occur until we understand the details of workout types. Now that we have the basic concepts of what we are trying to accomplish, the nest step is to delve into the details of each type of workout.

16

Creating and Manipulating Workouts

"Poor hitters make the best hitting coaches. They don't try to make you like them, because they sucked." Moneyball

Designing workouts is the step we all skip over. It's one of those jobs that appears so simple that we just gloss right over it. Everyone wants to know what the workout does and what adaptation it targets. That's the sexy part of coaching. Knowing that doing a 4mile tempo at X effort will give Y result is the basis of the majority of coaches' education, and it is an important first step. But once we understand what we are trying to accomplish when training, we need to stop and think about what it is we are creating.

The reality is that it's human nature to be stuck. We can only process so many items at once so it requires much less time and energy to simply give a workout we were given, have read, or saw someone else do than to come up with one ourselves. After all, if Roger Bannister did 10x400, and that's the stimulus we are looking for, then 10x400 it is. It's lazy coaching. My goal is to challenge you as a coach and prevent what I call lazy cookie cutter coaching. In order to accomplish this, we will go back to the beginning and cover the fascinating topic of workout design.

Traditionally in endurance coaching, we have decided what zone we want to target and then simply manipulated the speed and distance to target that zone. If we look at any of the handy training charts for workout design, they will typically look like something like this:

Zone	Speed	Rep length	Recovery	Volume
Lactate Threshold	HM race pace	5-20min segments	60-90sec	6000-10000m
VO2max	3k-5k race pace	800-1600m repeats	2-3min	3000-6000m
Supra-Vo2max	1500m race pace	400-600m repeats	1:1 to 1:3 work to rest ratio	1000-3000m

While there may be some variants, as some might include HR or lactate for instance, the principle is the same in that we pick a zone that gives the desired adaptation. Then we simply plug in a workout that fits the rep length, recovery, speed, and total volume. Not a lot of thought is given to exactly what the workout is beyond making sure it falls into this broad category.

The reality is that we need to take a slight step back from this zone-dominated system and instead realize that the workout details matter a little more than we have acknowledged in the past. The details matter because it decides the amount of stimulus and thus the overload we are applying and in what direction that overload is applied. It's not enough to hit the right zone. This becomes even more important when we step back and look at how a particular workout fits and changes throughout the season. We need to know if we are progressing that adaptation and if we are, then in what direction is it progressing from workout to workout.

If we look at models of stress and adaptation from the first part of this book, then we know that how much we overload influences how much we adapt, given that enough recovery is present. If we look at it physiologically, in order to improve a particular component we have to challenge homeostasis. So, we have to delve a little deeper into the depths of glycogen depletion to get the body to respond and make us utilize glycogen a little more efficiently. Or if we are improving strength, we need to have just enough micro-tears so that the body responds with repairing and making that muscle stronger. Essentially, we need to embarrass the body just enough so that it decides it is more prepared next time it faces that challenge.

Steps for Workout Design

Step 1: Adaptation and Direction

The first step therefore is to decide what adaptation we are in search of. This is where we combine knowledge of science and practical experience to decide what needs to be done. While this is covered in depth in the earlier sections of the book, the decision making on what adaptation is needed is dependent on the time of the season, the individual athlete's physiological makeup, and the race demands. These factors combine to let you know when it is best to work on the various components of endurance and speed. Then it becomes a simple decision of deciding what qualities to target, whether it's specific endurance, strength, biomechanical adaptations, or any other quality.

The other decision is based on what direction we want to improve a quality. For instance if we are training for the 5k and decide that we need to do specific endurance work, we may do 4xmile at 5:00 pace with 3min rest. We have decided that the goal is to work on specific endurance, but then the next time we do specific endurance work, we need to decide in what direction to progress the workout. Do we increase the volume or speed, or do we simply reduce the rest. This topic will be covered shortly, but it's important to know that what direction you choose to take the workout and thus the adaptation is a critical component in designing workouts.

Step 2: Build or Maintain

The next step is to decide whether the goal is to build or maintain the quality. As described at the beginning of this chapter, in my system we are either in a period of emphasis or maintenance. When we are emphasizing a particular component we are trying to improve its capacity, while when we are in maintenance mode the goal is obviously to do enough to simply maintain that parameter. This choice determines the volume and intensity of the workout in relation to what the athlete has done in the past. For example, if an athlete has done a 4mile tempo at 5:20 pace in the past, to maintain his high end aerobic abilities we might need to only do 3miles at 5:20 pace, while to build that parameter we might need to do 5miles at 5:20 pace or 4miles at 5:15 pace, depending on what direction we are trying to build that quality.

Once it has been decided to build a quality, the idea is to design a workout that embarrasses the body to some degree. We are assuming that once we complete the workout, we adapt to it if we provide enough recovery, nutrition, and support around the workout. So that the next time we do a workout trying to progress that same adaptation we have to change something to make it a slightly stronger stimulus. We change because if we did our job right, the body adapted. So if we did the exact same workout as before, we would presumably have less stress than before. As an example, if we did 10x400 in 60sec with 60sec rest and our lactate levels reached 18, the next time we did that same exact workout we would hope our lactate might max out at 17. We adapted, so now to keep adapting, something has to change. That is why the workout details matter.

Step 3: Degree of Overload

With this concept in mind, there are a couple of different questions that need to be asked when progressing one workout to the next. First, how big of a stimulus overload do we need? If the first time we did those 400's in 60sec with 60sec rest, do we try to do them in 55 now or 59? Or do we change every variable and try to do 12 in 58 with 40sec rest. The answer to that question depends on how big of an adaptation are you looking for. Theoretically, the greater the stimulus then the greater the adaptation, IF there is enough rest and support. The problem though is that you risk having the athlete fail, and you risk maladaptation because the athlete was pushed into overtraining and failed to adapt because the stimulus was too much or the recovery too short.

In general, I'm a big believer in very gradually increasing the stimulus of the workout. There are times when we can go for a big stimulus, but those should be planned in advance with ample recovery going in and coming out of it. So you might ask if there is a time we don't progress a workout or if we indefinitely increase the demands of the workout? The simple answer is that yes there is a time when we do not progress a workout or when we might even reduce the stress of the workout. The two scenarios where we would do this would be if we are trying to maintain a fitness component and are no longer trying to progress it and if we are trying to cement an adaptation. In maintenance mode, you may recall that it's easier to maintain a component then to build it up, so reduced workloads are often used as a maintenance workout.

When cementing a workout, you wouldn't progress the stimulus because you're trying to make sure that the athlete really has adapted.

Ultimately the progressing of workouts and training stimulus depends on how the athlete adapts. If the athlete isn't adapting, then don't progress it. It seems obvious, but it is a key concept to understand. How fast and far workouts progress depends on how the athlete adapts. It should be an athlete-driven process and not a purely mathematical one in which we simply increase the stress of the workout every single time.

Going to the Well

Before leaving this discussion and moving towards how to progress workouts, we need to briefly elaborate on what kind of effort the workouts should entail. There is a debate between training to complete failure versus having something left in the tank. The problem with training to complete exhaustion is that it is very hard on the nervous system, the endocrine system, the immune system, and psychologically. If we adapt to the huge workout, then as mentioned above, we get a large training adaptation. The issue is that it's a high risk, high reward venture. As previously mentioned, how hard the workout is should be determined by the recoverability, the degree of overload sought, and the time of the season.

We can use research on learning to give us some insight into this process. Both over and under stimulation of the brain have the same effect, and that is an inability to differentiate trivial and important stimuli. This explains why working too hard or not being challenged enough can lead to the same end result, apathy. This is an issue that teachers face every day, finding the right degree of challenge in the classroom to make sure that bright students are challenged enough to prevent apathy, while students on the other side of the coin aren't overly challenged so that they "overtrain" and get apathetic about the work.

The same concept applies to the challenge of training. We have this sweet spot that I'll call the optimal challenge window. This window shifts from day to day based on both psychological and physiological factors. What we are trying to do is find the right challenge based on what we are trying to accomplish. During very hard workouts we might want to push the envelope and work the higher edges of that window, while during moderate workouts we might want to be on the lower end. The key with this concept is that we are looking for an optimal challenge for our training goal. In general, we are looking for enough of a challenge to stimulate the adaptations we need, but not so much that we overwhelm the system.

External and internal factors can shift both the size of the window and also where it lies along the continuum of challenge. As coaches, we know this intuitively, as we've seen runners come out to a workout and not be able to handle something that they were fit enough to handle. When we delve deeper into the issue, most of the times, the reason for this perceived failure is because of lack of sleep, or a stressful test before, or some external factors. We have both negative and positive stressors that can increase or decrease the size of the window or shift its place on the continuum. We need to keep this in mind when planning workouts. When we are scheduling "go the well" workouts, for example, we need to ensure that the optimal window is shifted as far to the right as possible, as we want the challenge to be very high, but not so high that we are not at least somewhat able to handle it. Therefore, going into workouts like these, we need to be well rested both physiologically and psychologically.

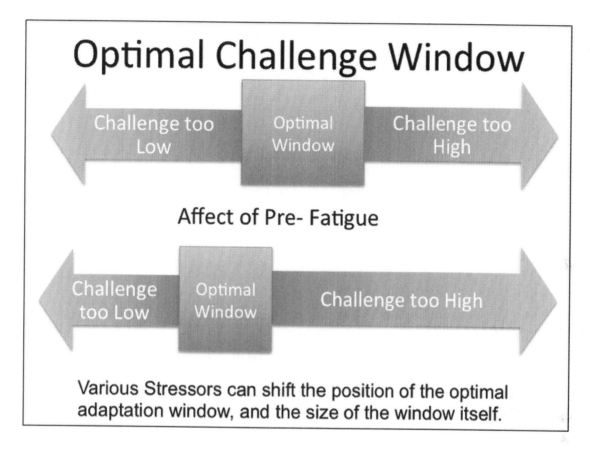

My High School coach, Gerald Stewart, called it going to the well. There are only so many times an athlete can go to the well before the well runs dry. For this reason, the majority of work should be done within your limits feeling like it was a good hard session but that you could have gone a little further or done one more repeat if need be. Remember that the goal of training is not to prove yourself in practice, but to cause progressive adaptation. Or as my High School coach would say, you need to win more workouts than you lose, meaning that you are in control of the workout, not struggling to hang on.

This train but don't strain idea popularized by Arthur Lydiard applies to the vast majority of the training. Occasionally, there will be a time when, to use a phrase Coach Stewart coined, you need to have a "see god" day. Races themselves are very intense efforts, so on rare occasions, the effort needs to be similar. Usually these see god days are reserved for a small number of key specific sessions that essentially function in the place of a race. The recovery going into and out of these sessions should be increased. Maximal effort workouts are the exception to the rule though, and for the vast majority of hard workouts, the motto of "train don't strain" applies. In essence, let the workout come to you, don't force it.

Choosing the Right Direction

Now that we know why we need to adjust workouts and how much to adjust them by, we can move onto the next step of how to do so. In the traditional model, we might change speed or rest or maybe volume up a bit. There's an over reliance on always trying to go faster on all workouts, so that is typically how people increase the stress of the workout. The problem with this line of thinking is that if that is the case then we really only adjust workouts in one direction. The reality is that how we change the workout alters what adaptation we get.

Once you are freed from the constraints of a zone-dominated system, you will quickly realize how many tools are available. The more tools in the toolbox, the more unique problems and situations you can solve. You are no longer constrained to that tiresome repeat of the standard workouts. But more importantly, it's to prevent the situation where you get to that point where something goes wrong, as it almost always inevitably does in distance running, and you have nowhere to turn because you are stuck in that little box of training and can't think outside of it because of the confines of the system you decided to marry. The goal is to embrace the freedom and creativity of being able to design workouts to work with you as a runner.

Given any run or workout, there are a few variables we have to manipulate. There is what I call the typical ones that every coach in the world uses and then there is a more complete list. There's nothing wrong with the typical list. It has proved its worth through the years and should be used during the vast majority of the manipulations of a workout. But the advanced list allows you to have fun, take adaptation to the next level, and really just allows for more tools in the toolbox.

The "Typical" List:
1. Rep distance
2. Total volume
3. Rest between interval
4. Speed

This shouldn't come as a surprise as these are the variables we have considered up until now. We typically focus on manipulating the volume, speed, and recovery of a particular workout or run. These are self-explanatory, and I won't belabor the point by explaining how to manipulate each workout. The key is understanding what changing each workout does.

Often, we don't take the time to think about how changing a workout affects adaptation because with the above manipulators it is almost intuitive. That being said, let's take a quick look. The simplest way to change a workout is by running the same type of workout just a little bit faster. When an athlete does this, we associate it with improved fitness, but what actually happens? If we're able to run the same interval set but faster, that means we've increased our ability to tolerate or accumulate fatigue. As a quick example, if we can do 10x400 with 60sec rest in 58 versus 60 before, we theoretically can now run 58sec per 400 and accumulate the same fatigue as if we were running 60sec. So we've increased our ability to tolerate fatigue and improved in the direction of speed.

On the other hand if we are able to do 10x400 in 60sec but now with 40sec rest, we've increased our ability to recover, which means we've improved our ability to clear or use fatiguing by-products. We're able to do the same total workload at the same speed but now need less recovery to do it, so we've increased our ability to recover which normally is tied to our aerobic system being able to clear things out better during the rest.

If we take the same workout and instead of doing 400's, we do 8x500m at the same pace with the same rest, now we've increased our ability to endure at that pace, or in other words we've increased our specific endurance for that speed. We're now able to lengthen the distance we can spend at a pace. So we're able to slow the buildup of fatigue slightly longer and increase our ability to endure. And lastly, if we were to do the same 400m workout but instead do 12 repeats, we've increased our general endurance. In other words our total workload capacity or stress capacity has increased. We're able to handle a higher total workload then before.

As I mentioned before, most of the changes that take place with these adaptations are self-evident. If we are able to increase speed, we improve in the direction of speed; if we handle longer reps, we increase our ability to endure, and so forth. The next step is to go over some of the more complex ways to manipulate a workout and expand the toolbox a bit.

The Entire Toolbox

The expanded toolbox is meant to open up the possibility of challenging the runner and adaptation in as many possible ways. That doesn't mean that we need to use every single workout manipulator listed below just because we have access to that tool. Instead, we should look towards using the right manipulator for the right adaptation. The reality is that we will use some of these manipulators much more so than others and may only need to call upon some of these very rarely. It is like painting a picture and having a full array of colors to use instead of the seven basic colors to choose from. We may only need the color teal once, but having the ability to, means that we can paint a more complete picture.

The key to remember is that how you manipulate the workout determines what adaptation we get, whether it's toward speed, or endurance, or how fatigue is handled and dealt with. Remember that the body adapts to what it is "embarrassed" by, so when using the manipulators below, think of the ways in which they would "embarrass" or challenge homeostasis. Then you have your answer on what direction the adaptation is taking place in.

The Full List of Manipulators:

1) Speed
    a. Within reps, workout
2) Recovery
    a. Length (between reps, between sets)
    b. Standing/jogging/steady/with "stuff"
3) Rep length
4) Terrain
    a. Hill, soft, hard, variable, etc.
5) Volume (total/sets)
6) Density
7) "Stuff"
    a. Aerobic/clearing
    b. Sprint
    c. Strength
8) Surges
9) Feedback manipulators
    a. Knowledge of splits, reps, distance of reps, total workout, terrain, etc.

Speed Manipulation

Before, we looked at manipulating speed as simply getting faster over the run or repeat, but there are more ways to look at speed than just this simple method. We can also change speed within repeats or within the total workout to get different adaptations. For example, we can either positive or negative split a workout. By negative splitting, we are working on recruiting more fibers as we go along and gradually ramping up the stress, as well as ingraining a positive psychological mindset towards finishing fast. On the other hand, we can "positive split" where we initially go out faster than our normal pace or have the first reps faster. This could be done to adapt to getting out fast in a race or to inject some fatigue or lactate into the system before slightly slowing and getting the body used to processing or dealing with that fatigue. In this sense, going out hard and then settling can be a way to train the removal and use of some fatiguing by-products.

We can go beyond these ideas and vary speed within the total workout too. Instead of simply going in one direction, we can vary the pace of each rep or set distance. For example, if we are doing 9x600m repeats at around 5k pace (1:48 for example), we might do every 3rd one in 1:42 to work on injecting speed and fatigue into the workout before settling back into race rhythm for the next few reps. Similarly, varying the pace within each rep allows for further challenge and adaptation. Instead of adapting to a steady rhythm and pace, vary it within the rep, creating the ability both mentally and physically to alter pace throughout a distance. If we were doing 4x2000, instead of running each rep at 5:00min mile pace, or 75sec a lap, we can work on our ability to handle a surge by going 80, 68, 75, 72, 70. Or from a physiological point of view, we could work on using lactate or fatigue with laps of 65, 75, 80, 75, and 70. Oftentimes, I will use varying paces within reps to work on tactical race preparation and what it entails to change rhythms biomechanically. We know physiologically that when we change out of a rhythm, it takes the body a little time to adjust the breathing, heart rate, etc. to the new level. So what we work on is physiologically getting the body to adjust more quickly without putting the athlete in a hole. And, biomechanically, what we work on is how increases in pace don't require some big elaborate change in running form but instead slight subtle adjustments, whether it's an increase in arm stroke or in turnover. The possibilities for pace adjustments are endless based on what physiological, psychological, or biomechanical component you are trying to adapt too.

The result of varying the pace can be many faceted. Depending how it's done, we can work on fatigue tolerance, removal, accumulation, or production. We can also work on numerous psychological components, such as getting runners used to going out over their head and staying relaxed, working on varying paces above and below their comfort rhythm, or finishing progressively faster. How you manipulate the speed determines what adaptation you get.

Recovery and "Stuff"

When we think about recovery between repeats, what first comes to mind is how long and whether it is jogging or standing. As you might expect, we can actually go far beyond this simple dichotomy and look at many ways to vary recovery. We can separate them into adjustments by length or style.

Adjustments of the length of the recovery should be self-explanatory, but most of the time people think of it only in terms of recovery between repeats. Instead, we can also vary the recovery by breaking the workout into sets and having much longer recovery between sets than we would between reps. By having long rest between sets, we can get the best of both worlds and challenge the athletes with shorter recovery, while ensuring that we can get an adequate volume of work done by inserting relatively longer breaks in the middle of the workout. Breaking workouts into sets is a great way to introduce a workout, with the goal over the next several weeks of being able to work down to doing the workout with no set breaks. For example, working down from 3 sets of 3x800 with 90sec rest with 5min between sets towards 9x800 with 90sec rest by the end of the season.

The way we vary the recovery impacts the workout demands and the subsequent adaptation. If we shorten the recovery, the aerobic demands of the workout actually increase. While this may seem counterintuitive, it occurs because there is no time for our anaerobic systems to recover between repeats. If instead we had a longer recovery, we'd have time for our anaerobic system to recover and fire back up, as well as our phosphagen system. While at the same time, especially if it was standing rest, our oxygen consumption and heart rate would drop, meaning that we'd need to spend the beginning of each repeat burning through our anaerobic system as we waited for our aerobic system to fully kick in gear. So recovery length manipulation not only matters in creating a stress to the system, but it also determines what system is stressed.

With style adjustments, we change how the recovery is done. The classic debate would be whether to stand or jog, but the reality is there are a slew of speeds between jogging and very fast running, but still slower than repeat pace. To start with the jogging versus standing question, the answer depends once again on what adaptation we are seeking out. As I mentioned above, if we jog, we keep heart rate, blood flow, and oxygen consumption elevated. So it creates a situation where the aerobic system doesn't go from fully engaged to resting as quickly, therefore making each subsequent interval more aerobic. Additionally, because of the increased circulation, the body gets to work on clearance and removal of fatigue by-products during the rest. While if we had standing rest, we'd create a situation where blood would pool more, so and we'd accumulate more fatiguing products going into the next interval. So this might be a better option when we are looking at adapting to accumulation of fatigue or from a psychological standpoint if we were looking at disrupting someone's rhythm running ability.

We can take this a step further and look at making the speed of the recovery more defined. Instead of specifying that an athlete simply jog, we can look at faster speeds that may shift the emphasis to being able to recover while still working fairly hard. For instance, if running repeat 800s at 5k pace, we might include a 400m recovery at a steady pace that is just slower than tempo pace. Now, during the recovery the body would have built up fatigue during the repeat and be barely slower than our lactate threshold. So, we'd be forcing our body to try to clear out the fatigue while it is still working at a highly demanding aerobic speed. The fact is, for every subsequent repeat we'd have ever increasing lactate levels being thrown into the body, and we wouldn't be able to clear things out very much on the recovery, so we'd get used to dealing with ever increasing fatigue. On the other hand, if we wanted to work on maximizing clearance, we might use a pace that is around marathon pace, so it is slow enough that we aren't at a steady state yet but fast enough that the aerobic system is fully revved up. The paces you can use are almost endless, from just slower to the repeat all the way down to a "sprinter shuffle."

Another way to change the style of the recovery is to add "stuff" to it. This non-technical term called "stuff" refers to inserting various other modalities, such as strength work, hills, sprints, or surges, into the recovery. We could insert strength work such as squats, lunges, or squat jumps into the recovery to work on strength endurance. The strength work would provide some fatigue in a non-specific way, meaning that the exact same muscle fibers aren't recruited. Similarly, we could make the recovery on a hilly loop or uphill to force an incomplete recovery and add a strength component.

If instead we wanted to stress a different system, like the neuromuscular system, during the recovery, we might add very short sprints. This would force increased muscle fiber recruitment, and you would then hope that those fibers were used and trained during the subsequent repeat. Finally, if we needed to clear out some fatigue during the recovery in hopes of having a faster next interval or to try to have an athlete salvage the workout, we might include a short surge or a few strides at a moderate aerobic pace.

"Stuff" can also be used in non-recovery situations too. An example of this might be to insert plyometric-like activity in the middle of a repeat. When working on kick development one of the goals is to increase fiber recruitment during the kick. To accomplish this, one workout I like is to do 500m repeats, where the middle 100m is done by bounding. The bounding is a way to increase the force component and thus recruit more muscle fibers. In a similar vein, we could add surges during the middle of an easy run to keep muscle tension high so that we don't get into the habit of slogging along. Or we could put surges in the middle of a repeat or at the end of a long run to work on increasing the pace when fatigued or glycogen depleted.

Terrain

Another way to manipulate a workout is by altering the terrain that it is done on. The first thing that pops into your head should be running hills. When we switch a workout to include hills, it increases the strength component of the workout and slightly changes the muscle fiber recruitment. The hill also dampens the amount of energy return a runner can get off the ground, so it changes the dynamics of the run. How steep the hill is determines the balance between strength/power and speed of the workout. Obviously a gradual hill means that speed can still be kept relatively high, that the mechanics of running are kept fairly normal, and that there are only slight increases to the strength demands of the run. The opposite is true for a very steep hill.

The desired adaptation determines what incline the hill should be. As a general rule, the degree of incline can almost be thought of in terms of the light weight versus heavy weight lifting paradigm. If we want to emphasize pure strength, we lift heavy. If on the other hand we want speed and explosiveness, we might lift a lower amount more quickly. And finally, if we want to maximize power, there is a sweet spot between how heavy the weight should be and how quickly we can move it. The same holds true for hills.

The other way terrain manipulation comes into play is in the degree of hardness, softness, and instability of the terrain itself. As I mentioned previously, if we have a very soft, absorbent ground like sand or thick grass, then we dampen how much energy return we can get from that ground. For some runners this may not be a problem at all, while for others it may sap all of their energy. This phenomenon can be seen in cross country where you have your "grinder" runners who have heavy foot plants and tend to run well on courses with rough terrain, and then you have your "bouncy" track style runners who run poorly on rough terrain but excel on the perfectly manicured and responsive golf course style courses. In training then we can replicate some of these effects by running on a variety of surfaces. We can choose hard surfaces for fast responsive running, or we can try to take it all away by running on thick grass or slippery gravel. Similarly, we can use sand or other surfaces occasionally to work on the stabilizers of the lower leg, though this should be adapted to very gradually.

Volume, Density, and External Manipulators

The last two workout manipulators are changes in the volume and density of the workout. While we have already looked at rep length changes, increases in volume can be thought of in more global terms. If we are able to handle a greater volume of work, given similar recovery and speeds, then we've increased our work capacity. Or to put it another way, we've increased the workload we can handle for a given stress load. An increase in work capacity not only makes us stronger and better able to absorb the work needed to reach the next level but also opens up the possibility for handling new stressors.

When looking at the volume of work done in each workout or run, I like to look at it in terms of how much total work we are doing for each type of workout. We can think of things globally, as in how many total meters or miles of specific endurance work can we do? So if we are training for the 3k and do 6x800 at 3k pace, then we obviously do 3miles worth of 3k work. If we are looking to increase work capacity, the next time we might do 7x800 for example. This is a simplistic demonstration, which should come as no surprise, but if we look at the volume of each type of workout it gives us an idea about where our work capacity strengths and weaknesses lie and how we can change them.

If we have a middle distance athlete who can handle tons of 400's at mile pace without any problem but falls apart halfway through any longer rep (i.e., mile repeats), then we might need to increase the volume on either side of those mile repeats to try and give them the work capacity needed to last. Increasing their threshold volume to 4 miles might help transfer some of that strength to be able to do the longer repeats necessary to hit their goal.

The other way to think of volume is within sets. Often times to bridge the gap between an introductory workout and a full-fledged workout, it's smart to start with a workout split into sets and then gradually take away the sets. In the example below, the total volume stays the same throughout, but the volume broken into sets changes, thus the stress of the workout is increased.

3 sets of (4x400 with 60sec rest) 3min rest between sets

2 sets of (6x400) with same rest

12x400 with 60-75sec rest

What changes in the above example is the density of the work. Density is best conceptualized as how much work is packed into the workout or the surroundings of the workout. It is essentially a combination of work done and the time taken to do that work. So if we have more activity jam packed into the entire workout, then the density is high. While if it's a relatively straightforward short and sweet workout, then density is low. If we look at the 400m repeats example above, in terms of total volume the workouts are exactly the same, but if we think of things psychologically, performing 12 400m repeats straight through is a lot more challenging than performing them with breaks. There is more work packed into the time period.

But what happens if we inserted hill sprints or squat jumps during the rest periods in between the sets? We've just increased the workload significantly, so the density goes up, and it might be a denser workout now than just doing 400's straight through. Now, we're doing consistent work over the entire longer time frame. We have more time, but we also have more work packed into that time, so the stress of that workout goes up. And it's not just the stress that matters. Why would we be concerned with density or try to adapt athletes in that direction? Similar to volume, density manipulations increase work capacity but also can be used to influence strength endurance, and recoverability.

Up until now, we've thought of manipulating the workout in terms of what goes on during that workout only. But what we do surrounding that workout matters too. Density includes not only what happens within the workout itself but also other activities within the training block. The adaptations to a particular workout change if we are doing the workout in a pre-fatigued state due to doing a workout the previous day or morning. So we have to look at the density of the training block.

Imagine if we had a 17-mile long run on a Saturday morning. Would the adaptations from that long run change if we had an easy 8 miles versus if we had a 6 mile threshold on Friday afternoon before? You bet they would. The reason is that now on that 17 mile run, we enter it in a pre-fatigued state. We start the run with lower fuel stores, with some muscle fibers having damage, and a whole host of other problems that we wouldn't have had with just an easy run the day before. What happens on the long run now is that we delve deeper into our glycogen stores, we access different muscle fibers, and we generally feel a bit more fatigued earlier. So the adaptations we get from that long run change depending on what we did the day before.

This same concept applies not only to workouts before long runs but to the entire training program. We could do hill sprints the day before a workout to change the neuromuscular demands or do some cruise 200's the morning before a hard repeat session or vice versa. What surrounds the workouts matters. And without sounding too obsessively detail orientated, what we do workout wise affects what we get out of our easy runs.

The surrounding density of the training can greatly affect the stress and subsequent adaptations. It's why you may be improving a ton even if you can only do that 5xmile workout at the same speed as a month ago if this time you did it in the middle of a 90mile week, as compared to 70, with hill sprints the day before. Therefore density within a training block is a great way to manipulate the demands of a workout without even having to touch the workout itself!

Which brings me to external manipulators. These are similar to density manipulators in that they may create a situation of pre-fatigue. Instead of doing them by increasing the density of the training, they are achieved by external means. One such way is to manipulate the recovery after a workout or run. Instead of fully recovering, we may use minimal recovery devices so that we create the pre-fatigue state discussed above. In fact, during the base and pre-competition phases of training, recovery is de-emphasized for this exact reason.

Another way to externally manipulate workouts is by using nutrition. When training for the marathon, we generally think of taking carbs during a long run as performance enhancing. But what if the adaptation we are trying to achieve is to work on fuel use efficiency and sparing glycogen. If that's the case, then we want to shift fuel metabolism, and the way to do this is to "embarrass" the system. So we need to delve deeper into the depths of glycogen depletion. To do this, we could do fasted runs where we wake up and don't fuel before a run so that we use our overnight fast as a way to train with less glycogen. Similarly, we may do really long runs without fueling support to push the stress of low glycogen further. It's a balancing act to determine when to do this and when to practice the race strategy of fueling, but the point is that we can use nutrition to manipulate the stressor of the workout.

Feedback Manipulators

Times, splits, seconds, minutes. They are so ingrained in our head as runners, sometime cruelly, that we cannot escape them. We become slaves to the watch and knowing exactly where we are during every workout and every race. But what happens if we take it all away?

The role of feedback in performance is an intriguing one. Current theories on fatigue posit that it is a combination of internal and external feedback that tells us how we feel at that moment during a race. We then use that momentary fatigue to compare with how we think we should feel at that moment, knowing that we have X amount left, and that determines if we drive on or slow down. There's more to it, and usually we focus on the internal feedback (lactate levels, glycogen stores, etc.) that we aren't exactly aware of but that we know our brain is constantly monitoring. We forget that the external feedback plays just as big of a role. So, the splits you hear, the people you are passing or getting passed by, the mile marker coming up; it all matters.

In training we give athletes set numbers of intervals at set paces with set rest breaks. They know exactly how fast they have to run for, when they are going to stop, how much rest, etc. In a race, you know the distance, but the pace could go all sorts of different ways. It could be tactical; you could have some crazy person go out hard, do a crazy surge, and so on. The athlete isn't in control, so we have to train the mental aspect during practice. We have to train them to deal with unknown external feedback, especially in championship style racing. How do we do this?

One way we can create psychological stress that in turn changes into physiological stress and adaptation is by manipulating the feedback that a runner receive in practice. We can manipulate the runner's knowledge of splits, rep length, recovery, or even the total workout. I call these blind feedback workouts, where we take away some form of external feedback depending on the desired adaptation.

We can further classify these into blind surges, blind distance, and blind splits workouts. During Blind surges, we try to replicate the uncertainty of a race where when surges occur the athlete has to decide to surge or not without knowing how long that surge might last. We are trying to work on acclimatizing the "central governor" of the runner to unknown outcomes and convincing the brain it's okay if we surge without knowing for how long it will last. Blind surge workouts can be done in multiple ways. First, if you are running with your athletes, you can surge at different intervals within a run or workout, with their only instructions to go with you no matter what and without telling them how far you will surge for. Another way is to simply blow a whistle whenever you want an athlete to surge and tell them to surge until you blow the whistle again. I often prescribe these during tempo or longer repeats.

During blind distance workouts, I prescribe an athlete a pace to run without instructing them on how far they will run that rep. By doing a workout in this style, we work on an athlete having that creeping uncertainty and anxiety that comes from not knowing how far they'll go. It really works on the mental strength of the athlete and helps them with working through tough patches of a race.

Finally, we have blind split workouts where we inform the athlete of the rep distance but withhold split information. The goal is to ingrain the ability to focus on how they feel and the rhythm of running. Oftentimes, this works well with athletes who hold themselves back by only rarely going outside of their own perceived ability level. By taking away the reliance on splits we allow for breakthroughs to occur. The famed coach Mihali Igloi was a proponent of using such workouts as he gave his athletes descriptors of how they should feel during each repeat, instead of using time goals.

Breaking Away

Once you break free from the constraints of thinking 400's equals anaerobic training, you can quickly see that how the workout is manipulated and created determines the stimulus and ultimately the adaptation. We can do 400's that range from completely anaerobic capacity work to simply a general aerobic stimulus and everything in between. This happens solely based on how we manipulate every single variable.

We have all of these different variables to tweak, and the training stimuli provided depends on the combination of all of them. The point isn't to overly complicate workout design but instead to change the paradigm. Instead of seeing workouts as a classification scheme where we do X workout in Y zone, we see workouts as a way to increase stress and drive adaptation. The way that stress is increased determines the direction of the adaptation the body takes. Therefore, it's a simple act of stress that leads to an adaptation. It's just up to you as the coach to paint the picture and take the adaptation the route you want it to go. It's about making the right decisions to continue adaptation in the correct directions for the goals of the athlete. Hopefully, you can see that it's not a tedious way to complicate training but instead a liberating simple idea that allows for freedom of creating and molding the athletes' physiology and psychology in the way necessary for them to reach their limits in running.

17

Individualizing Training

"When we categorize, we polarize." Leonard Mlodinow

Individualization is one of those buzzwords or so called principles of training that coaches frequently talk about. But what does this actually mean and do people actually adhere to this so called training law? You'll find that most people claim to adhere to it, but few actually do. It is very rare that a coach can completely adapt to the individual. Instead, most coaches try to adapt the individual to their training system, instead of adapting the training system to the individual. While this might seem like a difference in semantics, it is actually much more.

When most coaches think of individualization, they do the former and try to adapt their athlete to the training program. By this I mean that they have their own training model or system and they try to force the athlete into this model. For example, if someone was using a strict Lydiard system, he would try to get the athlete up to 100mpw, then follow it with hills, and so forth. The coach's idea of individualizing this program for the athlete would be to adjust the quantity or quality of the training, but the overall system would be the same. By doing this, the coach thinks he is adapting to the individual. However, all he is really doing is taking that same training model and putting the athlete in it.

Another form of individualization used by coaches is to adapt their training program based on the event the athlete runs. In doing this, coaches change their training system slightly based on the different track events. The athletes are put into groups based on the type of runner they are. If they are a 1500m runner, then their training would differ slightly from if they were a 5,000m runner. One such system, based on Frank Horwill's work, would use the 2 distances above and below the race distance as the main training paces. A 1500m runner would therefore train at race pace in addition to 400m, 800m, 5000m and 10km pace, while a 5000m runner would get rid of 400m pace and add half marathon pace. The problem with this type of individualization is that it assumes that every runner running a particular event is the same. So the coach is not adapting to the individual; instead he is adapting to an event.

These two commonly used methods of "individualization" suffer from the same problem; they are trying to fit the individual into the system or event. The key to true individualization is creating the training system around the individual runner's needs. In the chapter Theories of Training Adaptation, the scientific basis for the individuality of adaptation was discussed. We saw that recent research shows a wide range of adaptation responses to the same exact training stimulus. This should not come as a surprise, as in just looking at what affects adaptation it is clear that an individual's physiological makeup can significantly affect their response to a workout. Despite this fact, it is seldom acknowledged in either the coaching or research world. Scientists doing training studies continually look at the group as a whole and search for some mythic magical training intensity. Obviously accounting for every individual difference between people is impossible, but in this chapter, a practical model of true individualization will be introduced, and readers will learn how to apply this to their own training.

True individualization requires adaptation of the training system to the athlete. This means that the training system changes, sometimes entirely, based on the individual physiology of an athlete. If we look at physiology, it can be seen that individuals vary widely in a number of different aspects. Some of those aspects we are well aware of, such as the percentage of different muscle fibers an athlete has. Other aspects are probably unknown to us, such as some genetic limits or the total amount of adaptation energy a person has. Acknowledging that we do not have the whole picture figured out, it is important to make individual adaptations in our training based on the parameters that we do know.

Looking at it from a coaching perspective, I'm sure we have all had several runners who run around the same time for a distance, let's say the mile for example, yet some of those excel to a higher degree at faster races, while others excel at longer races. In essence, to reach the same mile time, some of the runners come at it from the speed side, while others come at it from the endurance side, and some seem to have a perfect mix at the mile. Do these runners all need the same exact training since they are running the same kinds of times for the same event? No.

In looking at the training done by different runners, the idea that different athletes need different training becomes clear. If we just look at one event, say the 1500m, we can see that we've had World Record holders and Olympic medalist succeed off of a wide range of training programs. Some used very high mileage, some used very low mileage. Others used endless repeats with lots of anaerobic training, while others were strength based. Peter Snell was a world record holder and gold medalist at 800m and 1500m using a Lydiard, high mileage approach. Lydiard is famous for saying that Snell won the 800m when he had the slowest 200m speed of anyone in the field. So that must be the right approach? On the other hand, Sebastian Coe succeeded with a program that included much lower mileage and much higher intensity interval workouts. He achieved similar success to Snell and did it more recently, so that must be the magic program? Nope. How can so many seemingly different programs produce great results for the same event? It's because the program worked for that individual. It may not have worked for another equally talented but different runner. Even the greatest training system will not work for every runner.

Snell succeeded off the Lydiard program probably for the very reason that Lydiard always used as proof his system worked: that Snell had the slowest speed. He needed the long aerobic training and came at the 800m from the endurance side. Coe on the other hand split mid 45's on 4x400m and was brought up slowly adjusting to higher and higher intensity training, so it makes sense that his approach worked for him. One last example is that of Jim Ryun. He achieved phenomenal times in the 800m, 1500m, and mile, yet there were scores of talented athletes who went to Kansas University who tried to copy Ryun's training and had little success. The reason? Bob Timmons system was well suited to Ryun who could handle large workloads, but other runners weren't physiological or psychologically the same as Ryun, so it did not suit them.

The best coach should be able to use a wide range of systems. They should be able to use a high mileage approach when that is needed and a low mileage/high intensity approach when that is needed. In essence, the best coach has no distinct system; he has general principles of training but is not locked into calling himself a "high mileage" coach for example. Instead, the best coach adapts to the individual giving him exactly what he needs. As it currently stands, most coaches are locked into one idea, and the runner has to get lucky and hope that he is physiological compatible with that system, because if he's not, good luck. While this may sound like a daunting task, how do we break away from having one dogmatic training system?

The answer is using a practical model for individualization. Combining observation of athletes training with the science gives us a simple model. Although good coaches have been practically individualizing training for years, the first integrated system of individualized training I came across was by Jan Olbrecht in *The Science of Winning*. Later, Italian coach Renato Canova developed a similar integrated model. Using those two models as a foundation and building upon it with both practical experience and science, a system of individualizing training based on muscle fiber type is described below. Am I saying that every runner needs to go get a muscle biopsy and figure out his or her muscle fiber type? No. Using muscle fiber type provides for an easily understandable model, especially when we combine it with the runner's goal event.

Muscle Fiber Type

Before delving into how to individualize based on muscle fiber type, let's briefly go over some important basics about muscle fibers. Fiber types are generally classified as Slow Twitch (ST) or Fast Twitch (FT) with several subdivisions of FT fiber types (FT-a,x,c are common classifications). The details of how these are classified are not important for the coach, so we'll skip this. While having distinct fiber type classifications is useful in research, the reality is that fiber types are more like a spectrum. On one side of the spectrum we have what we'd call a pure ST fiber and on the opposite is the pure FT fiber. In between these two extremes is a range of fibers with different ratios of FT/ST characteristics, and this is where the majority of fibers fall. Where exactly a fiber falls depends on its individual characteristics, which are things like mitochondria density, capillary density, oxidative and Glycolytic enzyme activity, creatine phosphate stores, and contraction velocity.

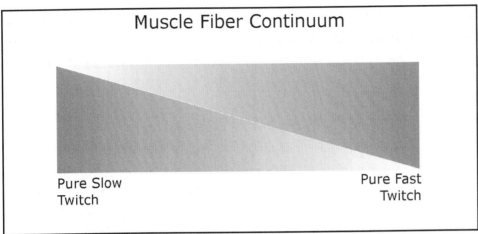

Along this continuum, fiber type can shift to either the aerobic (ST) or anaerobic (FT) side. With acute training, the shifts are very small, but with long term training a larger change can occur. How large a change is up for debate. Switching back to the science for a minute, for a long time Scientists thought that we could not change fiber types at all, then it became we can't switch fiber types from FT to ST. The reality is that we most likely can change fiber types; the reason why it can't be proven in humans is that it is a long process. Several pieces of evidence lead to this conclusion. First, animal studies on both rats and rabbits have demonstrated complete fiber type changes with chronic muscle stimulation. What they've found is that a large amount of damage is required for a complete transformation. Second, fiber type percentages have been altered in elite skiers as shown when they were tested during their beginning stages of training and then 7 years later. Put these two together, and it makes sense that a large amount of volume (or in other words, damage) is needed to change fiber types.

The second piece of important practical information regarding muscle fibers is how recruitment occurs. First, muscle recruitment is dependent not on speed or intensity, although they are related, but on force output required. The amount of force needed determines muscle activation. This explains why running slightly slower up a hill activates more muscle than running on the flat ground at a slightly faster pace. The easier to recruit fibers (ST) take up the work first, while the harder to recruit fibers are activated as force or duration increases. But this isn't always the case. There are instances when FT fibers are recruited before ST fibers, particularly in situations when a high amount of force is needed in a short amount of time, such as ballistics exercises or during sprinting. Similarly, the force rule of muscle fiber recruitment can be violated during prolonged activity when ST fibers fatigue (glycogen is depleted for example), and then the FT fibers are recruited to take up the slack, despite the relatively low intensity and force recruitment.

Muscle fiber, or more properly termed Motor Unit, recruitment for endurance events happens in a cyclical manner. That means within a whole muscle, some units are recruited to do the work and then they can cycle off and recover, while other units cycle on and take up the workload. At low intensities, the number of units active at the same time is very low, but as intensity increases more units need to be active at the same time to result in a great enough force output, thus fewer units are recovering or inactive. Additionally, as force recruitment increases the "resting" time between both activation and between individual contractions decreases. These concepts about muscle fibers and recruitment are important in obtaining a complete understanding of the next section, which is on how to individualize training.

The Slow Twitch vs. Fast Twitch Model

First, let's look at why we use fiber type and event for the model. Many coaches individualize based on event, but as mentioned earlier that assumes that every person who runs the same event is the same. That is simply not true. Still, it is a good idea to use event run to individualize because each event presents a different physiological demand. An 800m is going to require a completely different skill set then a 5k for instance. But there is something missing; something is needed that can distinguish the differences between runners who all run the same event. We need a simple, easily understandable parameter to explain those differences, and that parameter is muscle fiber type.

We are not using muscle fiber type in the strict scientific sense, but as a means of helping to separate runners. Each athlete will fall somewhere on the fiber type spectrum for this model. Finding out exactly where they fall is unnecessary but having a general idea of where your runner is on the spectrum will provide the basis for how to individualize. An easy way to figure out where each runner falls will be discussed shortly. General guidelines for each type are listed in the chart below and on the following page:

Slow Twitch Runners
• Have limited use of Anaerobic systems for end kick.

• Can handle faster easy runs for two reasons:
   o Better fuel system so burn fat at higher intensities, delaying glycogen use
   o Use ST fibers at higher intensities before having to recruit ST.

• Anaerobic Capacity, their ability to generate lactate, is naturally weak, so they need regular (but sparing) injections of faster running that generates some lactate. Strides, short sprints, etc.
• Performances are more consistent.
• Can maintain peak shape for longer
• Fewer competitions to reach peak performance
• Are better at jog recovery between workout reps than FT runner's because less reliant on Phosphagen and anaerobic systems.
• ST fibers do the work longer (at higher intensities) than a FT runner because they have more of them.
• Doesn't have to run as fast to recruit large percentage of fibers.

Fast Twitch Runners:

- High anaerobic capacity to use in kick IF he does not use it to stay on pace. If they have to delve into anaerobic capacity to stay on pace too much, they have no kick.
- Easier recovery runs to make sure that FT fibers aren't recruited.
- Will burn glycogen at a slower pace than ST runner because fuel system and fat burning not as developed.
- Lots of aerobic intervals at faster/moderate speeds to increase LT instead of threshold runs. (Example: 400s at 10k pace with very short active rest)
- Active rest prevents anaerobic system from recovering and being used
- More irregular in race performance
- Can maintain peak shape for a shorter period of time than ST runners
- Need more competitions to reach peak shape.
- Have to be more careful with intensity selection when training aerobically. Much easier to go over the edge and miss training stimulus. Also, easy for them to go out too quickly and produce lots of lactate.
- Standing recovery allows for them to go faster b/c of recovery of anaerobic and CrP system.
- Able to handle shorter intervals better than longer intervals.
- Have poor lactate management, poorer ability to use lactate as a fuel
- Have to augment (poorer) aerobic system by large amounts of energy from anaerobic system. Work to decrease amount of augmentation needed, so that can use more of that anaerobic capacity at end in kick.
- Will use FT fibers to help do the work at earlier intensities because have less ST fibers. Thus lactate is produced more and earlier than a ST runner.

The charts provide a general overview of the differences between a FT and a ST runner and some of the general training recommendations based on these differences. The reasons for the different needs are mainly due to 3 main factors:

1. The difference in anaerobic and aerobic capacities (i.e., Energy system contribution).
2. The difference in muscle fiber recruitment.
3. The strength of their fuel systems.

A FT runner will have a higher anaerobic capacity and a lower aerobic capacity. That means at slower speeds, our FT runner will need to supplement his aerobic energy production with some more anaerobic production. At each intensity, the FT runner will need the anaerobic system to pick up the slack for his poorer aerobic system. It is okay to an extent as this runner has a very large anaerobic system that can handle the increased workload to a large degree. On the other hand, the ST runner will rely heavily on the aerobic system and will not delve into using his anaerobic capacity until much higher intensities, and that anaerobic capacity will not last as long.

The second difference is in muscle fiber recruitment. At any given intensity, a FT runner will be recruiting more FT fibers than a ST runner. More FT fibers recruited means more use of the anaerobic energy pathways, more lactate production and less lactate clearance.

Lastly, the strength of the fuel systems will be different. A ST runner will be more effective at using fat as a fuel source and have a greater glycogen supply. That means, ST runners can handle longer runs and more mileage without completely depleting glycogen stores. It will also play a role in the speed of recovery or easy runs. A FT runner would burn more carbohydrate, thus depleting glycogen stores more than a ST runner at the same speed. This means that if the goal is to make sure recovery takes place, a slower speed will be needed for the FT runner.

How Fiber Type Impacts Each Training Workout

Before discussing the exact changes that need to be made for each type of runner, let's consider what sort of training modifications does fiber type require? Remember that workouts are designed for eliciting a specific adaptation. A simple example is that a long run is used to increase general endurance and enhance your ability to use fat as a fuel source. Where fiber type comes in is not in what the goal adaptation is, but what workouts are used to reach that goal adaptation. In the following paragraphs we'll look at some of our goal adaptations and how fiber type impacts what we do to reach those adaptations.

Long Run

The long run has become a sacred part of the runner's training schedule. Once a week, the runner religiously gets in a run that is the longest of the week. The goal of the long run varies based on what event you are training for, but its main goals are to build general endurance, change the fuel system, and get the musculoskeletal system prepared for all that pounding. While most runners need a long run, care needs to be taken in assigning the specifics of the run. A ST runner can handle a longer long run, a faster paced run, and more "stuff" added into the run. We don't want a FT runner running for too long or too fast for several reasons. First, FT fibers will start to get recruited after a prolonged period of time, thus training them more aerobically, which could be counterproductive for a FT runner. Second, because of their more inefficient fuel system, glycogen depletion will occur sooner, thus if a run is too long or too fast glycogen depletion will be significant and impact their subsequent training. The bottom line is too long or fast of a long run will negatively impact their anaerobic abilities to a large degree, which is what a FT athlete thrives off of.

High End Aerobic Endurance

Working down the aerobic ladder, the next training goal is usually something I refer to as high end aerobic endurance. This definition works well when discussing multiple events and is best thought of as improving steady endurance, such as lactate threshold, marathon pace, or similar intensities. Traditionally, workouts such as threshold runs, tempos, or progression runs have been used. However, the ways to develop high end aerobic endurance for ST and FT runners differs markedly. Running at or below the Lactate Threshold is the most commonly used workout, and it works extremely well for ST runners, but for FT runners too much running at the LT will decrease the runner's anaerobic capacity, which is vital to their success, and decrease their muscle tension which will leave their muscles feeling flat and non-responsive. For these reasons, FT runners should do a minimal amount of LT work and instead focus on broken tempos at 5-10sec per mile faster than threshold and on longer straight tempos at 15-30sec slower than threshold. In addition, progression runs work well for FT runners. Lastly, short surges or short intervals at 3k-10k speeds with short rests train the high end endurance of FT runners because it trains their FT fibers aerobically. In addition, for shorter event groups, it allows for training aerobically at speeds that are more specific.

On the other hand, ST runners thrive off of lots of work ranging from long steady runs at marathon pace to runs done at around threshold. Instead of full workouts at just faster than threshold, ST runners benefit from finishing off threshold runs with 5-10 minutes at a slightly faster pace. Finally, ST athletes benefit greatly from the inclusion of alternations. These workouts alternate running at 10k to threshold type paces with their "recovery" being running at a still steady pace that usually is at marathon pace or just slower. An example would be alternating 800m at threshold and 800m at marathon pace for 6 miles.

Alternations

FT runners do alternation work too, but how it is done differs. ST runners typically use alternations to build endurance at 5k pace or slower speeds, and their recovery portion is done at a moderate but still pretty fast pace. In addition, ST runners aim to build the alternations to include running longer segments of up to 1 mile or more. On the other hand, FT runner's alternation workouts differ in several key ways. First, the pace of the "recovery" portion of the alternation is drastically slower. Second, the total volume of work is lower, and often the alternations are split into sets instead of one long continuous session. Third, their alternation workouts include running at faster speeds up to 800m pace or faster for the hard segment. Fourth, the lengths of the segments are drastically shorter. For example, a FT 800m runner might do an alternation workout that includes alternating 100m at 800m pace and 100m slow for a mile, take a break and repeat. On the other hand a ST 5,000m runner might alternate 800m at 10k pace with 800m at marathon pace for 5 miles straight.

Speed Endurance/Anaerobic

A key difference in the types of runners is how much intensive speed work that they can handle. For simplicity's sake, we'll call this work "anaerobic". ST runners generally only need a small to moderate amount of anaerobic work to maximize their potential. Typically, when ST runners do a large amount of anaerobic work, their aerobic abilities degrade and suffer. The key is doing enough to maximize performance while still maintaining aerobic abilities. There are several possible solutions to this balancing act. The Lydiard way was to do a short period of anaerobic type work at the end of the season. While this works, it is risky and can often lead to a mistimed peak or a short peaking period. The second option is to include short cycles of anaerobic work followed by aerobic refresh periods to balance each other out. Another option is to do small spices of anaerobic work throughout the year without ever having a period heavily emphasizing it. Along the same lines, including small amounts of anaerobic work tacked onto the end of other types of workouts is another option. I generally prefer the latter two options and opt for small anaerobic workouts that do not tear the athlete down; in essence, a lot of mini workouts are performed. For example, 8x200 with 200 jog, starting at mile pace, and doing the workout periodically until you progress to faster than 800 pace works well. The volume is low enough that it does not seem to impair the aerobic system.

On the other hand, FT runners can handle more anaerobic work and need a longer buildup of this type of work. They can handle more intense workouts more frequently. For the workout specifically, longer rest periods are needed for FT runners.

Speed

Pure Speed refers to short intense sprints generally of a 100m or less and is something that both types of runners need. The FT runner needs it to maintain that stimulus on the harder to recruit Fast Twitch fibers, while a ST runner needs to work on this weakness to increase his recruitable fiber pool and neuromuscular system. The differences are in how much of this they can handle and the recovery periods between them. Let's split the pure sprint work between that done on a moderate hill and that done on the track. Both types of runners should do both kinds of sprints, but hill sprints are usually easier to recover from. ST runners should rely more on hill sprints with some occasional flat track sprints because they are looking more for the fiber recruitment benefits. FT runners should do a higher percentage of their sprint work on the flat ground as they are looking more at rate of force development and elastic energy use development. Additionally, FT runners should be given a longer recovery period between sprints as it takes them longer to replenish their phosphagen system than ST runners.

Specific Endurance Development

The development of specific endurance is another factor that depends on the runner's physiology. While specific endurance is also event specific, there are some general guidelines for how development differs with each group. FT runner's benefit mostly from coming at it from a short to long approach. That means that they start out with short segments that are at race pace and gradually extend the length of those repeats while keeping the pace relatively the same. ST runners on the other hand benefit more from a top down approach where they progressively increase the pace of their repeats until it reaches goal pace and then the recovery between repeats is shortened. While both types of athletes need both approaches, the fiber type classification will determine what approach receives more emphasis.

Another difference is in the volume of the workout. ST runners can generally handle more volume in total and in the set. FT runners' workouts should often be broken into sets with long rest periods between sets to allow for increased total workload. Alternations can be used for specific endurance development too, and the differences noted above apply here as well. ST runners should work at decreasing the difference in pace between their specific pace segment and their recovery segment, while FT runners should focus on hitting their specific pace segment, keeping the recovery very moderate, and increasing the length of their specific segment. Lastly, both types of runners benefit from mixed workouts, or what I call blend workouts, that mix paces during the workouts to develop specific endurance. FT runners benefit more from blends that include a wide range of paces, while ST runners benefit from blend workouts for specific endurance development that focus on a tightly grouped range of intensities.

Completing the Model

Lastly the total mileage and pace of recovery runs should differ between the two types of runners. FT runners need lower mileage than their counterparts because the higher mileage will dampen their anaerobic abilities and because they will have a harder time recovering because they do not have as developed a fuel system, thus glycogen depletion occurs quicker. On recovery runs, the FT runner is better served by doing short recovery runs, possibly even splitting the day's mileage into two short recovery runs. In addition, the pace should be kept lighter than the ST athletes. ST runners can run at a faster pace using primarily fat as fuel, so they can run their recovery runs at faster speeds without negatively effecting glycogen recovery for example.

But what really makes the model work is finding out where the runner falls in relation to the event they are racing. Basically, you are looking at how his speed and endurance compare to other runners racing the event. We can then classify the runner as being a FT orientated runner or ST orientated runner for that particular event. Once classified as a FT or ST orientated runner for that event, individualization can fully take place. Why is event group needed? Because an athlete who should be trained from the ST side for an 800m may need to be trained from the FT side if he decided to move up to a 3k or 5k. Or to put it differently, his endurance may be a strength at 800m, but it is not adequate, or it is a weakness, at 5,000m.

The goals for the athletes are the same; just how we accomplish them changes. Use the principles of what the differences between FT and ST runners are above and apply them to training athletes in specific event groups. This is the last refining step in the individualization process.

Listed in the charts below are examples and guidelines for each event group. As explained previously, General refers to work that is far away from the goal race, support refers to work that connects general and specific work, and specific refers to any work done at around race speed. Furthermore, it can either come from the speed side or endurance side, which is noted on the left side of the chart:

800m

	Fast Twitch Runner	Slow Twitch Runner
General	Easy surges thrown into easy runs	
Endurance side	Steady paced marathon pace type runs and progressive tempos, not much LT work	
Endurance side	Threshold runs 5-10sec per mile faster than LT . Avoid long LTs.	Moderate amount of threshold work split into segments
Endurance side	1500-10k paced short extensive intervals (ex: 100s at 1500m pace)	Longer repeats at 5k-10k speeds with longer rest periods
Speed side	Includes more pure sprint work and more of that done in the form of flat sprints on track	Sprint work includes more of a mix of hill sprints and flat sprints
Support		
Endurance side	Short Pace work 100s-200s at 800-1mile pace, extending the distance as you progress	Can handle longer repeats. More traditional 1mi-3k pace intervals.
Speed side	Split faster work into sets, with low volume within set and long rest between sets	More volume per set, shorter rest between sets
Speed side	More work done at paces faster than race pace	Moderate amount of faster than 800m pace. Low volume of total work.
Specific		
	Longer rest between reps/sets. Sets split into ~800m of work.	Sets can include more than 800m of work. Shorter rest periods.
	More intermixing of 800m speed and just faster	More intermixing of 800m speed and just slower

1500m

	Fast Twitch Runner	Slow Twitch Runner
General		
Endurance side	Minimal threshold type work, more work done at marathon pace or just faster than threshold	Lots of work at or just below Threshold
	Total volume of threshold work kept low	Can handle large volumes
	Long runs are shorter and easy	Long runs are longer and can include moderate paces or inclusion of surges at the end
Speed Side	Heavy emphasis on sprint work. Work to extend to speed endurance.	Emphasis on sprint work, starting with hill sprints progressing to some flat sprints. Minimal speed endurance.
	Strides or surges done frequently at the end of runs	Rhythm work (100s-200s at race pace) included throughout year
Support		
Endurance side	Extensive intervals with short jog rests at 1500-10k pace	Traditional longer repeats, more mixed workouts including faster and slower repeats in the same workout
		More Strength Endurance work
	Alternation workouts are short focused on race pace and steady	More longer alternation workouts focused on 3k-10k paces
Speed side	Speed endurance work emphasized (faster than 800m pace)	
	Speed workouts include more long rest, longer repeats	Workouts at 800m pace or faster are done with shorter repeats
	Can handle more often and larger volumes of work faster than RP	Small spurts of faster work done, instead of full blown workouts.
Specific		
	Longer specific period used	Low volume of anaerobic workouts
	Mix between short and long rest	

5,000m, 10,000m and Cross Country

	Fast Twitch Runner	Slow Twitch Runner
General		
Endurance side	Long runs kept relaxed and slower	Long runs can be faster and include more "stuff" (pickups, surges, etc.)
	Include more progression work starting at slower than threshold and progressing past threshold	
	Moderate mileage	Higher mileage
Speed Side	Sprint work should be very short (less than 8-10sec in length)	
	No or minimal speed endurance work	
Support		
Endurance side	Responds better to 5k-10k type paced work instead of lots of LT	Heavy emphasis on work done just below and right at lactate threshold
Speed side	Use lots of short intervals at moderate (1500-5k) speeds with short rest	Work at 1500-3k pace done using maintenance type short intervals
	Minimize large volumes of speed work (3k pace or faster) because they respond quickly to it, and it will negatively impact aerobic capacity	More use of 5k paced intervals as speed side support.
Specific		
	Alternations of specific speed and easy with easy being further away from specific speed.	Alternations of specific and steady pace with the steady being a pace much closer to specific race pace.
	Moderate length repeats (400-1mile) with longer rest periods for specific work	Long repeats (800-2mile) included at +/- specific race speed

Finding Your Fiber Type

Short of getting a muscle biopsy, which is very painful and invasive, there is no true way to find fiber type. And even if we did, it would truly vary from muscle to muscle. Thankfully, there are several simple tests that allow for an estimation of where you fall on the fiber type spectrum. By using the following tests, you'll be able to identify what kind of runner you are and begin the process of individualization.

Lactate Test

To start, let's look at the most invasive and expensive of the group, a lactate test. While a lactate test might sound like something reserved for only exercise scientists, a quality portable lactate analyzer can be purchased for a couple hundred dollars, or there are numerous performance testing businesses popping up which will provide lactate testing for around $50. The key is knowing how to test.

In determining what type of runner you are, a simple test can be used that Jan Olbrecht calls the anaerobic capacity test. In this test, you run between 400 and 600m all out. Following the test, lactate samples are taken starting at 3 minutes and every 2 minutes afterwards. The objective is to get a clear maximum lactate reading. There is a delay in lactate production in the muscles and accumulation in the blood, especially after a short test, so a max usually this occurs between 5 and 9 minutes, but you should continue to take lactate samples until a drop in lactate readings is seen. Once the maximum lactate is obtained, this can be used to ascertain where you fall on the fiber type spectrum. The lower the lactate levels, the more ST, while the opposite is true for FT. As a guideline a reading of 6 or less and you are about as ST as you can get. Between 6 and 9 and you are predominately ST. Anything between 10 and 14 and you have a mixture. Between 14 and 18 and you are more likely to be in the FT group, and anything above around 19 and you are definitely in the FT group. Combine this info with how fast the distance was completed, and a good picture develops of how the runner should be classified.

PR Comparison

A much simpler method is to compare the best times of a runner at distances above and below their primary event. This method relies on two things, first that the runner has had equal opportunities in racing events above and below his event and second, that a valid method of comparison is used. These two factors introduce some room for error so it is a less accurate approach.

There are many different methods used for PR comparison. Some of the more accepted methods include the IAAF performance tables which can be found on their website (IAAF.org), and two equivalency mathematical models. The first of the mathematical models is the Purdy calculator, which can be found through an Internet search, and the McMillan calculator, which can be found on mcmillanrunning.com. These systems are generally acceptable when comparing events 800m and up but are less accurate for distances below that. Use the athlete's primary event and compare his above and below distance PR's versus those that are calculated by the above methods. If his longer events are closer to, or even surpass, the predictions by more than his shorter events, then the athlete is a ST athlete for that event. The opposite is true if the shorter events are comparably better.

Performance Testing

There are several performance tests that can be done to determine what type of an athlete a runner is. The easiest is a simple sprint test over 100m, which will give an indication of an athlete's pure sprint speed. Since sprint speed is highly related to fiber type, the faster the 100m time, the more FT fibers the runner is likely to have.

Other tests that can be performed include power tests. Power tests give a strong indication of what fiber type grouping a runner belongs to because power is dependent on rate of force development. Rate of force development is highly related to fiber type, as FT fibers are able to produce large amounts of force more quickly than ST. Some power tests include a standing broad jump test and the 25-meter hopping test. The standing broad jump is self-explanatory and consists of seeing the furthest a person can long jump from a stationary position. While there is no set standardization of what is a good distance for distance runners, FT runners will be able to jump further. The 25 meter hopping test consists of hopping on one leg for 25 meters with the goal being to get past 25 meters in the fewest hops possible. The British Miler's Club developed this standardized test over 25 years ago and found that for world class 800m runners males needed to be able to cover 25m in 10 hops or less and females in 11.

Stride Mechanics

An often overlooked but very useful tool in individualizing a runner's training is in looking at their stride characteristics. Runners tend to develop a wide variety of running styles. While there is certainly a better way to run biomechanically, an individual's running form can provide us some clues as to what type of runner they are.

To start with, one of the major differences is in ground contact time. A FT runner will typically have a shorter ground contact time than a ST runner for the simple reason that they are able to generate force more quickly. Ground contact can be measured in any gait analysis lab, but since the focus of this section is on practical tests, by using a high speed camera you too can measure ground contact times. High speed cameras allow for filming at very high frame rates, or in laymen's times it allows for super slow motion video. While these cameras have been traditionally expensive, the Casio Exilim series has cameras as low as $130 that can shoot up to 1,000 frames per second.

To measure ground contact time simply have someone record foot strike using the high speed function. You can count frames from the time foot contact occurred to the time the foot leaves the ground, and then by using a little math convert the frame numbers to a time in seconds. Alternatively, use free motion analysis software to do this work for you. On my website, I explain in detail what program to use and how to use it, which can be found by searching for the post "Poor man's High Speed Video Analysis." Since ground contact times change with speed, do the analysis at the same relative speed for each runner. While there are no set ground contact time guidelines, research provides us some guidance for 800m and 1500m runners. In a series of studies by Hayes and Caplan, ground contact times were measured in 1500m races (average time 3:56) and 800m races (average time 1:55). In the 1500m, forefoot strikers ground contact time averaged .161sec, mid-foot strikers .169sec, and heel strikers .192sec. In the 800m, forefoot strikers averaged .156sec, mid-foot strikers .161sec, and heel strikers .177sec. These values can be used as references to compare your runners to.

Ground contact time is not the only characteristic that matters. How well a runner uses elastic energy also plays a role in individualizing their training. A runner with a bouncier, more elastic stride is typically a FT runner for his event, while a 'grinder' who has a flatter stride that people associate with 'strength' runners is typically a ST runner for his event. While there is no exact test to determine each type of runner, there are several things to look for. First is foot strike, an elastic runner tends to land higher up on their forefoot. Second is how the stride looks, an elastic runner will have more spring or bounce in their stride. In addition, they will use their Achilles tendon to a larger degree to provide for elastic energy. Lastly, compare how the runner tends to perform on hard surfaces, such as a track, versus soft surfaces, such as the grass. An elastic runner tends to perform much better on hard surfaces than soft due to his reliance on elastic energy.

Use any of these tests or a combination of them to help discern what type of runner you or your athletes are. While it is not an exact science, using several of these tests will allow for an accurate judgment of where a runner falls on the fiber type spectrum. This information combined with their event specialty can then be used to individualize their training.

18

Defining the Workouts

"The person who acquires more knowledge often develops an enhanced illusion of her skill and becomes unrealistically overconfident." Daniel Kahneman

Since the type of runner and the event that they are training for changes the particular workouts effects, there is no easy way to run down each type of workout for each specific purpose. Throughout the training section the emphasis has been on de-classifying workouts and getting your brain out of the habit of creating zones. Now, we reach the difficult part of having to discuss the variety of workouts available. In this chapter, what we are attempting to define is a variety of different ways to do workouts. The aim is to divide workouts into the ways they are traditionally used, such as distance runs, long runs, intervals, or tempo runs, and then discuss the variety of ways to do each workout and what effect each way will have on an athlete physiologically. I am not saying that we should do only Tempo runs to improve aerobic abilities. Instead, think of this as your toolbox. We have all of these ways to do a particular workout and manipulate it. Once this is done, we'll go through each event, from 800m to the marathon, and define how to progress from general to support to specific training.

Mileage and Recovery Running

Runners are obsessed with mileage due to the fact that it is easily measured and provides a way to quantify training. While it is a useful tool, it should not be a goal in and of itself. Instead the individual runs and workouts should be planned to provide the most benefits, and the mileage should be a result of those runs. That being said, mileage is still useful in measuring total volume stress. The biggest question is how to increase mileage. For various reasons, a so called 10% rule for increasing mileage has developed as a sort of law of training. Throw it out. Just like in adapting to interval training, weights, or any other stimulus, the individuality of what a runner can handle varies a lot. Some runners will be able to handle massive increases, while others need small increases. The 10% rule essentially assumes that we are all the same and at the same point in our training.

To aid you in this process of figuring out how to increase mileage, there are a few simple rules that can be followed. First, it is safe to increase mileage very rapidly to any level which you have been previously consistent at over the past 6-12 months. For example, if during the previous training cycle I maxed out at 100mpw during the base phase, then dropped gradually to 70mpw during the end of the season, and then took 2 weeks off, when I started back up I could rapidly increase up to 80-90mpw (because that's what I was most likely consistent at during the base phase). How rapidly depends on the person, but it is not unusual to be able to go from 2 weeks off of running post season to 50, 70, and then 85mpw in a 3 week period. When you should be more cautious about increasing mileage is when venturing into new territory. That is when slow and gradual adaptation occurs. As a general rule, when delving into new levels of mileage, add one mile per day of running to the schedule. Some will be able to handle a slightly more aggressive approach. The injury history, biomechanics, structural build, and nutrition (such as calcium levels) of the runner help determine how quickly they can increase mileage. With the topic of total mileage touched on, what makes up all of those miles?

Research and practical experience has demonstrated that with elite runners 70-80% of their training volume is either General or Recovery paced training. In Kenyan runner Moses Mosop's lead up to his Kenyan Cross Country Championship during the 4 months prior to his win, he averaged ~54% of his training done at recovery paces or slower and 27% of his training in the General category. Combined this resulted in 81% of his training being performed at General speeds or slower; in other words, over 80% of his training was performed at steady paces or slower. Lower caliber runners may be able to handle a higher percentage of their training to be done at more intense speeds due to their lower training volumes. With 80% of their training devoted to such low intensity running, let's first look at the various types of runs that fall into this category.

Normal Distance Runs

A normal distance run is just what it sounds like; it is a typical distance run and represents the most basic form of training. For almost every event, your typical distance run can be considered general training. The benefits of distance runs are almost entirely focused on aerobic adaptations, whether it is changes in capillarization, mitochondria, aerobic enzymes, or cardiorespiratory adaptations. In addition, distance runs can help to improve the fuel system, including changes in substrate use and glycogen storage. In a practical sense though, distance runs are necessarily for accumulating a sufficient amount of mileage and to enhance the other training. Many of the changes that occur with endurance training are the result of long term consistent training and can take years for full adaptation to occur, such as shifting muscle fiber types. Thus, the role of distance is to establish the general aerobic endurance.

The pace of the distance runs depends on several factors including the event your training for, what type of runner you are, and the purpose of the run. Before it is considered a true workout, distance runs can generally be run at speeds up to around 5% slower than marathon pace. As described previously, steady running is generally 5-10% slower than marathon pace, and easy running is up to around 25% slower than marathon pace. To keep it simple though, easy is a pace that could be run at without even concentrating. Breathing should be very easy, and a conversation should be possible. At steady pace it is still relatively easy, but some concentration is required. In other words, a small degree of effort is required to run at a steady pace. Conversation should occur but if you continuously talk for a long period of time, it will become noticeable that you need breaks in the conversation to catch your breath.

Recovery Runs

Recovery runs are very similar to normal distance runs, except the pace is slower and the duration is typically shorter. The purpose of recovery runs is, just as the name suggests, enhancing recovery. When used in the day following a more intense workout, a recovery run helps return the body to homeostasis and prepare the body for the subsequent work to be done the following day. Often overlooked, recovery runs work to enhance the supercompensation effect.

The pace of the recovery run should be slow enough so that it is enhancing recovery, not prolonging it. The intensity needs to be low enough so that minimal muscle damage is occurring and the primary fuel source is fat so as not to delay glycogen replenishment. The exact pace varies from individual to individual. Some athletes, such as many Kenyan runners, will do recovery runs at paces that would be considered ridiculously slow (8-9+min miles) for such elite athletes. On the other hand, some runners react poorly to such slow running because their biomechanics change and this causes a change in muscle tension, which can leave them feeling flat and tired the next day. For FT runners this is usually the case. The bottom line is pay attention to your body and how it reacts. Many runners get caught in a no man's land of training, where there is no difference between their recovery pace and their normal distance pace. This is a bad practice to get into.

The total distance of recovery runs is also an individual preference. The aim should be to do enough that it enhances how you feel the next day, but not so much that it hinders recovery. Generally, recovery runs range from just a couple miles to up to around 10 miles in length. Once you get over about 10 miles, for most people, no matter how slow they go, it is no longer enhancing recovery.

For some runners, another option is to do what I call split recovery runs. A split recovery run is when the total day's mileage is split directly in half into two separate runs. Many runners feel more recovered when doing two short runs as opposed to one single run. An example would be for a runner who needs 10 miles for the day, split it into morning and afternoon 5 mile runs. There are many elite level runners who do this. One possible explanation is that by splitting the runs, it allows for certain hormones beneficial to recovery to be released twice, thus keeping a steady hormonal trigger throughout the day. Another explanation is that splitting the runs reduces the impact on glycogen usage.

The bottom line is that the purpose of recovery runs is to enhance adaptation by taking you through the adaptation phase quicker and getting you prepared for the subsequent workout. The recovery runs and normal distance runs should make up the bulk of the training.

Adding "Stuff" to Runs

"Stuff" refers to strides, surges, pickups, or progressions during the run or workout. Stuff is best seen as an add on to another type of run or workout. They can be added on to normal distance runs, long runs, or included in more intense workouts. When added to a normal distance run, stuff is generally seen as not being very intense or taxing. On the other hand, with long runs or faster workouts, the add on can be a full blown intense session. How intense the add on is depends on the purpose of the run.

Strides

The most basic and commonly used addition is strides post run. Strides are short repeats of usually 100-150m in distance done at faster speeds with plenty of recovery. Generally, strides are done at between 5k and 1 mile pace depending on the goal. Strides after runs serve several functions. First, they are a way to maintain speed during periods of heavy aerobic running as they reinforce good biomechanics and the recruitment of Fast Twitch muscle fibers. Second, strides can be used to work on running form or work a little on muscle recruitment in a semi fatigued state since they are performed after a distance run. Lastly, strides are a way of altering muscle tension, which will be covered in a later chapter in detail, which basically means it is a way of getting "pop" in the legs so that the runner feels better the next day.

Surges

Along the same lines as strides is the addition of surges. Think of surges as strides in the middle of the run. Surges consist of a gradual increase in pace down to 5k pace or faster for approximately 15 to 60 seconds. The difference is that immediately following this surge, the runner falls back into his earlier distance run pace for between 1-3 minutes before repeating the surge. Surges are not meant to be a workout, but instead as a way to inject a little faster running into a normal distance run. Surges train the body to be able to make a smooth transition to a faster pace, a vital skill to be learned for racing, and train the body how to efficiently recruit additional fibers with a pace change. What separates surges from strides is that additional fiber recruitment occurs in the middle of the run. This allows for not only recruitment of these fibers but also the training of them as well since they can continue to be used in between each surge. In addition, surges start the process of training the body how to use lactate, as during the surge a small amount of lactate is produced, which then can be used during the following recovery portion. Lastly, surges serve as an excellent maintenance or transition method to faster paced running when coming off of the base phase.

Example and Progression of Surges:

8 mile run with 6x30sec surge w/ 2:30 easy after each in the middle
8 mile run with 6x45sec surge w/ 2:15 easy after each
8 mile run with 6x60sec surge w/ 2:00 easy after each

Pickups

The next addition is pickups, which refers to a gradual sustained increase in pace near the end of the run. A pickup simply refers to what one of my coaches referred to as "smelling the barn." It is an increase in pace over the final minutes of the run. Pickups serve both psychological and physiological purposes. Psychologically, it ingrains the habit of finishing runs strong. On the physiological side, pickups are a great way to get a slight increase in aerobic stimulus at the end of the run and to teach muscle fiber recruitment under mild fatigue. Pickups should be kept to a minimum in terms of total length if the run is to be considered easy or moderate. Longer pickups can be used as full-blown workouts, which will be discussed later. An example of a pickup would be to have the last 2-10 minutes of a distance run done at an ever increasing pace. The pace can progress down towards marathon pace or even lactate threshold.

Progressions

Lastly, progressions can be used to enhance the stimulus of a distance run, long run, or workout. Progression runs or workouts are a good way to get a slightly different stimulus. This occurs because the first part of the progression serves to pre-fatigue the body. Thought of in terms of muscle fibers, the first part will fatigue the easy to recruit fibers, thus forcing more Fast Twitch or harder to recruit fibers, which aren't normally trained, to get involved as the pace progresses. In place of a distance run, progression runs should be of moderate intensity, starting out at an easy pace and progressing to marathon pace or slightly faster by the end. The runners should feel invigorated at the end, not heavily fatigued from the effort. If they feel heavily fatigued, then the progression was too intense and serves as a workout in and of itself instead of replacing a moderate distance run. These should usually be reserved for use during base training periods when very few truly hard workouts are done. They serve as a great way of transitioning from general training to faster high end aerobic type work. Additionally, FT runners should use short moderate progressions in the place of distance runs on occasion throughout the season. For them, short progression runs allows for an aerobic stimulus that is a little more specific to their race pace.

Another way to mix paces is progressions, which was used in the context of long runs and normal distance runs. Progressions not only are long gradual workouts but can also include very short interval progressions. An interval progression would consist of running each split of a particular interval slightly faster. An example might be doing 4x800m starting at 5k pace but each 200m getting faster until you're down to mile pace by the end of each repetition. Similarly, progressions can simply be "kick style" in which athletes run the first part of the interval at pace and then accelerate to the finish for a designated portion of the interval. An example of this might be 4x800m with the first 600m at 2 mile pace and the last 200m accelerating to the finish. How the workout progresses is up to the coach and can be done in a myriad of ways, but for now progression runs and workouts include any run or repeat where the pace is progressively increased.

Knowing when to add "stuff" is important. For each event, we'll cover how and when to include such additions. In terms of using them in distance runs, some overall guidelines can be suggested. For the most part, the use of strides or surges should serve as an easy way to do some speed maintenance. Surges are slightly more intense than strides, so they better serve as a way to transition to faster workouts. Strides can be done very frequently, especially during the base phase, while surges should probably be limited to a maximum of 2x per week, decreasing in amount as more intensity is added. Pickups should be used even less. During the base phase, one to a maximum of two distance runs with a pickup per week is fine, and this should decrease to one every 1-2 weeks or so as the season progresses. Finally, progression runs are to be used the least. During a base phase they can be used once per week if no other intense workouts are done, and once every 2 weeks if other intense work is being done. During the season, they should be used as a sort of general aerobic maintenance every 2-3 weeks. For Fast Twitch 800-1500m runners, short progressions can be inserted more frequently, one every 1-2 weeks throughout the year.

Long Runs

The long run is typically the holy grail of distance runners. For the majority, it has its own dedicated day in which the long run is done religiously. While the long run is very important, sometimes I feel that it is given too much emphasis, especially for shorter distance runners. For the marathoner, there is no doubt of its importance. The long run mostly serves as a great way to increase general endurance, but for a marathoner it can be used as a specific workout too.

First, the long run provides many of the positive adaptations discussed in the Science section of this book, such as an increase in mitochondria, capillarization, improved fuel system, etc. The long run also provides the important benefit of preparing the body structurally. Additionally, if we look at muscle fiber recruitment during a long run it can be seen that this might be a way to train FT fibers aerobically. During a long run, the easiest to recruit fibers will do all the work to begin with, but as the duration extends, these will start to fatigue and run out of fuel. When this occurs, additional fibers will be recruited to take up the workload. If a run lasts long enough, then you will eventually get to the point where you are training fibers aerobically that seldom get recruited in such a way. If you think of what muscle fibers are doing the work during most of your normal distance runs, it's always the same ones since the duration does not extend too much more than an hour or so in most cases. This is not the case in the long run, which essentially serves as a way of making sure the majority of the muscle fibers get trained aerobically.

For the marathon runner, the most important benefits are the structural and fuel system changes. Structurally the muscles, bones, and joints adapt to the pounding necessary to run 26.2 miles. With each long run, those structures get more resistant to fatigue from the pounding, with the eventual goal of building a body that can handle a full marathon's worth of stress on the structural components. That is why the long run is progressively increased.

The main factor when running a marathon is essentially how well your fuel system is managed. First, a large carbohydrate store increases the fuel supply. Secondly, the percentage of fats used compared to carbohydrates plays a large role. The more that ratio shifts to fat at your desired marathon pace, the more likely it is you'll make it to the finish line without hitting the wall and running out of fuel. For the marathoner, the long run provides one of the ways in which to manipulate these variables.

Since adaptation does not occur unless the stimulus is strong enough, the total fuel system is rarely challenged. Due to its length the long run is the only workout done that will stress the total fuel supply. Following a long run, the body will adapt by increasing its glycogen storage, so that the dangerous decrease in glycogen does not occur next time. The body's other choice for preventing fuel shortage is to increase the amount of fat used at that pace. While this is not of major consequence at slower speeds, if we can get the body to change its fueling ratio at marathon-specific speeds, then performance will be improved. That is one of the reasons why we add "stuff" to long runs.

The same additions that can be added to distance runs can be tacked onto long runs too. Unlike most normal distance runs, long runs can be considered a workout. Therefore, when adding on stuff, it can be more intense as ample recovery time will be given following the run. The basic premise behind the additions is to force muscle fiber recruitment when fatigued and to put the body in crisis so that glycogen-related adaptations occur. Surges and strides are useful for ensuring most of the fiber types are recruited and, in the case of surges, trained. Doing these at the end of a long run is a good way to train the nervous system to send a strong enough signal to recruit fibers when tired. Pickups and progressions are a great way to train muscle fibers rarely recruited with a high end aerobic stimulus. Progression and pickups also are the best way to change the fuel system. The reason is that the first part of the long run depletes the fuel stores to a large degree, and then the body is put under a large amount of stress that leads to fuel system changes in the second half of the run when a progression or pickup is introduced. In essence, we are using the first half or ¾ of the run as a simple way to tire out the muscles that normally do the work and deplete the glycogen stores. The real key is the last additional bit which will then recruit and train the rarely used fibers and put the body in crisis with low fuel so that it will make necessary adaptations to prevent this from occurring again.

Long Run Details for Each Event

For shorter events and FT athletes the long run is simply there for maintenance and strengthening the muscles and joints for general training. The pace of the long run should be relatively easy and is not as important for other groups. Depending on the runner, going too long could hinder performance, especially for a FT runner. The longer the run is the more the harder to recruit muscle fibers will be asked to carry the work load. This is fine to an extent, but it is training these fibers to work very aerobically, which can be counterproductive for an 800m or even 1,500m runner. For this reason, for 800m runners, long runs should be kept to a maximum of around 13 miles, with 10 miles being about average. No additional "stuff" should be added, with the exception of maybe strides.

For the ST 1500m, 5k, and 10k runners, the long run increases in importance. These runners can handle upwards of 17-18 miles for the longer events with most long runs being in the 13-16mi range. These volumes pertain to runners training at a high level; for lower level runners the volume should be reduced to a suitable level. Unlike most books, I do not believe that the long run should be a set percentage of total mileage. Instead, think of the long run as a run or workout in and of itself and think of the desired benefit for that run. These runners will benefit from small additions that focus more on muscle fiber recruitment when tired, as opposed to fuel system changes. The chart below demonstrates a sample long run progression once mileage is built for these runners:

13 miles with 6x45sec surges with 1:45 easy between at the end
14 miles easy
13miles with 5min pickup down to marathon pace at the end
15 miles easy
12 miles with last 4mi progressive from easy to steady to final mile at marathon pace
14 miles with 6x100m strides after

The long run for the marathon runner is of central importance. It should be a main focus and main workout of the schedule. Early on, the emphasis should be on accumulating volume, up to around 22 miles, to prepare the body structurally. As volume reaches higher levels, additions should be introduced that focus on primarily the fuel system. Since this is a full blown workout for the marathoner, the additions will be longer and more intense than with the other runners. How to progress a marathoner's long run will be discussed in the marathon training chapter.

Lastly, before we move on from the long run, the timing of the long run should also be considered. As a rule of thumb, the more intense the long run, the more it needs to be treated as a separate workout with an easy day or two before and after. The marathoner almost always treats it as a workout and needs an easy day before and after. For the other events, it depends on the desired purpose and intensity. A long run the day after a workout works well to increase strength endurance. When this is done, the long run should be mostly recovery to easy pace with no or only small additions tacked on.

Tempo/Threshold Running

Whether it is called a tempo, threshold, or steady state run, these all refer to a longer sustained effort. The duration can be as short as 10 minutes to as long as 70 minutes, depending on the intensity. Similarly, the intensity can vary greatly from 10k pace to marathon pace or a little slower. While some try to pinpoint an exact intensity for these types of workouts, the fact is that the intensity varies with the purpose of the workout. To avoid confusion, I use the word tempo when talking about any long sustained effort, making sure to define the intended intensity, whether it is threshold (half marathon pace), a marathon pace run, or a long steady run.

The intensity is probably the hardest thing to keep under control for these types of workouts. For almost all of these intensities, the pace is slow enough so that it feels only comfortably hard. Given that we have an ingrained idea of hard work must equal better results, the tendency is to push the pace too much. For marathon pace runs for a marathoner, the pace is easily identifiable and of central importance. For runner's not training for a marathon or half marathon, it is often best to do these workouts by feel. Marathon pace runs should be moderate with breathing being elevated but under control. The runner should be able to say a few sentences in between breaths if they have to. The stressor in marathon pace runs is not the pace, but instead the distance.

On the other hand, threshold runs are slightly more intense. They once again should be comfortably hard, but under control. The breathing is more intense but should not be labored. A good way to test whether you are running above or below threshold is the talking test. You should be able to say one or two short sentences, such as "I feel good, I feel great. I want to communicate." Only towards the end of that sentence should the sensation to breathe again be present. The breathing test is a good way for the runner to receive instant feedback, and in fact when just beginning threshold training, it is best to forget about splits and focus on feel.

While many programs will give a set distance to cover or time to run for the threshold work, this sometimes causes the runner to be "holding on" during the latter portion of the workout. While this is fine in some instances, for the majority of the threshold work, unless used for specific training, the goal is a hard but under control workout that results in feeling invigorated, not torn down. To combat this "survival mode" phenomenon, I prefer to do what I call split threshold runs, where I give a total time needed to spend at threshold and the runners get to split it up with short breaks. How they get to this total time is not strict or that important. Since the goal is to have internal adaptations and not getting comfortable at some set pace, what is going on internally is what is most important. For this reason, athletes are told to keep running at threshold until they feel like they are going over the edge or slowing, then to stop and jog 1-3 minutes. Following the jog, they then continue to run at threshold until either the total time has been accumulated or they go over the edge again and have to stop and jog for a short period of time. For younger runners to prevent abuse of this trust, I will sometimes suggest how many times they are allowed to split it up. Generally, 25min or less I let them split it once, 30min twice, and anything over 3 times. What I've found is that this allows runners to have a slightly less stressing workout mentally, allows for the same adaptations as a threshold run with no breaks, and allows for a higher total volume of threshold work.

Progression of Thresholds

By using this method, progression is also quiet easy. Progress by increasing the total time to be spent at threshold each workout by several minutes. For example, in the early base phase the workout might be 15min total at threshold, which then progresses to 20min, 25min, and so on. Around 35min total is the maximum for well-trained runners without it being very taxing. Workouts that include over 35min of total work at threshold can be used, especially for half marathon runners, but should be used sparingly and with plenty of rest and recovery.

There are two other ways to progress thresholds that deserve mention. First, uphill thresholds should be used as a way to further enhance high end aerobic ability when it seems like a ceiling has been reached. By running the threshold session uphill the stress is slightly changed because there is an increase and change in muscle fiber recruitment when running uphill. While most of us don't have a hill long enough, using a treadmill is an effective way. Set the treadmill at 3-4% incline at a fast but comfortably hard speed; then increase the incline every 2 minutes until you get an intensity that feels like threshold according to the talk test. Another way to progress thresholds is by adding short surges during the threshold. The short surges of 20-60sec should be a gradual increase in the pace and then a return to threshold. This will allow for a small amount of lactate to be injected into the system and then used during the subsequent threshold section. Further details on how to implement and manipulate tempos or thresholds are included in each of the chapters on training for each event.

Sprints

On the opposite end of the spectrum from endurance or threshold work is pure sprint training. Since pure sprint training serves as general speed for each event, I'll cover it in depth here. The amount and type of sprint training that should be done depends on the event and type of runner, so the exact details of how and what will be covered in those events chapters. Sprint training for distance runners is essential, but few coaches utilize it. The reason given is usually injury concerns, but, like almost everything, when done correctly the injury risk is relatively low. What are the actual benefits of sprint training for distance runners?

One of the most important is in terms of muscle fiber recruitment. Sprinting is one of the only ways in which a distance runner is going to recruit a very large amount of his harder to recruit FT fibers. Why is this important? First, because in learning how to recruit these muscle fibers, you are increasing the recruitable fiber pool. Having those fibers available to jump in and do some of the work when those ST fibers are being overwhelmed will help an athlete sustain his pace for slightly longer. Second, it allows for the athlete to more easily recruit these fibers at the end of a race when it is time to kick. Lastly, a distance runner rarely stresses his CNS to such a high degree in such a short term. Since everything begins and ends in the brain and CNS, doing some work to deal with a high stress on the CNS could help with central fatigue.

Besides the muscle recruitment aspects of sprinting, there are mechanical benefits too. Sprinting provides an excellent platform to work on and improve running mechanics. You will find few athletes who sprint while landing on their heel like many do during distance running, so translating the mechanics of sprinting while landing (more) correctly to distance running can be done. Also, sprint training can improve the body's elastic energy storage and return system. The body will become better at stiffening the lower leg upon impact, thus improving energy storage and return. In addition, sprinting can improve ground contact time for distance runners.

The most important and overlooked part in successful utilization of sprint training is to actually teach someone how to sprint. Correcting mistakes early and establishing a good foundation on sprinting mechanics early on will save a lot of trouble later, not to mention make for a quicker progression. How to run correctly is covered in the Biomechanics chapter.

It goes beyond just having good running form though. Distance runners need to learn how to truly sprint. It is our nature to try and push harder or increase the effort when we want to run faster. However, this does not work for sprinting. There's a point where trying to increase the effort does more harm than good. When you see most distance runners sprint, they really try to bear down and force it. Compare this to the relatively relaxed sprinting of someone like Usain Bolt. Teaching the concept of relaxed sprinting is essential. To do this, I suggest having runners do their initial sprint training at sub-maximum speeds. A good speed is usually around 400m pace. It is still fast, yet since it is only 100m, the athletes can still get the concept of relaxation while moving fast. As they grasp the concept, increase the speed while trying to get them to keep the same relaxation.

Ideally, this step of teaching relaxed sprinting or relaxed fast running is the first step. However, in many cases, such as when working with a large group of HS runners, this can't be done. It is not the end of the world if you skip this first step. Why? Because, with the progression I've outlined below, it is very easy for runners to discover how to sprint with only minor coaching cues.

Progression of Sprint Training

The first step is Hill Sprints. These are becoming exceedingly popular for distance runners recently, thanks in large part to Renato Canova and later Brad Hudson. In reality distance runners, and even more so, sprinters have been doing short hill sprints for a long time, it's just never been popularized as a key to training.

Hill Sprints work as a great introduction to sprinting because it is almost impossible to get hurt doing them. One reason is that it is harder to sprint wrong while doing them. Sprinting up a hill requires correct foot placement and really emphasizes hip extension. Finally, by sprinting uphill the force requirement is much higher, thus more muscle fibers are recruited.

The slope of the hill depends on the purpose. A steeper slope is used for more strength and a gradual slope used when the goal is for speed. Since these are acting as an introduction for pure speed work, a moderate hill should be used initially before progressing to a more gradual one as time goes by. Start out with only a handful (4-5) of sprints that take 8-10sec and take full recovery in between. Full recovery is needed because these are max intensity repeats and that means at least 2-3min between each. To keep myself and athletes I've worked with from doing these with too little recovery, we used to play a rousing game of throw the rock at a pole to see who could hit the pole the most times during the entire hill sprint session. It may seem trivial, but it served its purpose of keeping the recovery long enough. For distance runners used to short recovery periods, it is often a task to get someone to rest long enough. The sprints are initially so short that most runners don't feel fatigued after the first couple, so they rush the recovery. So, to keep them from doing this, throwing rocks at a pole can be very helpful.

These hill sprints start during the base period and are done once perhaps twice a week. Each week, the number of hill sprints is increased until the runners get to around 10. Sometimes the length is also slightly increased (from 8 sec to 10 sec). After several weeks of hill sprints, the transition then shifts to flat sprints

Flat Sprints

The Hill sprints serve to prepare athletes for flat sprints. These are, preferably, done on the track. Even more so than with hill sprints, the tendency is for runners to try to tense up when running at maximum speed. To prevent this, I often say that these are to be done at around 95%. This prevents them from "forcing" the speed and overstraining to run fast.

To start with, the length of these sprints is generally 60m. Once again, full rest is needed, even more than with hill sprints. After building up to 8-10 hill sprints, I normally start off athletes with 4 flat sprints because they are more demanding physically and on the nervous system. Once flat sprints are introduced there is a gradual progression. For most runners transitioning to flat sprints, begin by alternating between doing hill sprints and flat sprints each week. After this the exact progression depends on the type of athlete and the event. Shorter distance runners (800-1,500m) and FT type runners benefit more from flat sprints, while ST runners tend to benefit more from hill sprints. Both groups benefit from following the initial progression of hill sprints first and then flat sprints. During this transition is when the emphasis and details of what kind of sprint work they should use changes.

Speed Endurance

The final step in the sprint progression is extending speed to speed endurance. This step is sometimes not used at all or greatly deemphasized depending on the goal event and athlete type. For shorter events and FT runners, speed endurance can serve as general endurance or speed support. While more will be covered in the event sections for these athletes, the progression should continue to speed endurance.

Speed endurance reps refer to max or near max sprints that last up to about 40sec or 300m in length. The goal is to extend your maximum speed. These can be done after both hill sprints and flat sprints or as a workout by itself. Which kind of sprints we will use depends on the training emphasis, goal, and time of the year. The general principles for adding speed endurance are the same for both types of sprints. First cut back on the pure sprints and initially add one rep of speed endurance at the end. For hill sprints, cut back from 10 to 5, and add in one 15-20sec sprint uphill at the end. For flat sprints, cut back from something like 5x100m to 3x60-80m with one 150m full sprint at the end.

The progression for speed endurance is similar to the other sprints. First add one or maybe two more reps. Then slightly increase the length of the reps up to a maximum of 250-300m. For almost every runner except FT 800m types, speed endurance sessions are best done in combination with pure sprint work. For FT 800m runners, a separate workout of entirely speed endurance work can be done.

6x8sec Hill Sprints
8x8sec HS
10x8sec HS
4x60m flat sprints
8x10sec HS
5x80m flat sprints
10x10sec HS
2x60m, 2x80m, 2x100m
8x10sec HS + 1x20sec
4x60m, 1x150m
2x60, 2x80m,100m, 150m, 200m
4x100m, 150m, 200m
Maintenance-Every ~2wks- 3-5x60m sprints and 2x150m OR 2x60m,100m,150m, 200m.

Interval/Repeat Workouts

Intervals and repeats are self-explanatory and should be familiar to all runners reading this book. The only confusion that could occur is that some coaches differentiate the meaning of intervals and repeats based on the speed and rest taken. Instead, in this book they will be treated as the same with the specifics of rest and intensity given in the details of the workout.

Briefly, intervals refer to running segments of various lengths with rest periods in between. These workouts can also be broken into sets. Sets allow for a larger rest period inserted in the middle of the workout, for example instead of doing 10x400m with 60sec rest, breaking it into sets would make the workout 2x (5x400) with 60sec rest between repeats, and 5min between sets. These workouts can be manipulated in an endless number of ways depending on the purpose of the workout. The intensity, rest periods, set numbers, and how paces change or progress are all factors that can change the purpose of the workout. Contrary to popular belief intervals are not only for speed or anaerobic development but can be used for aerobic support or even general endurance development. The manipulation of the intervals determines its effect. Next, a couple of the common ways to use intervals will be discussed.

Aerobic Intervals

Aerobic intervals are interval sessions that are manipulated in such a way that while you may be running at faster speeds, the metabolic stress and the adaptation is an aerobic one. To accomplish this goal, the interval distance is kept very short, with short rest periods in between intervals, a low total volume, and possibly long rest periods between sets. While the details differ on the desired result, the interval distance is generally kept less than 600m and is often in the 100-200m range. While the pace is faster than what is usually considered an aerobic workout, because of the aforementioned manipulations, the paces can be as fast as even 800m pace, and the benefits are almost entirely coming from the endurance side. It is best to think of this as a mini workout or as easy pace/rhythm work where the runners learn how to run relaxed at a faster pace.

This type of workout is ideal for 800-1,500m and FT type runners as it allows for running at a pace that is closer to specificity yet highly aerobic. That is why these types of workouts can serve as general or aerobic support for those events. Similarly, for longer event groups, aerobic intervals allow for running at speed type intensities without the negative stress of an intense workout. That's why they are a great way to transition into harder interval sessions or to use as a maintenance type workout throughout the year. Lastly, they work well during the peaking period to provide just enough stimulus and can function as a way to ingrain race pace.

Another use for short aerobic intervals is to teach the body to use lactate as a fuel and enhance recovery. Lactate can be used as an energy source through the lactate shuttle. One goal of training is to teach your body how to use lactate as a fuel at higher intensities. The best way to do this is through alternation work, but another option is to use aerobic interval work in the middle of a more intense interval session. This can be accomplished by inserting moderate 100-300m segments in the middle of an interval as part of the "recovery." Instead of doing 4x800m at 3k or 5k pace with 2-3 minutes rest, change the rest to 100m jog then 3x150m at 10k-threshold pace with 50m jog then 100m jog and start the next 1000m. These types of aerobic intervals were developed in the 1950's by world class coach, Mihaly Igloi.

Besides promoting lactate use/clearance, it also aids in recovery. If you see a runner struggling during an intense workout and you still want him to get in more volume of training, a good way is to insert a couple of short aerobic intervals. By doing the short aerobic intervals, the athlete gets in some work, which helps him mentally, and aids in recovery.

An example of this would be if during 6x800m at 5k down to 3k pace the athlete is struggling hard after 4, insert 3x200m at 10k-LT w/ easy 200m. Then give him 2min rest and finish with the last 2x800. For these intervals use relaxed 100s, 150s, 200s, 300s, etc. at 3k to threshold type paces in the middle of workouts, or in between sets, such as inserting 150m easy strides in between sets of 2x5x400 at mile pace w/ 60sec recovery. While the details of how to use aerobic intervals will be discussed in the chapter on each event group, below are some examples of aerobic intervals and their uses:

Aerobic Interval Examples:

Use	Example
Race pace Rhythm for miler	For miler: 8-10x200 at mile pace w/ 200m jog
Endurance support for 800m runner	2x(6x150) at 3k down to 1mi pace w/ 50m jog between reps, 400m jog between sets.
Direct aerobic support for 800m runner	2 x(8x100) at 1mile pace w/ 30sec rest in between reps, 5min between sets.
Speed Maintenance or Transition for 5k-10k runner	3x(400m, 200m) at 3k pace w/ 200m jog between everything

Hill Repeats

One way to progress and overload a workout is to add a hill component to it. The hill component slightly changes the stress due to a different muscle fiber recruitment pattern. Hills increase the force required, so a greater number of fibers are recruited.

The incline of the hill obviously plays a role. The more gradual the hill, the more the emphasis is on speed, while the steeper the hill the more strength plays a role. Almost any type of workout can be done as a hill work if the goal is to add a strength component. Longer hill (400+ meters) repeats are great for enhancing strength endurance, while shorter and faster repeats (less than 400m) work well to increase the speed side of the component or specific speed endurance.

In addition to doing straight hill repeats, hills can be blended into the workout so that portions of the workout are done on the flat ground and portions on a hill. By doing the workout this way, you are introducing a strength component that will force muscle fiber recruitment during the hill session and then train those fibers during the flat ground. An example of this would be to do 400m repeats with every 400m alternating between being on flat ground and on a hill.

Lastly, hill repeats are useful as a way to transition to faster work and to delay a peak. Often runners and coaches get in trouble with peaking early because they do too much specific or speed type work too quickly. One workaround to this problem is to make more of the speed type sessions be hill repeat sessions. Use your imagination, and use hills as a way to further progress a workout.

Alternations

Alternations were briefly covered in the Individualization chapter, but to refresh, they consist of alternating a faster and a slower segment with no rest in between. Or as the namesake says, alternating faster running with recovery segments. One key point is that the recovery segment is not a slow jog but is a steady effort that allows just enough recovery so that the subsequent faster portion can be completed. Alternations can be used for anything from marathon pace running to all the way down to 400m pace. The difference lies in the lengths of the two segments and the paces of each.

The basic premise behind alternation work is that the slower segment does not allow for full recovery; the athlete has to work to stay on target during the slower segment. Oftentimes it is not the faster segment that gives athletes problems; it is the slower segment. In looking at the lactate fatigue theory, alternations work to progressively adapt the body to working at higher and higher steady lactate levels because lactate is produced during the faster portion and then if the recovery portion is done at a steady pace, lactate remains elevated. In elite athletes, alternations can be used to develop a lactate steady state at 5k to Half Marathon paces.

The faster the paces of the alternation segment lengths will be, the shorter the segment lengths for the fast portion. They can be as short as 50m for 400m pace, but usually in the 100-400m range for 800-1,500m pace. For 5k-10k pace the faster lengths can start at 200-400m but generally progress to 800-1,000m lengths for 5k pace and up to 1mile or slightly more for 10k pace. For the half and full marathon, the lengths can span several miles. As you have probably noticed, the idea is to progress these workouts as fitness improves. Progression can be done in several ways including increasing the pace of the recovery portion, increasing the length of the faster portion, or decreasing the length of the recovery portion.

Early on, the recovery portion lengths are much longer than the faster portions, but as the season progresses the goal should be to make the two segment lengths come together so that eventually the faster portion length is longer than the recovery portion. Similarly, the pace of the recovery portion should start off far away from the faster portion and inch closer as the season progresses. Initially the recovery portion can be a pace that is done on steady distance runs, but it should work its way down to close to marathon pace or faster depending on the goal. The recovery portion's pace impacts what is worked on in terms of lactate. If the pace is slower, then the body is training to use lactate during the recovery portion. If the pace is more intense, or close to lactate threshold, then lactate is in balance during the recovery portion and the body is learning how to deal with a higher lactate steady state. The former would be useful for a marathon or general endurance, while the latter would be useful for a 1,500-10k runner's specific endurance. Total volume depends on the type of alternation workout done and at what level the athlete is at. Start with modest lower volumes and increase progressively. A good rule of thumb for all paces shorter than half marathon is to max out the volume at around that race distance or slightly longer for the 5k-10k paces and around 1.5x race distance for the shorter race paces.

Alternations can be used for every purpose, running the gamut from aerobic support to specific endurance to speed endurance. How to exactly use alternations for each purpose will be covered in that event group's chapter. For some general guidelines, alternating race pace with a steady effort can develop specific endurance. Aerobic support and direct endurance support for most events can be done by alternating two close but aerobic speeds (such as 10k and marathon pace). Direct speed support can be done by alternating a pace that is faster than specific with a steady recovery portion (such as the classic 200m at mile pace, 200m at steady pace for a 3k runner). Lastly, speed endurance (also general speed, or anaerobic support for some groups) can be accomplished by alternating a near max speed for a short distance of 50m with a short recovery distance (of 50m in this example) where the runner simply relaxes and takes his foot off the gas. These speed endurance alternations are very intense, thus volume is limited to around 400m per set, and only a handful of sets are done.

Example Progression of Alternation Workout for 5k Specific Endurance:
- 4 miles of alternating 200m at 5k pace w/ 1400m at steady pace (5:50 pace)
- 4mi of alternating 400 at 5k pace w/ 1200m at steady pace (5:45 pace)
- 4mi of alternating 600 at 5k pace w/ 1000m at steady pace (5:40 pace)
- 4mi of alternating 800 at 5k pace w/ 800m at steady pace (5:40 pace)
- 4mi of alternating 900 at 5k pace w/ 700m at steady pace (5:40 pace)

Combo Workouts

Combo workouts mean exactly what it sounds like. It is the combining of two or more different workout types or intensities. As an example for a 5k runner looking to work on aerobic support and pure speed, a runner might do 20 minutes at threshold followed by 6x10sec sprints.

Another example would be to combine 1,000m repeats at 5k pace with a set of 200's at mile pace at the end. The combo does not have to just be two intensities but can include several different ones. For an aerobic refresh, a combo workout might be 10min at marathon pace, 7min at threshold pace, 4min at 10k pace, and 2min at 5k pace.

Combo workouts are mostly used as transitions or maintenance work, but occasionally they are used when a specific adaptation is required, such as strength endurance. To use as a transition workout, simply do ¾ of the intended workout and then add in a small segment at the next categorization level. For example in transition from aerobic support to direct support for a 5k runner, they would do 25min at threshold followed by a short break and 5min at 10k pace. The latter portion would act as an introduction to direct support (10k pace). Similarly, the combining of several different intensities or categorization levels provides an excellent maintenance stimulus. The aforementioned aerobic refresh workout is a prime example of a maintenance workout.

Blend Workouts

Blend workouts are when two or more different intensities are intermixed and serve as a way of connecting them. Most training programs move abruptly from one type of workout to another; instead there should be some form of connection that integrates the various workout types. Blend workouts are one way to accomplish this and are very useful for transitioning and bringing the speed and endurance component together. There are several different ways to use blend workouts. The changes of paces back and forth within the workout cause several unique physiological events. First, muscle fiber recruitment is constantly changed, as are lactate levels. During the faster portion, more fibers are recruited, and more lactate is produced. Then during the slower portions the runner has to deal with higher lactate levels than normal at that pace. Essentially, by doing the workout this way, the metabolic stress that is seen during the race is mimicked and can be introduced much earlier.

In addition, muscle fibers that are recruited during the fast portion, likely extend their endurance during the slower portion. Depending on the desired adaptation, the difference in pace can be quiet large or quiet narrow. Generally a long and short segment is included in blends. You can blend with an equal 1 to 1 ratio of long and short or change the ratio to include more long or short segments depending on what the focus is. An example of a blend workout would be 1000, 400, 900, 300, 800, 200 with the long segments at 5k pace and the short at mile pace with 3min rest between. An example of a complex blend is: 900 (5k pace), 400(1mi pace), 800 (3k pace), 300 (800 pace), 500 (1mi pace). The possibilities are endless as to how these are manipulated and depend on the desired goal. While more in depth discussion on how to use blend workouts will be covered shortly, there are several options as to what paces you choose and how to progress including:

1. Start with slower paces at both the long and short segments and progress downwards.
    a. This starts as aerobic support for race pace and progresses to specific endurance and then to speed endurance
2. Start with the extremes and progress towards specificity. This means it starts as general or special support and then progresses towards specific endurance.
    a. In this case, the early workouts train for fiber recruitment and progressively train endurance of those fibers.
    b. For example: start with LT+ hill sprints, progress to 10k/1600 then to 5k/3200 if the 5k is your specific pace.

Maintenance Workouts

I've mentioned before that all categories of training are included during each phase of training; it is just the emphasis that changes. Once something is built, it takes much less work to maintain it. Given this concept, once a component is built and the emphasis changes, it goes into maintenance mode. That means that a small stimulus needs to be applied every ~2 weeks depending on what that component is. The question is how much is needed for a maintenance mode?

A good rule of thumb is that maintenance workouts should be about ½ to ¾ of what the workout for that component was when you were building it. For example, for threshold runs, if you built up to 30min total, then 15-20min total would serve as maintenance. Since it takes less of a stimulus, a good way to maintain various components is to use combo workouts to combine two or more paces. The one exception to this rule is long runs. While volume can be decreased slightly for maintenance long runs, it should not be cut as dramatically as seen in other workouts because the volume itself is the stimulus. Instead of cutting the distance by up to a half, only a few miles should be taken off during a maintenance long run. The difference is that a maintenance long run should occur at an easy pace.

For the maintenance of most aerobic components (general endurance, aerobic support, and direct endurance support) a moderate fartlek or a breakdown interval session does the job well. Simply use a descending ladder to hit each intensity once or twice to serve as maintenance. An example for maintaining general endurance and aerobic support for a 5k runner would be 10min at marathon pace, 7min at threshold, 5min at 10k, 3min at 10k with a couple minutes jog in between. For general endurance for many events, long runs serve as maintenance, or even slight pickups during distance runs will have the same effect.

On the other hand, the speed side is often best maintained with easy intervals or rhythm work. These workouts do not have to be extremely taxing. 100s-400s with relatively long rest at anaerobic support and direct support paces accomplish the goal. 6x300 switching between 1mile and 800 pace is an example for a 3,000m runner. Additionally, a short segment can be added on as a combo to the end of other workouts, such as doing a set of 4x200 after a threshold. Pure speed is the easiest to maintain as doing a set of hill sprints or doing flying 100m repeats after a distance run or event specific workout is never hard to fit in.

Specific Workouts

Before explaining how to bring this all together for each separate race distance, the concept of specific endurance needs to be thoroughly explained. There are several universal concepts on building specific endurance that apply to every event. As mentioned previously, specific endurance refers to increasing the length that a runner can last at a given pace. This is best understood using the fatigue theories discussed; specific endurance is increased when fatiguing factors at race pace are reduced, the rate of accumulation of fatiguing factors is decreased, and/or the maximum amount of fatiguing factors that a runner can withstand over the entire race distance is increased.

With specific endurance training, the goal is to progress the training so that the runner can adapt to an ever increasing workload. If the runner is able to handle a higher workload via changes in interval length, total volume, rest periods, or speed, then one of the three adaptations happened which resulted in an increase in specific endurance. The runner either reduced fatigue products at race pace, decreased the rate of accumulation of fatigue, or increased the maximum amount they could withstand. What occurred depends on how the specific endurance workout was progressed. There are several different ways to go about creating and developing specific endurance. Most runners should come at specific endurance development from at least two different ways. Each event and runner type will respond slightly better to a different method of development.

The pattern of development is to start with very small spices of specific work during the base phase, such as surges or rhythm intervals, and gradually increase the workload until it reaches its highest 2 weeks before the peak race.

The different methods of developing specific endurance include:
- **Alternations**
- **Bottom up**- Intervals are run at specific pace and the length is progressively increased
- **Top down**- The distance of the intervals is present, the pace is progressively increased to a more specific pace
- **Blend**- Use blend workouts to work from the extreme pace of endurance and speed in the same workout and bring them together.

The easiest way to develop and progress specific endurance is figure out what the starting point is and then decide where you are going with the workout. In other words, determine what is the last specific workout that is needed for your race. This last workout provides the destination. If you have the starting point and the finish point, coming up with the in between is relatively simple. In designing a final workout, keep in mind that you want it to be a challenging workout that is highly specific to the race. That means relatively long intervals at the pace they want to run with relatively short rest in between. Examples of final specific workouts for each group are listed below:

Example Final Specific Workouts:

800m	1500m/1mile	5k	10k	Marathon
2x(200,600) with 75sec rest and 5-6min	2x800m w/ 2min rest at 1mile pace	3x1mile w/ 2min rest at 5k pace	2mi, 2x1.5mi w/ 3min rest at 10k pace	8mi easy, 12mi at Marathon Pace

Bottom Up Method

The bottom up method starts with short intervals with very short rest in between reps, but the reps are split into sets so that it is feasible. In addition, the total volume of the session matches the total volume of the final workout from the beginning. To progress, the distance of the reps is gradually increased and the numbers of sets are diminished. Below is an example of this progression.

Bottom up Method for 5k:

3 x (4x400) at 5k w/ 30sec rest. 5min b/t sets
3x(3x600) at 5k w/ 40sec rest. 5min b/t sets
2x(3x800) at 5k w/ 45sec rest. 5min b/t sets
2x (1000,800,700) at 5k w/ 45sec rest. 5min b/t sets
5x1000 at 5k w/ 60-75sec rest

Top-Down Method

The top down method is also the traditional way to increase specific endurance. Roger Bannister's advisor/coach Franz Stampfl was one of the earlier advocates of this system. For Americans it is better demonstrated in the Bowerman or Oregon method of training in which intervals were run at date pace that progressively increased to goal race pace. An example would be to start by doing 400's at 68sec in the fall and progress to doing 400's at 60sec at the end of the season for a miler aiming at 4 minutes. The central idea is that the distance is there and the pace is increased or the rest manipulated. Since the pace starts off slower than goal pace, the early sessions serve as aerobic or direct support training and only later become specific endurance training. An example of this type of progression for a mile runner with a goal of running 60sec pace is:

- 10x400m with 30sec rest in 68
- 10x400m with 45sec rest in 66
- 10x400m with 60sec rest in 64
- 2x(5x400m) with 60sec rest and 3min between sets in 62
- 2x(5x400m) with 60sec rest and 3min between sets in 60
- 10x400m with 75sec rest in 60
- 10x400m with 60sec rest in 60
- 2x(5x400m) with first set in 60, second in 59 with 60sec rest and 3min between sets.

Alternation Method

The alternation method of creating specific endurance consists of alternating one segment at specific pace and the other at a recovery pace. Like in the other specific work, the amount of specific work is gradually increased. This is done by increasing the length of the specific segment and/or decreasing the length of the recovery segment. In addition, the recovery segment's pace can be increased so that it is closer to specific pace. These alternation workouts provide a different kind of stimulus than traditional race pace work and is a great way to create specific endurance. Below is an example of a progression of alternation workouts:

- 4 miles of alternating 200m at 5k pace w/ 1400m at steady pace (5:50 pace)
- 4mi of alternating 400 at 5k pace w/ 1200m at steady pace (5:45 pace)
- 4mi of alternating 600 at 5k pace w/ 1000m at steady pace (5:40 pace)
- 4mi of alternating 800 at 5k pace w/ 800m at steady pace (5:40 pace)
- 4mi of alternating 900 at 5k pace w/ 700m at steady pace (5:40 pace)

Blend Method

The Blend method consists of using workouts to emphasize the extremes of speed and endurance and then bring them together. By doing the workouts this way, the early focus is on developing support from each side, while getting more specific as the workout progresses. The blend workout does not have to culminate in an entire specific workout, but instead can keep more elements of the endurance or speed side depending on whether the goal is to develop strength endurance or speed endurance at specific paces. An example for a miler trying to run 60sec quarters is as follows:

- 4x(1200,Hill Sprint) with 1200 at 10k pace and 3min rest between everything.
- 3x(1,000, 200) with 1min rest between reps, 3min between sets, 1000m at 5k pace and 200 at 800 pace
- 3x(800, 300) with 1min rest b/t reps, 3min b/t sets, 800 is at 3k pace, 300 at mile pace.
- 3x(600,200) with 45sec rest b/t reps, 3min b/t sets, 600 and 200 at mile pace.

Putting it Together

Combining the different ways of developing specific endurance is a good way to diversify the stimulus and makes sure that every runner gets a training stimulus that is effective. Certain methods will be better for different runner types and events. Any of the combinations can work, but below is an example of combining the alternation and bottom up method.

During base phase: 8x30sec at race pace w/ 2:30 easy in the middle of an easy 8 mile run. Then progress to:

- 3 x (4x400) at 5k w/ 30sec rest. 5min b/t sets
- 4mi of alternating 400 at 5k pace w/ 1200m at steady pace
- 3x(3x600) at 5k w/ 40sec rest. 5min b/t sets
- 4mi of alternating 600 at 5k pace w/ 1000m at steady pace
- 2x(3x800) at 5k w/ 45sec rest. 5min b/t sets
- 4mi of alternating 800 at 5k pace w/ 800m at steady pace
- 5x1000m at 5k pace w/ 90sec rest

Lydiard Style Time Trials

Although not a style of progression to create specific endurance, Lydiard style time trials are a good way to bring everything together as the last specific workout. A Lydiard time trial is when you complete the race distance at a very strong, but under control pace or when you run at or near goal pace for around ¾ of the race distance. In the former type, you are adjusting to running a strong pace for the entire race distance. The pace of such an effort should be about 2-4% slower than your actual race pace over that distance. The latter method is used to adapt to running race pace for a longer period of time than normal in training. Oftentimes, past around the halfway point a runner is in new territory in terms of how far they have run at that pace before. By doing a trial at around ¾ of the event, the runner gets to experience that feeling in practice. These time trials are also good feedback on how a runner is developing and where to go from there on with the training.

All of these methods in creating specific endurance work well. Which one you use depends on the type of athlete you have (remember FT vs. ST) and what you are trying to accomplish. For example, using the alternation approach will probably be more suited to a ST athlete because the 'rests' are kept at a decent pace. A FT runner might not be able to accomplish the workout because he won't recover as quickly on the rests. On the other hand, using some of the alternation progression might help that FT athlete work on his weakness and improve his ability to deal with lactate while running at a steady pace. Consider this example and the athletes themselves when choosing your preferred progression.

19

Bringing It All Together: Periodization

"No matter how successful you are, change is always good. There can never be a status quo."
Billy Beane

It is finally time to put everything together. All of the workout types, goals, and theories are defined. Now let's look at how to mix everything together and come out with the best race performance possible. Training is not something that occurs in a one-season vacuum that ignores all training done before or to be done after. Instead, training interacts and is fluid in nature. We will take the all-encompassing approach and look at how training should develop throughout ones career as well as within the season.

The Big Picture: Periodization Within a Career

One major problem with most training theories is that they have one overarching model of training and there is little variation. What they are basically saying is that with only minor adjustments in volume or intensity a developing High School runner should follow the exact same program as a Master's runner. Knowing that the goal of training is to change runners on a physiological level and knowing the changes in our physiology as we develop, how can the same program be optimal for all runners? The answer is that it can't. Instead we'll outline the ideal development of training as an athlete grows. Obviously, we do not live in an ideal world, so sometimes certain phases of the training have to be accelerated in the real world, but the concepts and progressions hold true.

Legendary distance coach Joe Vigil is fond of saying that American runners are tens of thousands of miles behind our African counterparts when we start running. His point is that by the time our runners start in High School, the African runners have accumulated a large volume of training by living an active lifestyle. Whether this consists of running several miles to and from school every day or performing hard work on the land, African runners are establishing a very large general fitness base. Several prominent coaches have stated this as the reason for their dominance.

During these developmental years, the analogy is always that you are laying a foundation on which to build your house. The larger and better constructed the foundation, the more room for the intricacies of the house. The finishing touches of the house are the more intense workouts that are added once official training begins. The African runners' foundation is much larger, so they have more room to add these finishing touches. The second problem is that once Americans start training, we take the opposite approach and try to add the finishing touches before developing the foundation. This is often seen in Junior High or even High School track where the focus is on specific interval training with little attention paid to developing a general endurance or speed base. Let's look at exactly how a runner should develop in terms of mileage, intensity, density, training distribution, and focus.

The mileage question is always the first to be asked. The answer is that it depends on the person and their event, but some overarching principles remain. Total volume should be progressively increased throughout a runner's career until he reaches the point that is necessary for maximizing his potential in that event. How long it takes depends on the goal event, but for most non-marathon runners max mileage can be progressed to within 5-7yrs of beginning serious training.

Maximum mileage needs for event specialist (low end is for FT athletes, high end for ST):

800m:	1500m:	5k:	10k:	Marathon:
35-80mpw	60-100mpw	75-110mpw	85-120mpw	90-140mpw

However, there comes a point where mileage is counterproductive. Once a large volume of training has been done there will be diminishing returns, and the same amount is no longer needed to maintain the stimulus. In addition, more and more of the training will be shifting from general to more specific. Thus, a mileage drop is needed. This once again depends on the goals of the athlete, but once an athlete hits his peak mileage, a drop in mileage can occur the next season or mileage can be kept constant for a year or two before that drop occurs. For master's athletes this is of particular importance. Master's athletes should cut back on their mileage levels due to changes in how they recover.

The next idea is how does intensity and focus change throughout the years. Beginning runners should focus on the extremes and have a much higher percentage of general training. The goal should be to gradually increase the amount of general aerobic running they are doing and perfect their general speed. Other types of work can be done but it should be low volume and low stress. By approaching it this way, the runners will develop a large aerobic system, gradually adapt their musculoskeletal system for the demands of running, and impart neuromuscular development and good biomechanics through pure speed training. Or simply put, the first couple of years should be spent on laying a foundation on which to develop a better runner.

As athletes progress, the percentage of their training devoted to general training should decrease as more emphasis should be put first on support paces and later on specific paces. During the time period when the runner is shooting for his best performances (i.e., post collegiate 25-34yrs or so for pro runners), the emphasis should be on specific training with slightly reduced mileage to allow for this. As athletes get older, more emphasis is needed on pure speed training, as speed losses with older endurance athletes are common. To help combat this, speed and strength training designed to maintain strength levels, Fast Twitch fiber numbers, and neural recruitment is a necessity.

Lastly is the concept of density. Density refers to how much intensity can be handled within a period of time. A common measurement is how many intense workouts can be done per week. Surprisingly, younger athletes with their superior recoverability can handle higher levels of density. That does not mean that they necessarily need it though. During the early post-collegiate years, density should probably be highest since a large base has already been established yet the athletes are young enough to still recover well. In general density should decrease as one ages and loses the ability to bounce back and recover as quickly.

Within Season Periodization

The next step is looking at how to plan training for one season. While the basic ideas of periodization have been mentioned before, an in depth look is needed. With older models of periodization you basically had one training period focused on one training goal, and the subsequent period focused on an entirely different goal. An example would be a base period focused on aerobic running, followed by a threshold period, then VO2max, then a speed phase.

Unlike this traditional model, in the following method there is rarely a period of training where only one or two types of work are done. The only exceptions are when coming back from a break post season or coming back from a long layoff. Instead, during each training period, the vast majority of the training components are included; the only thing that changes is their emphasis. The result is that peak fitness is never incredibly far away like in the traditional model, and also peak racing can be sustained for a longer time period. This is a necessity in modern track and road racing as athletes no longer plan for just one big race per year but have many important competitions scattered throughout.

The training periods can be broken down into a base phase where general training is emphasized, a pre-competition phase where support training is emphasized, and a competition phase where specific training is emphasized. While I am breaking down the season into phases for the purpose of easy conceptualization, in reality they are really blends; they are not distinct and abrupt phases but rather blend into each other.

Base Period

During the base period, the emphasis is on developing the foundation for all subsequent training. The goal is to establish all the necessary components but not to start putting them together yet. This means creating not only an aerobic base but also a musculoskeletal base and a neuromuscular base. This means that general endurance and speed training are emphasized while specific and support intensities are introduced.

For developing general endurance, the important part is duration, not necessarily intensity. The goal should be to increase total mileage and duration of work to appropriate levels. Contrary to popular dogma, the 10% rule of increasing mileage has little value. The rule of thumb is that mileage can be progressively increased rather rapidly up to the amount that the runner has successfully maintained in the past. For experienced runners coming off a layoff, this could mean a jump from not running to 70mpw in 2-3 weeks. Where mileage increases are a concern is when venturing into new territory. When increasing mileage to a level above this, it is best to add one mile per day to your running. The goal for mileage during the base period is to progressively increase to maximum level for the season.

The long run also should be progressively increased to its maximum duration during this phase. Once the long run reaches its maximum length, then intensity or add-ons should be considered. For most event groups aerobic support training should be gradually introduced after an initial 2-4 week period of mostly mileage and general speed. Initially this could be introduced as pickups or gradual progressions. As the athletes progress, the introduction of Lactate Threshold (LT) runs should be done for the majority of events. These should be progressively increased during the latter base phase and continue through to the early pre-competition phases.

General speed would start with strides first to get the runner neurally and biomechanically ready for faster work. Following a week of this, runners can then include hill sprints initially, eventually progressing to flat sprints or some combination of each. Towards the latter end of the base phase, anaerobic support or, for shorter events, speed endurance is introduced. It is done mostly in the form of add-ons or combo work.

While general endurance and speed are emphasized, small spices or introductions of specific work should be included. For the majority of events, this will be something as simple as strides or surges during a distance run, but during the latter base phase this could include some rhythm work.

Lastly, during the latter parts of the phase, transition into the pre-competition period should be done with small spices of aerobic/anaerobic and direct support thrown in. This is usually done in the form of some sort of add-on or combo work depending on what the support paces are. For example, a LT run might be cut down by 10min in length but have a 5min segment at aerobic support pace added on.

Pre-Competition Phase

The pre-competition phase represents a transition in emphasis to support paces. The goal of this phase is to start to bring together and assemble the components built up during the base phase. The amount of general endurance training will decrease to maintenance levels. What this means is that for most events, mileage is reduced slightly and the longer high end aerobic training is reduced to maintenance levels. The long run, unless it is of central importance to the event, is used as a maintenance tool for general endurance. That means that additions to it are limited and most of the time it serves as a long easy run. The exception is that it can occasionally be turned into a long steady or progressive run for maintaining high-end aerobic general endurance.

The early part of the pre-competition phase consists of carrying on the aerobic support work introduced during the base phase and transitioning that to direct support work. Transition can occur in the form of alternations getting faster, blending workout, or combo workouts. On the speed side, for shorter events speed endurance should be maintained early on and transition to direct speed support. For longer events, pure speed goes into maintenance mode with it being done maybe once every 2 weeks depending on the goal. Lastly, during this phase the specific endurance progression should be introduced. The goal is to take the introduction or maintenance specific work done during the base phase and start to progress it towards the end goal during the last part of the specific period.

Competition Phase

The Competition phase is all about having all of the components assembled and simply shining them up to operate at peak performance. The general endurance and mileage drop slightly. More importantly, because of the increase in intensity, the density of training has to be manipulated. Density should decrease due to the higher level of emphasis put on specific workouts. That means more recovery training and more time between intense sessions.

The goal during this phase is to do everything to enhance specific endurance and specific speed endurance. The progression of specific endurance is continued with a new workout every 10-14 days. This is accompanied by some blend work introduced to combine the specific pace with direct speed so that specific speed endurance is increased. This is important because it enhances the ability to finish off a strong pace. Direct and aerobic/anaerobic support are relegated to maintenance duty and often used as a combination workout. These are general guidelines for periodization; specifics for each event are covered in their chapters.

Lengths of Phases

To determine the lengths of phases first start with your peak workout and work backwards to determine how much time you have. The lengths of each phase will depend on the level of the athlete, the type of athlete, and the goals. Slow Twitch athletes can hold peaks longer than FT athletes so that should be taken into account. Additionally, the base built determines how much specific work can be done. The greater the general foundation is the more specific work can be done. Lastly, the lifetime fitness of an athlete plays a role. As a rule, the more lifetime training volume underneath their belts, the less time is needed during the general period.

Certain phases can be lengthened if needed by introducing what I call a refresh period. A refresh period refers to a 7-14 day period where the focus returns to general or support training. This can be strategically implanted during the specific period to make sure the athlete's performance is sustained.

As a guideline, the specific period can last 6-10 weeks, the support period 4-8 weeks, and the general period 3-8 weeks depending on what the focus is. These can be shortened and lengthened based on the athlete's needs and goals and are not set in stone. It ultimately depends on how much time is needed to build and progress to where you need to be.

Special Training Periods

In addition to the normal training phases and workouts, there are a couple of different special short periods of training that can be introduced throughout the training period. The use of these special periods is to shift the focus to one particular aspect to try and maximize it.

One type of special training phase is what I call a refresh period. A refresh period is a short period of time (usually 3-10 days) in which the emphasis is put entirely on one or two training goals that have not been addressed in a while. The goal is to give a boost to that particular area. The aerobic refresh period is designed to refresh the athlete aerobically. This is of particular use in the middle of a long competitive season or when trying to prolong a peak. During an aerobic refresh, general and support endurance work is done. On the opposite side is the Anaerobic Refresh, which is a short period of time when you go back to general speed or speed endurance work to maintain each or to bring the anaerobic system to a higher level during a period of de-emphasis. Lastly, a general refresh period is when general endurance and general speed are given complete emphasis during a short period of time. As mentioned previously, refresh periods are very useful in prolonging a peak or in the middle of a European-like competitive season in which there are frequent races followed by a gap in racing and then more racing.

Another type of special period is what is called a special block of training. Used in swimming and by running coaches such as Percy Cerutty and Renato Canova, it is a very intense short period of time that tries to take advantage of the supercompensation effect. The period can be as short as one day, where a double workout is done, or consist of a weekend of intense training. The blocks should consist of two or more, depending on their length, hard workouts aimed at different purposes. A commonly used block is the double workout day where a hard workout is done in the morning and then another hard workout is done in the afternoon. What workout to use depends on the training goal, but it is generally best to use workouts for slightly different goals. One use would be to work on the direct endurance support in the morning or the direct speed support in the afternoon. Another possibility is to do a specific workout in the morning and then a shorter faster workout in the afternoon. In the latter example, speed endurance when tired would be trained. These blocks are useful to try to take an athlete to the next level. The key is to take extra rest both before and after the block.

The takeaway message for both career long and within a season periodization is that a foundation of general training allows the athlete to handle more support training, which in turn allows for higher quality and volume of specific work to be done. The training process is a continual build with the ultimate process in enhancing specific endurance. If there is a weak link in the foundation or support structure, then no matter how much specific endurance training is done, improvement will not be seen. At that point, the weak link would have to be addressed. That is why we must return to general and support work periodically throughout the years to ensure that the foundation is stable enough to build our specific endurance.

Within Days/Weeks Periodization

Bill Bowerman popularized the idea of alternating hard and easy training. This was a great leap forward in training theory, as it applied the principle of adaptation, mainly that a stress is needed but adaptation takes place only with adequate recovery. Two problems with a literal interpretation of the hard/easy principle, which Bowerman did not even practice himself, are that it does not mean that the alternation occurs day after day and that there are intensities between hard and easy.

The first problem is easily solved. The amount of recovery or easy training after a workout should be directly proportional to how intense or draining that workout is. That means the harder the workout, the more recovery needed. Recovery does not mean a day off but rather some level easy training. The one slight exception to this rule is when doing a special supercompensation block of training. The rest between double workouts or a weekend of intensity is purposely inadequate as we are trying to accumulate a large stress. However, after the special block, the recovery deficit needs to be repaid, and the principle holds true.

The second problem is that there are many shades of grey between easy and hard training. Instead of having a strict strong modulation of hard and easy days, most programs combine two to three hard workouts per week, 1-2 medium workouts, and several easy runs. Of course, we are still classifying using three units, instead of two, but the point is don't get caught up in a polarized system of very hard workouts with very slow running.

While training is usually defined in the week because it is a common measurement, it's not necessary. Workouts should ideally be designed and placed based on when they are needed and how much rest is needed afterwards, not because Mondays and Thursdays are always workout days and Sundays are long runs.

In general, most athletes can handle a week that includes 2 hard workouts and 2 medium workouts with the rest being a combination of distance runs and recovery runs. An example of such a set up would be hard workouts such as specific endurance work on Monday and a Threshold run on Friday. For the medium days, Wednesday could be an aerobic interval workout such as pace 200's or hill sprints, while Saturday would be a long easy run. Sunday would then be a designated recovery day consisting of only slow recovery running or a day off, while the rest of the week would be filled with a mix of easy to moderate distance runs and recovery runs.

Singles Versus Doubles

The debate over whether to run once or twice per day is a constant in the world of running. The singles advocates will point to Lydiard's statements of having to keep "prolonged pressure on the heart" and to successful coaches like Mark Wetmore. The doubles advocates will point to the Kenyan runners who run two sometimes three times per day regularly. But what is the answer?

The answer is both are needed. There is a time and a place for doubles and singles. And no, there is no magic mile per week threshold that one has to surpass to begin doubles. Low mileage runners sometimes need doubles just as much as higher mileage runners. The question is when do we need doubles?

It is common sense to think that one 8mi run is better than two 4mi runs and that definitely holds true when building general endurance. During a period of time when the focus is on general aerobic base building, it makes sense that you want that longer stimulus. That means a longer single run or doubles where there is one long single run and a shorter recovery run are most likely the way to go. However, once the intensity starts to increase and you are no longer running only miles, is it better to do one 8-10mi or two 4-5mi runs during an easy or distance day?

I think most people automatically assume a single run or a single longer run plus a shorter recovery run is better. Not many people consider an even or near even doubles split. I didn't either, except that I was forced to do split double runs early on in my career. Due to circumstances at my High School, we trained twice a day and generally split our mileage right down the middle. Why did we do this? First off, we had Cross-Country practice first period, so running in the morning made sense. We also had after school practice, so it made sense to run again. Second, and perhaps most importantly, we were restricted to running on our campus, which meant all running was around a 1.5mi loop. We were all running 60-70-80mpw at times, so no one wanted to run 8mi straight doing loops, as it was mind numbing to do that every day. If I go back and look at my logs, they are littered with days of 4.5/4.5, 5/5, and 6/6 during the school year. During the summer, when general endurance was being built, it looked much different, 9/4 or 8/5 mileage splits were the norm.

Fast forward a couple of years, and the High School runners I coached at the school followed the same approach. I noticed that as long as we built general endurance in the summer with longer runs and included a long run every week during the school year, there was no negative impact on endurance, even though most runs were only 5 miles in length. Conventional wisdom would expect the aerobic system to be the one that took the hit if the mileage is split in half, but this has never happened.

My High School and the athletes I coach are not the only examples of runners who have done split mileage for easy days. World class marathoner Kenny Moore's log is filled with recovery days consisting of very short doubles of 3 and 3 or 4 and 4. The key was that Kenny was hitting his workouts every couple days and had a good long run.

This brings us to the key point. Splitting distance days seems to enhance recovery for most runners once general endurance is built. That means, longer distance runs are probably best for building general endurance, but once this is built the emphasis switches. Thus, to maintain general endurance, the stimulus needed is much lower. That means split recovery days in combination with a long run on the weekend will be enough to maintain general endurance, and the split distance days will enhance recovery.

What happens when you split it with shorter doubles is that it enhances recovery. The runs are shorter so that the degree of mechanical and oxidative damage that occurs is kept to a minimum. Second, and perhaps most importantly, splitting may aid in glycogen replenishment. It is much easier to restore glycogen stores after an easy 4-5mi run then after a 10mi run. Yes, you run twice, so you have to replenish glycogen twice, but I'd argue that it is easier to replenish glycogen twice with several hours in between. Lastly, running twice may mean that you get a hormonal release twice in the day, which could improve recovery.

If we look at growth hormone release during easy running, there's a swift rise initially for the first 30-40min of a run, and then it levels off significantly to 60min. One study showed an increase of about 550 percent from 0-40min, yet from 40-60min it only went up another 40-50percent. This is but one example of the hormonal triggers of exercise, but it provides insight into why split runs may enhance recovery.

Doubles=Training in a Depleted State?

The recovery aspects cover short split doubles, but what about longer doubles that higher mileage runners do, such as 9mi and 7miles. One theory is that the longer initial run creates a pre-fatigued state for the second run. While it is reasonable to expect that when doing short doubles of 4-6miles the runner will be recovered for the second run, when doing a longer run first, that might not be the case.

Some researchers have suggested that training in a fatigued state may enhance subsequent adaptations. It has been found that training in a glycogen depleted state enhances gene transcription of several markers of training adaptation (Yeo et al., 2008; Hansen et al.,

2005). Low muscle glycogen amplifies the activation of signaling proteins, in particular AMPK and MAPK. Both of these proteins control adaptations such as mitochondria biogenesis.

In two studies on training every day versus training twice every other day, increases in enzyme activity have been more significant in the twice every other day group. In the study by Hansen, they used knee extensor exercises with one leg being trained every day and the other twice every other day (2005). The twice every other day leg group showed significantly better time till exhaustion at the end of the training, along with increased enzyme activity.

In the study by Yeo, they compared two different groups using cycling as the means of training (2008). The groups performed either easy or interval training, with the once every day group alternating each day between hard and easy. The twice every other day group performed an easy ride early, then the interval session. In their study glycogen content, fat oxidation, and CS and HAD enzyme activity were higher in the twice every other day group, but performance was equally increased in both groups.

What these studies and their findings suggest is that occasional training in a depleted state may lead to increased adaptations. This shouldn't be surprising if you just understand the basics of training and adaptation. What you are doing when training is putting a certain amount of stress on the body. During recovery the body responds to that stress by increasing its defenses against that stress. So it should not be surprising that training in a glycogen-depleted state produces more stress than normal. The body then adapts. The thing to remember is that the adaptation is specific to the stress and requires recovery. Without recovery, those adaptations aren't taking place. It's a balancing act.

While this may be thoroughly confusing, the takeaway message is to include several different kinds of runs using singles, short doubles, and long doubles. As general guidelines, singles or a double including a longer segment are much better for building general endurance. Shorter split doubles are better for enhancing recovery and therefore should be used as maintenance during pre-competition or competition portions of the season when intensity is high.

Peaking

Often the hardest part is not just getting in top shape but getting in top shape on the right day. This art is referred to as peaking. It is referred to as an art because it is very unscientific and requires good manipulation of the training. We know that workouts generally take between 7-10 days at the shortest before we see their benefits. So it would make sense then to do a hard workout about 10 days out and then just simply rest since we can't gain any fitness, right? Not exactly.

The goal of peaking is to allow rest and recovery to invigorate the runner mentally and physically, while still doing enough work to maintain fitness and to keep his body from overreacting. This overreacting is often seen by long distance runners, whose body paradoxically goes into a hibernation like state as they feel tired, heavy legged, and flat even though their rest has increased. The cause of this is a concept called muscle tension, which will be discussed shortly. Given this knowledge, the two key pieces of information we need to figure out are: 1) how long do we need before fatigue has dissipated and 2) how much training do we need to do to prevent this overreaction.

There are two basic approaches to peaking, which I'll term tapering and sharpening. Tapering is the classic or research based method. In this method, total volume is dropped significantly, while intensity is increased significantly. Sharpening takes the approach of maintaining or only very slightly dropping total mileage and decreasing the volume of the intense workouts slightly. Additionally, the density of the training is decreased, allowing more recovery in between harder sessions. Essentially, in sharpening, there is only a slight change in the training from the previous weeks of training, and those changes are mainly reducing the intensity and density slightly to allow for more recovery.

What type of peaking strategy is used depends on what type of athlete they are (FT or ST), their psychology, and their event. A FT type runner generally needs a longer peaking period and responds better to a classic taper. A ST type runner usually does best with a shorter peaking period and a sharpening phase. While this generally holds true, the event being trained for also matters, as does the training they have done to this point. The taper length and degree is proportional to how difficult the training has been up until the taper point. If the athlete is barely hanging on and in a state of barely functional overreaching, they may need a larger and longer taper than someone who is generally non-fatigued and handling the training.

Research on tapering with sprinters and more recently with more endurance type athletes shows that after a dramatic taper there is a shift in the muscle fiber type. If you remember back to the muscle fiber continuum chart, a dramatic and longer taper causes a slight shift towards the FT end of the fibers. This may be beneficial for a FT athlete or someone training for a shorter event but could be very harmful for a ST athlete or even a FT athlete training for a longer event. A dramatic taper for ST/longer distance events can cause a small erosion of the aerobic abilities, which is not what we want most of the time. In addition a large taper will alter muscle tension, which will be discussed shortly. For these reasons, I prefer a short sharpening phase for the majority of runners. There is less risk, and if done correctly just as high of a reward. The exception is for select FT athletes or those athletes who seem to be over trained, which should not happen if training is planned correctly. The sharpening period should consist of more recovery between intense work and only a slight drop in volume. For reasons to be discussed, it's important to maintain a similar training schedule, meaning don't suddenly cut out all doubles if the athlete is used to doubling.

The event also matters as that determines the relative importance of aerobic or anaerobic abilities. A common mistake is to always use faster work no matter the event to peak. The problem is that as discussed this faster work can shift the body to work more anaerobically. For instance, in peaking for a marathon, the last thing a runner needs is a decent volume of faster work in the week leading up to the race as that basically sends the signal to burn glycogen to a higher degree. Similarly, a lot of longer slower work might not be ideal for most 800m runners.

Lastly, the psychological makeup of the athlete plays a role. Some runners require the confidence from their recent hard workouts, while others can be satisfied by the long-term training that they have accumulated. Be careful in cutting training back to a high degree with runners who derive confidence from their workouts. The goal with these type of runners should be to cut back enough to give rest but not so much that they start to panic about losing fitness. The workouts done during the sharpening or even tapering phase should have the goal of getting the athlete to feel right on race day.

Muscle Tension

We've all experienced a race where we completely fell apart from the start of the race and felt completely off despite going into the race with training going well. How does it happen? If I knew exactly, I'd be a genius, but one thing that plays a large role is muscle tension. It partly explains why we feel good one day and flat the next. Have you ever wondered why most coaches have you do strides the day before a race? Through experience, most have figured out that if you do just a little faster stuff the day before a race, you feel really good the next day. One of the reasons is muscle tension.

So, what is this mysterious muscle tension? This might anger some of the scientist types, but its best to keep things simple. We can get incredibly complex on explaining what resting muscle tension is and how it can be altered, but when we do that it loses its practicality in application to the real world. With that in mind, here's the useful simplified way to look at muscle tension.

Within your muscle fibers, there is an optimal length for force production. This is known as the length-tension relationship, and it varies considerably based on a lot of factors. So, in simplistic terms if it's 10% too low, you may only be able to generate 90% force, while if it's 10% too high, you will generate less force.

Your body controls the resting tension through a variety of mechanisms, mainly through muscle spindles. If you want an example of this, go sit on your bed with legs extended for a while. When you get up and jog around, your quads are tight. Why? Because they've been shortened for a long time because of the way you were sitting. Similarly, what happens after you sit in a car or airplane for a while? Your hamstrings are tight because they've been in a shortened position for a while. Because these muscles have been in a shortened state for a while the body adjusts the resting tension. These are examples in a passive state, but it works very similarly in a dynamic state like running.

For running think of it like this, if we do a lot of long slow running or even a lot of threshold like running, the body is not worried about high force development, it is worried about efficiency. The length/tension needed for maximal force development is going to be different than that needed for a lot of medium force contractions. Your body is amazing at adapting, so if you do a lot of work where only moderate contractions of mainly Slow Twitch and a little Fast Twitch-a fibers, then it's going to adjust and optimize efficiency for this type of contraction. If you do this type of training continuously, then one day decide to perform a race that is much faster (let's say 1500m pace), you feel flat for that 1500m because your muscles are pre-conditioned to be most efficient at a lot of moderate contractions. . Your tension wasn't right going into it.

You know how you feel super bouncy or have a pop in your stride or you feel flat? That's muscle tension. If you feel super bouncy, your tension is probably high. If you feel really flat and non-responsive, your tension is probably low. The last week or so before the big race, you're not going to gain any fitness, so why workout and not just rest? Wouldn't it make sense to just store up all that energy and be ready to race? Well, if you've ever backed off too much for a race, you know what happens. You feel horribly flat. The reason is the whole tension relationship was messed up. The last week is about altering tension, not gaining fitness. It's about getting a runner to the line with his muscles in the optimal place.

What's optimal? It depends completely on the race and the person. In general, the shorter the event, the higher the tension needed and the longer the race, lower the tension needed. This only makes sense if we think it about it logically. Having tension that is for high force might be great, but is it most efficient for an activity that takes a lot of small contractions? No. Similarly, with sprint events, having tension that is optimal for max force may seem like a great idea, but if it's too high, then it might take longer to contract, thus resulting in a decrease in power. Not something we want.

And it is going to vary for each individual. Each individual will have a different fiber type makeup that will alter his optimal tension. If we have an individual with a lot of Fast Twitch fibers, he's probably going to need to be at a higher tension than someone with a lot of ST fibers, even if they are running the same race. Here are some simple guidelines for altering muscle tension, listed from those that will affect it the most down to the least.

Increase Tension	Decreases Tension
Sprint work, both flat sprints and hill sprints	Longer duration runs
Weight training	Very taxing workouts
Ballistic/Power work	Threshold work
Faster Pace/rhythm work	Moderate paced aerobic running
Strides or Running in spikes or on harder surfaces	Soft surface running (sand, heavy grass, wood chip trails)
Plyometric or reactive training	

Now modifying tension and getting it right on the exact day is a work of art. It's hard to do. As a coach, you've got to be acutely aware of how the runner looks and feels. Look at their stride to see how responsive it is and ask the runners how it feels. To what degree you alter tension depends on how far out you are from the competition. What I've found works best is if big changes are needed in altering tension, go for changes further out from the race, then as the days get closer, go for small/tweaking changes. This generally works much better than waiting till the day before to try to make big changes in tension.

In looking at training there are a few options:
1. Increase tension dramatically- Sprints or hill sprints for example.
2. Increase tension slightly- ex: 8x200 at 2mi down to 1mi pace
3. Tension is good-maintain- either do race pace work, or blend work that has athletes do some moderate running and some fast running (ex: fartlek with 5min moderate segments to start and end with 10sec segments fast)
4. Decrease tension slightly- short threshold run
5. Decrease tension dramatically- long run or long threshold run

What you do depends on what the athlete needs and how far out you are from a race. As I said, go for big changes far out (3-7days) and small changes closer. If big changes are needed closer to a race, know how an athlete reacts to certain types of training. For example, he might get sore from flat sprints so while that may raise tension, it makes him sore so it's useless. Generally with distance runners, you'll almost never use option 5, unless it's for a marathon. Below I'll give you some examples of how this works:

If it's Monday and an athlete is crazy bouncy, well, you might do something that slightly lowers tension (i.e., a short threshold run) then come back Wednesday or Thursday with some short pace work, such as 200s at 3200 down to mile pace. The threshold run lowers tension, then later in the week, the pace work maintains tension or prevents the continued lowering from the threshold work combined with easy distance running.

If it's Tuesday or Wednesday and they look pretty good, you might just do something to maintain tension. A combo workout is a great idea in these circumstances. My favorite is 5min medium, 5 easy, 5 medium, 5 easy, 5min of 10sec sprint 50sec easy. Then do strides the day before to raise tension a little and you're good. If it's early in the week and they look flat, then faster work or sprints should be done. You have to be careful with sprints because if they haven't done them in a while they'll get sore, so that would take away from the purpose.

Generally with true distance runners it's about raising tension because the mileage we do keeps it pretty low. Middle distance runners are a little trickier. Tension should also play a role in the pace of the strides done the day before a race.

I'll give you an example of when I nailed it with one of my top runners, Ryan. Going into the Nike regional meet, Ryan was feeling flat on that Sunday and Monday. So, the only workout we did was Tuesday. A mile in 4:33 on trails, then 5x 8-10sec hill sprints. The mile was just there to get some confidence and keep the body reminded of what it feels like to work pretty good and get out fast and relaxed. The real key was the hill sprints, which consisted of just 40-50 seconds of total work. But they alter tension a lot. Come Saturday, his legs felt great, and he had his best race of the year, winning regionals and advancing to nationals where he ended up 12th. Now if only it was always that easy.

To offer a summary of the peaking process before a major race, first do your last hard specific workout between 14 and 10 days out from the race. Around 7 days out a moderately intense or a low volume intense workout can be done. The key is to keep the volume low so that tension changes aren't enormous and delayed fatigue isn't likely. Within a week of the performance, the goal should be to manipulate muscle tension to get the athlete feeling right on race day.

As far as mileage goes, do enough that they do not feel flat, as large drops in mileage also alter tension. For the majority of runners, it is best not to make drastic changes in their routine. For FT athletes, they respond better to bigger tapers than ST athletes, so that is another factor to consider. The bottom line is that peaking is an art form and an individual process. Find what works best for your runners.

How to race in Europe (or peaking when racing several times a week)

I always wondered how the professional runners who seemed to race several times per week at times maintained peak fitness when racing on the European track circuit. I finally got to witness some of the different approaches when coaching professionals who competed on the European circuit. What I found is that it can be applied to runners of all levels.

The key is doing just enough to get by and no more. Because of the frequency of racing, the races themselves also act as the toughest specific track workout of the week. That means, the in between time is spent almost entirely doing maintenance and rhythm work. The workout volume is kept low, and the intensity depends entirely on how much time is separated between races. The longer the time period, the more intense or "normal" the workout is. For the most part, race pace 200s, 300s, and 400s maintenance style are the staples, with an occasional longer interval done to keep the feeling of a sustained effort. If there is a larger gap between races, then some "refresh" training is often done. Full workouts at a variety of intensities that haven't been touched upon in a while are refreshed.

How does this apply to others? In particular, High School runners often have to race several times per week or even have 4 important races in a row every weekend; take the European racing season approach. Do enough to maintain what you have built up and stop trying to squeeze in another workout here or there. Instead, cut the volume of your typical workouts to a maintenance level and let the racing take care of itself.

Finalizing the Plan

While each coach has their separate method to the madness, here is how I go about setting up the training plan on paper.

1. Get a calendar showing the entire training period.
2. Identify the peak race.
3. Fill in known races.
4. Design your big key workouts for specific, supports, general, pure speed, etc.
5. Design the progressions of workouts to reach that key workout for each category
      a. This takes skill as you need to know how long you are taking to develop each attribute and how often you want to do a workout that focuses on that attribute.
6. Design maintenance workouts for each category to be used once its emphasis is decreased.
7. Decide how to transition and connect (blends) each category.
8. Next, look at the calendar and decide roughly where the base, pre-comp, and competition phases lie.
9. Starting 10-14 days out, start with final specific endurance workout and work back to the beginning placing a specific workout roughly every 2 weeks (10-20 day range is normal)
10. Insert any special blocks (such as aerobic refresh) of training
11. Using the training periods (base, pre-comp, competition), insert your key general training workouts at the end of the base phase, your key aerobic/anaerobic support in the middle of the pre-competition, the key direct support workout at the end of the pre-competition, and the specific work has already been taken care of.
12. Once these key workouts have been set, working backwards, insert the progressions that get you to these key workouts. For direct supports, a new workout every 10-14 days is generally the guideline, while aerobic/anaerobic supports and pure speed training can occur more frequently (on avg. every 7-14 days).
13. Following the key workouts, insert the maintenance workouts every 2-4 weeks depending on the type.
14. Fill in any workouts designed for a special reason (i.e., kick development, strength endurance, etc.)
15. Fill in the medium training days
16. Determine easy days/mileage.
17. This is the guiding plan! Be prepared to rip it apart and adjust along the way.

20

Training for Each Event

"To coach a top athlete you need to be an explorer. An explorer, because always you must discover something new. When you suppose that you feel protected with what you already know, you no longer have the possibility to overtake your limits." Renato Canova

After making it this far, it is finally time to go through the details of training for each event. In the following sections, we will go from the base phase to peak race with workout examples, progression of workouts, and sample training plans for each group. While I'll provide the framework, it is important to remember the one principle that should be ingrained in you by this point, individualization. I'll take you through the training for the event as a specialist, or someone who's right in the middle in terms of Fast Twitch versus Slow Twitch. It's your job to use the concepts and suggestions found in the individualization chapter to put the final touches on the training.

800m

The 800m is an event where the difference between the runner coming at it from the speed side and the runner coming at it from the endurance side is drastically different. It almost requires two entirely different methods of training. That makes it difficult to come up with one streamlined specialist way to train for the 800m, so I strongly advise you to go back and look at the Individualization chapter in regards to the 800m.

Endurance Side Development

The 800m runner's endurance training differs from most other event groups. Unlike other events, normal easy, steady, or moderate running is very far away from 800m specificity. That does not mean that it is not important, it just means different and unique ways of developing general endurance are required.

The 800m runner needs a solid base of mileage and a moderate long run (9-12miles for most). The total amounts of each depend on the type of runner he is, as a FT runner can get away with moderate mileage in the 40-50 range, while a ST 800m runner needs top peak in the 70-80mpw range. As far as general endurance development for FT type of runners, the 800m runner should do very limited amounts of LT work as it will decrease his anaerobic abilities. During their distance runs, more "stuff" should be added instead of only long, consistent distance runs. The frequent inclusion of strides, surges, and moderate pickups/progressions are a necessity.

During the base phase, an 800m runner should focus on easy progression runs and aerobic intervals. The aerobic intervals, particularly for a FT runner, work to increase general endurance at a pace much closer to specificity. During the early base phase, simple fartleks of short 30sec-2min fartlek intervals at 10k pace will suffice. These should progressively increase in length and increase in pace down to 5k pace as the base proceeds. These can eventually be turned into full interval sessions during the pre-competition phase at 10k-5k paces but longer rest periods and shorter intervals should be used than for the same sessions with longer distance runners. Similarly, shorter aerobic intervals, such as 100-150m repeats at 3k down to mile pace with short rest between reps and long rest between sets work well to transition to support work as you get closer to the pre-competition phase.

As mentioned already, the early pre-competition phase for the endurance side of things should focus on 5k-10k pace workouts and aerobic intervals. In addition combo workouts involving a step down in paces from LT to 3k can be used. During the latter part of the pre-competition phase, the short aerobic intervals can be lengthened to 200-800m intervals at 3k down to 1mile pace for support. Additionally, combo and blend workouts should be implemented that combine the speed and endurance supports. In this way, a blend workout would focus on longer segments at 3k-1mile pace with a few shorter segments at 800m pace thrown in. These blend workouts will go a long way towards ensuring the 800m runner has the necessary endurance at specific paces.

Speed Side Development

Speed is vital for a good 800m runner. For this reason, a lot of importance is given during the base phase in developing first speed and then, during the pre-competition phase, speed endurance. Initially, hill sprints are used as a way to develop speed and strength. These should be progressively increased in number until they get to around 10 total. Hill sprints can be done once or even twice per week for 800m runners. Once this occurs, the transition to flat sprints is made. Flat sprints should be started with shorter 60m lengths and increased to 100m. For the majority of 800m runners, doing one session of flat sprints per week is enough, but for some FT runners or those emphasizing speed development, another set of hill sprints can be added on some weeks. During this phase it is best to not get caught doing solely flat sprints every week. Once every 2-3 weeks, switch these for hill sprints to give the athlete a different stimulus and a break from the monotony.

The next step should occur during the pre-competition phase and is speed endurance, which includes at first adding on one to two longer segments of 20-25sec after a hill sprint session. The next step is to add one or two 120-150m segments after a reduced flat sprint session. Finally, progress in such a way that the ratio of speed endurance to pure speed tips in the favor of speed endurance, with the segment lengths getting gradually longer. In the final stages of the pre-competition phase the speed endurance work can shift towards 400m pace work as the segment lengths get above 200m. During the competition phase, especially for a FT runner, some full 400m +/- pace work should be done. Keep the volume low and the rest periods between such work very high. For most 800m runners, this type of work only needs to be done once every 2-4 weeks.

Specific Development

Initial specific work during the base phase should consist of strides or short segments. The specific progression should begin during the pre-competition phase. It is best to start with very short segments for the 800m runner. For FT runners, the segments should be broken into low volume sets equaling around 800m worth of work. An example of a starting workout would be 2-3 sets of 8x100m at 800m pace with 1 minute rest. From here, increase the segment lengths gradually, keeping the set volume around the same. Manipulation of the recovery or the order of the longer reps (such as in the case of sets of 600/200m or 200/600m) are ways to progress and adapt this workout.

The last step is specific speed endurance, in which workouts slightly faster than 800m pace are done, or mixing 800m pace and slightly faster is used in blend or combo workouts. Specific speed endurance is often the deciding factor in the 800m, as the last 200m of the 800m is decided not by who has the best kick but who slows down the least. One way to do this in a combo fashion with the specific endurance work mentioned above is to change the last segment of each set to be done at a faster speed. This is a great way for not only 800m runners but all event groups to develop specific speed endurance. Another option is to develop high intensity strength endurance, which is mentioned in the chapter on Workouts for Specific Reasons.

Maintenance

General endurance should be maintained with aerobic intervals/fartleks and combo work. Easy additions to distance runs can also serve this purpose with progressions, pickups, and surges. Speed should be maintained more frequently than with other events, particularly for FT runners. The addition of short sprints or hill sprints after distance runs or other workouts is one way to go about it. Specific endurance during the base phase or during peaking phases can be maintained via short specific intervals and rhythm work. 100-300m repeats with relatively long rest are one example.

See appendix for examples/progressions for each workout type.

800m Training Plan

Monday	Tuesday	Wednesday	Thursday	Friday	Saturday	Sunday	MPW
Base Period- Plan for well trained runner maxing out at 65mpw							
Note: To hit mileage some recovery/secondary runs after workout days need to be added to schedule. Warm-ups/cool downs not listed.							
8mi+strides	6mi	8mi +strides	6mi	6mi+strides	8mi	Off	40
7mi+strides	6mi	Run+ 8x10sec Hill Sprints	6mi	8mi+strides	10mi	Off	45
7mi Moderate Progression run	7mi	Run+ 10x10sec Hill Sprints	5mi	12x200 at 3k pace w/ 200m jog	10mi	Short recovery run	50
4x(60,45,30 w/ 30sec easy) w/ 3min b/t sets at 10k-5k pace	6mi	Run+6x60m Flat Sprints	5mi	10min MP, 7min LT, 5min 10k pace w/ 4min easy between	9mi w/ strides	Short recovery run	50
15-20min LT	7mi	6x80m Flat Sprints	8mi	Distance run w/ 8x30sec surges	11mi	Short recovery run	55
4x3:30 w/ 3min rest at 10k pace	4mi	8mi +strides	Run+6x100m Flat Sprints	7mi easy progression run	12mi	Off	45
20min of alternating 2min at 10k/ 2min at steady pace	7mi	5x(400, 200) at 3k pace w/ 200m jog	9mi	Hilly Fartlek- 2x4min,2x3min, 2x1min at 10k, 5k, 3k pace w/ 2min rest	10mi	Short recovery run	60
3x(8x100m w/ 45sec rest at 800m pace) 4min rest b/t sets	8mi	Run+ 4x100m, 2x150m sprints, speed endurance	3mi/3mi	8mi easy progression down to marathon pace	12mi	Short recovery run	60

Pre-Competition Period

2x(800, 2min rest, 400m) w/ 3min rest at 10k/5k pace	8mi	Run+ 4x150m w/ full recovery speed endurance	4mi/4mi	3x(500,400,300 w/ 1min rest) 4min b/t sets-1mi pace	10mi	Short recovery run	60
3x400m Alternating 50m at 400m pace, 50m cruise with 4-5min rest	8mi	500 (1mi), 150(800m), 400 (1mi), 100m (400m), 300 (1mi), 100 (400m) w/ 3min rest	5mi	5mi/3mi	6mi progression run Marathon pace to 10k	Off	55
3x(4x200) w/ 75sec rest and 4min rest, 800m pace	7mi	4x200m at 400m pace	4mi/4mi	Hill Repeats-2x2min (5k) 2x90sec (3k) 2x60sec (1mi) 2x30sec hard w/ jog down recovery	10mi	Short recovery run	50
4x400, 2x400, 1x400 w/ 60sec rest b/t reps, 5min b/t sets (paces-1mi, just faster than 1mi, 800m)	7mi	4mi/4mi	3x (600(3k),300(1mi), 300(800)) w/ 2min rest b/t reps, 4min b/t sets	6mi/3mi	12mi	Short recovery run	50
3x(3x300) w/ 90sec rest and 4min rest at 800m pace	6mi	2x300 (1mi), 3x200m (800m) w/ 200m jog	6mi	3mi w/ strides	Race	Off	40

Competition Period

9x150m at just faster than mile pace w/ 150m walk	6mi	250,200,150, 100m w/ 5-8min rest, 400m pace	8mi	Distance run w/ moderate progression	9mi w/ strides	Short recovery run	50
4x(200, 100m jog, 100m) w/ 4min rest. 200's at 800pace, 100m kick in.	6mi/4mi	alternation: 4 laps of 200m (1mi)/200m (steady), 3min rest 1x200m alternating 50m fast/50m cruise	5mi	3mi w/ strides	Race	Short recovery run	45
800 (1mi), 500(800m), 250(400m) w/ long rest	5mi/4mi	8mi +strides	6mi moderate progression run +6x10sec hill sprints	7mi easy progression run	10mi w/ 6x30sec surges	Off	55
3x(400,400) w/ 75sec rest and 5min rest	5mi/4mi	12x200m w/ 200m jog at 3k-1mi pace	5mi	3mi w/ strides	Race	Short recovery run	45
2x(500, 100m walk, 200m) with 6-8min rest. 500m at 800m pace, 200m kick in.	5mi/4mi	7mi	2x80, 2x100, 2x150m sprints w/ long rest	4mi/3mi	9mi w/ strides	Off	50
2-3x(600, 200) w/ 75sec rest and 5min	8mi	6mi + strides	4mi/4mi	3mi w/ strides	Race	Short recovery run	40
2x(300,100m cruise, 100m) w/ 300 at 800m pace, 100m kick. 5min rest between,	6mi/4mi	3mi/3mi	300,200,150 w/ 4min rest (800, just faster than 800, 400)	8mi + strides	Off	4-6mi	50
4x200m 800m pace down w/ 200m jog	3mi/3mi	distance run w/ 100m strides at 800m pace	5mi	3mi w/ strides	**Peak 800m Race**		35-40

1,500m/ 1mile

The 1,500m or mile is the classic track event. Whenever a non-runner asks about your running, the question of "what's your mile time?" seemingly always pops up. The mile represents an event that requires very high levels of speed and endurance to be successful at it, not to mention a high tolerance to pain. Due to this, more than any other event it requires a balance of both sides of the spectrum to reach peak performance.

Endurance Side Development

Like with all events the first step is a short (~2 weeks) introductory period that includes only mileage and strides. After this, the base phase of training starts. As always, the emphasis is on general endurance and general speed.

Mileage and long runs are of varying importance depending on where the runner falls on the classification scale. For either group, mileage should reach its maximum at the end of the base phase with a small decline and leveling off for ST type runners and a more drastic decline as the training progresses for FT runners. The long run should increase reaching a moderate length of 12-17 miles (depending on the runner type) during the base phase and should be used solely as maintenance after that. For the FT runner, no add-ons should be included in the long run, while the ST runner can do easy add-ons of limited volume.

Since general endurance is best developed through high-end aerobic running at marathon to threshold pace, that is the emphasis throughout the base period. ST runners in particular should do a high amount of marathon pace (MP) and LT running. To start with progression runs working down from a steady pace through MP to LT should be done. These should be rather informal at first and develop into structured LT workouts. LT workouts can be done once per week during the base phase with the goal of slowly increasing the time spent at LT. Start with around 15min total time spent at LT and progress upward to around 30min. Once this level is reached, adding in faster work at 10k pace will serve as a transition to support training or adding in hill sprints or moderate hill repeats at the end can develop strength endurance.

As explained in the individualization chapter, FT runners should limit the amount of running done at LT and instead should develop general endurance through progression runs, fartleks at just faster than threshold, and aerobic intervals. Aerobic intervals should be done during the base phase and consist of short (30-90sec) bouts of running at 3k-10k pace with equal or more jogging rest in between. These aerobic intervals can be lengthened during the pre-competition phase to serve as aerobic support and direct aerobic support. Following the base phase, general endurance should be reduced to maintenance through fartleks, short thresholds, aerobic intervals, combo and blend workouts.

During the pre-competition phase, on the endurance side, aerobic intervals should be lengthened to form full-blown support workouts at 10k down to 5k speeds. On the endurance spectrum, the transitioning of the LT work to fartleks or intervals at 10k pace initially and 5k pace later should continue. Alternations using 5k-10k pace are an excellent way to develop aerobic and direct endurance support for the ST miler.

During the latter pre-competition phase, the support should start shifting towards faster work including 5k down to 3k pace. This can be done in any number of ways using any of the different workouts. Blend workouts, in particular mixed blend sessions, are particularly useful as a way to develop support. An example of a mixed blend workout would be: 1000, 500, 800, 400, 600, 300 with the three longer segments being run at progressively faster paces (10k, 5k, 3k) and the same with the shorter segments (3k, 1mi, 800). Workouts like this are a great way to bring together the supports on the speed and endurance side. As the training phase progresses, this workout can be progressed via bringing together of the paces toward 1,500m pace from the speed and endurance side.

Speed Side Development

Speed plays a much larger role in the 1,500m than in longer events. For this reason, greater emphasis is given to developing general speed and in maintaining speed during the base phase. Speed development should begin early in the base phase through short hill sprints. As these are progressively lengthened, flat sprints should be introduced. Unlike with longer events, milers can move almost entirely to flat sprints at this point. Flat sprints should be increased up to 100m in length by the end of the base phase. From here, most milers will need at least some speed endurance training. For ST milers, keep the total volume limited to adding a handful of speed endurance segments at the of a general speed session. For FT type runners, whole sessions of speed endurance can be done. These sessions should start out with 120m sprints and progressively increase to 200 to 250m sprints. Only the FT type runners need to progress to 250m sprints. The total volume should be kept moderate to low (400-800m of total work is a good guideline). This speed endurance work should be started at the end of the base phase and continued into the early pre-competition phase. When speed or speed endurance is emphasized, it should be performed once per week.

In addition to pure speed endurance, a maintenance level of speed support work should be done during the base phase. This initially can be strides before or after runs or workouts. During the pre-competition phase low volume amounts of speed support should be done in the form of 800m pace +/- running. A good way to accomplish this is to take the rhythm 200's done during the base phase and start progressively increasing their speed down to 800m pace. At first start with just the last one or two intervals and increase this until the majority of the workout is done at 800 pace by the end of the pre-competition phase. Additionally, as mentioned earlier, the use of blend workouts of both endurance and speed support paces works well during the pre-competition phase.

During the competition phase, sprint and general speed work is in maintenance mode, while specific speed endurance is emphasized. Specific speed endurance should include the combining and/or blending of race pace speeds with work faster than race pace. This can be done in the form of combo, blend, or progression intervals. The goal should be to mix mile and 800m pace together in workouts to increase specific speed endurance.

Specific Development

Race rhythm is incredibly important for mile runners. To establish this race rhythm early and to start on the development of specific endurance, aerobic intervals or rhythm work at 3k to mile pace should be done in the forms of 100-200m repeats with longer rests (200m jogs for example) during the base phase.

The official progress of specific work should start during the pre-competition phase using one of the specific development methods. For milers, combining the top down and bottom up method usually works well. Alternations for specific development, such as Oregon's famous 30/40 workout (alternating a 30sec 200 and a 40sec 200m) are best used as final touch ups on specific endurance, not necessarily in creating it.

In addition, as mentioned already, blend workouts are a good way to bring together the support paces to form specific endurance. The last specific endurance session can be a time trial or longer repeats. With the majority of specific work for a mile, the repeat length is relatively short (600m or shorter), so sometimes it helps to top off specific endurance with a low number of longer repeats at mile pace. An example would be to run a 1,000 or 1,200m time trial at race pace followed by some short 200's. Another possible workout would be 2-3x800 with 3-4min rest between at mile race pace. These longer specific intervals are very intense, so plenty of recovery before and after should be given.

The ability to finish strong in the mile is paramount to success. For this reason, the kick development workouts described in the chapter on workouts for a specific reason can be used. Additionally, specific speed endurance should be developed during the competition phase. FT runners will need a greater amount of this type of work then ST runners. This is best accomplished through combo or blend workouts consisting of combining mile pace and work slightly faster. Very short alternations, with 100m segments for example, are good for developing specific speed endurance. In this case, the fast segment should be just faster than mile pace, and the slow segment should be around 5k-10k pace. An example for a 4-minute miler, would be to alternate 13.5-14sec 100's with 17-18sec 100s for 800m then take a rest and do it again.

Maintenance

For the 1,500/mile runner, endurance maintenance work can be done through combo work. Periodically include combo work that focuses on threshold, 10k, and 5k paces. A good way to do this is through longer fartleks or combo workouts. Additionally, the long run and occasional moderate tempo runs can serve to maintain general endurance for the ST runner.

On the speed side, pure speed can be maintained with hill sprints or flat sprints done every 2-4 weeks either as a separate workout or tacked on to the end of another workout. Oftentimes combining general endurance and general speed maintenance into one workout is a good idea. Speed support can be maintained through blend workouts or simple rhythm workouts such as 100s-200s at 800m paces with a 200-400m jog in between. During the pace phase, maintenance specific work can be done in the form of surges, aerobic intervals, or rhythm work.

See appendix for examples/progressions for each workout type.

1,500m/1mile Training Plan

Monday	Tuesday	Wednesday	Thursday	Friday	Saturday	Sunday	MPW
Base Period- Plan for well trained runner maxing out at 80mpw							
Note: To hit mileage some recovery/secondary runs after workout days need to be added to schedule. Also warm-ups/cool downs not listed							
7-9mi distance run	7mi distance run	10mi distance run+strides	7mi	9-10mi	10mi run	4-6mi recovery run	50-55
7-9mi distance run	7mi distance run	9mi+Hill Sprints 6x10sec	8mi	9mi distance run w/ 5-10min pickup	11mi run	4-6mi recovery run	60
moderate 8-10mi progression run	5mi/5mi recovery	9mi+Hill Sprints 8x10sec	8mi	5mi/5mi recovery	12mi long run	5-7mi recovery run	65
15min LT	5mi/5mi recovery	Run+Flat Sprints- 6x60m	9mi	Distance Run +8x30sec surges	13mi long run	5-7mi recovery run	70
20min split LT	5mi/5mi recovery	Run+Hill Sprints 6x10sec +2x20sec	7mi/4mi	Distance Run +8x45sec surges	12mi long run+ strides	6-8mi recovery run	70
25min split LT	5mi/5mi recovery	Run+Flat Sprints- 5x100m	8mi/5mi	Distance run+ 6x200m w/ 200m at 3k pace	11mi run w/ 30sec surges	6-8mi recovery run	75
15min LT, 5min at 10k, 2x60sec at 5k	6mi/6mi recovery	Run+Hill Sprints 6x10sec +20sec, 25sec,30sec speed endurance	9mi/5mi +strides	Strength Endurance Hill Circuit	13mi long run	8-10mi recovery run	80
6mi Marathon Pace	6mi/6mi recovery	Flat Sprints- 3x100m, 3x150m	6mi/6mi recovery	Strength Endurance Hill Circuit	14mi long run	8-10mi recovery run	80

Pre-Competition Period

1.5mi,1mi, 800m w/ 4min rest at 10k down to 5k pace	6mi/6mi recovery	5mi moderate progression run	5mi/5mi recovery	9mi distance run	12mi w/ 40sec surges	8-10mi recovery run	70
4x(4x400m) w/ 40sec rest b/t reps, 4min b/t sets at 5k-3k pace	6mi/6mi recovery	8-10x200m at mile pace w/ 200m jog	7mi/4mi	Strength Endurance Hill Circuit	13mi long run	OFF	65
Alternating 200m at mile pace, 200m easy for 2miles	5mi/5mi recovery	300,250, 200m at 800m down to 400m pace w/ 5min rest	7mi/4mi	Run+8x10sec Hill Sprints	10mi run	8-10mi recovery run	70
3x(400,300,200) w/ 60sec rest) w/ 3-4min b/t sets	5mi/5mi recovery	7mi/4mi	Long hill repeats at 3k effort (6x2min w/ jog down recovery)	7mi/4mi	10mi run w/ middle 20min at LT	8-10mi recovery run	60
1000 (5k), 500 (1mi), 700m (3k), 300 (800m), 600 (3k), 200 (800m) w/ 3-4min rest	5mi/5mi recovery	8x200m at 1mi down to 800m pace	7mi run	4-6mi w/ strides	Race	OFF/short recovery run	55

Competition Period

3x(500, 300 w/ 60sec rest) w/ 4min b/t sets	5mi/5mi	10min steady, 8min MP, 6min LT, 4min 10k pace w/ 2-3min easy b/t	6mi/6mi recovery	Run+ 4x100m flat sprint, 1x200m speed endurance	10mi run	6-8mi recovery run	70
4x800m w/ 2min rest at 3k pace, 4x200m at 800m pace w/ 200 jog	7mi/3mi	3x600(5k), 3x200(1mi), 3x500 (3k), 3x200 (800) w/ 90sec b/t reps, 4min b/t sets	7miles recovery run	5-6mi+strides	Race	6-8mi recovery run	60
Alternating 400m/100m (5x) w/ 400 at mile pace, 100m easy	5mi/5mi	9mi run	20min LT, 3min rest, 5min at 10k pace, 5xHill Sprint	5mi/5mi recovery	12mi long run	6-8mi recovery run	70
600m (1mi), 200 (800m), 500 (1mi), 200 (800m), 400m (first 200m at mile, last 200m kick in) w/ 2-4min rest	5mi/5mi	Fartlek-5min MP, 5min Easy, 5min MP, 5min Easy, 5min of 15sec hard w/ 45sec easy	8mi easy	4-6mi w/ strides	Race	OFF/short recovery run	55
3x(600/200 w/ 60sec rest) 4min rest b/t sets, 1mi pace	5mi/5mi	6mi/6mi recovery	2x600 (5k), 300(1mi), 2x500(3k), 200(800), 400(1mi), 150(400m) w/ 2-3min rest	8mi distance run	11mi run	6-8mi recovery run	60
Alternation: 1700m, 1300m, 900m, 500m w/ 5min rest (alternating 200m-steady/ 200m 1mi, and finishing w/ extra 100m kick in on final segment	8-9mi run	8x200m at 3k to 1mi pace w/ 200m jog	5mi/5mi recovery	4-6mi w/ strides	Race	OFF/short recovery run	50
7mi distance	3x800 w/ 5min rest at mile pace	5mi/5mi recovery	4mi/4mi	2x300,200,100 m w/ 3min rest at 800m pace	10-11mi run	6-8mi recovery run	55
5mi/5mi	2x400m(1mi) w/ 45sec rest, 4x200m at mile down to 800m pace w/ 200m jog	7-9mi run+strides	6-7mi easy	4mi w/ strides	**Peak 1500m**		50

5,000m

The 5k is a unique event that can be approached from the endurance or speed side. Throughout history endurance type 1,500m runners and 5k runners who could also run the 10k have done equally well in this event. The two prime examples for 1,500m types who have excelled at the 1,500m are 2004 Olympic 1,500m and 5,000m Champion Hicham El Guerrouj and double world champion in the 1,500 and 5k Bernard Lagat. On the other side of the coin, there are examples of world record holders and Olympic gold medalists Haile Gebrselassie and Kenenisa Bekele who dominated both the 5k and 10k. The 5k represents probably the most commonly targeted event, as it is a staple distance in road racing, High School Cross Country, and on the track.

Endurance Side Development

General endurance is developed through a number of different ways for a 5k runner. The most important ones are through total mileage, long runs, and high-end aerobic tempo/threshold running. Mileage should steadily increase throughout the base phase, hitting its maximum at the very end of this period. From there, a slight reduction by 10-20% should gradually occur until a comfortable steady level is maintained all the way through the specific period with short drops preceding major races.

The long run follows a similar pattern to mileage. The early focus should be on accumulating distance and worrying about intensity later. For this reason, the first 4-5 weeks of the base phase should be focused solely on increasing the length of the long run. It is best to do this very gradually by perhaps a mile per long run. After this, "stuff" is added on. That means including at first strides, then surges, and finally pickups at the end. For a 5k runner, the long run is not a main priority, so the add-ons should be moderate, culminating in at most a 10-15min pickup for the majority of runners. Typically during the late base phase a pattern of two long runs with add-ons, one easy long run without, works well. During the early pre-competition phase this pattern should be reversed and by the end of the pre-competition, add-ons should be eliminated from the long run as its sole purpose is maintenance of general endurance from there on out.

High-end aerobic running can serve both as general endurance and aerobic support for the 5k, depending on the pace. Early on this should be done in the form of natural progression runs down to marathon pace. Midway through the base period, these should be replaced with threshold runs. Threshold runs should start at 15-20min of total time and progressively increase until a maximum of around 30-35min total. Once that level is reached, then threshold lengths can be reduced and turned into combo workouts with short segments at 10k pace added if the goal is to transition to direct support work.

In addition, a longer marathon paced or steady/hard run should be done at the end of the base period. This serves as a great feedback tool to tell if the runners' general endurance levels are high enough or if more work needs to be done. The run should be between 7-10 miles and can replace the long run. This will give a good indication of where to go at the end of the base phase.

Moving down to support paces initial direct support work can be done as 10k paced fartleks, alternations, traditional intervals, or my favorite choice blends. The best early option is fartlek work because it promotes running by feel, which makes it an easier transition to slightly faster workouts. Alternating 10k and threshold pace is a great way to transition from aerobic support to direct support, and can later be progressed to a specific alternation (by increasing the speed of the faster segment to 5k pace).

My favorite though is blend workouts. By doing blend workouts with longer segments at 10k pace and shorter segments at 3k pace, it is a great way to get work done at both direct supports (speed and endurance side). Additionally, the paces of the longer segments can be gradually increased to turn it into a specific or specific speed endurance session.

Lastly, from the endurance side of things, strength endurance plays a large role for the 5k. See the chapter on workouts designed for a specific purpose for more information. For strength endurance development, long runs serve the early foundation. During the base phase hill circuits can be done. As we get into the pre-competition phase, inserting hill sprints in between sets of direct support or blend workouts will do the job. Finally, during the specific period, hill sprints between sets of specific work or the addition of long hill repeats will finish off the development of strength endurance.

Speed Side Development

From the speed of things, the first step is hill sprints. These will develop general speed and provide our multifaceted base. Start out with a low number (4-5) and progress upwards each week until 8-10 is reached. Once this goal is accomplished, it's time to convert that speed to flat sprint speed. Every other week perform flat sprints instead of hill sprints, starting with 60m sprints and progressing to 100m. From here speed endurance can be developed through combo work by adding on longer sprints to hill or flat sprints. Not much of this is needed unless it is a very FT type runner.

Speed should also be maintained with strides and surges throughout the training. During the pre-competition phase, some short work at 1600m-3k pace should be included. For a 5k runner, this isn't meant to be an intense "anaerobic" workout but instead as a simple neural and biomechanical introduction to faster work. 100-400m repeats with plenty of recovery work well in this case. During the later pre-competition phase, starting to blend this 3k-1600m pace with 5k pace work is a good idea. It will create specific speed endurance and the ability to surge if done within the repeat itself.

Specific Development

Specific work should be done in the base phase as strides and surges. The inclusion of 30-60sec surges during the base phase serve as a great specific work introduction and can later be transformed into the more formalized aerobic intervals, such as cruise 200's. The first real specific workout should begin during the early pre-competition phase, and depending on your specific endurance development choice, it should consist of relatively small spurts of specific paces. These can be in the form of alternations such as 200m at 5k pace and 600m at a steady pace for 4 miles, or it can be done in the form of short intervals, such as 400's at 5k pace with short rest between reps and long rest between sets. Either way, progress the specific workouts upwards in terms of specificity every 10-15 days, and slightly more frequently during the specific period. For the 5k, it is best to come at it from several different ways, so my suggestion is to use several different methods, alternating each method type.

Lastly, specific work can benefit during the competition period by including blend work. Blend work is a great way to progress from the supports to the specific training. For 5k runners, blend work can often serve as a finishing touch when done in a way that promotes specific speed endurance. By combining longer segments at race pace with shorter segments at 3k or faster paces, you develop speed endurance at race pace. To finalize race preparation, use blend type workouts where the pace blending occurs within each repeat itself. This teaches the ability to accelerate off of race pace and can be done with workouts such as 4x600m repeats with the first 400m of each 600m at 5k pace and the last 200m a progressive kick down to 3k or 1 mile pace.

Maintenance

For the 5k runner, endurance maintenance work can be done through combo work. Periodically include combo work that focuses on marathon pace, threshold pace, and 10k pace. A good way to do this is through longer fartleks or combo threshold workouts. In addition, shorter marathon pace runs in the 5mi range do a good job of maintaining general aerobic endurance.

On the speed side, pure speed can be maintained with hill sprints done every 2-4 weeks and some faster strides. Speed support paces can be maintained through blend workouts or simple rhythm workouts such as 300s or 200s at 3k and mile paces with a 200-400m jog in between. Finally, put it all together. Below is a full training cycle for a 5k runner:

See appendix for examples/progressions for each workout type.

5,000m Training Plan

Monday	Tuesday	Wednesday	Thursday	Friday	Saturday	Sunday	MPW
Base Period- Plan for well trained runner maxing out at 90-100mpw							
Note: To hit mileage some recovery/secondary runs after workout days need to be added to schedule. Also warm-ups/cool downs not listed							
10mi distance run+ strides	8mi/5mi	10mi distance run+strides	5mi/5mi recove	9-10mi	11-13mi run	6-8mi recovery run	70
9-10mi distance run	9mi/5mi	9mi+Hill Sprints 6x10sec	6mi/6mi recove	8mi Progression Run	13mi long run	8mi recovery run	75
Run+Hill Sprints- 8x10sec	9mi/5mi +stride	9mi/4mi	9mi Progression Run	5mi/5mi recovery	14mi w/ strides	8mi recovery run	80
LT 15min total w/ warm-up and cool down	9mi/5mi	Run+Hill Sprints 10x10sec	9mi/5mi	5mi/5mi recovery	13mi w/ 4x30sec surges	8mi recovery run	80
LT 20min split total	6mi/6mi	Run+Flat Sprints- 6x60m	9mi/5mi	Strength Endurance Hill Circuit	15mi Long Run	8-10mi recovery run	90
LT 25min split total	9mi/5mi	Run+Hill Sprints 6x10sec +2x20sec	9mi/5mi	Normal run+ 6x200m w/ 200m jog strides	16mi Long Run	8-10mi recovery run	90
LT 30min split total	9mi/5mi	Run+Flat Sprints- 5x100m	10mi/5mi +strides	6mi/6mi recovery	14mi w/ 5min pickup	8-10mi recovery run	95
LT 30min split total	9mi/5mi + stride	10mi/6mi	Strength Endurance Hill Circuit	6mi/6mi recovery	16mi Long Run	8-10mi recovery run	100

Pre-Competition Period

LT 20min,3min easy, 5min at 10k pace	9mi/5mi	Alternation 800 at 10k/800 steady for 5mi	6mi/6mi recovery	9mi/5mi	12mi medium long runs	8-10mi recovery run
						90
3x(4x400) w/ 30sec rest, 3-4min b/t sets, 5k pace	9mi/5mi	10-12mi run+ strides	5mi/5mi recovery	7-8miles at MP	8-10mi recovery run	8-10mi recovery run
						80
2000, 400, 1200, 400, 1000 (10k pace for long, 3200 pace for short) w/ 2 and 4min rest	9mi/5mi	Run+12x200m at 3k pace w/ 200m jog	5mi/5mi recovery	Strength Endurance Hill Circuit	14mi w/ 6x45sec surges at the end	8-10mi recovery run
						80
Fartlek- 6,3,5,2,4,1 w/ 2min easy- at 10k pace w/ 40sec surge down to 5k pace in the middle of each rep	6mi/5mi	Run+ flat sprint work (2x60m, 2x80m, 1x120m at 90-95%)	7mi/4mi	4-6mi w/ strides	Race	OFF/short recovery run
						60
Strength Endurance Hill Circuit	6mi/5mi	Alternate 400 at 5k, 800 steady, 4-5x	10mi	9mi/5mi	14mi w/ 5min pickup	8-10mi recovery run
						80

Competition Period

3x(600,400,600) w/ 40sec rest, 3-4min b/t sets, 5k pace	8mi/5mi	6x10sec Hill Sprints	6mi/6mi recovery	1600, 600, 1200, 4, 800 w/ 3min rest (paces-10k, 3k, 5k, 15, 5k)	10mi run	6-8mi recovery run	75
15min LT, 4min rest, 4x60sec uphill w/ jog down rest	7mi/5mi	4x(300/200) w/ 200jog 3k down to mile pace	7mi/4mi	5-6mi	Race	6-8mi recovery run	65
1600(5k), 400(1mi), 1200(5k), 300(1mi), 600(first 300 at 5k, last 300m kick in w/3min rest	9mi/4mi	Aerobic Refresh: 10min MP 7min LT 5min 10k pace 3min 5k pace w/ 3min easy between	6mi/6mi recovery	5mi/5mi recovery	14mi run w/ 6x30sec surges w/ 1:30 easy in the last 2miles	7-9mi recovery run	80
Alternation 600 at 5k, 600m steady, 4x	9mi/4mi	9x300 w/ 100m jog rest (alternate 3k pace, 1mi pace)	8mi easy	4-6mi w/ strides	Race	6-8mi recovery run	65
2x (800,800,400) w/ 45sec rest, 3-4min b/t, 5k pace	5mi/5mi	6x10sec Hill Sprints + 2x20sec hills	6mi/6mi recovery	LT 20min total + 2x400m with 3min rest, 2x200m w/ 3min. Faster work at 3k-1mi pace	8-9mi recovery run	13mi long run	75-80
5mi/5mi + strides	8-9mi run	2x(800,1k, 400) at 5k pace w/ 1:30-45 rest, 4min rest b/t sets	5mi/5mi recovery	4-6mi w/ strides	3k-5k Race	OFF/short recovery run	65
Alternation-800 at 5k pace/400m steady (4x)	5mi/5mi	8-9mi run	800 (3k), 400 (1mi), 500 (3k), 200 (800) w/ 2min rest	4mi/4mi	10-12mi run	6-8mi recovery run	60
6mi/6mi	800m at 5k pace, 300m jog, 2x400, 2x200 at 5k down to 1mile pace w/ 200m jog	7-9mi run+strides	6-7mi easy	4mi w/ strides	**Peak 5k**		55-60

10,000m

The 10k is an event that requires a very high level of endurance, but to be competitive at the elite level, it also requires the ability to change gears off of fast paces. In the past, longer distance runners were simply told to run a very high amount of mileage and then top it off with some interval training. With the top 10k runners and even marathoners, being competitive all the way down to the 1,500m, times have changed. A combination of speed, endurance, and strength endurance are required for maximum performance.

Endurance Side Development

The foundation for good 10k racing is a highly developed aerobic system. The long run and total mileage play large roles in establishing general endurance. As with all events, mileage should be progressively increased to maximum by the end of the base period. For ST 10k runners, the mileage should stay relatively constant with only a small drop of 10% or less during the pre-competition and early competition phases. A FT 10k runner should have a more substantial drop in mileage, up to 20%, but it should remain relatively high. It is only during the peaking phase when a FT runner can see significant mileage drops, while a ST runner should only see very slight decreases. As far as the total amount for elite 10k runners, the range varies widely from 80-90mpw for a FT to up to ~130 for a ST runner.

The long run also has more importance for a 10k than with the shorter events. The progression starts the same with a focus on increasing the distance (up to 14-20mi) first and then adding in "stuff." From here it diverges, as the long run should be thought of as an additional workout during the base and even early pre-competition phases before tapering off to maintenance as the competition phase begins. Until now, all other events have stopped with add-ons before they became full blown workouts. For the 10k, the progression should continue so that the stimulus is much higher. This is done by increasing the end pickup during the long run to up to 30-40minutes of steady to marathon pace work. Additionally, the long run is often replaced with a long tempo run of up to 10-12 miles in length that should start at a steady pace and progress to marathon pace or slightly faster. Lastly, alternations can be added to long runs instead of pickups or long tempos.

Because of the long runs increased intensity, it is best to cycle the long run every week. By cycling, I mean to establish a rotation of one easy long run the first week, a long run with moderate add-ons the second, and a long run with major add-ons or a full-blown long tempo the third. The cycle does not have to be based on an easy long run every 3 weeks but instead should be adjusted to the individual and how they recover. During such a system, the workouts surrounding the long run would also change. During the easy long run week, two "hard" workouts could be done, while during the hard long run week it is best to include only one other focus "hard" workout and include more moderate workouts instead. An example of such a cycle would be the following:

- 16mi easy
- 15mi with 25min pickup at the end
- 14miles total, 2mile warm up, 10mi tempo, 2mi cool down
- 16mi easy

The long runs with pickups or long tempo runs are one way to create aerobic support. Long alternation workouts are another great way. These can initially serve as aerobic support and be progressed to serve as direct endurance support and eventually specific endurance. The way to do this is to start with the "hard" segments at marathon pace and the recovery segments only very slightly slower and, as you progress, shorten the hard segments and increase the pace, first to LT and finally to 10k pace. Once at 10k pace, a specific endurance progression can take place, increasing the distance of the hard segments or reducing the recovery. Aerobic support should take place during the latter base phase and continue into the pre-competition phase. Once in the pre-comp phase, transitioning towards direct support should be done.

Lactate Threshold (LT) runs should be included and emphasized during the pre-comp phase. The goal is to use split LT runs and increase them to up to a maximum of 40 minutes total spent at LT for elites and 5-10min shorter for others. As discussed previously, alternations can also serve as direct support. For 10k runners, using some sort of add-on stimulus to LT runs near the end of the pre-comp are beneficial. Possible choices include hilly or uphill LT runs, surges during LT runs, progressions at the end of the run, or adding another segment for combo work. Adding on short segments of 10k paced work at the end of a threshold run is a good way to transition towards specificity.

Lastly, strength endurance is an important part of successful 10k training. During the base phase hill circuits can be done that include running at aerobic paces and doing various general strength exercises. Other possible options include runs on very hilly routes, aerobic hill fartleks, and uphill threshold runs. During the pre-comp phase, these can be made a little more specific by adding on hill repeats to the end of various workouts. Lastly, shorter more intense hills can function to enhance high intensity speed endurance and then doing specific combo work where you separate intervals at 10k pace with short to medium length hills can develop specific strength endurance.

Speed Side Development

General speed development for most 10k runners is done for biomechanical and neural reasons. The neural reasons are why 10k runners should still do hill sprints once a week during the base phase. The hill sprints will function to increase the muscle fiber pool, increase force development, and prevent injuries. Unlike with shorter events, some 10k runners will not need to progress to flat sprints. Instead the goal should be to increase the number done. Hill sprints perform the vital function of maintaining speed when all of the mileage being done is pulling the body towards only slow/aerobic adaptations. Sprint work helps to counterbalance this out.

Additionally, during the base phase establishing good biomechanics and comfort at faster paces is a must. With the high amounts of mileage being run, it is easy to get flat, loose responsiveness in the muscles and develop poor biomechanics. To counteract this, during the base phase easy speed work should be done in the form of surges, strides, aerobic intervals, and rhythm work. Start with introducing strides and surges to distance runs and progress to adding an easy set of aerobic intervals to the week. These intervals can be 100-400m intervals starting at 1mi to 5k paces. Plenty of recovery should be given, and the effort should not be hard as the goal is to teach the ability to run at a faster pace while being relaxed and under control.

During the pre-competition phase the use of aerobic intervals and other such strategies should continue. The aerobic intervals can branch off to form full 5k paced workouts. One way to incorporate direct support (5k paced) work is to use the early couple of workouts of a 5k specific endurance progression. Another way is in the form of combo and blend workouts, which have been covered before. During the competition period, the 5k paced work should be used in combination with specific 10k work to create specific speed endurance. There are several possibilities including blend and combo workouts or hill repeats.

Specific Development

Specific endurance development for the 10k begins in earnest during the pre-competition phase. Prior to the beginning of the progression, surges, pickups, and progressions create a base on which to build during the base phase. Any of a combination of the specific endurance progressions can be used. In particular, a Lydiard style time trial over 5-6k at just faster than 10k pace is a useful way to end the specific endurance development. This can often be easily accomplished by doing a small 5k road race at just faster than 10k effort 2 weeks before the 10k. For elite runners, alternations can create a MaxLASS (lactate steady state) at around 10k pace, which will enhance a runner's ability to close fast in a race.

For specific speed endurance, the combining of specific work and 5k pace work is what should be done. Once again, how to do this is only limited by your imagination. One way that focuses on the ability to finish is by progressing within an interval. For example, doing 1600m repeats with the first 800m at 10k pace and the next 800m at 5k pace works well. Similarly, combo workouts that are done in ladder form and focus on finishing at faster 3k-5k paces will accomplish the job. Finally, blend workouts are another good choice. Blend longer segments at 10k pace with shorter segments starting at 5k pace and get faster as the workout goes along, or substitute the faster work for hill repeats. An example of a blend workout could be 1600, 2x300 at 5k pace, 1200, 400 at 3k pace, 1000, 2x200 at 1mile pace with the longer segments being at 10k pace and taking 3-4min rest after the long segments, and 1-2min after the short.

Maintenance

General endurance is maintained through the use of long runs. Long run volume should be kept high as a form of maintenance throughout the pre-comp period with occasional moderate add-ons. Additionally, shorter marathon paced runs or progression runs top off general endurance and should be done once every 2-4 weeks. Similarly, threshold runs or some mixed combo or progression run should be used to maintain direct and aerobic support.

Due to the large volume of endurance work, hill sprints should be used pretty frequently for most 10k runners, as it can be their only very fast stimulus during certain training periods. Thus, hill sprints or a similar stimulus should be done once every 7-14 days. Specific endurance can be maintained through easy intervals and fartleks during the base phase or during the peaking process.

See appendix for examples/progressions for each workout type.

10,000m Training Plan

Monday	Tuesday	Wednesday	Thursday	Friday	Saturday	Sunday	MPW
Base Period- Plan for well trained runner maxing out at 100mpw							
Note: To hit mileage some recovery/secondary runs after workout days need to be added to schedule. Also warm-ups/cool downs not listed							
10mi distance run+ strides	8mi/5mi	10mi distance run+strides	5mi/5mi recovery	9-10mi	12-13mi long run	6-8mi recovery run	70
9-10mi distance run	9mi/5mi	9mi+Hill Sprints 6x10sec	6mi/6mi recovery	8mi Progression Run	14mi run	8mi recovery run	80
Run+Hill Sprints- 8x10sec	9mi/5mi +strides	9mi/4mi	9mi Progression Run	5mi/5mi recovery	14mi w/ w/ 6x30sec surges	8mi recovery run	80
LT 20min split total	9mi/5mi	Run+Hill Sprints 10x10sec	9mi/5mi	5mi/5mi recovery	13mi w/ 5min pickup	8mi recovery run	85
LT 25min split total	6mi/6mi	Distance run + 8x30sec surges	9mi/5mi	2x4mi at Marathon pace w/ 5min b/t sets	15mi Long Run	8-10mi recovery run	90
LT 30min split total	9mi/5mi	Run+Hill Sprints 6x10sec +2x20sec	9mi/5mi	Normal run+ 6x200m w/ 200m jog strides	15mi w/ 10min pickup	8-10mi recovery run	90
LT 35min split total	9mi/5mi	7mi/6mi recovery runs	10mi/5mi +strides	6mi/6mi recovery	17mi long run	8-10mi recovery run	100
LT 25min split, 3min easy, 2x800 w/ 30sec rest at 10k pace	9mi/5mi + strides	10mi/6mi	8x200 at 5k down to 3k pace w/ 200m jog	6mi/6mi recovery	8-10mi at Marathon Pace	8-10mi recovery run	100

Pre-Competition Period

Alternation 5-6mi of 400m (10k)/ 1200m steady	9mi/5mi	4x(400,200m jog, 200) at 5k down to 3k pace w/ 200m jog	6mi/6mi recovery	9mi/5mi	1mi medium long runs	8-10mi recovery run
						90
20min LT, 3x3min uphill w/ jog down recovery	9mi/5mi	5mi/5mi recovery	4x6min(first 4min at LT, last 2min at 10k) w/ 4min rest	9mi/3mi	8-10mi recovery run	8-10mi recovery run
						80
2x(5x3min w/ 1min easy) w/ 4min easy b/t sets at 10k	9mi/5mi	8x10sec Hill Sprints	5mi/5mi recovery	5x400, 5min rest, 4x400m, 5min rest, 3x400m at 5k pace w/ 40sec in b/t reps	14mi w/ 6x45sec surges at the end	8-10mi recovery run
						80
3x(500(5k), 300(3k), 200 (1mi)) w/ 1min b/t reps, 4min b/t sets	6mi/5mi	10-12x200 at 3k pace w/ 200m jog	7mi/4mi	4-6mi w/ strides	Race	OFF/short recovery run
						70
Alternation 5-6mi of 600m at 10k pace/ 1000m steady	6mi/5mi	3x800 at 5k, HS, 2x800, HS	10mi	9mi/5mi	14mi w/ 5min pickup	8-10mi recovery run
						80

Competition Period

25min LT run	8mi/5mi	6mi/6mi recovery	7mi/5mi	8mi Progression Run	10mi run	6-8mi recovery run	75
6x1mile at 10k pace w/ 3-4min rest	7mi/5mi	7min LT, 2x3min at 10k, 2x45sec at 5k pace w/ 2-3min rest	7mi/4mi	5-6mi	Race	6-8mi recovery run	70
1mi (10k), 600 (5k), 1200 (10k), 600 (3k), 1mi (10k), 2x400 at 3k/1mi w/ 3min rest	9mi/4mi	6mi/6mi recovery	Distance run w/ 8x45sec surges	5mi/5mi recovery	15mi Long run	7-9mi recovery run	80
Alternation 5-6mi of 800m 10k 800m steady	9mi/4mi	8x200m at 3k down to 1mile pace w/ 200m jog	8mi easy	4-6mi w/ strides	Race	6-8mi recovery run	65
4mi MP, 3min easy, 15min LT	5mi/5mi	8x10sec Hill Sprints	6mi/6mi recovery	3x(600,600,400) w/ 40sec rest at 5k pace, 3-4min b/t sets	8-9mi recovery run	13mi long run	75-80
2mi w/up, 3x2400m w/ 4min rest alternate 400m LT 400m 10k to 5k	8-9mi run	6min (LT), 3Easy, 3min (10k), 6E, 2x400 w/ 45sec rest at 10k, 2E, 4x10sec w/ 50sec rest	5mi/5mi recovery	4-6mi w/ strides	Race	OFF/short recovery run	70
1mi LT, 2mi 10k, 1mi LT, 1mi 10k down w/ 3-4min rest	8-9mi run	4mi/4mi	5x800 w/ 2:30 rest at 5k pace, 4xHill Sprints	5mi/5mi recovery	10mi run	6-8mi recovery run	60
6mi/6mi	5min LT, 5min easy, 2x3min at 10k pace w/ 2min easy, 60sec, 45sec, 30sec w/ 2min easy at 5k down to 3k pace	8-9mi run+strides	6-7mi easy	4mi w/ strides	**Peak 10k**		55-60

Marathon

Unlike all of the other events covered, fuel use is the major cause of fatigue in the marathon. This creates a situation where we not only have to train to be able to run at our goal pace for the entire race, but we also have to train the fuel system to be able to have enough fuel to run at that pace for 26.2 miles. To improve the fuel system we must either increase the total supply, decrease the rate of glycogen use at race pace, or some combination of both. To accomplish these goals, the training must be developed in two different ways; one focused on developing enough endurance at race pace to last aerobically and biomechanically, and another focused on the fuel system issues. Or, in plain English, we must train to be comfortable at marathon pace, and train so that we don't hit the wall.

Endurance Side Development

The foundation of a good marathon is built on a large base of general endurance. General endurance is not only needed to lay the foundation of aerobic development but also to establish a biomechanical base. One often overlooked factor for marathon performance is withstanding the pounding and subsequent muscle damage that occurs over 26.2 miles. Due to the pounding and large amount of eccentric contractions, particularly on hilly courses, muscle damage will occur. As muscle damage increases, efficiency decreases, so it negatively affects performance. High mileage and long runs are not only used for aerobic endurance, but they also serve to prepare the body to withstand the stress of running such a long way. The base period should focus on increasing the distance of the long run and total mileage. Total mileage should progressively increase, reaching maximum during the later part of the pre-competition, and remaining very close to max until the tapering phase. Volume is needed first, and then intensity can be built upon this volume.

General endurance should be focused initially only on easy running and increasing the total volume, but it should progress to the inclusion of steady paced running. This progression can start with short pickups at the end of runs and then include moderate progression runs or longer steady paced tempo runs. The long run should increase progressively in distance without concern over pace initially. Only during the pre-competition period should the intensity of the long run start to be a focus. Initially, moderate surges, pickups, and progressions should be added, while during the later pre-comp phase a specific progression should be introduced that includes marathon paced running during the long run.

Unlike other events, the direct endurance support is actually a pace that is faster than marathon pace. Half marathon pace or Lactate Threshold pace serves as direct support. The reason is that paces around LT serve to increase our high-end aerobic abilities. This sets the stage for increasing our specific marathon speed. If the opposite approach were taken, focusing on marathon pace or slightly slower first and then focusing on LT work, two problems would arise. First, in this approach, the latter LT work would increase the rate of glycogen use, which would not be a good idea for the marathon. Second, there is only a small gap between marathon pace and LT, and by doing marathon pace work first, there is less room for improvement of the marathon pace. Instead if LT is developed first, then it increases the gap between LT and marathon pace, which then allows for the subsequent marathon specific work to close that gap during the competition period.

Therefore, during the pre-competition phase the focus should be on developing the LT. This does not mean runs solely at LT but rather an array of paces surrounding LT. Runs at LT and slightly faster than LT will work on developing the aerobic abilities of the muscle fibers in slightly different ways. The faster work will focus more on the development of more Fast Twitch muscle fibers, while slightly slower than LT will focus on the Slow Twitch fibers. Additionally, work slightly faster than LT will induce a small amount of ever increasing lactate into the system. To work on lactate use as fuel use alternations, which can improve the fuel system by delaying glycogen use, these alternations should consist of alternating at just faster than LT and just slower than LT.

Lastly, strength endurance is an important part of successful marathon training. During the base phase hill circuits, hilly runs, or uphill runs can be used for development from the endurance side. This type of work can be continued during the pre-competition phase, in particular uphill LT runs or hilly LT runs are useful. Hilly LT runs will lead to a similar response as alternations done just above and below LT. During the uphill portion an increase in lactate will occur even without an increase in effort because hills cause an increase in FT muscle fibers. During the downhill or flat section, if run at LT, then the lactate created during the uphill portion can be used. In addition, strength endurance should be developed from the speed standpoint, which will be discussed shortly.

Speed Side Development

Speed development for the marathon functions to improve biomechanical efficiency, increase the amount of muscle fibers available to do the work, increase strength and power, and above all to make marathon pace feel as relaxed as possible. During the base period, hill sprints are used to increase strength, power, and neural recruitment. In addition, short surges or aerobic intervals at 5k, 3k, and 1mi pace are used. These are not full workouts but should rather be thought of as for biomechanical reasons.

The pre-competition period is when anaerobic support and direct support work are brought to maximum. 5k-10k paced work is done both for biomechanical reasons and to improve aerobic abilities, specifically to increase the amount and rate of aerobic energy that can be supplied. This can initially be done by progressive or combo work, and later through aerobic intervals, longer intervals, and alternations. To start with, adding on a short segment at 10k pace to an LT work is a good way to introduce 10k pace, while extending the cruise work done at 3k paces during the base phase to include short intervals at 5k pace work can serve as its introduction. The development of speed support can be done by using the first part of the specific endurance progressions for the 5k and 10k races. The only difference when taking this approach is to stop the progression earlier and to use more blend workouts. In this way, alternations, blends, or combo workouts can also be included. The end goal is to increase high-end aerobic abilities and establish a level of comfort at faster paces.

During the specific period, this work needs to be kept to a minimum. The reason is that larger doses of 5k, 10k, and LT work shifts the fuel system to rely more on glycogen. This happens because when running at these faster paces the fuel supply is never the issue; therefore the body is worried about what the best way is to supply energy rapidly, not on how to conserve it for a marathon. Therefore, only short maintenance work should be done.

Lastly is the issue of strength endurance from the speed perspective. Initially, the foundation of strength endurance is developed through hill sprints. From here, hill circuits work well, as do blend and alternation work at 5k-10k paces. Additionally, medium length hills (200-600m) at 1mi-5k effort during the base or early pre-competition phase will convert some of that pure speed to high intensity strength endurance. As we go later into the pre-competition period, longer hills at 5k-10k paces can be used to develop both direct speed support and strength endurance. Finally, during the competition phase, uphill tempo's or hilly long runs put the finishing touches on specific strength endurance.

Specific Development

Running at or slightly faster and slower than goal marathon pace is the key intensity for many of the adaptations that are necessary for improved marathon performance. Specific development comes in several forms. First, the ability to endure for 2 hours or more comes from progressively increasing the distance of the long run to that length. Second, and most importantly, is the development of specific endurance by extending endurance at marathon pace.

During the base phase, marathon pace is included for short periods of time at the end of runs in the form of moderate pickups and progressions. Specific endurance for the marathon is usually built in two different ways. First, alternations or long fartlek segments are used. In alternations, we generally start with short alternations of around 800m at marathon pace alternated with an equal segment at a just slower pace. From here, the marathon pace segment increases progressively up to a max of around 4 miles, while the recovery segment generally stays between 800-1mile in length. In addition, the total volume of these alternations starts at a relatively low distance of 6-7miles and increases to up to 18-20miles worth of total work. If alternations were used to develop direct endurance support, then one option is to continue the progression of those workouts by progressively slowing and lengthening the faster segment until it is at marathon pace, then building specific endurance from there.

The second way is through longer tempos or progressions. Early on, progressions will only end with a small portion at marathon pace, but as the season progresses, more and more of the run should be done at marathon pace or slightly faster. Progressions usually serve as a great introduction or transition to marathon pace. Long Tempo's should start out as simple pick-ups at the end of distance runs before becoming a workout in and of themselves. These tempo runs should start fairly short at around 6 miles and progressively increase. For a straight marathon paced tempo, the maximum volume varies by level and athlete type. A general rule is to work up to near 13-18mi, though such a workout is very stressful and should only be used sparingly. Depending on the purpose of the workout, these can either be done on their own or as an add-on to the long run. By doing them as an add-on to the long run, the first portion of the long run will serve to fatigue the runner and deplete their glycogen stores. Due to this pre-fatigue, the fuel system will be stressed to a higher degree, forcing adaptations in either fuel capacity or usage.

While some long runs or long workouts should include practicing fuel intake, particularly your one or two key longer workouts, some long runs and marathon pace runs should be done without taking in supplemental fuel. The reason is that we are trying to decrease glycogen stores during longer runs because that is the signal for adaptation. When the body encounters low glycogen, it triggers a response (see Chapter: The Genetics of Training) that causes adaptations to prevent the body from encountering low glycogen at the same intensity and duration as before. Supplemental fuel such as gels or sports drinks would impede this trigger. It is a balancing act of perfecting fuel intake and avoiding supplemental fuel. A good rule is to alternate whether supplemental fuel is taken in or not.

Maintenance

While maintenance work for the marathon was mentioned in the previous sections, I'll briefly go over it again. General endurance is maintained through the use of long runs and high mileage. While many long runs include specific work, every 2-4 weeks depending on the phase, a long run should be of almost entirely easy running. Aerobic Support is similarly maintained with easy to steady distance running.

Direct endurance support is maintained mostly through end of the workout pickups and progressions. During the competition phase, maintenance style threshold runs can be included. For anaerobic support, maintenance includes short aerobic intervals that are limited in volume to keep from them affecting the fuel system during the competition phase. Direct speed support is similarly maintained through short aerobic intervals or as a form of combo work. General speed is maintained through strides, hill sprints, and short aerobic intervals or rhythm work.

See appendix for examples/progressions for each workout type.

Marathon Training Plan

Monday	Tuesday	Wednesday	Thursday	Friday	Saturday	Sunday	MPW
Base Period- Plan for well trained runner maxing out at 120-130mpw							
Note: To hit mileage some recovery/secondary runs after workout days need to be added to schedule. Also warm-ups/cool downs not listed.							
8-10mi	9mi/4mi	Run+6x10sec Hill Sprints	5mi/5mi	8-10mi	14mi Long run	6-8mi recovery	70
8-10mi	9mi/7mi	Run+8x10sec Hill Sprints	10mi w/ last 5mi pickup	9mi/7mi	15mi easy	8-10mi recovery	80
12x200 at 3k down to 1mi pace w/ 200m jog	9mi/5mi	Run+8x10sec Hill Sprints	7mi steady	9mi/7mi	16mi w/ 8x45sec surges	8-10mi recovery	90
9mi/7mi	20min LT	10mi/4mi	8x(400/200) at 3k pace w/ 200m jog	8mi/8mi	17mi easy	8-10mi recovery	100
6mi/6mi	alternating- 6mi-400m(just faster than LT)/1200m (steady)	9mi/7mi	Strength Endurance Hill Circuit	7mi/7mi	18mi easy	Off	70-80
25min split LT	9mi/7mi	8mi/7mi	3x(3x600) at 5k pace, 30sec rest, 4min rest	8mi/7mi	13mi w/ last 4mi progressive	8-10mi recovery	110
Strength Endurance Hill Circuit	7mi/6mi	800m(just faster than LT)/800m (steady)	10mi/6mi	8mi/7mi	20mi easy	8-10mi recovery	110

Pre-Competition Period

Run+10x10sec Hill Sprints	8mi/8mi	30min split LT	9mi/6mi	9mi/9mi	alt- 8mi-800m(LT)/800m (MP)	8-10mi recovery	100
9mi/9mi	3x(800,400,800 w/ 40sec rest) 5k pace, 3min rest	7mi/7mi	Run+8x10sec Hill Sprints	6mi easy	15-20k Race	Off/short recovery	70-80
9mi/9mi	35min split LT	10mi/8mi	9mi/7mi	18mi w/ 10x60sec surges in the last 4mi	8mi steady/5mi easy	8-10mi recovery	115-125
10mi/8mi	15min LT,3min rest, 2x5min uphill (10k effort), 2x3min uphill (5k effort) w/ jog down recovery	9mi/8mi	10mi/5mi	5mi easy, alternation 9mi of 800m(just slower than LT)/800m (MP)	7mi/7mi	8-10mi recovery	110-120
2mi LT, 1mi (10k), 6x10sec hill sprints	7mi/7mi	8mi w/ 7x30sec surges/ 6mi easy	6mi/4mi	6mi easy	Half Marathon Race	Off/short recovery	70-80
10mi/5mi recovery	9mi/7mi recovery	5x4min uphill at 10k down to 5k effort w/ 3min easy, 6x8sec hill sprints	12mi/ 6mi	9mi/9mi	4mi easy, alternating 6x1mile/800m (MP/steady), 4mi easy	8-10mi recovery	120-130

Competition Period

9mi/7mi	10-16x200 at 5k down to 1mi pace w/ 200m jog	12mi easy	8mi steady/6mi easy	10mi/8mi	5mi easy, 14mi progression down to MP	8-10mi recovery	120-130
6mi steady/8mi easy	9mi/5mi	5mi easy, alternating 5x1.5mi/800m (MP/steady)	7mi/7mi	9m/9mi	2mi (10k), 1mi(5k), 800 (3k), (2x400 w/60sec rest) (1mi), w/ 4min rest	8-10mi recovery	110-120
9mi/9mi	6mi MP,1mi 10k, 4mi MP, 1mi 10k w/ 4min rest b/t	9mi/9mi	12mi steady	7mi/7mi	18-20miles easy	8-10mi recovery	110-120
9mi/5mi	2mi (LT), 1.5mi (10k), 1mi (5k), (4x300 w/ 200m jog) (1mi) w/ 4min rest	9mi/9mi	Run+8x10sec Hill sprints	10mi easy	5x (2mi at MP /800m steady)	Off/short recovery	90-100
7mi/7mi	Morning-6mi +7mi at MP Afternoon-6mi+25min LT	6mi/6mi	9mi/4mi	7mi alternating 400m at LT, 1200m at MP	7mi/7mi	8-10mi recovery	110
9mi/5mi	16mi hilly run-progression from easy to just faster than MP	6mi/6mi	Run+8x200 at 5k/3k pace w/ 200m jog	9m/7mi	4x3mi at MP w/ 800m steady	8-10mi recovery	100-110
9mi/5mi	7mi at MP w/ 1min surge down to LT every mile	6mi/6mi	7mi/4mi steady	9mi/6mi	6mi at MP	10mi Recovery	80-90
10mi/4mi w/ 30sec surges	8mi/4mi	7mi easy w/ 5-10min pickup to MP at the end	5-6mi easy	4-5mi easy	**Peak Marathon Race**		60-70

21

Special Workouts and Strength Training

"One of the big mistakes when you are able to improve using a program is to suppose you can continue to improve using the same type of program. Instead, you must change the program! Because, why are you able to (improve)?" Renato Canova

Strength Endurance: The Key to Developing a Kick

One key to developing a kick is the idea of strength endurance. Strength endurance is the ability to maintain strength (force production) during fatigue, or in other words the ability to use your strength for longer. For simplicity's sake, in terms of running think of it as combining exercises/runs that require a larger amount of strength with an element of endurance. Before getting into the details of actually creating a strength endurance session, let's look at some of the science behind it.

We have all admired and wondered how certain runners are able to maintain perfect running form while their legs are searing with pain on the final homestretch of the race. There are many hypotheses about how the athletes are more aerobic or better able to deal with the (wrongly) accused poison lactic acid, but what actually happens during the final straight away?

Studies by Numella have looked at strength endurance by looking at muscle activity and force production changes during fatigue in runners. In one study he demonstrated that force production capacities decreased by about 25% at the end of a 400m, and this decrease correlated with increases in by-products. In addition to the strength reduction there was an increase in ground contact time and a decrease in ground reaction forces during the latter portion of the race. These findings confirmed that the ability to maintain a high level of strength, also known as strength endurance, could be vital in maintaining speed during the final stretch of the race. However, at this point it is still theoretical. It makes sense that maintaining strength levels longer would prevent slow down because force production into the ground would be maintained longer, and thus ground contact times would not decrease as fast. Getting form theory to practice required another study.

In the last study, Miguel and colleagues compared explosive strength and explosive strength endurance of fast runners (48sec or better for 400m) to slower runners (49sec or slower).

They measured the attributes with a series of vertical jumps and a 30 second continuous jump for height to measure strength endurance. By comparing these two groups, it could be seen if faster runners had more strength endurance than slower ones. Not surprisingly, the faster runners had significantly better explosive strength and strength endurance. The better strength endurance allowed the faster runners to maintain ground contact times during the end of the race. With the association established, it can be safely concluded that higher levels of strength endurance help combat fatigue during the latter part of a 400m race.

How do we actually develop strength endurance? Here's my 3-step cheat sheet guide to strength endurance and kick development:

1. Increase maximum fibers recruited
2. Improve ability to use for prolonged time
3. Learn to recruit them under high acidity

Developing A Strength Endurance Program

In developing a program for strength endurance it is important to remember that our main goal is to be able to finish races faster. In terms of strength endurance, this means maintaining strength levels for longer, maintaining ground contact, and maintaining proper running mechanics, or, in essence, resisting the muscular and neural effects of fatigue.

An obvious but often overlooked aspect of developing strength endurance is the need for a satisfactory level of overall strength from which to develop the endurance. If there is not a decent base of strength to work off of, then it cannot be extended to last very long. The general strength needed can be developed by sprint, plyometric, and explosive power/ballistic training. As mentioned previously, such training as sprint work will increase the total recruitable muscle fiber pool. This first step is needed before strength endurance can be developed.

Strength Endurance Development

Once this base of strength is developed, the focus must be switched to extending the strength, i.e., converting it to strength endurance. The first step in this conversion is adding an endurance component to the strength work. Just being able to recruit more muscle fibers does not guarantee success. The strength gains are useless unless they can last for a period of time that can aid the athlete. It does the athlete no good to recruit more fibers if they don't last long enough to be used during a race. Also, increasing the proportion of fibers that can be used is another key in developing strength endurance.

The concept of non-specific lactate accumulation is also important when discussing the benefits of strength endurance work. Arthur Lydiard was one of the earliest coaches to note that high levels of lactate work seemed to have a negative effect on aerobic abilities. This led to an overreaction to avoid all faster workouts or higher lactate work during the base phase. The key is not in completely avoiding faster or moderate lactate work but in ensuring balance between the faster work and the aerobic work. One way to transition or introduce higher lactate work is through circuits. When completing circuits, the exercises will introduce some lactate into the system. Since the exercises are not specific to running, most of the muscles producing the lactate are slightly different from those used when running, or they are being recruited in a different way than when running. That means we aren't training the specific running muscle fibers to produce or deal with lactate directly. As a result, none of the negative effects on the aerobic abilities occur. Additionally, during the subsequent running session, lactate use can be trained, as the muscle fibers can be trained to take up and use the lactate from the blood stream. Non-specific lactate work is a great way to train not only strength endurance but also moderate lactate accumulation during the base or early pre-competition phases when we do not want to negatively affect the aerobic system.

Strength endurance work can be separated in terms of how specific it is to the goal of running a race. For simplicity's sake it can be divided into three categories: general, high intensity, and specific strength endurance.

General Strength Endurance

In general strength endurance work, the goal is to start the process of extending our ability to use a high proportion of our strength over a longer period of time. The exercises and runs are not specific in terms of type, intensity, or duration. The possibilities of creating general strength endurance are almost endless. Briefly we will go through some of the different methods.

Hills are one of the tried and true methods that have been used almost since the inception of our sport. Runs over hilly courses at easy to moderate speeds are a great way to work on general strength endurance. Because the speed and intensity are not close to race speed, it falls into the general category. Hills offer a wide variety of options which include simple runs over hilly terrain, easy to moderate repeats of running up and down a portion of a hill, uphill strength endurance circuits, and longer moderate repeats uphill.

Circuits are another great way to develop general strength endurance. The Italian coach Renato Canova developed a great progression of circuits in more recent years, while Arthur Lydiard had his famous hill circuits in the 1960's. The first step in creating a strength endurance circuit is a rather simple one. Take general exercises and add an endurance component. One simple way to accomplish this is to separate each set of exercises with a run. The pace of the run should be easy at first and then progressively increased as you develop general strength endurance to more specific strength endurance. A good place to start is to have both the exercises and run at roughly 70% effort. The length of each set of the circuit depends on the event that the athlete will run. The longer the race, the longer the circuit should be. A general rule of thumb is to have each repetition be as long as an aerobic interval workout would be for that athlete. For example, a 10k runner who does 5x 2000m repeats would do a circuit that is approximately 5-6 minutes in length and do this circuit 5 times with appropriate rest in between.

Another option that a coach has is to do the circuits uphill. This will further increase the strength component, and thus fiber recruitment, during the running portion of the circuit. This makes it so that not only do the exercises have a strength component, but the running portion does too. With the hill, more muscle fibers will be recruited than during a flat ground circuit.

In terms of what exercises to use during a circuit, it depends on what you want to accomplish during the workout. The focus can be on the legs, arms, core, or overall body endurance. In addition, you can make the exercises focus on a specific component, for example if the athlete tends to lose bounce when tired he can do more explosive exercises, such as various hops. The key to deciding what exercises to use and the sequencing are to evaluate the athlete and what their needs are. Watch your athletes finish races and see what portions of their running mechanics break down. That will give you a good idea of what the focus should be on.

Another way to increase strength endurance is in the use of long runs. Long runs done the day after a hard workout will help accomplish this goal because of the residual fatigue of the workout. The muscles will not be fully recovered by the next day after the workout, and in doing a long run you are working heavily on the endurance component. Also, because the athlete goes into the run pre fatigued, more and different muscle fibers will have to be recruited (and thus trained aerobically) to sustain the workload during the latter part of the long run. In a similar vein, doing strength work then immediately following it with a run at an easy to moderate intensity will increase strength endurance levels. The strength workout will recruit different muscles than just running would and will fatigue them. Then by going for a run afterwards, those muscles are worked on aerobically, or other muscles have to cycle in and be recruited to take up the workload.

High Intensity Strength Endurance

Once a base of general strength endurance has been established it is time to increase the intensity. This can be accomplished by altering the circuits or by including longer hill repeats. Hill repeats (200-600m) that are very intense (mile effort or faster) with long recoveries are one way to improve high intensity strength endurance. My High School coach, Gerald Stewart, was a fan of using 300 and 400m repeats up a moderate hill with a slow jog down. Towards the end of the session, your body is trying to maintain fiber recruitment for running uphill under heavily fatigued conditions. In strength endurance circuits, there are several different ways of adding the intensity to the circuits. Either you can increase the intensity of the exercise itself, increase the intensity of the run connecting the exercises, or increase both. What method you use depends on the goal of the circuit.

Adding intensity to the exercises themselves will recruit additional muscle fibers and increase the strength component of the workout. In addition, since the recovery between the exercises, the run, is performed at a moderate intensity the muscles do not get full recovery.

Because of this lack of recovery and the fact that the strength requirement is higher, the athlete is teaching his body how to recruit additional fibers while becoming progressively fatigued. This is a great way to train the body to maintain high fiber recruitment over a longer duration. The key difference between this type of work and general circuits is that the athlete is fatiguing at a much higher rate. Thus he is training his muscles to be able to last longer, but this time at a much higher intensity.

Another way to increase the intensity is to increase the speed of the running part. The running part is then the main part of the workout, and the exercises at a medium intensity serve as the recovery portion. In doing the circuit this way, the focus is on running, thus it is more specific.

The exercises then serve as a way of forcing fiber recruitment after the fibers have been heavily fatigued during the running part. When running at a high intensity, the athlete is quickly fatiguing the fibers used and rotating new ones in to take their place. The force requirement can only be so much, and with the continued fatigue, the athlete cannot keep recruiting new fibers. To try to force the body to change up the recruitment and recruit more of its supply (remember, the athlete never reaches full fiber recruitment), exercises are used. The exercises, such as various plyos or bounds, will force additional and slightly different muscle fiber recruitment due to the explosiveness of the activity and the fact that the force requirement is higher. In this type of circuit, the goal is obviously to try to translate to specific high intensity strength endurance.

Sample Circuit

200m run
10x squat jumps
100m run
50m bounding
70m running
50m skipping
200m running

For General strength endurance the runs and exercises are moderately hard in nature, so that the paces would be around 10k effort. During the High Intensity strength endurance circuit, the runs and exercises would be performed at much higher intensities and have longer recovery between each circuit.

Kick Development

The final step is a continuation of high intensity strength endurance work, only in the most specific way. The goal is to reach a high level of fatigue, then try to force fiber recruitment under these conditions, and then continue to run, thus training those fibers to be recruited during running under such conditions.

Following these guidelines, we want to do some running that causes fatigue then go immediately into an activity that forces fiber recruitment, and then go immediately into running. We don't want a long delay between the running and exercise, so that leaves us with a couple of basic options. First, if you are fortunate enough to have a place where there is a flat section, a short hill, then it levels out at the top of the hill, that is perfect. Run at a fast pace for 30sec on the flat to the hill, then sprint up the hill and continue that sprint for 15-20sec at the top of the hill. For the rest of us who aren't fortunate enough to have such an arrangement, the best way to go about it is by using bounding in the middle of intervals. A workout I often use is to run sets of a broken 500m, with 200m fast, 100m bounding, and 200m kick in. Run the first 200m at around 800m pace, go straight into bounding, then straight into 200m kick in. For most runners 2 sets will do, but with more experienced runners 3 or 4 can be used. There are many variations of this type of work, just use your imagination.

Lastly, we want to teach the athlete how to kick. Learning how to gradually accelerate and change the running mechanics during the last part of the race is a skill that needs to be learned. To begin with, added segments at faster paces, such as those used during specific speed endurance work, teach the athlete how to change paces when fatigued. The problem is that in reality when we kick it isn't an abrupt change; therefore we must work on progressing from race pace to a faster pace within the interval itself. Teach this gradual progression with an emphasis on how to change mechanics at first during short workouts that progress from race pace to a kick. Research shows that each runner has a particular signature in how they kick. They use a preferred change in stride length and rate, and it is often in the opposite direction of their preferred running style. This means that if they rely heavily on a very quick turnover during the run, that is likely maxed out, so they will try to lengthen their stride during the kick. Train so that each athlete has the ability to change either rate or length so that they have more options in their arsenal.

The goal is to lengthen the interval. An example would be to start with 200m segments with the first 100m at race pace and the last 100m being a kick in and progress to where athletes are running 1000m intervals with the first 800m at race pace (for the 2mile or 5k for example) and the last 200m being a gradual kick in. As for biomechanical cues, teach the runners that the arms dictate what the legs do, so lengthen and increase the arm stroke using it to control the tempo. The bottom line is that this progression will teach a runner how to increase his kick and be ready to race.

Creating a MaxLASS at Race Pace

For elite runners, a MaxLASS is a lactate steady state at 5k or longer race pace. We are accustomed to thinking about the fastest speed that we can have a lactate steady state as being lactate threshold or around half marathon pace. However, research done by Renato Canova has demonstrated that well-trained elite runners can create a steady state for a short period at 5k and 10k race pace. This has been given as one reason why African runners can finish the latter part of their race at much faster paces, closer to their top end speed, than their western counterparts. Remember that while lactate doesn't cause fatigue, it corresponds with fatigue, so that is why a lactate steady state is important. It essentially means that fatigue products are at a steady state too. While there is much research to be done, by using Canova's research we can come up with an idea about how to create a MaxLASS for elite runners.

The caveat to developing a steady state is that it only can occur in well-trained runners who are very fit. One hypothesis is that the lifetime aerobic base of Africans allows them to create such a steady state. Combining this with what we know about the dynamics of lactate, a very well-developed aerobic system is a requirement. Thus two prerequisites to developing this special MaxLASS are a very high level of general endurance and a well-developed lactate threshold. Additionally, Canova demonstrated that a high level of strength endurance is the third requirement. Once these three components are created, then they have to be put together. Therefore, our steps for creating a lactate steady state are as follows:

1. Develop a high level of General Endurance.
2. Develop a high Lactate Threshold.
3. Develop Strength Endurance.
4. Top it off with Specific Endurance and specific endurance combined with strength endurance.

In America or any Western country we will never be able to generate the natural aerobic base that African runners have since our society is built on convenience and inactivity. Instead, we have to do it in organized fashion. For all runners that means a focus on first increasing general endurance. This means a smart gradual progression of volume of training and a good deal of easy to moderate high end aerobic endurance work. The longer moderate workouts such as sustained tempos, thresholds, and progression runs help make up the gap of general endurance. Other ways of increasing general endurance have been covered throughout the book.

The next step is to increase the lactate threshold. Once again, this has been covered throughout the book, but to briefly rehash, transition marathon pace and progression work into LT workouts, then increase the quantity of total LT work and then the frequency of LT workouts. From here, add in hilly LT runs or uphill LT runs and combo work with some running at just faster than LT. To top off the threshold, some faster work needs to be done, including long intervals at 10k pace and aerobic intervals at 3k-5k paces.

At the same time as threshold development, strength endurance development should be started. How to develop strength endurance was discussed earlier in this chapter. It is the combination of a well-developed LT and strength endurance that allows for the final step.

The last step is to use alternations to create a lactate steady state. Start with alternations at race pace and a steady pace. The goal is to first progress the pace of the steady portion of the alternation and then increase the lengths of the race pace portion. The aim is to increase the steady portion pace to near LT. When this is done, the body will be trained to deal with the lactate that is produced during the race pace portion of the segment. If progressed well, the body will adapt by gradually reducing the amount of lactate in the blood at race pace, eventually creating a steady state.

Creating a MaxLASS is one of the keys for world class 5k and 10k performance. While the number of runners who reach this level is minimal, all runners can still benefit from taking this approach. In the end, while a steady state will not be created for most runners, decreasing the lactate accumulation at steady state will be beneficial, as that means that fatigue products are accumulating at a slower rate.

Strength Training for Endurance Athletes

Strength training evokes a polarized response from coaches, runners, and scientists with some emphasizing it and others completely neglecting it. Furthermore, among those who do strength training, there is no consensus on what the best approach is. So, what is an athlete to do? Ask most distance runners, and they'll say a high rep low weight approach is the best strength training program, but in reality this is far from the truth.

I'm always hesitant to write about strength training for endurance runners, because while it does help, it has to be implemented correctly. Before delving into how that is done, there are some overarching rules with strength training. First, running is king, and the strength work should not take away from the running. If strength work starts to interfere with your more important running sessions (after a short adaptation period to strength training obviously), then the strength training should be decreased. Second, strength training is highly individual. I'll discuss how to individualize the training later in this chapter, but it is important to recognize that unlike with running, not every single strength training method is needed by every runner. While heavy training, power training, and plyometrics can all provide benefits, their importance for each individual differs greatly. Especially with heavy training, some runners need it because they need the neural benefits, while others can minimize or skip that type of training because it is not important for their event or their individual physiology. Keep these rules in mind throughout this chapter.

Before getting into how a runner should strength train, let's cover the biggest fear of runners: weight gain. Gaining muscle mass is the number one reason why runners don't want to strength train. This fear of bulking up is largely unfounded if trained properly. This is clear to see when we look at how muscle mass is developed.

A Weighty Matter

An increase in muscle size is called Hypertrophy. As long as runners avoid work that causes hypertrophy there will be little to no change in muscle size. So, the answer is simple, don't do work that increases muscle size. The practical application is a little more difficult.

Hypertrophy is largely dependent on muscle protein breakdown. A large amount of protein needs to be degraded to create a supercompensation like effect during recovery where protein synthesis occurs. This supercompensation effect leads to greater protein synthesis and thus an increase in muscle size. Total protein breakdown is a function of the rate of protein breakdown and the amount of time (or in other words total amount of reps) spent lifting. In general, the heavier the weight lifted the higher the rate of protein breakdown. So this means that heavy lifting creates hypertrophy right? Most runners come to this conclusion, but they forget the second part of the equation, the time or total work part. When lifting heavy weights, the rate of breakdown is high, but the number of total reps is very low, so the total protein breakdown is not very high. Instead, to maximize protein degradation, and thus hypertrophy, a lift that is of a moderately heavy weight (50-65% of 1RM for example) for a moderate amount of reps (6-12 for example) is done. It is no coincidence that body builders use mostly these in between weights and rep numbers. For a distance runner, the plan should be to avoid this in between zone and to limit the total workload to avoid hypertrophy.

But the story does not stop there as caloric intake and protein balance play a large role. In order for this supercompensation to take place, enough extra protein needs to be lying around to cause a large amount of protein synthesis. For most distance runners they are either at neutral or a slight negative protein balance due to the large volume of running they are doing. Thus, for most runners doing higher volumes of training, they have little to worry about as far as weight gain goes no matter what. Just like in training for endurance, strength training is highly individual too. Fast Twitch runners are more likely to have enough spare protein lying around to build muscle, so they have to be more cautious.

In their case, diet plays a large role, particularly after the strength workout. In looking at the signaling pathways for adaptations, we know that Amino Acids act on the same pathway (mTOR) that causes an increase in muscle size. Branched Chain Amino Acids (BCAA) can activate the mTOR pathway, particularly when taken after a strength training workout. So following resistance training it is probably not a good idea to refuel with BCAAs if the goal is not to increase muscle fiber size.

Another factor that plays a role is the timing of training. Once again, research shows that one of the key determinants of an increase in muscle size is continual high levels of mTOR activation. Fortunately for runners, the signaling pathway that is activated with endurance training (AMPK) not only works to increase mitochondria, but also to inhibit the strength gaining mTOR pathway. The mTOR pathway does not reach its highest activation during the workout but instead steadily increases and peaks after post workout. It is this near constant prolonged activation that stimulates muscle growth. Unlike mTOR, AMPK is highest during the endurance work and decreases once glycogen is replenished. What this means is that if the goal is to minimize muscle size gains, an easy way to achieve this is by doing strength training first followed by some easy endurance work. By timing the training in this way, the AMPK activation during the endurance training will inhibit the mTOR pathway and not allow it to stay elevated for very long post strength training.

How to Strength Train

The goals of strength training for endurance athletes should be to improve injury resistance, gain neural adaptations such as increasing muscle fiber pool, and improve rate of force development (RFD). These adaptations combine to improve efficiency, speed, and strength endurance. The bases of any strength program for runners should start with movement and act as an almost pre-habilitation program. The scope of how to identify individual needs and exercise selection for runners is beyond the scope of this book. I highly recommend Jay Dicharry's *Anatomy for Runners* as a valuable text to lay the foundation. This movement-based foundation should function much like your base phase of running would. Get the basics down and establish movement and foundational strength before progressing to training for performance. The training discussed in the rest of the chapter is the next step once the movement-based training is done.

As I have mentioned previously, if we look at fatigue from a neural and muscular perspective, fatigue can occur when muscle fiber recruitment decreases and when force development cannot occur in a quick enough time (thus longer ground contact times when fatigued). If we can increase the amount of fibers available to do work, decrease their relative percent of force while running by increasing their strength, and improve our power to maintain force development, then performance is improved.

Running, even long distance running, is mostly a function of power and thus RFD. Maximum force development takes at minimum .3-.4 seconds. If we look at ground contact times for sprinters, they are generally around .1 seconds, and for distance runners during races, times are .13-.17 seconds. This clearly demonstrates that while maximum force is nice, it is really about how quickly we can exert the force needed to maintain our pace. In other words the RFD plays a large role.

In addition to force development, increasing the muscle fiber pool can also play a role in enhancing performance. A larger pool of fibers means more potential fibers to cycle in and handle the workload. Since we know that force requirement is what determines muscle recruitment, it only makes sense that heavy lifting or high force activities will maximize fiber recruitment. Increasing the fiber pool while lifting is nice, but where it really benefits runners is when this is translated to an increase in the recruitable fiber pool when actually running. This can be done through sprinting and sets up the runner for an increase in strength endurance. Essentially, lifting to increase the recruitable fiber pool serves as the base of strength endurance training, which is invaluable for runners.

The way to accomplish these goals is not the traditional high reps, low weight method. Instead, start with the complete opposite, higher weight low reps. The reason is that when lifting heavy for only 1-6 reps, the enhancements in strength are almost entirely neural. The heavy weight challenges the nervous system without having a high total volume to elicit enough of a protein response to trigger changes in muscle size. Therefore, heavy training with low reps is the way to go for neurally induced gains in strength and muscle fiber recruitment.

Neural improvements occur via several mechanisms. Muscle force is regulated by four basic factors: the amount of muscle recruited, the firing frequency of the fibers, the recruitment pattern at the motor unit level, and the motor programming of several muscle groups working in synch. Recruitment pattern at the motor unit level refers to how motor unit recruitment occurs and whether it is in a cyclic fashion like in endurance activities or in a synchronous fashion like in power events. At the whole body level, the motor programming refers to how well a group of muscles interact and work together to produce force for a particular movement. An example of improved motor programming can be seen when the muscle opposite of the one doing the work learns to relax. In beginners, you'll often see what is called co-contraction. Co-contraction is when the muscle doing the work and its opposing muscle are contracting at the same time. This is obviously more inefficient than if the opposing muscle would relax and thus not resist the movement.

Exercise Selection

With heavy lifting, the focus should be on the prime movers used in your sport. For runners that means the legs (quads, hamstrings, glutes, etc.). The use of full body movements instead of muscle isolation is also important. That means, lunges, squats, cleans, dead lifts, split squats, and a myriad of other choices. The exact exercises to use are beyond the scope of this book, but it is important to maintain proper form when lifting, so if you cannot complete a lift with proper form, do not do that lift.

Remember that the goal of this first phase of strength training is to function in the same way that general endurance or speed functions. It sets the table for the important adaptations later. The benefits are for total muscle recruitment and similar neural adaptations, thus it is a general not specific adaptation. We aren't overly concerned with having the movement mimic the activity exactly because the general gains will be converted to the specific movement later. We just need the exercises to be similar enough in muscle use that we can gradually transition to a specific running exercise. For example, heavy squats increase total recruitable motor units, then power training is done in a slightly more specific way to work on muscle recruitment in a short period of time, but then it really comes together during plyo/sprint sessions when you train recruitment in a way that strongly relates to running (i.e., sprinting).

The volume will vary with each individual, but for distance runners the idea should be to get the most gains with a minimal physical and psychological commitment. For that reason, I prefer to keep all strength training sessions short, taking around 30-45 minutes to complete. For this reason, most runners can do between 2-4 exercises with 1-2 sets of each exercise when lifting heavy. The rep total should be low within a set. Training should not be done to failure, as research has demonstrated that non-hypertrophy strength and power gains occur when performing exercises not to failure. This means to stop the lift before performance during the lift decreases. Also, the subsequent fatigue, muscle damage, and cortisol levels are much lower. The weight lifted depends on the runner but should be moderately challenging. There is no need to overload the runner, as heavy for them is different than heavy for a regular lifter. Lifting for most runners is akin to lifting for untrained athletes, so a relatively heavy load will be a completely new stimulus.

Power Training

The neural heavy lifting strength training forms the base off of which to work. Once the base is established training shifts to power development or ballistic training. The goal here is once again to work on fiber recruitment, but this time with an emphasis on force development in a relatively short time, otherwise known as power. The goal is to improve RFD by using exercises that become more and more similar to running in terms of muscle function. Additionally, ballistic training offers a great way to recruit FT fibers, as it can violate the size principle of recruiting ST fibers first then FT. By teaching recruitment of FT fibers first, this can later be translated into recruitment of those harder to activate fibers when under heavy fatigue. This is done through specific or high intensity strength endurance work.

The goal of power training is to maximize power output. Power exercises consist of explosive movements that take place in a short period of time with a light to moderate external weight. Power work often gets confused with plyometric training. The difference is that power training is concerned with a single explosive movement followed by a brief period of rest and then repeating the explosive movement. On the other hand, plyometrics consist of a series of movements one after another with the goal in minimizing the time spent on the ground.

Even more so than with heavy lifting, we want to focus on movements that are similar to running. Start with more general exercises and work towards more specific. That means starting with double-support (two legged) exercises initially before progressing to single leg explosive exercises. There is a lot of mixed research on what kind of added weight creates the highest power output, so weight selection is often a problem. With runners though, it is best to start with a moderate amount of weight and gradually decrease the amount of weight until it is relatively lightweight. For many runners this might mean start with doing jump squats with only the bar and progressing downwards until doing single leg jumps with a 15-20lb dumbbell.

Distance runners do not need to concern themselves about maximizing power to a large degree with a heavier external load because of the short amount of time for force development to occur when running. As mentioned earlier, start with double-support exercises and progress to single support ones. Some exercises to consider include squat jumps, split squat jumps, box jumps, and standing long jumps. Additionally, very steep hill sprints are another way to train for power, and in a more specific way.

Once again, the total amount of work should be relatively low. 2-4 exercises with 1-2 sets of each exercise should be the general guideline. The total amount of reps depends on the exercise, as those done with heavier weights can max out at 4-5 reps, while lighter or no external loads can have as many as 10-12 reps. The external load should be light and max out at around 30% Body Weight and can be as low as no external load. Once again, the training should not be done to failure but instead be stopped before performance and therefore power drops. The rest between each rep can be short 30-90 seconds with long rest between sets.

Plyometrics

The last addition to our strength training arsenal is the most specific, plyometrics. For runners plyos are any movement that has the focus of minimizing ground contact. A whole variety of hops, skips, jumps, and bounds make up the plyos runners use. These exercises teach the body how to impart enough force in as short a time as possible, or in other terms maximizing our rate of force development. Additionally, they help with utilizing the stretch shortening cycle, the stretch reflex, and therefore elastic energy storage and return. They represent the last step in converting the muscular force development into specific running improvements.

Running by itself is a plyometric event. With that in mind, the volume and complexity of plyos should be kept low as we are already getting thousands of foot contacts per day running. Additionally, since running is a plyometric event itself, what's the best and most specific plyo to do? Sprinting! The ground contact times are about as low as you can get, a large amount of force is generated in a very short time, and it is as specific as you can get.

Additional plyometric exercises can be used as a way to bridge the gap from power work to sprinting. Remember that with plyos we are concerned with keeping ground contact short. Because of this and the fact that distance runners don't need to train for large eccentric contractions, don't use moderate or high box or depth jumps in a plyometric-like way. Plyo box jumps are different than power box jumps in one crucial factor: with power box jumps, you simply jump up to the box and then step down, but with plyo box jumps, the exercise continues so that as soon as you land on the top of the box, you drop back down to the ground and try to explode upwards to the top of the box again. This is largely used to train jumpers how to withstand large amounts of eccentric force and is not as important in runners. Therefore, stick to simple plyometric exercises such as the various single or double support hops.

Individualization

Once again, individualization plays a large role on what kind of strength training is done. The same classification system based on fiber type and event works well with strength training too. In general, the shorter the event and the more FT, the more strength training takes on importance. On the other hand, ST or long distance runners can use more running workouts, such as sprints or steep hill sprints, for their strength training.

FT runners respond differently to strength training than ST runners. Generally, they will be a higher responder to muscle size growth due to the fact that FT fibers are easier to increase in size. Additionally, it is likely that they will have lower volumes of training to inhibit strength gains, more likely to be in a positive protein balance, and have higher levels of anabolic hormones. For these reasons, with FT runners if muscle size increase is to be avoided, limit the total volume of heavy weight training of each session and then follow it with a short cool down of aerobic running. FT runners can also handle a higher load of power and plyometric training. This is because they generally can handle higher levels of nervous system fatigue than a ST runner. ST runners generally should do a lower volume of work per workout and do strength training less frequently. While a FT runner can strength train 2 to maybe 3 times per week, ST runners should train once to a max of twice per week when using the above methods.

Lastly, the exact exercises used for strength training also differ. For ST runners, more of the strength training can be done through running specific activities. For example, very steep hill sprints can be used as a method of power development. From there, the hill steepness can gradually decrease until the runner does flat sprints. In this way, the emphasis slowly shifts from power development to a plyometric like effect.

How to Progress and Integrate With Running

Detailing the exact workouts and progressions for strength training is beyond the scope of this book. Some general guidelines can be given. As mentioned previously, the running sessions are the most important, and therefore strength training should solely supplement this work, not take away from it. If you have never lifted before, start with doing body weight general strength, perfecting and mastering the technique, and establishing the motor programming for the lifts.

For this reason, the strength training should be planned to occur so that it does not interfere with the more important running sessions. That means planning the strength training so that delayed soreness does not impact subsequent training. This problem is largely taken care of by adapting to strength training early in the base phase when there are few intense running sessions. As a guide, most runners will be fine with 2 strength training workouts per week initially. As the season progresses this can decrease to one and finally be replaced and maintained entirely through the maintenance sprint training done during the competition phase.

As discussed already, the initial phase should consist of a longer general strength and movement-based program. Once that has been established the runner can either move towards a neural development phase or shift into power/plyo. The decision to do heavier/neural training depends on the athlete's physiology, level of development, and the goals for the training. Often with long distance or ST athletes, the neural phase will be de-emphasized.

When first done, heavier weight lifting can drain runners, as they are not use to nervous system fatigue. Therefore, heavy training should be introduced early on in the base when not much other training is done. The bulk of your heavy training should be done during the base phase where running intensity is low. As intensity of your running increases, start decreasing the volume of heavy training and shift towards ballistics/power training. This is easier to recover from than heavy training. During the late base phase and early pre-competition phase the power work can be done using moderate external weight. As the pre-competition phase progresses, this should shift to more specific power work with a light external load or no extra weight at all. During the competition phase, plyos should be the emphasis. Finally when in the middle of peak racing, maintenance plyo work can be done, or the maintenance sprint work that is done can be used to maintain the strength adaptations too. During this phase, no heavy strength training should be done.

Another option is to shift the focus so that the neural strength and power work can be converted into strength endurance. Essentially, the neural gains serve as the base for strength endurance, while the power and plyometric work can be intermixed with endurance work in the form of circuits.

Just like in running, it's a good idea to do some sort of maintenance training with heavy or power work once you transition away from it. This can be as little as one set of heavy lifting before some power or plyo work every 3-4 weeks. For power work, hill sprints serve as a great maintenance, as well as jumps with low or no weight, such as a standing long jump. Once racing is entering its peak phase, the amount of strength training should be minimal. For some runners it can be dropped completely, for others they will need a little stimulus because they are adapted to it and get flat when it's not there.

Lastly, I'd like to point out that these ideas on strength training are not new. Percy Cerutty, who was the eccentric Australian coach of numerous world-class runners, made use of heavy training. His most notable pupil was Gold Medalist Herb Elliott, whom many consider to be one of the best milers in history. Middle distance star Sebastian Coe was a firm believer in heavy lifting, strength circuits, and plyometric training. According to his strength coach, George Gandy, Coe would develop to where he could complete 2 sets of 5x full squats at 1.5x his body weight. George Gandy has gone on to coach many of Great Britain's top distance runners including 1500m runner Lisa Dobriskey and holds on to these strength training beliefs. He has stated that what he wants out of strength training is the same thing that sprinters or throwers want; his point is that power matters. These are just a few examples of world-class coaches and athletes utilizing similar strength training paradigms with success. The information has just been slow to reach the masses.

Strength Training Sample Progression and Plan

Phase	Main Strength Workout	Outside "strength" work
Introduction	Movement based, general strength. Establish balance and movement patterns.	
Base	2 days per week of: 2 sets of 4-5 reps progressing w/ full rest between of Full Squats and cleans.	Hill Sprints
Pre-Competition	1-2 days per week of: 2 sets of 6-10 reps of the following: Squat jumps (external weight=30% Body weight), standing long jump (holding dumbbells 20% BW), box jump (holding dumbbells 10-15% BW) w/ 30-90sec between reps, 3-4min b/t sets	Flat Sprints and Strength Endurance Circuits
Late Pre-Comp	Body weight only 1 day per week of: 1 set of 6-10 reps of standing long jump, box jump for height, single leg squat jump. And 1 set of 5 reps for two plyo exercises (double leg hops, double leg tuck jumps)	Flat Sprints and High Intensity Strength Endurance Circuits
Competition	1 day per week of 1 set of 6-8 reps of 3 plyo exercises: double leg hops, single leg hops, bounding	Specific Strength Endurance, sprints
Peaking	None or maintenance	Hill sprints/ flat sprints for maintenance

Why High Rep Low Weight Training Doesn't Make Sense

The majority of high rep, low weight training is done in a way to isolate a muscle or a group of muscles to enhance muscular endurance. The problem with this is if we think back to the fatigue models of exercise, fatigue does not happen on an isolated level. It is an integrated process whether you believe that fatigue happens directly on a muscular level or indirectly via central nervous system control.

When training a muscle with the high rep method, the benefits are largely local muscular endurance, meaning endurance of that specific muscle recruited in that specific way. There is very little transfer of local muscular endurance to a dynamic activity like running for several reasons, including the fact that muscle activation and recruitment is vastly different. Additionally, isolated local muscle fatigue causes fatigue in a different way than when fatigue occurs during a dynamic activity like running. So, it is essentially training to resist fatigue that will not occur when running.

High repetition work can be beneficial when combined in strength endurance circuits. This happens because the strength exercises are causing some level of local fatigue and then immediately the specific activity of running is done. In this way, the strength works to create a low level of pre-fatigue to ensure that more fibers are trained for endurance during the actual running portion that follows.

Arms and Core

For the arms, training should not be the heavy strength training, but rather as general maintenance in the form of body weight or light exercises for general strength such as push ups and dips, or simple medicine ball tosses. The reason is that we are not trying to develop force development with the arms. They are simply there to assist the legs in movement and provide counter balance.

Core training has reached fad level. The reality is that core does not mean abs and is a nebulous term. For our purposes it will refer to the entire torso and connection to the legs. There are many problems associated with core training. First, the core does not function in isolation, yet most try to use isolation movements to train the core. When isolated, the muscles of the core function in an entirely different way than during running or any dynamic activity. During running, the core functions as a connector between the upper and lower body, a stabilizer, and it aids in energy transfer. Many coaches or trainers have taught the idea of bracing the core during exercise. When this is done, breathing can be impaired as the lower part of the diaphragm cannot enlarge, and rotation is impeded. While a large amount of rotation of the trunk is not wanted, there has to be a small amount of rotation to compensate for the forward/backward motion of the opposite arms and/or legs. The idea of drawing the spine in or bracing creates an unnatural and machine-like running style. Additionally, it causes co-contraction, which would decrease efficiency while running.

Stability is another issue. For a long time, there was a search for the most important stabilizing muscle. Unfortunately, the body does not function in isolation. The trunk is stabilized by a whole myriad of different muscles, and the degree that each muscle type functions as a spine/trunk stabilizer changes depending on the exercise.

One other popular argument for the core is that a strong core prevents an athlete's form from breaking down. The problem with that logic is that core muscles are not what is fatiguing when racing. The breakdown of form is a symptom of fatigue and happens as a result of fatigue elsewhere. The runner tries to compensate for or fight the fatigue by making changes in their stride, either consciously or subconsciously. For instance, if stride length starts to decrease, you often see over swinging of the arm stroke. Are the arms fatigued? No, the runner is just trying to compensate. This can also be seen with the forward or backward lean during heavy fatigue. Is the runner's back fatiguing so much that he can't keep upright during the final 100m of the race when so many runners lean back? No, he's just trying to compensate for reduced stride length and/or frequency. To combat form breakdown, we have to learn how to deal with fatigue and learn to stay relaxed, not fight it, and above all don't compensate. Ironically, most of the time, it is trying too hard that causes form breakdown.

Last but not least is the question of how to train the core. My belief is that a little goes a long way. Even when running, the so-called core muscles work at a low level for a prolonged time. The best way to train the core for the event is probably through running at various speeds. Research by Behm, Cappa, & Power (2009) supports this idea, as the level of muscle activation of certain core muscles was higher when running than with traditional core exercises. Additionally, full body movements seem to train the core better than traditional crunches or planks to a large degree. In particular the strength training already discussed does a good job. The heavier training increases core strength, while the power and plyometric work trains the core to work reactively and absorb and transfer energy. In another set of studies, it was found that full body exercises such as squats and dead lifts provided much higher muscle activation than traditional core work such as crunches, back extensions, planks, and stability ball work.

The use of stability training or unstable devices such as bosu balls or swiss balls have become en vogue in core training. Training on unstable surfaces challenges balance and proprioception, which is a good thing, but it also causes some problems. First off, training on an unstable surface increases the activation of the antagonist (the opposing) muscle. What this means is that the muscle working directly opposite of the muscle that is doing the work is activated. This obviously isn't a desired outcome as it is in effect working against what you are trying to do. Essentially, this co-contraction is like driving with the parking brake on. Second, when performing unstable training, improper muscle recruitment patterns are established. This is particularly true when performing weighted exercises on an unstable platform. As mentioned earlier, doing exercises on an unstable surface does not increase muscle activity compared to doing the same exercise on a stable surface. Several studies have found that for a variety of core exercises ranging from full body movement lifting to traditional core activities like back extensions, muscle activation of the working muscles is decreased when done on an unstable surface compared to on a stable one. As mentioned before, antagonist muscle activity is increased, which proponents of unstable training sometimes cite as additional muscle activity, neglecting to disclose that we don't want that kind of additional muscle activity when training. Leave the unstable training for balance, proprioception, and pre-habilitation training. Keep it away from your standard strength training.

What this practically means is that functional full body movements are the way to train the core. This can be either be done through heavy weight lifting such as that described earlier, or by lower general strength full body workouts and circuits. Exercises such as various lunges, body squats, and rotational and reactive medicine ball work fit the bill. Planks and other such stabilizing exercisers can be used as a sort of maintenance core work. With core, a little goes a long way. I've found that many runners can be fine with almost no additional specific training aimed at the core, while others are fine with 2-3x a week of about 20 minutes worth of work. After all of this discussion, it's important to remember that the "core" is activated and trained while running to a larger degree than with many core exercises.

The takeaway message is that while core training and even lifting can be beneficial they are not the most important part of the training. They are called supplemental training. Do not give them more attention than they deserve. This doesn't mean you shouldn't do them; it just means to prioritize and focus on the running first and add in the additional stressors as they can be handled.

22

The Biomechanics of Running

"Too much concern about how well one is doing in a task sometimes disrupts performance by loading short-term memory with pointless anxious thoughts." Daniel Kahneman

Distance runners and coaches seem to hate the topic of running form. Most subscribe to the idea that a runner will naturally find his best stride and that stride should not be changed. However, just like throwing a baseball or shooting a basketball, running is a skill that must be learned. The problem with learning how to run is that there are so many wrong ideas out there. This is partly due to the complexity of the process and partly due to a lack of understanding of biomechanics. It's my belief that the wide range of "correct" ways to run has led to this apathetic attitude towards running form changes by most athletes and coaches. Instead of being dogmatic that there is one way to run, the goal here is to provide a model. Not unlike what we did in creating event race models, we should take this generalized model and fit it around the individual variation of our runners.

The argument that running is a natural movement that should not be corrected is easy to dispel. First, we know that even simple outside influences such as what running shoe you wear impacts gait dramatically. In a society where we grow up wearing shoes from a young age and spend most of our time walking around on man-made surfaces, it is a stretch to think that a decade or more of living in this way does not change our mechanics. Second, if we look at the fields of motor control and motor learning more evidence can be seen. In learning movement we often learn by imitation of what we see and from sensory feedback. Since most people aren't taking their kids to see world class runners at track meets, we are stuck with seeing the "joggers" in the neighborhood or horribly running players in more popular sports, such as baseball, as our childhood running models. The second method of motor learning is done by using feedback. A simple example of this is learning not to touch something hot. The first time a child puts his hand on the hot stove, he learns quickly that that wasn't a good idea. Similarly, if a child develops correctly, he would quickly learn that landing heel first when running is not a good idea. It hurts to over stride and slam your heel down into the ground when running barefoot. But since we grow up wearing heavily cushioned shoes, the cushioning eliminates this negative feedback. There is no longer a consequence for heel striking, so why should we avoid it?

Lastly, motor control studies provide some interesting insights. In comparing the controlling mechanisms of running and walking in humans and animals, some interesting differences are apparent. In animals such as cats, control at the spinal cord level plays a much larger part than in humans (Duysens & Van de Crommert, 1998). In animals that have spinal lesions, they can regain much of their gait functioning when trained on a treadmill, while humans with spinal lesions can only partially mimic the walking motion. The thought behind this is that humans rely more on a mixture of higher-level control in the brain and lower level control in the spinal cord than animals do. Some have hypothesized that this means that animal gaits are more reflexive and therefore naturally or instinctually ingrained than humans who rely more on higher level brain control.

The benefits of changing form are enormous. As discussed in the Science section of this book, changes in mechanics can enhance efficiency. Additionally, running correctly can reduce the injury risk, and, perhaps most importantly, increase basic speed. What I've found is that many distance runners who say they have no speed in reality just don't know how to use their natural speed. They never learned how to sprint correctly, so it is their mechanics holding them back not their speed. The goal of this section is to outline what proper running form is and note some of the common misconceptions. Unlike most methods of running, the following is based on research, science, observation, and practical experience. It is based on the system that world-renowned biomechanics expert and sprint coach Tom Tellez has used for many years in developing gold medalist and world record setting runners, and I am much indebted for the information he provided.

For practical reasons, coaches and scientists separate the running stride into various phases. While this is needed so that the idea can be conceptualized it often promotes a fragmented approach to learning proper biomechanics. Instead, a whole body integrated approach is needed. Looking at the body as a whole is required because of how the body interacts. Every so called phase impacts the next phase, and the movement of one body segment impacts completely different body segments. When looking at running form from a segmented point of view, we are relying on the principle that each segment works in isolation, and that is simply not true. Therefore, while breaking the stride into phases allows for better descriptive ability, when looking at how we function when running it is best to look at how the body interacts as a whole.

How to Run

To go through the entire running cycle, we'll start with when foot contact is made and go through the full stride. Foot contact should occur on the outside edge of the foot and depending on speed either at the mid-foot or forefoot. The initial contact on the outside of the foot is generally not felt and instead for practical reasons should be thought of as a simple mid/whole foot landing. Contrary to what most people believe, initial foot contact should not occur on the heel even when running slow. As discussed in the Science section of this book, heel strike results in a higher braking force, reduced elastic energy storage, and a prolonged ground contact. By hitting forefoot or mid-foot the braking action is minimized, and the initial impact peak is reduced. Additionally, the landing should occur in a neutral position at the ankle, as that sets up the calf and Achilles for optimal use of elastic energy. Once landing has occurred, it is important to allow the foot to load up. Often, the mistake is made in trying to get the foot off the ground as quickly as possible, but remember that it is only when the foot is on the ground that force is transferred into the ground. While having a short ground contact time is beneficial, it should be a result of transferring force faster and not of getting quick with the foot. Loading up the foot means allowing it to move through the cycle of initial contact to fully supporting the body. Since initial contact is on the outside of the foot, the support will move inwardly. With forefoot strikers, the heel has to settle back and touch the ground to allow for proper loading of the Achilles and calf complex. Holding the heel off the ground and staying on the forefoot will not allow for the stretch reflex on the Achilles-calf complex to occur.

After the initial loading phase, propulsion starts to occur and the foot begins to come off the ground. The center of pressure should move forwards with the big toe acting as a locking mechanism before the foot leaves the ground. This locking ensures that the foot acts as one entire unit, allowing for greater propulsion. Unlike what many suggest, do not try to get any extra propulsion out of pushing off with the toes consciously. It is too late in the running cycle to net any forward propulsion and will result in simply making your stride flatter. Instead, the forward propulsion should come from the hip, and the foot should be thought of as being along for the ride, which we will discuss shortly. Essentially, once the hip is extended, leave the foot alone.

During this entire process, the calf and Achilles tendon can utilize the stretch shortening cycle and stretch reflex phenomenon. Upon foot contact the Achilles-calf complex goes from a neutral position to fully stretched upon mid-stance to fully contracted upon toe off. This cycle allows for energy storage upon ground impact and release upon take off. In essence, the complex acts like a spring as it stores energy that comes with ground contact and then releases it when ground contact is broken. A common mistake is to stay too high up on the balls of the feet and never let the heel touch the ground. When this occurs, the Achilles-calf complex is not fully stretched and thus you are losing out on the elastic energy return. Similarly, if a runner is too quick with the foot, meaning they try to rush it off the ground, elastic energy is lost because the foot and Achilles were not properly allowed to store and the release energy. Likewise, the arch in the foot also stores elastic energy as it is initially compressed and then subsequently rebounds. This mechanism happens because of its elastic properties.

While foot contact is occurring, the emphasis in your mechanics should shift to the hip. The extension of the hip is where the power comes from, not from pushing with your toes or other mechanisms that are commonly cited. The hip should be thought to work in a crank-like or piston-like fashion. The speed and degree of hip extension is what will partially control the speed. A stronger hip extension results in more force application and greater speed, thus how powerfully and rapidly the hip is extended helps to control the running speed. Once the hip is extended, the foot will come off the ground, and the recovery cycle will begin.

In coming off the ground you are trying to optimize the vertical and horizontal component of the stride. If you think too much horizontally, you will flatten out and not come off the ground, thus losing airtime and stride length. If you think too much vertically, you will be high up in the air for too long and almost bounce along, not having a very big stride length. Thus it is important to optimize the angle and extend the hip so that you have a slight bounce in your stride. A good cue for this is to look at the horizon. If it stays flat, you are too horizontal. If it bounces a lot, you are too vertical. The best analogy is to think back to your High School physics class and remember how to get the greatest distance when firing a cannon ball. The angle has to be optimized, not minimized.

Once the hip has extended, the recovery phase starts. When the hip is extended correctly, it will result in the working of a stretch reflex mechanism. This is best thought of as a sling shot where you stretch the sling shot back and then let it go. The result will be that it shoots forward very rapidly. The hip works in much the same way. If you extend the hip you are putting it in a stretch position. With the slingshot, if instead of letting it go, you tried to move it forward, the sling shot band would come forward much more slowly. The same applies for the hip.

With the combination of the stretch reflex and the basic passive mechanical properties of the lower leg, the recovery cycle of the leg will happen automatically. The lower leg will lift off the ground and fold so that it comes close to your buttocks (how close depends on the speed you are running) then pass under your hips with the knee leading. Once the knee has led through, the lower leg will unfold and it is then the runner's job to put it down underneath them. Ideal landing is close to the center of your body and directly underneath the knee.

Trying to actively move the leg through the recovery phase is another common mistake and will only result in wasted energy and a slower cycling of the leg through the recovery phase. Two other common mistakes are to try to lift the knees at the end of the recovery cycle and to kick the lower leg to the butt at the beginning of the recovery cycle. Neither idea is sound, as they are essentially like trying to push the sling shot forward in our analogy instead of just letting it go. Active lifting of the knee lengthens the recovery cycle with no added stride length benefits. Instead, the knee should be allowed to cycle through and lift on its own. It should not be forced upwards because that cycle through of the knee is a result of the stretch reflex. Similarly, pulling the lower leg to the butt simply wastes energy, as the hamstrings have to be put to work in doing this action. Instead, the folding up of the leg should be thought of as a passive activity. How close the lower leg comes to the butt depends on the amount of hip extension.

This phenomenon may seem strange and is sometimes a hard concept to grasp. After all, who has the patience to not do anything during the recovery phase? But research has demonstrated that both muscle activity during the recovery phase and energy use (the recovery phase only uses 15% of the whole stride's energy) show that the leg is largely cycling through entirely because of reflex-like phenomena and passive mechanics.

Research on patients with spinal lesions has demonstrated the effect of the stretch reflex and passive dynamics on gait. Even though the patients have lost the use of their lower legs, if put on a treadmill their legs will work in walking motion as long as hip extension is initiated by someone. If a therapist simply manually extends the hip and then lets it go, the leg will have a slight folding up as it cycles forward automatically. The forward movement and folding up of the leg is a result of the stretch reflex on the hip and passive mechanics. The fact that the leg folds up slightly at all shows that it is a simple mechanical issue and does not occur due to active muscle contraction. As a simple experiment, play around with a simple two-jointed object, pushing the top joint forward and see what the lower joint segment does. If it's moving forward at sufficient velocity, it's going to fold up because of simple physics and mechanics.

Once the knee has cycled through, the lower leg should drop to the ground so that it hits underneath your knee and close to your center of gravity. When foot contact is made, it should be made where the lower leg is 90 degrees to the ground. This puts it in optimal position for force production. The leg does not extend outwards like is seen in most joggers, and there is no reaching for the ground. Reaching out with the lower leg results in over striding and creates a braking action. Another common mistake is people extending the lower leg out slightly and then pulling it back in a paw like action before ground contact. In using this paw back technique, the idea is to try to get quick with the foot and create a negative acceleration. This is incorrect and does not lead to shorter ground contact times or better positioning for force production. Instead the paw back motion simply engages the hamstrings and other muscles to a greater degree than necessary, thus wasting energy. The leg should simply unfold and drop underneath the runner.

This paw back phenomenon was originally taught because of the idea of trying to create backwards acceleration. This concept does not hold up as the braking forces are still the same upon foot contact. Moreover, the paw back was created through misinterpretation of scientific data. Coaches saw that the hamstrings were active during the latter portion of the in flight recovery phase and assumed that meant the hamstrings were contracting, thus pulling the lower leg back. Instead, the hamstrings were active due to stiffening the muscle-tendon unit in preparation for ground contact and in aiding the slow down of the unfolding of the lower leg. The muscle stiffness manipulation occurs for two reasons; first to absorb elastic energy as a stiff system can utilize elastic energy better, and second because of a process called muscle tuning. Muscle tuning is the body's way of preparing for landing. In essence it acts as an in built cushioning system to minimize the muscle vibrations that occur during landing. The body uses feedback and sensory information to tune the cushioning so that ground reaction forces are essentially the same whether in a cushioned shoe or when running barefoot. When running barefoot, muscle tuning takes place so that the in built cushioning can absorb more of the force.

So far we have only talked about the lower body, but the lower and upper body are linked together as one unit. The interaction between the upper and lower body plays a very large role. First, you should run with an upright body posture with a very slight lean forward from the ground, not from the waist. The arms and legs should work in a coordinated fashion. When the left leg is forward, the right arm should be forward and vice versa for the left arm and leg. But it goes beyond just the arms and legs working in opposition; when they both stop, forward and backward motion is also coordinated. When the arm stops moving forward and is about to reverse direction, the opposite leg should reach its maximum knee height before starting its downward movement. Similarly, when the arm reaches its maximum backward movement before switching directions and coming forward, the opposite leg and hip should be at their maximum extension backwards.

The arm swing occurs from the shoulders, so that the shoulders do not turn or sway. It is a simple pendulum-like forward and backward motion without shoulder sway or the crossing of the arms in front of your body. On the forward upswing the arm angle should decrease slightly with the hands in a relaxed fist. On the backswing they should swing back to just above and behind your hip joint for most running speeds. As the running speed increases, the arm will swing back more, eventually culminating in going back and upwards in sprinting.

The integration of the arms and legs is crucial. Often we see something happening with the leg that is incorrect and immediately work on fixing the problem by adjusting how that particular leg is working. For example, if an athlete extends out with the lower leg, we immediately try to correct them by having them put their foot down sooner. Instead, the problem seen with the leg could simply be the symptom. The real cause could be in the arm swing. A delayed arm swing or a swing with a hitch in it causes a delay or hitch in the opposite lower leg. If you watch someone run, the arms and legs are timed up so they work perfectly in synch. If the runner has a problem with their arm swing that causes a delay in the typical forward and backward motion, such as turning it inwards or shoulder rotation, then the opposite leg must compensate for this delay. In many cases, the opposite leg extends outwards as a form of compensation. Therefore, it is important to look at the whole body and understand that the arms and legs are synched together and interact, so a problem in one of them may simply be a way of compensating. We need to figure out if the issue in the arm or leg movement is coming from that spot or if it is a result of the body attempting to counterbalance itself.

Summary of Running Form:
1. Body Position- upright, slight lean from ground. Head and face relaxed.
2. Feet- As soon as knee comes through put the foot down underneath you. Land mid or forefoot underneath knee, close to center of the body.
3. Arm stroke- controls rhythm, Movement from the shoulder without side to side rotation
4. Hip extension- extend the hip and then leave it alone.
5. Rhythm- Control rhythm and speed through arm stroke and hip extension.

Changing Your Mechanics

Knowing how to run is one thing, but how do you go about changing running form. One popular method is to break the running stride into segments and do drills to improve that segment. However, this method does not work well. If you recall, each part of the running cycle impacts the next. The body works as a whole, not as a bunch of different segments. When drills are used, they may mimic visually what happens when running, but that is all. Due to doing drills in isolation, the muscle fiber recruitment pattern is much different. There is little contribution of the stretch reflex, the stretch shortening cycle, or elastic energy storage and return. An example would be the use of butt kicks. When doing the drill, the lower leg kicking to the butt is accomplished by contracting the hamstring. When the lower leg coils up towards the butt when actually running, it's a result of the hip extension and some stretch reflex, among other contributors. Therefore, the drill has very little actual transfer to the actual running. For this reason, drills are not as useful for improving mechanics because they do not replicate the running form biomechanically, neurally, or muscle recruitment wise. Instead, running form should be worked on when actually running.

To accomplish this, cues are provided to the runner. A cue is a simple task to focus on while running. Possible examples including putting the feet down, dropping the foot beneath you, extend the hip, or any other cue that helps reinforce proper running technique. What cues are used depends on what problem needs to be corrected. The athlete should focus on one or two possible cues at a time so that they do not get overwhelmed. The goal is to ingrain proper running form to the point where they no longer need the cues.

The process of using cues is simple and consists of a trial and error method. The first step is to identify what is wrong with a runner's stride and then figure out how to change it. This will help identify what cue to focus on. Sometimes when giving cues it helps to overemphasize the point, such as telling a runner to feel like they are putting their feet down behind them when correcting foot strike. Since "normal" is incorrect, such as reaching out and heel striking in this example, sometimes overcorrecting is necessary initially.

The athlete should do short strides focusing on one cue at a time. Each stride should be video recorded or analyzed by the coach. If after a cue is given, the runner makes a positive change in the running form, then that cue is successful for that athlete, and they should focus on that cue until it becomes ingrained. If that particular cue does not result in the desired change, the coach should come up with a slightly different cue, essentially a different way of communicating the desired effect. All runners will respond to a cue slightly differently; that is why it is important to come up with several different ways to say the same thing. An example of several different cues to tell a runner who needs to switch from heel striking to a flat foot or mid-foot strike are: put your feet down underneath you; put your feet down behind you; drop the foot as soon as the knee stops going up; when the knee comes through start thinking foot down; feel choppy with your stride.

Once a successful cue is found, then the goal is to ingrain that running style. To do this, start slowly. For distance runners, have the athlete focus for short periods of times during distance runs. Breaking it down into short segments of focusing on form does not make the task feel as daunting for a distance runner. Additionally, during aerobic intervals or rhythm work, have a few intervals where the focus is on running correctly, regardless of time. Also, use strides before or after workouts as a means of getting in some extra form work time to ingrain good mechanics. The last step is transitioning those changes to stressful situations. When running under stress, such as in a race, we tend to revert back to old habits. Having the focus of running with good mechanics during low key competitions or during a time trial setting is a good way to start this transition. As long as it is gradually and consistently worked on, changes in running form can happen. The key is to make gradual changes and to prepare for the alterations in form by conditioning your body. For example, if foot strike is to change, we need to make sure that the surrounding musculature is ready for this change in shock absorption duties. After all, we don't want to simply switch our form to one where a muscle is used to a higher degree than before without preparing that muscle for the increased load.

Problem	Possible Causes
Excessive back kick	-Too much forward lean -Active pulling of foot to butt
Short/Flat stride	-Excessive extension of the entire leg -Trying to toe off (trying to generate force by pushing off of foot, instead of force coming from the hip)
Very little hip extension	-Trying to get quick with the feet and pulling them up early
Reaching out with the lower leg/ heel striking	-Excessive/slow back kick -Leaning backwards -Delayed opposite arm swing because of the arm movement -Excessive shoulder rotation
Angle of swing leg too large or small	-Hip extension either too great or too small (for too large of an angle- i.e., foot stays low and doesn't come up the butt)

Cues

Problem	Cues
Reaching out with lower leg/ heel striking	-Put Feet down behind you -As soon as the knee stops, drop the foot to the ground
Hip extension	-Think of the hip as a crank -Think of the hip as working in a piston-like forward and backward motion
Flat/Short Stride	-Think more vertical -See the horizon bounce very slightly -Do not push off the ground as long
Excessively Bouncy Stride	-Watch horizon and try to limit it to a slight bounce -Think more horizontal
Paw back	-Leave the lower leg alone. It's just along for the ride. -Be patient. Don't try and get quick.
Dorsiflexion of the foot	-Leave the ankle alone -Keep the ankle in a neutral position

Appendix

Specific Endurance Workout progression examples:

800m

Top Down	Bottom Up	Alternations
(For goal 800m at 56sec pace)	3x(8x100m) at 800m pace w/ 45sec b/t reps, 3min b/t sets	100m surges down to 800m pace during a 3mile threshold.
4x600m at 60sec pace w/ 3min rest	3x(6x150m) w/ 60sec and 4min rest	Alternating 100m (800m pace) and 800m at marathon pace (4x)
5x400m at 58 pace w/ 200m jog	3x(4x200) w/ 75sec rest and 4min rest	Alternating 100m at 800m pace and 300m at marathon pace (8x)
600, 500, 500, 400 w/ 2min rest at 58 pace	3x(3x300) w/ 90sec rest and 4min rest	Alternating 200m at 800m pace, 200m steady (6x)
3x(400,90sec, 200m) at 56-57 pace w/ 5min b/t sets	3x(400,400) w/ 75sec rest and 5min rest	2x900m of alternating 200m at 800m pace, 100m easy, w/ 3min easy b/t sets
2x(600,90sec rest, 300m) at 800m pace w/ 7min b/t sets	2-3x(600, 200) w/ 75sec rest and 5min	

1500m/Mile

Top Down	Bottom Up	Alternations
(For goal of 60sec pace)	9x300 w/ 100m walk/jog	Alternating 100m at mile pace, 400m steady/marathon pace for 2.5 miles
4x(4x400 w/ 30sec rest) at 64-65, 3min b/t sets	3x(400,300,200) w/ 60sec rest) w/ 3-4min b/t sets	Alternating 200m at mile pace, 200m easy for 2 miles
3x(5x400 w/ 40sec rest) at 63-64 w/ 3min b/t sets	4x200, 3x300, 2x400, w/ 60sec rest	Alternating 200m at mile pace, 200m at 10sec slower per 200m for 2 miles
12x400 at 63 w/ 60-75sec rest	3x(500, 300 w/ 60sec rest) w/ 4min b/t sets	Alternating 300m at 1mile pace, 200m steady for 3,000m
2x(5x400 w/ 45sec rest) at 61 w/ 2min b/t sets	2x(5x400 w/ 60sec rest) w/ 3-4min rest	Alternating 400m/100m (5x) w/ 400 at mile pace, 100m easy
10x400 at 61-62 w/ 60sec rest	3x(600/200 w/ 60sec rest) 4min rest b/t sets	2x3000m w/ 5min rest alternated this way: 500(1mi pace)/500m steady, 400m(1mi), 400m steady, 300m (1mi), 300m steady, 200m (1mi), 200m steady, 100m (1mi), 100m steady
10x400m at 60sec w/ 60sec rest	3x800 w/ 4min rest at mile pace	

5000m

Top Down	Bottom Up	Alternations
6x1mile at threshold with 1-2min rest	3 x (4x400) at 5k w/ 30sec rest. 5min b/t sets	4 miles of alternating 200m at 5k pace w/ 1400m at steady pace
5x1mile at 10k pace w/ 2-3min rest	3x(3x600) at 5k w/ 40sec rest. 5min b/t sets	4mi of alternating 400 at 5k pace w/ 1200m at steady pace
3x1mile at 10k, 2x1000m at 5k pace w/ 3min rest	2x(3x800) at 5k w/ 45sec rest. 5min b/t sets	4mi of alternating 600 at 5k pace w/ 1000m at steady pace
1xmile at 10k, 1mile at 5k, 2x1000m at 5k w/ 3min rest	2x (1000,800,700) at 5k w/ 45sec rest. 5min b/t sets	4mi of alternating 800 at 5k pace w/ 800m at steady pace
3x1mile at 5k pace w/ 3min rest	5x1000 at 5k w/ 60-75sec rest	4mi of alternating 900 at 5k pace w/ 700m at steady pace

10000m

Top Down	Bottom Up	Alternations
6 mile Threshold runs	2x(5x3min w/ 1min easy) w/ 4min easy b/t sets at 10k pace	6-7mi total-alternating:400 (10k pace),1200-(marathon pace)
4mi LT, 3-4min rest, 2mi at 10k pace	Fartlek- 6,5,4,3,4,5 w/ 3min easy in between at 10k pace	6-7mi total alternating: 600 (10k),1000-(Marathon Pace)
3x1.5mi at 10k pace w/ 5min rest	6x1mile at 10k pace w/ 2-4min rest	Alternation: split into 4mi, 3mi w/ 3min rest of: 800m (10k) and 800m (marathon pace)
2x2mile,1mile at 10k pace w/ 4-5min rest	2mi, 1.5mi, 1mile, 1mile w/ 3min rest at 10k pace	Alternation: split into 3x2mi w/ 2min rest of: 1000m (10k) and 600m (marathon pace)
3x2mile at 10k pace w/ 5min rest	3miles at 10k pace, 5min rest, 800 to 1mile hard	4x2k alternating 10k pace and Threshold pace w/ 2-3min b/t repeats

Marathon

Top Down	Bottom Up	Alternations
Starting point: 18mi long run and 8-10mi steady distance runs	5mi MP run w/ warm-up, cool down	alt-10mi of 800m (MP)/800m (steady)
16mi long run w/ last 15-20min progression to MP	4mi easy+ 7mi MP	alt- 6x (1mile/800) (MP/steady)
10mi progression from steady down to MP	4mi easy+ 9mi MP, 2mi easy	alt- 5x1.5mi/800m (MP/steady
16mi w/ last 25-30min at MP	5mi easy + 2x5mi MP w/ 10minutes easy b/t	alt- 5x2mi/800m MP/steady
12mi progression run from steady down to MP	3mi easy + 5,4,3 MP w/ 7min easy b/t, 2mi easy	4x3mi w/ 800m MP/steady
5mi easy, 7mi MP, 5mi easy	4mi+7mi, 5mi MP	
11mi MP run	5mi+12mi MP	
3mi easy, 5mi MP, 1mi easy, 5mi MP, 3mi easy	14mi MP workout	
13-15mi MP run		

Specific Speed Endurance

800	1500/1mile	5k
3x400m Alternating 50m at 400m pace, 50m cruise with 4-5min rest	800-mile pace,5min rest, 2x400 at 800m pace w/ 4min rest	4x600 (5k pace) 4x300 (3k pace) 4x500 (5k pace) 4x200 (1mi pace) 2min b/t reps, 6min b/t reps
4x(200, 100m jog, 100m) w/ 4min rest. 200's at 800pace, 100m kick in.	4x(400,200 jog,200) w/ 3min rest between sets. 400 at mile pace, 200 at 800m pace	3x(1200, 1min rest, 400m) at 5k and 3k down to 1mi pace, 5min rest b/t sets
2x(500, 100m walk, 200m) with 6-8min rest. 500m at 800m pace, 200m kick in.	2x800m alternating every 100m. 100m-800m pace and 100m 10kish pace. w/ 5min rest	9x300m w/ 100m jog rest switching between a 300 at 5k pace and a 300 at 3k to 1mile pace
4x300m w/ 3-5min rest (first 200m at 800m pace, last 100m kick in)	2 sets of 600, 300, 500, 200 (1mi,800, 1mi, 800 paces) w/ 2min rest b/t reps, 4min b/t sets	1600, 2x400, 800, 2x300, 600 (5k,1mi,5k, 800,3k paces) w/ 3min rest

10k	Marathon
Fartlek at 10k effort; 6, 2, 5, 3, 1 with equal rest. Surge down to 5k pace in middle of each rep for 20sec.	8-10mi progression run from marathon pace to threshold
4x(1mile,1min rest, 400m) w/ 4min rest, miles at 10k pace, 400m at 5k down to 3k pace	10mile marathon pace run w/ surges to threshold for 1min every mile
5x1200m w/ 3min rest (first 800m at 10k pace, last 400m at 5k down to 3k pace)	Marathon pace alternations: 3x2mile/1mile/1mile at MP/LT/steady
	2x (5mi at MP, 2min rest, 1mile at 10k pace) w/ 3min rest between
	6mi easy, 8mi at MP, 1mi finish hard

Combo Workout Examples:

General End + Gen Speed	Ex: 20min LT, 8x10sec hill sprints
Connect direct Supports	Ex for 5k: 4x5min at 10k pace w/ 3min rest, 5min rest, 4x60sec at 5k down to 3k pace
Specific speed Endurance	For mile: 5x400m at mile pace w/ 75sec rest, 3x300 at 800 pace w/ 90sec rest
Specific + direct speed support	For mile: 3xalternation of 400 at mile pace, 800m steady, 5min rest, 300,200, 150 at 800m pace down w/4min rest
Endurance + strength endurance	20min LT, 5min rest, 4x60sec uphill w/ jog down recovery
Direct endurance support + Specific endurance	For mile : 4x800m w/ 3min rest at 3k pace, 5min rest, 400,300, 200 at mile pace w/ 90sec rest

Blend Workouts:

800m Blend

Direct Support Connection	500 (1mi), 150(800m), 400 (1mi), 100m (400m), 300 (1mi), 100 (400m) w/ 3min rest
Specific Speed Endurance	4x(200, 45sec rest, 100m) w/ 200m at 800 pace, 100m faster. 4min b/t sets
Specific End. Support	500 (1mi), 200 (800), 400 (1mi), 300 (800), (500-first 300 at 1mi, last 200m at 800) w/ 2min rest

1500m Blend

Direct Support Connection	1200 (5k), 400 (1mi), 800m (3k), 300 (800m), 600 (3k), 200 (800m w/ 3-4min rest
Specific Speed Endurance	600m (1mi), 200 (800m), 500 (1mi), 200 (800m), 400m (first 200m at mile, last 200m kick in) w/ 2min rest after longer repeat, 4min after shorter
Specific End support	1200 (3k), 500(1mi), 800(3k) 300(1mi) w/ 3min rest

5k- Direct Supports to Specific Speed Endurance

Direct Support connection	2k, 400, 1600, 400, 1200 w/ 3-4min rest (long-10k pace, short-3k pace)
	1600 (10k), 600 (3k), 1200 (10k), 400 (1mi), 800 (5k) w/ 3-4min, paces in parentheses
	3x (1600,2min rest, 400) w/ 4min rest. 1600m at 10k pace, 400m at 2mile pace
Specific Speed End	1600 (5k), 600 (3k), 1200 (3k), 300 (1mi), 600 (5k), 200 (1mi) w/ 3-4min rest
	1600 (5k), 400 (1mi), 1200 (5k), 300 (1mi), 600 (1st 300 at 5k, next 300 progress to 1mi) w/ 3-4min rest
	2000 (10k pace), 400 (3k), 160 0(5k), 300 (1mi), 1000 (3k) 200 (800) w/ 3min rest

10k Blend

Direct Support Connection	1600, 400, 1200, 400 ,1000, 400, 800, 200 w/ 2min rest (longer at threshold, shorter at 5k pace)
Specific Speed Endurance	1600, 600, 1600, 500, 1600, 400, 1600 w/ 2-3min rest (longer at 10k pace, shorter at 5k down to 3k pace)

Marathon Blend

Direct Support Connection	2mi (LT), 1mi (10k), 1.5mi (LT), 1000m (10k), 1mi (LT) w/ 3min rest
Specific Speed Endurance	4mi MP, 1mi (LT), 4mi MP, 1mi (10k) w/ 3min easy between

Aerobic Intervals:

For all (change pace for event)	8x30sec surge w/ 2:30 easy in middle of 8mi run
	8x45sec surge w/ 2:15 easy in middle of 8mi run
	8x60sec surge w/ 2:00 easy in middle of 8mi run
	3x(10x100m w/ 15-25sec rest), 3min b/t sets at 800-5k pace depending on purpose/event
	3x(6x150m) w/ 20-35sec rest, 3min b/t sets at 800-5k pace depending on purpose/event
Insert in middle of workout to prolong workout while enhancing recovery	For 5k: 4x800m at 5k pace w/ 4x150m at LT w/ 50m jog rest in between each rep.
	For mile: 3x(3x400 at mile pace w/ 100m jog b/t reps), between sets 50m jog, 4x150m at 10k pace w/ 50m jog
	For 10k: 4x1000m at 10k pace w/ 2min rest, 3x200m at LT w/ 100m easy, 2x800m at 5k or faster w/ 2min rest
Rhythm work	200's-400s at race pace w/ 200m jog- ex: 8x200 at mile pace w/ 200 jog

Pure/General Speed progressions:

Pure speed	6x8sec HS
	8x8sec HS
	10x8sec HS
	4x60m flat sprints
	8x10sec HS
	5x80m flat sprints
	10x10sec HS
	2x60m, 2x80m, 2x100m
	8x10sec HS + 1x20sec
Speed Endurance	4x60m, 1x150m
	8x10sec HS +2x25sec
	2x60, 2x80m,100m, 150m, 200m
	4x100m, 150m, 200m
Maintenance- Every 2-5wks (depends on athlete/season)- depends on if it's more speed or speed endurance, but an example: 3-5x60-80m sprints, 2x150m OR 2x60, 100m, 150m, 200m.	

Long Run Progressions:

Mid Distance- FT type	Mid Distance- ST type	Long Distance (10k-marathon)
8mi easy	11mi easy	14mi easy
9mi easy	12mi easy	15mi easy
10mi easy	13mi easy w/ strides	16mi easy
11mi easy	14mi easy	14mi w/ 6x45sec surges
8mi easy progression	14mi w/ 8x30sec surges	14mi w/ 10min pickup
10mi easy	14mi w/ 5min pickup	17mi easy
10mi w/ strides	12mi easy	15mi w/ 15min pickup
9mi easy progression	15mi w/ 7x45sec surges	3mi, 8mi Marathon pace, 3mi

Threshold Progression (general, aerobic, or direct support)

	Natural progression runs
	15min LT
	20min split LT
	25min split LT
	30min split LT
	35min split LT
	Then choose direction you want to go, including:
Connect to faster pace	20min split LT, 5min rest, 5min at 10k pace
Add stimulus	30min uphill LT workout
Strength Endurance	25min LT, 5min rest, 4x60sec hill repeats with jog down rest

Maintenance Workouts:

Aerobic Maintenance:

General Endurance	Depending on event: Easy long runs; 5mi at MP; 20min LT;
Complete Aerobic Refresh	10min-MP, 7min-LT, 5min-10k, 3min-5k w/ 3min easy b/t
High End Aerobic Maintenance	12min MP, 10min LT, 5min 10k pace w/ 2-3min easy b/t
Aerobic support (for 5k,1500) maintenance	1.5mi- 10k pace, 1mi at slightly faster, 1000m (5k pace), 600m (3k pace) w/ 3min rest
Aerobic supports for 800m	8x(400/200) at 5k-3k pace w/ 200m slow jog between all

Specific Maintenance:

For 800m	1-3 sets of 8x100m at 800m pace w/ 100m jog rest, 4min b/t sets
For 1500m	2x(6x200m w/ 200m jog) 3min b/t sets at mile pace
For 5k	600,500, 4x400m w/ 200m jog
For 10k	1000,800, 600, 400 with 200m jog at 10k pace
For Marathon	3x2miles at MP with 3min easy in between

Speed/Anaerobic Maintenance:

Speed-support	8-12x200m at 3k down to 800m pace w/ 200m jog
General speed-speed endurance	300, 200, 150, 100 w/ 4min rest (800 pace for first 2, 400m pace for last two)
General/Pure Speed	6-8x10sec Hill Sprints
General/Pure Speed	2x100, 2x80, 2x60m flat sprints
General Speed/ Speed Endurance	2x80m, 2x100m, 2x150m sprints

Combo Maintenance:

easy fartlek (5min medium, 5 easy, 5 medium, 5 easy, 5min of 15sec surge every 1min)
5min (LT), 3min (10k), 60, 45, 30, 15sec at 5k,3k, 1mi, 800m paces w/ 60-90sec rest b/t all
3x1mile w/ 60sec rest (MP, LT, 10k), 4x200 (5k,3k, 1mi, 800m) w/ 200m jog

Workouts for a Special Reason:

Strength Endurance Workouts:

3x800m w/ 2min rest (10k pace), 6xHill Sprints, 3x800 w/ 2min rest (10k pace) 6xHS
3 sets of 4x400m w/ 45sec rest at 5k pace. In between sets, perform 3x60m flat sprints w/ 3min rest
4x60sec, 4x45sec uphill at 3k-1mile effort w/ jog down rest
10-15x 20sec uphill at mile effort w/ jog down rest
800 flat, 400m uphill, 600m flat, 400m up, 800m flat with 2min rest between all, 5k effort on long, 1500m effort on short

Strength Endurance Circuits:

General Strength Endurance	High Intensity Strength Endurance
90sec Marathon Pace	Done up a long gradual hill
10x squats	35sec 10k pace
40sec MP	8x full squats
10x lunges	35sec 5k pace
40sec MP	8x skipping for max height
15x push ups	35sec 5k pace
40sec MP	8x hops
10x burpees	35sec 5k pace
40sec MP	8x squat jumps for max height
20m bounding	100m kick in
100m hard	
Do 3x with slow jog down rest between	Do 3x with slow jog down rest

Kick Workouts:

2x(200m at 800 pace, 100m bound, 200m kick in) w/ 6min rest
2x(500m at mile pace, 100m bound, 200m kick in) w/ 5-6min rest
2x(300m flat at 1mile pace, 100m sprinting uphill, 100m sprinting on flat at top of hill) w/ 5min rest
4x1000m w/ 4min rest (first 700m at 5k pace, last 300m kick in)
3x800m w/4min rest first 600m at 3200m pace, last 200m at mile
600m, 100m jog, 100m kick in, 10-15min rest, 500m, 100m jog, 200m kick in all at 800m pace

Special Block:

For Marathon Specific Endurance:	Morning: 10mi w/ last 6mi at MP Afternoon: 10mi w/ 2x3mi at MP w/ 3min easy rest
For 5k specific strength endurance:	Morning-3x2k w/ 4min jog rest, LT to 10k pace Afternoon- 10x400 at 5k-3k pace w/ 200 jog
For mile speed and specific endurance:	Morning- 3x(800,400,200 at 3k, 1mi, 800 w/ 3min rest) 5min b/t sets Afternoon- 6x200m at 1mi down to 800 pace w/ 200m jog
Combining general Speed and Endurance	Morning- 25min split LT Afternoon- 8x10sec Hill Sprints

Aaron, E. A., Seow, K. C., Johnson, B. D., & Dempsey, J. A. (1992). Oxygen cost of exercise hyperpnea: implications for performance. *J Appl Physiol, 72,* 1818–25.

Abernethy, P. J., Thayer, R., & Taylor, A. W. (1990). Acute and chronic responses of skeletal muscle to endurance and sprint exercise. A review. *Sports Med, 10*(6), 365–389.

Acevedo, E. O., & Goldfarb, A. H. (1989). Increased training intensity effects on plasma lactate, ventilatory threshold and endurance. *Med Sci Sports Exerc, 21,* 563–568.

American College of Sports Medicine. (2009). American College of Sports Medicine position stand. Progression models in resistance training for healthy adults. *Med Sci Sports Exerc, 41*(3), 687–708.

Ando, S., Kokubu, M., Nakae, S., Kimura, M., Hojo, T. & Ebine, N. (2012). Effects of strenuous exercise on visual perception are independent of visual resolution. *Physiol Behav.* 106

Ardigo, L. P., Lafortuna, C., Minetti, A. E., Montgoni, P., & Saibene, F. (1995). Metabolic and mechanical aspects of foot landing type, forefoot and rearfoot strike, in human running. *Acta Physiol Scan, 155*(1), 17–22.

Arellano, C.J. & Kram, R. (2011). The effects of step width and arm swing on energetic cost and lateral balance during running. *J Biomech, 44*(7), 1291-5.

Arellano, C. J. & Kram, R. (2012). The energetic cost of maintaining lateral balance during human running. *J Appl Physiol.* 112, 427-434.

Baden, D. A, McLean, T. L., Tucker, R., Noakes, T. D., & St Clair Gibson, A. (2005). Effect of anticipation during unknown or unexpected exercise duration on ratings of perceived exertion, affect, and physiological function. *Br J Sports Med, 39*(1), 742–746.

Basset, F. A., & Boulay, M. R. (2000). Specificity of treadmill and cycle ergometer tests in triathletes, runners and cyclists. *Eur J Appl Physiol, 81*(3), 214–221.

Bassett, D. R. & Howley, E. T. (1997). Maximal oxygen uptake: 'classical' versus 'contemporary' viewpoints. *Medicine and Science in Sports and Exercise, 29,* 591–603.

Bassett, D. R. & Howley, E. T. (2000). Limiting factors for maximum oxygen uptake and determinants of endurance performance. *Medicine and Science in Sports and Exercise, 32,* 70–84

Beall, C. M., Decker, M. J., Brittenham, G. M., Kushner, I., Gebremedhin, A. & Strohl, K. P. (2002). An Ethiopian pattern of human adaptation to high-altitude hypoxia. *Proc Natl Acad Sci, 99*(26), 17215–17218.

Bebout, D. E., Hogan, M. C., Hempleman, S. C., & Wagner, P. D. (1993). Effects of training and immobilization of O2 and DO2 in dog gastrocnemius in situ. *J Appl Physiol, 74,* 1697–1703.

Belli, A. & Hintzy, F. (2002). Influence of pedaling rate on the energy cost of cycling in humans. *Eur J Appl Physiol, 88,* 158–162.

Beneke, R., Hutler, M., & Leithauser, R. (2000). Maximal lactate steady-state independent of performance. *Med Sci Sports Exerc, 32*(6), 1135–1139

Bentley, D. J., Roels, B., Thomas, C., Ives, R., Mercier, J., Millet, G., & Cameron-Smith, D. (2009). The relationship between monocarboxylate transporters 1 and 4 expression in skeletal muscle and endurance performance in athletes. *Eur J Appl Physiol, 106*(3), 465–471.

Berg, K. (2003). Endurance training and performance in runners. *Sports Med, 33*(1), 59–73

Bickham, D. C., Bentley, D. J., Le Rossignol, P. F., & Cameron-Smith, D. (2006). The effects of short-term sprint training on MCT expression in moderately endurance trained runners. *Eur J Appl Physiol, 96,* 636–643.

Billat, L. V., (2001). Interval training for performance: A scientific and empirical practice. Special recommendations for middle and long-distance running. Part II: Anaerobic interval training. *Sports Med, 31*(2), 75–90.

Billat, L., Sirvent, P., Lepretre, P. M., & Koralsztein, J. P. (2004). Training effect on performance, substrate balance and blood lactate concentration at maximal lactate steady state in masters endurance runners. *Pflugers Arch, 447,* 875–883.

Billat, V. L., Fletchet, B., Petit, B., Muriaux, G., & Koralsztein, J. P. (1999). Interval training at VO2max effects on aerobic performance and overtraining markers. *Med Sci Sports Exerc, 31,* 156–163.

Billat, V., Demarle, A., Paiva, M., & Koralsztein, J. P. (2002). Effect of training on the physiological factors of performance in elite marathon runners. *Int J Sports Med, 23,* 335–341.

Billat, V., Leptretre, P. M., Heugas, A. M., Laurence, M. H., Saijm, D., & Koralsztein, J. P. (2003). Bioenergetic characteristics in elite male and female Kenyan runners. *Med Sci Sports Exerc, 35*(2), 297–304.

Billat, V., Sirvent, P., Py, G., Koralsztein, J. P., & Mercier, J. (2003). The Concept of Maximal Lactate Steady State A Bridge Between Biochemistry, Physiology and Sport Science. *Sports Med, 33*(6), 407–426.

Bishop, D., Jenkins, D. G., McEniery, M., & Carey, M. F. (2000). Relationship between plasma lactate parameters and muscle characteristics in female cyclists. *Med Sci Sports Exerc, 32*(6), 1088–93.

Bompa, T. 0., & Haff, G. G. (2008). *Periodization: Theory and methodology of training.* Champaign, IL: Human Kinetics.

Bonacci, J., Chapman, A., Blanch, P., & Vicenzino, B. (2009) Neuromuscular Adaptations to Training, Injury and Passive Interventions: Implications for Running Economy. *Sports Med, 39*(11), 903–921.

Bridge, M. W., Weller, A.S., Rayson, M. & Jones, D.A. (2003). Responses to exercise in the heat related to measures of hypothalamic serotonergic and dopaminergic function. Eur *J Appl Physiol.* 89(5):451–9.

Brooks, G. A., Fahey, T. D., & Baldwin, K. (2004). *Exercise Physiology: Human bioenergetics and its application.* McGraw-Hill.

Brooks, G. A., & Mercier, J. (1994). Balance of carbohydrate and lipid utilization during exercise: the "crossover" concept. *J Appl Physiol, 76*(6), 2253-2261.

Buick, F. J., Gledhill, N., Froese, A. B., Spriet, L., & Meyers, E. C. (1980). Effect of induced erythrocythemia on aerobic work capacity. *J Appl Physiol, 48*(4), 636–642.

Bulbulian, R., Wilcox, A. R., & Darabos, B. L. (1986). Anaerobic contribution to distance running performance of trained crosscountry athletes. *Med Sci Sports Exerc, 18*, 107–113.

Busson, T. (2003). Variable dose-response relationship between exercise training and performance. *Med Sci Sports Exerc, 35*(7), 1188–1195.

Calbet, J. A., Boushel, R., Radegran, G., Sondergaard, H., Wagner, P. D., & Saltin, B. (2003). Determinants of maximal oxygen uptake in severe acute hypoxia. *Am J Physiol Regul Integr Comp Physiol, 284*(2), 291–303.

Calbet, J. A., Lundby, C., Koskolou, M., & Boushel, R. (2006). Importance of hemoglobin concentration to exercise: acute manipulations. *Respir Physiol Nerubiol, 151*(2-3), 132–140.

Canova, R., & Arcelli, E. (1999). *Marathon training: A scientific approach.* Rome: Marchesi Grafiche Editoriali.

Cappellini, G., Ivanenko, Y. P., Poppele, R. E., & Lacquaniti, F. (2006). Motor patterns in human walking and running. *J Neurophusiol, 95*(6), 3426–3437.

Castle, P. C., Maxwell, N., Allchorn, A., Mauger, A. R., & White, D. K. (2012). Deception of ambient and body core temperature improves self paced cycling in hot, humid conditions. *European Journal of Applied Physiology.* 112(1), 377-385.

Cavanagh, P. R., & Williams, K. R. (1982). The effect of stride length variation on oxygen uptake during distance running. *Med Sci Sports Exerc, 14*(1), 30–35.

Chang, Y. H. & Kram, R. (1999). Metabolic cost of generating horizontal forces during human running. *J Appl Physiol, 86*(5). 1657-62

Chapman, A. R., Vicenzino, B., Blanch, P., & Hodges, P. W. (2008). Patterns of leg muscle recruitment vary between novice and highly trained cyclists. *J Electromyogr Kinesiol, 18*, 359–371.

Chapman, R., Stray-Gunderson, J., & Levine, B. D. (1998). Individual variation in response to altitude training. *J. Appl. Physiol, 85*(4), 1448–1456.

Coe, P., & Martin, D. (1997). *Better Training for Distance Runners.* Champaign, IL: Human Kinetics.

Coffey, V. G. & Hawley, J. A. (2007). The Molecular Bases of Training Adaptation . *Sports Medicine, 37*(9), 737-763.

Conley, D. L., & Krahenbuhl, G. S. (1980). Running economy and distance running performance of highly trained athletes. *Med Sci Sports Exerc., 12*(5), 357–60.

Costill, D. (1967). The relationship between selected physiological variables and distance running performance. *J Sports Med Phys Fitness, 7*, 61–66.

Costill, D., & Trappe, S. (2002). *Running: The athlete within.* Traverse City, MI: Cooper Publishing Group.

Coyle, E, F., Martin, W. H., Bloomfield, S. A., Lowry, O. H., & Holloszy, J. O. (1985) Effects of detraining on responses to submaximal exercise. *Journal of Applied Physiology,* 59, 853–859.

Coyle, E. F. & Joyner, M. J. (2008). Endurance exercise performance: the physiology of champions. *The Journal of Physiology, 586,* 35–44.

Coyle, E. F., & Holloszy, J. O. (1995). Integration of the physiological factors determining endurance performance ability. *Exercise and Sport Sciences Reviews,* Baltimore, MD: Williams & Wilkins, pg. 25–63.

Coyle, E. F., Sidossis, L. S., Horowitz, J. F., & Beltz, J. D. (1992). Cycling efficiency is related to the percentage of type I muscle fibres. *Medicine and Science in Sports and Exercise,* 24, 782–788.

Creer, A. R., Ricard, M. D., Conlee, R. K., Hoyt, G. L., & Parcell, A. C. (2004). Neural, metabolic, and performance adaptations to four weeks of high intensity sprint-interval training in trained cyclists. *International Journal of Sports Medicine,* 25, 92–98.

Czerwinski, S.M., Martin, J.M., and Bechtel, P.J. 1994. Modulation of IGF mRNA abundance during stretch-induced skeletal muscle hypertrophy and regression. *J Appl Physiol* 76, 2026–2030.

Dallam, G. M., Wilber, R. L., Jadelis, K., Fletcher, G., & Romanov, N. (2005). Effect of a global alteration of running technique on kinematics and economy. *J Sports Sci, 23*(7), 757–764.

Dalleau, G., Belli, A., Bourdin, M., & Lacour, J. R. (1998). The spring-mass model and the energy cost of treadmill running. *Eur J Appl Physiol, 77,* 257–63.

Dalleck, L. C., Kravitz, L., & Robergs, R. A. (2004). Maximal exercise testing using the elliptical cross-trainer and treadmill. *Journal of the Exercise Physiology, 7*(3), 94–101.

Daniels, J. (2005). *Running Formula.* Champaign, IL: Human Kinetics.

Daniels, J. T., Yarbrough, R. A., & Foster, C. (1978). Changes in VO2max and running performance with training. *Eur J Appl Physiol, 39,* 249–54.

De Koning JJ, Foster C, Bakkum A, Kloppenburg S, Thiel C, et al. (2011) Regulation of Pacing Strategy during Athletic Competition. PLoS ONE 6(1).

De Morree, H.M., Klein, C., & Marcora SM (2012). Perception of effort reflects central motor command during movement execution. *Psychophysiology, 49*(9): 1242-53.

Dempsey, J. A., & Wagner, P. D. (1999). Exercise-induced arterial hypoxemia. *J Appl Physiol, 87*(6), 1997–2006.

Dempsey, J. A., Hanson, P., & Henderson, K. (1984). Exercise-induced arterial hypoxemia in healthy humans at sea-level. *Journal of Physiology (London), 355,* 161–175.

Dery, M. C., Michaud, M. D., Richard, D. E. (2005). Hypoxia-inducible factor 1: regulation by hypoxic and non-hypoxic activators. *The International Journal of Biochemistry & Cell Biology, 37,* 535–540.

Duffield, R., Dawson, B., & Goodman, C. (2005). Energy system contribution to 1500- and 3000-metre track running. *J Sports Sci, 23*(10), 993–1002.

Duysens, J. & Van de Crommert, H. W. (1998). Neural control of locomotion; Part 1: The central pattern generator from cats to humans. *Gait & Posture, 7*(2), 131–141.

Ekbolm, B., Goldbarg, A. N., & Gullbring, B. (1972). Response to exercise after blood loss and reinfusion. *J Appl Physiol, 33*(2), 175.

Esteve- Lanao, J., Foster, C., Seiler, S., & Lucia, A. (2007). Impact of training intesnity distribution on performance in endurance athletes. *Journal of Strength and Conditioning Research, 21*(3), 943–950.

Esteve-Lanao, J., Rhea, M. R., Fleck, S. J., & Lucia, A.(2008). Running-specific, periodized strength training attenuates loss of stride length during intense endurance running. *Strength Cond Res, 22*(4), 1176-1183.

Esteve-Lanao, J., San Juan, A. F., Earnest, C. P., Foster, C., & Lucia, A. (2005). How do endurance runners actually train? Relationship with competition performance. *Med Sci Sports Exerc, 37*(3), 496–504.

Faude, O., Kindermann, W., & Meyer, T. (2009). Lactate threshold concepts: How valid are they? *Sports Med, 39*(6). 469–490.

Fiskerstrand A., & Seiler, K. S. (2004). Training and performance characteristics among Norwegian international rowers 1970-2001. *Scand J Med Sci Sports, 14,* 303–310.

Fitts, R. H., & Widrick, J. J. (1996). Muscle mechanics: adaptations with exercise training. *Exerc Sport Sci Rev, 24,* 427–473.

Fletcher, J. R., Esau, S. R., & Macintosh, B. R. (2009). Economy of running : beyond the measurement of oxygen uptake. *J Appl Physiol,* Oct 15. [Epub ahead of print].

Franch, J., Madsen, K., Djuhuus, M. S., & Pedersen, P. K. (1998). Improved running economy following intensified training correlates with reduced ventilatory demands. *Med Sci Sports Exerc, 30,* 1250–1256.

Garcin, M., Mille-Hamard, L., & Billat, V. (2004). Influence of aerobic fitness level on measured and estimated percieved exertion during exhausting runs. *Int J Sports Med., 25*(4), 270–277.

Garcin, M., Mille-Hamard, L., Devillers, S., Delattre, E., Dulfour, S. & Billat, V. (2003). Influence of the type of training sport practiced on psychological and physiological parameters during exhausting endurance exercises. *Percept Mot Skills, 97*(3-2), 1150–1162.

Gaskill, S. E., Serfass, R. C., Bacharach, D. W., & Kelly, J. M. (1999). Responses to training in cross-country skiers. *Medicine and Science in Sports and Exercise, 31,* 1211–1217.

Gibala, M. J., Little, J. P., van Essen, M., Wilkin, G. P., Burgomaster, K. A., Safdar, A., Raha, S., & Tarnopolsky, M. A. (2006). Short-term sprint interval versus traditional endurance training: similar initial adaptations in human skeletal muscle and exercise performance. *J Physiol, 575*(3), 901–911.

Gilbert, K. L., Stokes, K. A., Hall, G. M., & Thompson, D. (2008). Growth hormone responses to 3 different exercise bouts in 18- to 25- and 40- to 50- year-old men. *Appl Physiol Nutr Metab, 33*(4), 706–712.

Girardo, O., Millet, G. P., Slawinski, J., Racinais, S. & Micallef, J. P. (2013). Changes in Running Mechanics and Spring-Mass Behavior during a 5km Time Trial. *Int J Sports Med.* Apr 2. Epub ahead of print.

Gledhill, N. (1982). Blood doping and related issues: a brief review. Med. Sci. Sports Exerc., 14, 183–189.

Gledhill, N. (1985). The influence of altered blood volume and oxygen transport capacity on aerobic performance. *Exerc. Sport Sci. Rev.,* 13, 75–93.

Gonzalez-Alonso, J., Teller, C., Andersen, S. L., Jensen, F. B., Hyldig, T., & Nielsen, B. (1999). Influence of body temperature on the development of fatigue during prolonged exercise in the heat. *Journal of Applied Physiology*, 86, 1032–1039.

Goodall, S., Gonzalez-Alonso, J., Ali, L., Ross, E. Z., & Romer, L. M. (2012). Supraspinal fatigue after normoxic and hypoxic exercise in humans. *J Physiol*. 590(11), 2767-82.

Hagberg, J. M., Allen, W. K., Seals, D. R., Hurley, B.F., Ehsani, A.A., & Holloszy, J.O. (1985). A hemodynamic comparison of young and older endurance athletes during exercise. *Journal of Applied Physiology*, 58, 2041–2046.

Hansen, A. K., Fischer, C. P., Plomgaard, P., Andersen, J. L., Saltin, B., Pedersen, B. K. (2005). Skeletal muscle adaptation: training twice every second day vs. Training once daily. *J Appl Physiol*, 98(1), 93–99.

Hargreaves, M., & Spriett, L. (2006). *Exercise Metabolism*. Champaign, IL: Human Kinetics.

Harms, C. A., Wetter, T. J., McClaran, S. R., Pegelow, S. R., Nickele, G. A., Nelson, W. B., Hanson, P, & Dempsey, J. A. (1998). Effects of respiratory muscle work on cardiac output and its distribution during maximal exercise. *J Appl Physiol*, 85, 609–18.

Harms, C. A.,Wetter, T. J., St Croix, C. M., Pegelow, D. F., & Dempsey, J. A. (2000). Effects of respiratory muscle work on exercise performance. *J Appl Physiol*, 89(1), 131–8.

Hawkins, M. N., Raven, P. B., Snell, P. G., Stray-Gunderson, J., & Levine, B. L. (2007). Maximal Oxygen Uptake as a Parametric Measure of Cardiorespiratory Capacity. *Med Sci Sports Exerc*, 39(1), 103–107.

Henriksson, J., & Reitman, J. S. (1977) Time course of changes in human skeletal muscle succinate dehydrogenase and cytochrome oxidase activities and maximal oxygen uptake with physical activity and inactivity. *Acta Physiol Scan*, 99, 91–97.

Hickson, R. C., Dvorak, B. A., Gorostiaga, E. M., Kurowski, T. T., & Foster, C. (1988). Potential for strength and endurance training to amplify endurance performance. *J Appl Physiol*, 65(5), 2285–2290.

Hickson, R., & Rosenkoetter, M. (1981). Reduced training frequencies and maintenance of increased aerobic power *Med Sci Sports Exer*, 13(1), 13–16.

Hill, D. W. (1999). Energy system contributions in middle-distance running events. *J Sports Sci*, 17(6), 477–483.

Hilty, L., Langer, N., Pascual-Marqui, R., Boutellier, U. & Lutz, K. (2011). Fatigue-induced increase in intracortical communication between mid/anterior insular and motor cortex during cycling exercise. *Eur J Neurosci*. 34(12), 2035-42.

Hilty, L., Jancke, L., Luechinger, R., Boutellier, U. & Lutz. (2011). Limitations of physical performance in a muscle fatiguing handgrip exercise is mediated by thalamo-insular activity. *Human Brain Mapping*. 32(12), 2151-60.

Hoffman, R. L. (1999). Effects of training at the ventilatory threshold on the ventilatory threshold and performance in trained distance runners. *J Strength Cond Res*, 13, 118–123.

Holloszy, J. O. & Coyle, J. (1984). Adaptations of skeletal muscle to endurance exercise and their metabolic consequences. *J Appl* Physiol, 56(4), 831–838.

Horoqitz, J. F., Sidossis, L. S., & Coyle, E. F. (1994). High efficiency of type I muscle fibers improves performance. *Int J Sports Med*, 15(3), 152–157.

Hudson, B., & Fitzgerald, M. (2008). *Running faster from the 5k to the marathon*. New York: Broadway Books.

Hurley, B. F., Hagberg, J. M., Allen, W. K., Seals, D. R., Young, J. C., Cuddihee, R. W., & Holloszy, J. O. (1984). Effect of training on blood lactate levels during submaximal exercise. *J Appl Physiol.*, 56(5), 1260–1264.

Inbar, O., Weiner, P., Azgad, Y., Rotstein, A., & Weinstein, Y. (2000). Specific inspiratory muscle training in well-trained endurance athletes. *Med Sci Sports Exerc*, 32(7), 1233–1237.

Inham, S., Whyte, G., Pedlar, C., Bailey, D., Dunman, N., & Nevjill, A. (2008). Determinants of 800-m and 1500m running performance using allometric models. *Med. Sci. Sports Exere.*, 40(2), 345–350.

Issurin, V. (2008). Block periodization versus traditional training theory: a review. *Journal of Sports Medicine and Physical Fitness*. 48, 65–75.

Iwasaki, K., Zhang, R., Zuckerman, J. H., & Levine, B. D. (2003). Dose-response relationship of the cardiovascular adaptation to endurance training in healthy adults: how much training for what benefit? *J Appl Physiol*, 95, 1575–1583.

Jacobs, I, Kaiser, P., & Tesch, P. (1981). Muscle strength and fatigue after selective glycogen depletion in human skeletal muscle fibers. *Eur J Appl Physiol Occup Physiol*, 46(1), 47–53.

Jelkmann, W. (2004). Molecular biology of erythropoietin. *Internal Medicine*, 43, 649–659.

Jemma, J., Halwey, J., Kumar, D. K., Singh, V. P., & Cosic, I. (2005). Endurance training of trained athletes- an electromyogram study. *Conf Proc IEEE Eng Med Biol Soc.* 7(1), 7707–7709.

Jewell, U. R., Kvietikova, I., Scheid, A., Bauer, C., Wenger, R. H., Gassmann, M. (2001). Induction of HIF-1 alpha is response to hypoxia is instantaneous. *FASEB J*, 15(7), 1312-1314.

Johnson, B. D., Babcock, M. A., Suman, O. E., & Dempsey, J. A. (1993). Exercise-induced diaphragmatic fatigue in healthy humans. *J Physiol*, 460, 385–405.

Jung, A. P. (2003). The impact of resistance training on distance running performance. *Sports Med, 33*(7), 539–552.

Kainulainen, H. (2009). Run more, perform better—old truth revisited. *J Appl Physiol, 106*(5), 1477–1478.

Ker, R. F., Bennett, M. B., Bibby, S. R., Kester, R. C., & Alexander, R. M. (1987). The spring in the arch of the human foot. *Nature, 325*(7000), 147–149.

Klausen, K. L., Andersen, B., & Pelle, I. (1981). Adaptive changes in work capacity, skeletal muscle capillarization, and enzyme levels during training and detraining. *Acta Physiol. Scand.* 113, 9–16.

Koltyn, K. F., Focht, B. C., Ancker, J. M., & Pasley, J. (1998). The effect of time of day and gender on pain perception and selected psychobiological responses. *Medicine and Science in Sports and Exercise, 30(5),* Supplement abstract 30.

Krib, B., Gledhill, N., Jamnik, V., & Warburton, D. (1997). Effect of alterations in blood volume on cardiac function during maximal exercise. *Med Sci Sports Exerc, 29*(11), 1469–1476.

Kushmerick, M. J., & Davies, R. E. (1969) The chemical energetics of muscle contraction II. The chemistry, efficiency, and power of maximally working sartorius muscle. *Proc R Soc Lond Ser B,* 1174, 315–353.

Kyrolainen, H., Belli, A., & Komi, P. V. (2001). Biomechanical factors affecting running economy. *Med. Sci. Sports Exerc.,* 33(8), 1330–1337.

Lacombe, V., Hinchcliff, K. W., Geor, R. J., & Lauderdale, M. A. (1999). Exercise that unduces substantial muscle glycogen depletion impairs subsequent anaerobic capacity. *Equine Vet J Suppl,* 30, 293–297.

LaManca, J. J., & Haymes, E. M. (1993). Effects of iron repletion on VO2max, endurance, and blood lactate in women. *Med Sci Sports Exerc,* 25(12), 1386–1392.

Larsen, H. B. (2003). Kenyan dominance in distance running. *Comp. Biochem. Physiol. A Mol. Integr. Physiol.* 136, 161–170.

Laursen, P. B. (2004). Training for intense exercise performance: high-intensity or high-volume training? *Scandinavian Journal of Sports Science and Medicine,* (in review).

Laursen, P. B., & Jenkins, D. G. (2002). The scientific basis for high-intensity interval training: optimising training programmes and maximising performance in highly trained endurance athletes. *Sports Med,* 32(1), 53–71.

Laursen, P. B., Blanchard, M. A., & Jenkins, D. G. (2002a). Acute high-intensity interval training improves Tvent and peak power output in highly trained males. Canadian *Journal of Applied Physiology, 27,* 336–348.

Laursen, P. B., Shing, C. M., Peake, J. M., Coombes, J. S., & Jenkins, D. G. (2002b). Interval training program optimization in highly trained endurance cyclists. *Medicine and Science in Sports and Exercise, 34,* 1801–1807.

Legaz Arrese, A., Serrano Ostáriz, E., Jcasajús Mallén, J. A., & Munguía Izquierdo, D. (2005). The changes in running performance and maximal oxygen uptake after long-term training in elite athletes. *J Sports Med Phys Fitness, 45*(4), 435–40.

Leskinen, A., Hakkinen, K., Virmavirta, M. Isolehto, J., & Kyrolainen, H. (2009). Comparison of running kinematics between elite and national-standard 1500m runners. *Sports Biomech, 8*(1), 1–9.

Levine, B. D., Lane, L.D., Buckey, J.C., Friedman, D.B., & Blomqvist, C.G. (1991). Left ventricular pressure-volume and Frank–Starling relations in endurance athletes. Implications for orthostatic tolerance and exercise performance. *Circulation, 84,* 1016–1023.

Lieberman, D. E., Venkadesan, M., Werbel, W. A., Daoud, A. I., D'Andrea, S., Davis, I. S., Mang'eni, R. O., & Pitsiladis, Y. (2010). Foot strike patterns and collision forces in habitually barefoot versus shod runners. *Nature, 463*(7280), 531-535.

Lydiard, A. (1998). *Running to the Top.* Auckland, NZ: Meyer and Meyer Sport.

Mainwood, G. W. & Renaud, J. M. (1985). The effect of acid-base balance on fatigue of skeletal muscle. *Can J Physiol Pharmacol, 63,* 403–416.

Manzi, V., Castagna, C., Padua, E., Lombardo, M., D'Ottavio, S., Massaro, M., Volterrani, M., Lellamo, F. (2009). Dose-response relationship of autonomic nervous system responses to individualized training impulse in marathon runners. *Am J Physiol Heart Circ Physiol, 296*(6), 1733–1740.

Marcora, S. M., Staiano, W., & Manning, V. (2009). Mental fatigue impairs physical performance in humans. *J Appl Physiol, 106,* 857–864.

Marzo, F., Lavorgna, A., Coluzzi, G., Santucci, E., Tarantino, F., Rio, T., Conti, E., Autore, C., Agati, L., & Andreotti, F. (2008). Erythropoietin in heart and vessels: focus on transcription and signalling pathways. *J Thromb Thrombolysis, 26,* 183–187.

Mayhew, J. L. (1977).Oxygen cost and energy expenditure of running in trained runners. *Br J Sports Med,* 11, 116–121.

Mauger, A. (2013). Fatigue is a pain- the use of novel neurophysiological techniques to understand the fatigue-pain relationship. *Front Physiol.* 4: 104.

McConnel, A. K., & Sharpe, G. R. (2005). The effect of inspiratory muscle training upon maximum lactate steady-state and blood lactate concentration. *Eur J Appl Physiol*, 94(3), 277–284.

McConell, G. K., Lee-Young, R. S., Chen, Z. P., Stepto, N. K., Huynh, N. N., Stephens, T. J., Canny, B. J. & Kemp, B.E. (2005). Short-term exercise training in humans reduces AMPK signalling during prolonged exercise independent of muscle glycogen. *Journal of Physiology* 568, 665–676

Midgeley, A. W., McNaughton, L. R., & Jones, A. M. (2007). Training to enhance the physiological determinants of long-distance running performance: can valid recommendations be given to runners and coaches based on current scientific knowledge. *Sports Med*, 37(10), 857–880.

Midgeley, A. W., McNaughton, L. R., & Wilkinson, M. (2006). Is there an optimal training intensity for enhanving maximal oxygen uptake of distance runners?: empirical research findings, current opinions, physiological rationale and practical recommendations. *Sports Med*, 36(2), 117–132.

Mikkola, J., Rusko, H., Nummela, A., Pollari, T., & Hakkinen, K. (2007). Concurrent endurance and explosive type strength training improves neuromuscular and anaerobic characteristics in young distance runners. *Int J Sports Med*, 28, 602–611.

Millet, G. P., Jaouen, B., Borrani, F., & Candau, R. (2002). Effects of concurrent endurance and strength training on running economy and VO(2) kinetics. *Med Sci Sports Exerc.*, 34(8), 1351–1359.

Millet, G., Jaouen, B., Borrani, F. & Canau, R. (2002). Effects of concurrent endurance and strength training on running economy and Vo2 kinetics. *Med Sci Sports Exerc*, 34, 1351–1359.

Molinsti, M. (2009). Plasticity properties of CPG circuits in humans: impact on gait recovery. *Brain Research Bulletin*, 78(1), 22–25.

Modica, J.R. & Kram, R. (2005). Metabolic energy and muscular activity required for leg swing in running. *J Appl Physiol*, 98, 2126-2131.

Monteiro, A. G., Aoki, M. S., Evangelista, A. L., Alveno, D. A., Monteiro, G. A., Picarro Ida, C., & Ugrinowitsch, C. (2009). Nonlinear periodization maximizes strength gains in split resistance training routines. *Strength Cond Res*, 23(4), 1321–1326.

Morgan, D. W., Bransford, D. R., Costill, D. L., Daniels, J. T., Howley, E. T., & Krahenbuhl, G. S. (1995). Variation in the aerobic demand of running among trained and untrained subjects. *Med Sci Sports Exerc*, 27, 404–409.

Morgan, D., Martin, P., Craib, M., Caruso, C., Clifton, R., & Hopewell, R. (1994). Effect of step length optimization on the aerobic demand of running. *J Appl Physiol*, 77, 245–251.

Mostardi, R. A., & Campbell, T. A. (1981). Effects of training once vs. twice per day and improvement in maximal aerobic power. *Ohio J Sci*, 81(5), 207–211.

Noakes, T. D. (2003). Commentary to accompany training and bioenergetic characteristics in elite male and female Kenyan runners. *Med Sci Sports Exerc*, 35(2), 305–306.

Noakes, T. D. (2007). Determining the extent of neural activation during maximal effort: comment. *Med Sci Sports Exerc*, 39(11), 2092.

Noakes, T. D. (2007). The central governor model of exercise regulation applied to the marathon. *Sports Med*, 37(4-5), 374–377.

Noakes, T. D. (2008). How did A.V. Hill understand the VO2max and the "plateau phenomenon"? Still no clarity? *Br J Sports Med*, 42(7), 574–580.

Noakes, T. D., & Marino, F. E. (2008). Does a central governor regulate maximal exercise during combined arm and leg exercise? A rebuttal. *Eur J Appl Physiol*, 104(4), 757–759.

Noakes, T. D., & Marino, F. E. (2009). Point: counterpoint: maximal oxygen uptake is/is not limited by a central nervous system governor. *J Appl Physiol*, 106, 338–339.

Noakes, T. D. (2012). Fatigue is a brain-derived emotion that regulates the exercise behavior to ensure the protection of whole body homeostatis. *Frontiers in Physiology* 11(3).

Okano, A. E., Fontes, E. B., Montenegro, R. A., et al. (2012). Brain stimulation modulates the autonomic nervous system, ratings of perceived exertion and performance during maximal exercise. *J Sports Medicine*

Ord. P & Gusbers, K. (2003). Pain thresholds and tolerances of competitive rowers and their use of spontaneous self-generated pain coping strategies. *Perceptual and Motor Skills*. 97, 1219-1222.

Paavolainen, L. M., Nummela, A. T., & Rusko, H. K. (1999b). Neuromuscular characteristics and muscle power as determinants of 5-km running performance. *Med Sci Sports Exerc*, 31, 124–130.

Paavolainen, L. M., Nummela, A. T., & Rusko, H. K. (2000). Muscle power factors and VO2max as determinants of horizontal and uphill running performance. *Scand J Sci Sports*, 10, 286–291.

Paavolainen, L. M., Nummela, A. T., Rusko, H. K., & Hakkinen, K. (1999c). Neuromuscular characteristics and fatigue during 10-km running. *Int J Sports Med*, 20,1–6.

Paavolainen, L., Hakkinen, K., Hamalainen, I., Nummela, A., & Rusko, H. (1999a). Explosive strength-training improves 5-km running time by improving running economy and muscle power. *J Appl Physiol*, 86, 1527–1533.

Pate, R. R., Macera, C. A., Bailey, S. P., Bartoli, W. P., & Powell, K. E. (1992). Physiological, anthropometric, and training correlates of running economy. *Med Sci Sports Exerc*, 24, 1128–1133.

Peltonen, J. E., Rusko, H. K., Rantamaki, J., Sweins, K., Nittymaki, S., & Viitasalo, J. T. (1997). Effects of oxygen fraction in inspired air on force production and electromyogram activity during ergometer rowing. European Journal of Applied Physiology, 76, 495– 503.

Peltonen, J. E., Leppavuori, A. P., Kyro, K. P., Makela, P., & Rusko, H. K. (1999). Arterial haemoglboin oxygen saturation is affected by F(I)O2 at submaximal running velocities in elite athletes. *Scand J Med Sci Sports*, 9(5), 265-271.

Pette, D. & Vrbova, G. (1999). What does chronic electrical stimulation teach us about muscle plasticity? *Muscle Nerve*, 22, 666–677.

Peukker, H., Cojard, A., Putman, C. T., & Pette, D. (1999).Transient expression of myosin heavy chain MHC1 alpha in rabbit muscle during fast to slow transition. *J Muscle Res Cell Motil*, 20(2), 147–154.

Power, S. K., Lawler, J., Dempsey, J. A., Dodd, S., & Landry, G. (1989). Effects of incomplete pulmonary gas exchange on VO2max. *J Appl Physiol*, 66, 2491–2495.

Powers, S. K., Lawler, J., Dempsey, J. A., Dodd, S., & Landry, G. (1989). Effects of incomplete pulmonary gas exchange of VO2max. *Journal of Applied Physiology*, 66, 2491–2495.

Purkiss, S. B. A., & Robertson, G. E. (2003). Methods for calculating internal mechanical work: comparison using elite runners. *Gait and Posture*, 18, 143–149.

Quinn, T. J., Klooster, J. R., & Kenefick, R. W. (2002). Can intermittent exercise maintain or enhance physiological benefits gained from previous traditional exercise? *Medicine and Science in Sports and Exercise, 34(5),* Supplement abstract 510.

Rhea, M. R., Ball, S. D., Phillips, W. T., & Burkett, L. N. (2003). A comparison of linear and daily undulating periodized programs with equated volume and intensity for strength. *J Strength Cond Res, 16*(2), 250–255.

Ricci, J., & Léger, L. A. (1983). VO2max of cyclists from treadmill, bicycle ergometer and velodrome tests. *Eur J Appl Physiol Occup Physiol, 50*(2), 283–289.

Romer, L. M., McConnel, A. K., & Jones, D. A. (2002). Inspiratory muscle fatigue in trained cyclists: effects of inspiratory muscle training. *Med Sci Sports Exerc,* 34(5), 785–792.

Rowland, T. (2009). Endurance athletes' stroke volume response to progressive exercise: A critical review. *Sports Med*, 39(8), 687–695.

Rusko, H. (1992). Development of aerobic power in relation to age and training in cross-country skiers. *Med Sci Sports Exerc*, 24, 1040–1047.

Rusko, H. K., Tikkanen, H. O., & Peltonen, J. E. (2004). Altitude and endurance training. *Journal of Sports Sciences,* 22:10, 928 – 945.

Saltin, B. (1973). Oxygen transport by the circulatory system during exercise in man. In Limiting Factors of Physical Performance, edited by J. Keul. 235-251. Stuttgart: Georg Thueme Verlag.

Saunders, P. U., Pyne, D. B., Telford, R. D., & Hawley, J. A. (2004). Factors affecting running economy in trained distance runners. *Sports Medicine, 34*(7), 465–485.

Saunders, P. U., Telford, R. D., Pyne, D. B., Peltola, E. M., Cunninhgam, R. B., Gore, C. J., & Hawley, J. A. (2006). Short-term plyometric training improves running economy in highly trained middle and long distance runners. *J Strength Cond Res.,* 20(4), 947–954.

Schlader, Z.J., Simmons, S.E., Stannard,S.R., & Mundel,T. (2011). The independent roles of temperature and thermal perception in the control of human thermoregulatory behavior. *Physiol.Behav.* 103, 217–224.

Scholz, M. N., Bobbert, M. F., van Soest, A. J., Clark, J. R., & van Heerden, J. (2008). Running biomechanics: shorter heels, better economy. *Journal of Experimental Biology*, 211, 3266–3271.

Seiler, S., & Tønnessen, E. (2009). Intervals, thresholds, and long slow distance: the role of intensity and duration in endurance training. *Sportscience*, 13, 32–53.

Selye, H. (1978*). The Stress of Life*. McGraw-Hill.

Sheel, W. A. (2002). Respiratory training in healthy individuals: physiological rationale and implications for exercise performance. *Sports Medicine.* 32(9), 567–581.

Shephard, R. J. (2009). Is the measurement of maximal oxygen intake passé? (2008). *Br J Sports Med*, 43, 83–85.

Simmons, S., & Freeman, W. A. (2006). *Take the Lead: A Revolutionary approach to Cross Country*. Simmons & Freeman.

Sinnett, A. M., Berg, K., Latin, R. W., & Noble, J. M. (2001). The relationship between field tests of anaerobic power and 10-km run performance. *J Strength Cond Resm* 15(4), 405–412.

Smith, T. P., Coombes, J. S., & Geraghty, D. P. (2003). Optimising high-intensity treadmill training using the running speed at maximal O(2) uptake and the time for which this can be maintained. *Eur J Appl Physiol*, 89(3-4), 337–343.

Smith, T. P., McNaughton, L. R., & Marshall, K. J. (1999). Effects of 4-wk training using Vmax/Tmax on

VO2max and performance in athletes. *Med Sci Sports Exerc*, 31, 892–896.

Soungatoulin, V., Beam, W., Kersey, R., & Peterson, J. (2003). Comparative effects of traditional versus periodized intensity training on cycling performance. *Medicine and Science in Sports and Exercise, 35*(5), Supplement abstract 185.

Spenser, M., & Gaston, P. (2001). Energy system contribution during 200- to 1500-m running in highly trained athletes. *Med. Sci. Sports Exerc., 33*(1), 157–162.

Spurrs, R. W., Murphy, A. J., & Watsford, M. L. (2003). The effect of plyometric training on distance running performance. *Eur J Appl Physiol. 89*(1). 1–7.

Stallknecht, B., Vissing, J., & Galbo, H. (1998). Lactate production and clearance in exercise. Effects of training. A mini-review. *Scand J Med Sci Sports, 8*(3), 127–131.

Stephenson, D. G., Lamb, G. D., & Stephenson, G. M. (1998). Events of the excitation-contraction-relaxation (E-C-R) cycle in fast- and slow-twitch mammalian muscle fibres relevant to muscle fatigue. *Acta Physiol Scan, 162*(3). 229–245.

Stone, M. R., Thomas, K., Wilkinson, M., et al. (2012). Effects of Deception on Exercise Performance. *Med Sci Sports Exerc. 44*(3), 534-541.

Stepto, N. K., Hawley, J.A., Dennis, S. C., & Hopkins, W. G. (1999). Effects of different interval-training programs on cycling time-trial performance. *Medicine and Science in Sports and* Exercise, 31, 736–741.

Stockman, C. & Fandrey, J. (2006). Hypoxia induced erythropoietin production: a paradigm for oxygen-regulated gene expression. *Clinical and Experimental Pharmacology and Physiology, 3*, 968–979.

Svedenhag, J., & Sjodin, B. (1994). Body-mass-modified running economy and step length in elite male middle and long-distance runners. *Int J Sports Med, 15*(6), 305–310.

Tanser, T. (2008). *More fire: How to run the Kenyan way.* Yardley, PA: Westholme Publishing.

Teunissen, L., Grabowski, A., & Kram, R. (2007). Effects of independently altering body weight and body mass on the metabolic cost of running. *The Journal of Experimental Biology, 210*, 4418-4427.

Tesarz, J., Schuster, A. K., Hartmann, M., Gerhardt, A., & Eich, W. (2012). Pain perception in athletes compared to normally active controls. *Pain, 154*(6), 1253-1262.

Tesarz, J., Gerhardt, A., Schommer, K., Treede, R., & Eich, W. (2013). Alterations in endogenous pain modulation in endurance athletes: *Pain, 154*(7), 1022-1262

Thomson, J. A., Green, H. J., & Houston, M. E. (1979). Muscle glycogen depletion patterns in fast twitch fibre subgroups of man during submaximal and supramaximal exercise. *Flugers Arch, 379*(1), 105–108.

Tucker, R., Kayser, B., Rae, E., Raunch, L., Bosch, A. & Noakes, T. (2007). Hyperoxia improves 20 km cycling time trial performance by increasing muscle activation levels while perceived exertion stays the same. *Eur J Appl Physiol, 101*(6), 771–781.

Tucker, R., Rauch, L., Harley, Y. X. R., & Noakes, T. D. (2004). Impaired exercise performance in the heat is associated with an anticipatory reduction in skeletal muscle recruitment. *Eur J Physiol, 448*, 422–430.

Ugrinowitsch, Carlos. (2013). Cerebral And Muscular Oxygenation During Different Modes Of Exercise. ACSM conference 2013

Vickers, R. R. (2005). Running economy: comparing alternative measurement tools. *Naval Health Research Center*. Report 05-14.

Volianitis, S., McConnel, A. K., Koutedakis, Y., McNaughton, L., Backx, K., & Jones, D. A. (2001). Inspiratory muscle training improves rowing performance. *Med Sci Sports Exerc, 33*(5), 803–809.

Vollaard, N. B. J., Constantin-Teodosiu, D., Fredriksson, K, Rooyackers, O., Jansson, E., Greenhaff, P. L., Timmons, J. A., & Sundberg, C. J. (2009). Systematic analysis of adaptations in aerobic capacity and submaximal energy metabolism provides a unique insight into determinants of human aerobic performance. *J Appl Physiol, 106*, 1479–1486.

Wagner, P. D. (1995). Limitations of oxygen transport to the cell. *Intensive Care Med, 21*(5), 391–398.

Warddrip, E. M. & Kram, R. (2012). Disintegrating the metabolic cost of human running: weight support, forward propulsion, and leg swing. *American Society of Biomechanics Conference.*

Weston, A. R., Myburgh, K. H., Lindsay, F. H., Dennis, S. C, Noakes, T. D., & Hawley, J. A. (1996). Skeletal muscle buffering capacity and endurance performance after high-intensity training by well-trained cyclists. *Eur J Appl Physiol, 75*, 7–13.

Weyand, P. G., Sandell, R. F., Prime, D. N. & Bundle, M. W. (2010). The biological limits to running speed are imposed from the ground up. *J Appl Physiol, 108*, 950–961.

Williams, J. S., Wongsathikun, J., Boon, S. M., & Acevedo, E. O. (2002). Inspiratory muscle training fails to improve endurance capacity in athletes. *Med Sci Sports Exerc, 34*(7), 1194–1198.

Williams, K. R., & Cavanagh, P. R. (1987). Relationship between distance running mechanics, running economy, and performance. *J Appl Physiol, 63*(3), 1236–1245.

Wilmore, J. H., Stanforth, P. R., Gagnon, J., Rice, T., Mandel, S., Leon, A. S., Rao, D. C., Skinner, J. S., & Bouchard, C. (2001). Cardiac output and stroke volume changes with endurance training: the HERITAGE Family Study. *Med Sci Sports Exerc, 33*(1), 99–106.

Wilt, F. (1964). *Run, Run, Run*. Track and Field News.

Wright, S., & Weyand, P. G. (2001). The application of ground force explains the energetic cost of running backward and forward. *J Expl Biol., 204*(10), 1805–1815.

Yamamoto, L. M., Lopez, R. M., Klau, J. F., Casa, D. J., Kraemer, W. J., & Maresh, C. M. (2008). The effects of resistance training on endurance distance running performance among highly trained runners: a systematic review. *J Strength Cond Res, 22*(6), 2036–2044.

Yeo, W. K., Paton, C. D., Garnham, A. P., Burke, L. M., Carey, A. L., & Hawley, J. A. (2008). Skeletal muscle adaptation and performance responses to once a day versus twice every second day endurance training regimens. *J Appl Physiol, 105*(5), 1462–70.

Yoshida, T., Udo, M., Chida, M., Ichioka, M., Makiguchi, K., & Yamaguchi, T. (1990). Specificity of physiological adaptation to endurance training in distance runners and competitive walkers. *Eur J Appl Physiol*, 61, 197–201.

Zoll, J., Ponsot, E., Dufour, S., Doutreleau, S., Ventura-Clapier, R., Vogt, M., Hoppeler, H., Richard, R., & Fluck, M. (2006). Exercise training in normobaric hypoxia in endurance runners. III. *Appl Physiol*, 100, 1258–1266

<u>About the Author</u>

Steve Magness is a runner, coach, exercise scientist, and most recently a writer. He has been a serious runner since the age of 14 and has had numerous running accomplishments ranging from holding the Texas High School mile record (4:01.02) to qualifying for NCAA nationals as an individual in Cross Country.

Steve is currently the Cross Country coach at the University of Houston. In only one year as the coach at UH, he has guided 3 athletes to qualifying for the 1st round of the NCAA championships in the 800m, and has had athletes set a school record in the 3,000m and top 5 all time times in the 800, 1,500, mile, 3,000, and 3,000m steeplechase. In addition to collegiate coaching, Magness coaches professionals Jackie Areson who was 15th at the 2013 World Championships in Russia, Asics steeplechaser Sara Hall, and 4 time USATF championship qualifier in the 1,500m Tommy Schmitz. Magness has also acted as a consultant for training, science, medical, and nutrition advice to numerous other world class runners and triathletes and as a consultant for the development of coaches' education for several countries.

He has also coached on the high school level where he had numerous regional and state qualifying teams and individuals. His most recent team was nationally ranked and finished 2nd at the Texas state meet. Additionally, an individual from that team was 12th at nationals in Cross Country and the TX state champion in the 3200m.

Steve is a 2007 suma cum laude graduate from the University of Houston with a B.S. in Exercise Science and a 2010 graduate of George Mason University with a M.S. in EFHP-Exercise. While writing is a more recent undertaking, he has written articles for IAAF's *New Studies in Athletics*, Running Times, Competitor magazine, Men's Health, and Runner's World. Additionally, he maintains the popular running website www.ScienceofRunning.com.

For more articles on training distance runners and the science behind endurance visit:
www.ScienceofRunning.com

8945290R00190

Printed in Great Britain
by Amazon.co.uk, Ltd.,
Marston Gate.